RECLAIMING VIRTUE

Also by John Bradshaw

CREATING LOVE
FAMILY SECRETS
HOMECOMING
HEALING THE SHAME THAT BINDS YOU
BRADSHAW ON: THE FAMILY

RECLAIMING VIRTUE

How we can develop
the moral intelligence to do
the right thing at the right time
for the right reason

John Bradshaw

BANTAM BOOKS

Grateful acknowledgment is given for permission to reprint from the following:
Excerpt from "Love after Love" by Derek Walcott, from *Collected Poems, 1948–1984*. Copyright © 1987 by Derek Walcott. Reprinted by permission of Farrar Straus & Giroux and Faber and Faber Ltd.
Excerpts from *Montessori: A Modern Approach* by Paula Polk Lillard, copyright © 1972 by Schocken Books. Used by permission of Schocken Books, a division of Random House, Inc.
Excerpt from *Phoenix: Therapeutic Patterns of Milton H. Erickson* by David Gordon and Maribeth Meyers-Anderson. Copyright © 1981 by David Gordon and Maribeth Meyers-Anderson. Reprinted by permission of Meta Publications, www.meta-publications.com.

RECLAIMING VIRTUE
A Bantam Book / May 2009

Published by Bantam Dell
A Division of Random House, Inc.
New York, New York

Book design by Melissa N. Sutherland

Library of Congress Cataloging-in-Publication Data
Bradshaw, John, 1933–
Reclaiming virtue : how we can develop the moral intelligence to do the right thing at the right time for the right reason / John Bradshaw.
p.   cm.
Includes bibliographical references and index.
ISBN 978-0-553-09592-0 (hardcover)
1. Virtue.   2. Integrity.   3. Moral development.   I. Title.
BJ1521.B73 2009
170—dc22   2008054502

Printed in the United States of America
Published simultaneously in Canada

www.bantamdell.com

10   9   8   7   6   5   4   3   2
BVG

To my beloved wife,
Karen Ann, whose smile
must be something like God's.
Her goodness is beyond question.
And to the memory of my mother
and my Elliot grandparents' fierce
and unwavering virtue.

Contents

RECLAIMING VIRTUE

PROLOGUE

MAGNIFICENT MORAL MOMENTS

Since the beginning of time, men and women have told stories about bravery, loyalty, justice, and the dignity and enduring strength of humans. We have a natural hunger for such stories. They bring us hope about the goodness and generosity of the human spirit. They help us withstand hardship, suffering, and calamity.

Dr. Robert Coles, a renowned Harvard child psychiatrist and author, calls these stories "magnificent moral moments." What follows are ten such moments.

THE FIRE DEPARTMENT CULTURE

Rumor had it that some of their fellow firefighters might still be alive in the wreckage of the World Trade Center. For three days the four men had been working side by side for sixteen hours at a stretch. They attacked the rubble with blowtorches in a desperate attempt to uncover one or more of the firefighters who had disappeared when the towers collapsed.

Suddenly, the men heard shouting: "They made it! They made it!" They flipped up their goggles, but they could not see past the smoking mounds before them. They returned to work with renewed vigor. Only later did they learn that two firefighters who'd been buried in the rubble had been rescued.

As they began their journey home in the late afternoon the four men were startled to see crowds standing along the highway, waving flags and applauding them as heroes. They were puzzled because they regarded themselves as doing what any firefighter would have done.

These men exemplified what William M. Feehan, New York City's first deputy fire commissioner on September 11, 2001, called the "fire department culture":

> There is a fire department culture—and it's a very special culture. When you have a department whose men and women are expected to be ready at a moment's notice, to put their life on the line, to go to the aid of a stranger even when it means you may put yourself in dire peril, I don't think you can pay people to do that. There has to be something beyond money that will make them do that.

Survivors later reported that as they came down the stairs from the eighty-first floor of the North Tower, firefighters passed them going *up* in an attempt to rescue others. "I was praying to die fast," reported Rich Picciotto, commander of Manhattan's Eleventh Battalion, who survived the collapse of the World Trade Center's North Tower. Later, Kerry Kelly, FDNY chief medical officer, said in her opening statement to the U.S. Senate: "In the first one hundred years we filled a wall with the names of fallen firefighters. On the eleventh of September we created a new wall."

One of the names on the new wall was that of William M. Feehan, who died while working at his command center in the South Tower of the World Trade Center on September 11.

RUBY BRIDGES

Ruby Bridges was only six years old when she was enrolled in the formerly all-white William Frantz School in New Orleans. Ruby was among the first black children to initiate desegregation in New Orleans, and the only black child at William Frantz.

It was November 1960, only five years after Rosa Parks precipitated the civil rights movement by claiming her right to sit anywhere she wanted on a segregated bus in Montgomery, Alabama. New Orleans was still a hotbed of racial hatred.

People wanted to *kill* Ruby Bridges and her family and had no reluctance saying so over and over again. Little Ruby went up against tremendous hate, prejudice, and pressure. In *The Moral Life of Children,* Robert Coles tells Ruby's story.

> For days that turned into weeks and weeks that turned into months, this child had to brave murderously heckling mobs, there in the morning and there in the evening, hurling threats and slurs and hysterical denunciations and accusations. Federal marshals took her to school and brought her home. She attended school all by herself for a good part of a school year, owing to a total boycott by white families.

Coles was perplexed by Ruby's behavior. How could she handle such hatred and rejection? Her teachers had started to wonder how she could persist under the barrage of threats, bigotry, and scorn she was experiencing. How could a child this age have such inner strength, courage, and perseverance?

A white teacher at Ruby's school told Coles that one day she was standing in a classroom looking out the window and saw Ruby Bridges coming down the street.

> The crowd was there, shouting, as usual. A woman spat at Ruby but missed; Ruby smiled at her. A man shook his fist at her;

Ruby smiled at him. Then she walked up the stairs, and she stopped and turned and smiled one more time! You know what she told one of the marshals? She told him she prays for those people, the ones in the mob, every night before she goes to sleep.

Coles refused to believe that Ruby's moral strength could be sustained solely by prayer, especially when she was all alone at school. Coles knew that Ruby was a member of a solid church community and that she loved and trusted her pastor and her parents, but even so, Ruby's strength still did not fit into any of the known psychoanalytic theories or moral developmental models. Coles reluctantly accepted that Ruby Bridges exemplified a "new reality," transcending any theory he had of a six-year-old child.

Ruby's parents certainly had unusual moral courage. They had left their life as sharecroppers in hopes of finding a better life in the city, but their lives were put in jeopardy for enrolling their child in a formerly all-white school. Ruby's father was fired from his job, and even her grandparents were forced to move off the land they had farmed. Ruby's mother was not well educated, but it was she who helped clarify Coles' confusion. On one occasion she told him:

"There's a lot of people who talk about doing good, and a lot of people who argue about what's good and not good." Then she added that "there are a lot of people who always worry about whether they are doing right or wrong." Finally, there are some other folks: "They just put their lives on the line for what's right, and they may not be the ones who talk a lot or argue a lot or worry a lot; they just *do* a lot!"

HUGH THOMPSON AT MY LAI

Looking down from his helicopter, Warrant Officer Hugh Thompson couldn't figure out what was happening in the Vietnamese village of My Lai. It was March 16, 1968, and he and his crewmen were flying low, trying to draw enemy fire so the gunship flying above them could locate and destroy the enemy. On this day, no one was shooting at them, but below in the village there were bodies everywhere. Then, as they hovered a few feet over a rice paddy, the team watched a captain approach a young woman lying on the ground. He nudged her with his foot and then shot her.

The helicopter crew reacted with horror. They saw dozens of bodies piled up in an irrigation ditch. Thompson set his helicopter down near the ditch. He saw that some of the figures in the ditch were still moving, and asked a sergeant who was standing nearby if he could get some of his men to help the wounded civilians.

The sergeant suggested just putting them out of their misery, and when a stunned Thompson called to the commanding officer, Lieutenant William L. Calley Jr., for help, he was told to mind his own business. Calley's troops began firing into the ditch. Thompson was horrified. He still didn't know the whole story, but whatever was going on seemed terribly wrong.

When C Company (Charlie Company), 1st Battalion, 20th Infantry of the 11th Light Infantry Brigade had moved into the hamlet of My Lai on a search-and-destroy mission, they were looking for Vietcong soldiers to destroy. There were none there, not a single combatant. They'd found only unarmed women, children, and old men.

As Thompson climbed back into his helicopter, he faced the truth of what was happening. A war crime—a slaughter—was taking place, and American soldiers were the criminals.

As Thompson's helicopter lifted off, he saw elderly men,

women, and children running toward a small bunker for shelter, being chased by Americans. "We thought they had about thirty seconds before they'd die," Thompson's door gunner, Lawrence Colburn, recalled.

He landed his helicopter between the U.S. troops and the bunker. With fury, he confronted the company commander and asked for help escorting the children to the bunker. The commander refused and made clear his intent to kill the Vietnamese civilians. Thompson told his two crewmen, Colburn and crew chief Glenn Andreotta, to shoot any American who interfered. The ground troops held their fire as Thompson coaxed the Vietnamese to come out. Thompson got on the radio and pleaded with the larger gunship to land and pick up the five children and four adults, which it did in minutes.

"There was no thinking about it," he said. "It was just something that had to be done, and it had to be done fast."

Before he took off, he saw something moving in the mass of dead bodies in the irrigation ditch—a child about four years old. Thompson, who had a son of his own, was overcome by emotion. He asked Andreotta to get the child. Andreotta waded through the bloody dead bodies and pulled the boy out. They flew the child to a nearby field hospital.

Thompson immediately reported the incident to his superiors, but the investigation that followed was cursory and failed to precipitate any action or consequences.

Charlie Company had killed five hundred to six hundred unarmed Vietnamese civilians in My Lai. A substantial number of unarmed civilians were murdered in other nearby hamlets by other U.S. troops.

There was undoubtedly a massive cover-up of this entire massacre. It seems that only Thompson, Colburn, and Andreotta actually fought to save innocent human lives. A year later, Vietnam veteran Ron Ridenhour, who had heard about these incidents from a member of Charlie Company, wrote to several congressmen about the atrocities. This action finally exposed the truth of the cover-up.

It wasn't until March 6, 1998, thirty years after the incident and after internal debate within the Pentagon, that Thompson and Colburn received the Soldier's Medal in a ceremony at the Vietnam Veterans Memorial in Washington, D.C. Andreotta had been killed in Vietnam and received the medal posthumously.

For Thompson and Colburn, a more rewarding moment came in 1999, when they went back to My Lai to dedicate a school and a peace park. There they met a young man, Do Hoa, the boy they had rescued from the ditch.

DR. MARIA MONTESSORI

Maria Montessori decided to pursue a medical degree in the face of great opposition. In late nineteenth-century Italy, women were simply not supposed to be doctors. But she persisted, and in 1896 she became the first woman to graduate from the University of Rome's medical school. After she received her degree, she became interested in what were then called "defectives"—the mentally retarded and people suffering with nervous and mental disorders. Working with such "defective" children in clinics in Paris and Rome, she began to experiment with ways to educate them.

After a time, she arranged for some of her "defective" students to take the standard examinations in reading and writing given to Roman schoolchildren. When they passed successfully, others hailed a "miracle," but Montessori said it was "only because they had been taught in a different way."

Montessori knew she had discovered something of deep significance—a secret about children that had been completely overlooked. The secret had to do with the child's innate and unique intelligence, what she would later describe as the absorbent mind of the child. She found that the so-called defective children could be helped in their psychic development simply by changing the environment in which their learning took place.

Montessori then began to question the current approach to educating normal children. She suspected that they were being "suffocated, held back" by their schools. Why, she argued, shouldn't normal students as well achieve far greater results in a changed environment? Four years later she was able to test her theory.

On January 6, 1907, in a section of Rome noted for its crime, ignorance, illiteracy, and poverty, she began her work. On that day in the midst of about sixty unruly and frightened children, Montessori spoke to the crowd of notables who had come to the opening of her new child care center, the Casa dei Bambini. She read from the epistle of the mass of the day: "Arise, shine; for thy light is come, and the glory of the Lord is risen upon thee." Montessori was to care for the children while their illiterate parents were working. In her speech, she suggested that perhaps the children's home might become a "new Jerusalem," which would bring a new light into the educational process. Within a year, Montessori's deprived students were flourishing. Children as young as three and four years old were reading, writing, and behaving with self-respect.

Montessori came to believe that every child's true nature is characterized by order, spontaneous self-discipline, and harmony with others. Every child, she observed, is innately intelligent and moral. What is essential is a right environment, one that is run by unbiased adults and set up to stimulate the child at age-appropriate levels, taking advantage of their readiness to learn.

Montessori's innovative techniques and her methods slowly began to spread. Today Montessori schools exist all over the world.

ANDY DUFRESNE: THE SHAWSHANK REDEMPTION

Works of the artistic imagination can deeply stir our moral sentiment, and one of my favorite movies is *The Shawshank Redemption*. The hero, Andy Dufresne, has been wrongfully convicted of his wife's murder and sent to Shawshank Prison for life. Because of his banking and accounting background, he is enlisted by the warden to fix the books for the warden's crooked scheme, which involves using the inmates for contract construction work and skimming money off the top for himself.

After Dufresne has served fifteen years of his sentence, a newly admitted inmate says that he was in another prison with a man who bragged about killing Andy's wife. Andy reports this to the warden, but the warden, fearing his lucrative scheme might be exposed if Andy were exonerated, discourages any further investigation. Even though Andy swears to keep his secret, the warden puts him in solitary confinement and later has the new inmate murdered.

Andy suffers great pain and disappointment, but after he's released from solitary confinement, he tells his friend Red that he will never give up hope: "Hope is a good thing, maybe the best of things, and no good thing ever dies." Strengthened by this hope, Andy has been secretly working on a tunnel through the sewer line of the prison, digging it out inch by inch with a tiny rock hammer.

In the climactic scene of the movie, we see Andy crawl through five hundred yards of sewer line filled with human waste. As he comes out of the sewer, he stands in the midst of a driving rain, throws off his prison clothes, and spreads his arms wide as he looks to heaven. His hope never died and proved to be his redemption. After thirty years in prison, he has escaped. He had also documented the warden's crooked scheme and sent the evidence to the authorities. As the police are knocking at the warden's door to arrest him, he commits suicide. Andy is completely exonerated.

HENRY DAVID THOREAU

Henry David Thoreau was born in 1817 in Concord, Massachusetts. He described himself as a philosopher of nature and was known for his extreme individualism, his preference for simple, austere living, and his revolt against a government that legalized the institution of slavery. In his essay "Civil Disobedience," published in 1849, he wrote: "I cannot for an instant recognize that political organization as my government which is the slave's government also."

To express his opposition to slavery and to the Mexican-American War, which would extend slavery into a vast new area, Thoreau had refused to pay his poll tax for six years. In July 1846 he was arrested, jailed, and fined. While his fine was paid by a relative and he was in prison only overnight, he had acted on his beliefs and was willing to take the consequences. "There are thousands who are *in opinion* opposed to slavery and to the war," he later wrote, "who yet in effect do nothing to put an end to them . . . [and] sit down with their hands in their pockets."

In "Civil Disobedience," Thoreau described his experience and set forth his belief in principled resistance to authority. When a government or any civil authority is immoral, he argued, one must not obey it. Indeed, he said, it is a person's moral duty to a higher law to disobey. His simple but eloquent words became a lasting call to individual conscience, internal moral reform, and just action.

This one man, Henry David Thoreau, whose conscience guided him to take action against gross injustice, became the moral model for the two great nonviolent revolutions of the twentieth century: Mohandas Gandhi's Indian independence movement and the civil rights movement led by Dr. Martin Luther King Jr.

ABRAHAM LINCOLN

Abraham Lincoln, the sixteenth president of the United States, embodied the extraordinary leadership that led to the greatest moral moment in the making of democracy in the United States of America. The Lincoln Memorial in our nation's capital is a grand monument not just honoring a president but also symbolizing a unique moment of change when the collective conscience of our people's innate ethical sensibility triumphed over moral legality and biblical literalism. The clear distinction between what is moral because it is legal (moral legalism) and what is truly moral (ethical sensibility) is a critical distinction in the process of reclaiming virtue.

Lincoln was born into a world where human slavery was justified by many as being in the Bible. It was legal in many states in the Union and guaranteed by the Constitution. It now seems absurd that anyone could justify slavery while proclaiming the grandeur of the U.S. Constitution, with its emphasis on human rights and equality.

Lincoln was morally repelled by slavery, but he believed in the rule of law and the Constitution. After he was elected president, he arrived in Washington on a secret train surrounded by guards. As he swore his oath of office, the soldiers of General Winfield Scott lined the rooftops of adjacent buildings. Two weeks prior to Lincoln's inaugural speech on March 4, 1861, seven southern states had joined together as a new confederation under Jefferson Davis. It's hard to imagine the inner turmoil Lincoln must have felt. In his first inaugural address, he sought above all to save the Union. He appealed eloquently for reconciliation. He called upon "the mystic chords of memory stretching from every battlefield and patriot grave to every human heart," and he hoped that all the people would be guided by "the better angels of our nature."

Sixty-four days after his inauguration, four more states

seceded from the Union. The Civil War, the costliest war in human lives in American history, began.

Lincoln never gave up. He continued to exhort his countrymen throughout the ghastly nights of conflict between North and South. After the battle at Gettysburg he gave one of the greatest speeches in American history. And yet the Gettysburg Address was severely criticized by his fellow politicians.

By December 1862 the Northern war effort was faltering and public opinion was turning against the war. Lincoln was faced with one of the most critical and momentous moral decisions ever to confront any leader in world history. It was clear to Lincoln that the freeing of the slaves and the saving of the Union were now inseparable.

Lincoln, the backwoodsman who'd had to teach himself to read, who was shy, physically awkward, and slow to speak, moved his fellow citizens to action with profound rhetoric. In ending his annual speech to Congress in December 1862, he said:

> The dogmas of the quiet past, are inadequate to the stormy present.... As our case is new, so we must think anew, and act anew....
>
> [W]e cannot escape history. We of this Congress and this administration, will be remembered in spite of ourselves.... We *say* we are for the Union.... The world will not forget that we say this. We know how to save the Union. The world knows we do know how to save it. We—even *we here*—hold the power, and bear the responsibility. In *giving* freedom to the *slave,* we *assure* freedom to the *free*—honorable alike in what we give, and what we preserve. We shall nobly save, or meanly lose, the last best hope of earth.

Lincoln found both the will and the words to usher in a new moral era in American history.

MORRIE SCHWARTZ

Many magnificent moral moments come from our life experiences, especially the experience of suffering, and most especially, the experience of those who are in the process of dying. There are many such moments in *Tuesdays with Morrie,* Mitch Albom's conversations with his old teacher.

As the book begins, Albom's frantic drive for success has taken him to the pinnacle of his career as a sportswriter. He occasionally thinks of the man who was his favorite professor in college, but he has not been in touch for years—until he turns on the TV late one night and hears Ted Koppel say, "Who is Morrie Schwartz?" During the *Nightline* interview that follows, he learns that Morrie is dying of ALS, a progressive and inevitably fatal disease.

Mitch's professional success and affluence have not brought him any real inner contentment, while Morrie's life experience has taught him a great deal about what is important in life and what is not. Mitch's conversations with his former professor force him to question what his current worldly success would mean if he were dying.

The fact that we are all going to die brings us face-to-face with questions about the meaning and purpose of our lives. Death and dying are our teachers. They ask us to question our values and our commitments. The following exchange between Mitch and Morrie touched me deeply:

He asked to see the hibiscus plant on the ledge behind him. I cupped it in my hand and held it up near his eyes. He smiled.

"It's natural to die," he said again. "The fact that we make such a big hullabaloo over it is all because we don't see ourselves as part of nature. We think we're human because we're something above nature."

He smiled at the plant.

"We're not. Everything that gets born, dies." He looked at me.

"Do you accept that?"

Yes.

"All right," he whispered, "now here's the payoff. Here is how we *are* different from these wonderful plants and animals.

"As long as we can love each other, and remember the feeling of love we had, we can die without ever really going away. All the love you created is still there. All the memories are still there. You live on—in the hearts of everyone you have touched and nurtured while you were here. . . .

"Death ends a life, not a relationship."

What starts out as a courtesy visit to an old professor who is dying turns out to be a profound experience that helps Mitch Albom clarify his own priorities about life.

JOHNNY PAGNINI

Sometimes the bravery of another person seems beyond understanding. I interviewed one such person, Johnny Pagnini, on my talk show, *The Bradshaw Difference*. Here is how he told his story:

Last year in California, I was driving a friend home after a Sunday afternoon of driving motorcycles. It was about 8:00 P.M. I noticed a swerving car to my left. The driver sat alone up front; but in the back, a man and a woman seemed to be wrestling. My concern grew as I approached the car. I soon realized that this was no lover's quarrel. This man was punching the woman in the face. I put my high beams on. The woman stared back at me. Our eyes locked for a moment. It is a face that I will never forget. It was the swollen bloody face of ultimate terror. Quickly her assailant shoved her head below the seat. But I had seen all I needed to—I was not going to let this car get away.

The back door of the car swung open and I saw the woman's legs fly out of the car. I thought that they were trying to push her out. But I found out later that she felt that she was dead no matter what and was just trying to end it quickly. These guys had abducted her, told her that they were going to rape and kill her. This guy in the backseat already had his pants pulled down and was trying to rape her when I put my high beams on. I thought that she was going to fall out of the car. We were going about 75 miles per hour. I thought that she might survive the fall but would surely be run over by a car. So I started swerving across the traffic lanes trying to slow down traffic on the freeway. It was working, but the guys were getting away.

So I sped up and caught them again. I knew that I needed to get a good look at them, so I pulled up alongside of them. I figured that if they had a gun, this was the time they were going to use it. They didn't. The chase continued for several hours on and off the freeway. At one point, they slowed down and shoved the woman out of the car. I continued to chase them. There was no way I was going to let them get away.

Finally, I ended up in front of them on the freeway and they rammed my car. I screamed at people on the ramp to call the cops. Someone finally did. These guys were arrested and convicted.

SUSAN KRABACHER

Some people think Susan Krabacher is a candidate for sainthood. Unlike Mother Teresa, who was never invited to a party at the Playboy Mansion, "Mama Blance" (literally "mother with blond hair"), as she has been called by the Haitian locals, Susan was the *Playboy* Miss May of 1983 and hung out with the *Playboy* crowd for a decade, acting, modeling, and doing promotional work. It was a mixed blessing that allowed her to escape from her bondage to an emotionally troubled and severely abusive Christian fundamentalist mother and her sexually abusive paternal grandfather. "You become very mature," writes Susan in her book *Angels of a Lower Flight,* "when sex is forced on you at age four." Susan did what many who are sexually abused at an early age do: she turned to sex and sexuality as the only way she knew to experience attention and self-esteem.

Susan deteriorated during her time as a Playboy Bunny, chronically using drugs and finally marrying a physically and emotionally abusive man who was sexually addicted, a control freak, and an out-and-out criminal. When he went to prison, she separated from him, but then went to work as the cook and house servant of an angry, resentful octogenarian.

A turning point came when Susan married her divorce lawyer, Joseph Krabacher, and settled into a lush lifestyle in Aspen, Colorado. But something in Susan did not want her epitaph to read "Miss May 1983." After watching a TV show on children in Mongolia, she was passionately moved to do something to help and care for poor children. A church friend suggested that she think about Haiti, which her friend described as ten times poorer than Mongolia.

Writing about Haiti, Susan says:

> Today Haiti is unknown to most of the world.... About 80 percent of Haitians live in abject poverty.... The average annual salary is $350, less than $1 a day.... The unemployment rate is more than 70 percent.... The average life expectancy in Haiti is fifty-three.... More than 10 percent of Haitian children will die before age four. Some 7 percent of children in Haiti are believed to be enslaved. Some 300,000 children as young as age three consistently suffer sexual, emotional, and physical abuse.

The slum called Cité Soleil, just outside the city of Port-au-Prince, has been described as 250,000 people living on a garbage dump. When Susan first saw Cité Soleil, she insisted that she had to know what the people there have to go through. So she slept in a filthy hovel with a family of seventeen. The next day, her friend said, "I couldn't even hug her, she smelled so bad." Susan was filled with purpose. She had expected to find poverty, but nothing could have prepared her for the children's ward at the state-run hospital in Port-au-Prince. "I walked in," she said, "and saw probably 100 little cribs with dying children in them."

Violent crime, corruption, and political unrest make Haiti a place of audacious evil. Susan describes it as the embodiment of hell. For Susan the abused children were not just out there; she had experienced severe child abuse herself. "One day in my childhood," she writes, "there was a moment of clarity: I knew that someday I would do something significant, more significant than all these people who were hurting me could ever imagine. I promised it to God—I would fix it so no child ever suffered like I had again." She soon realized that the poor in Haiti were literally dying of starvation. In 1994, two orphaned babies she was trying to nurse back to health died, an experience that moved her into a total commitment.

Susan and her husband, Joe, established the Mercy and Sharing Foundation, a nonprofit agency that today cares for more than 1,600 children at three orphanages, three schools, and a medical clinic in Haiti. They have spent hundreds of thousands of dollars of their own money to fund this endeavor. Nadia François, a minister of social affairs in the Haitian government, says, "She has given life and comfort to a lot of kids who would otherwise be left, perhaps to die."

I'll return to a discussion of these magnificent moral moments in the body of this book. Each of them, inspiring in itself, is part of a larger tapestry I'd like to create concerning the meaning of moral intelligence and the life of virtue.

Part I

What Is Moral Intelligence?

INTRODUCTION

THE BETTER ANGELS OF OUR NATURE

The mysterious complexity of our life is not to be embraced by maxims...to lace ourselves up in formulas of that sort is to repress all the divine promptings and inspirations that spring from growing insight and sympathy...from a life vivid and intense enough to have created a wide fellow-feeling with all that is human.

—George Eliot

Magnificent moral moments often move us to tears. They can make chills run down our spine; sometimes they inspire us to change. Why is this? These stories seem to touch something deep within us, a part of us that is naturally attracted to what is good and virtuous.

The psychologist Erik Erikson writes: "Men have always shown a dim knowledge of their better potentialities by paying homage to those purest leaders who taught the simplest and most inclusive rules for an undivided mankind."

Abraham Lincoln evoked the source of this dim knowledge with his phrase "the better angels of our nature."

Is this dim knowledge of our better potentialities a unique kind of moral intelligence that is part of human nature? If it is part of our nature, why is it that so few people develop it fully? And if the rules taught by our purest leaders are so simple, why have I found it so hard to live virtuously? These questions are among the overarching concerns that have prompted me to write this book. I have other concerns, some of which are more personal.

MY STRUGGLES WITH RIGHTDOING AND WRONGDOING

For the first thirteen years of my life, I was a model child. I was a straight-A student, the president of my class every year in elementary school. I was my mother's favorite, always willing to help around the house, and the boy who cut the neighbors' lawns and helped them with their groceries. I was the nuns' favorite too, president of the Sodality of Our Lady, the society in Catholic schools that honors the Blessed Virgin Mary. I was considered a perfect little Catholic boy and the pride of my family.

But during early puberty all this good-boy behavior developed a dark side. My mother could no longer tolerate my father's drinking and womanizing and divorced him. I was shattered, and gravitated to other guys whose fathers were alcoholic and whose parents were divorced. We began to drink and frequent brothels. It was a Jekyll and Hyde existence: I was president of the senior class and second academically during my first two years of college, but I ran with a crowd that drank almost every day. I helped my mother financially but stole money from the place where I worked. By the age of twenty, I was a full-blown alcoholic and had a sordid history of sexual experience with prostitutes.

As the pain of drinking and out-of-control sexuality intensified, I hit what is called in addiction programs an "early bottom." I decided to follow the advice of the elementary school nuns and several priests, who had suggested that I had a "calling" to serve God. I entered the seminary at age twenty-one and became an exemplary but rigid novice, praying on my knees for three or four hours at a time, and fasting to a point where my physical health was threatened. After four years of this moral and spiritual rigidity, I began to loosen up. I secretly started drinking and stealing drugs from the seminary pharmacy. Over the next five years, this behavior escalated, becoming so bad that I was sent to two psychiatrists, both of whom advised me to give up the pursuit of the priesthood. I had struggled with the demands of living a life of poverty, celibacy, and obedience for nine and a half years, but I was afraid to leave. It was only during my graduate work, after studying the Greek philosopher Aristotle's *Nicomachean Ethics,* that I was inspired to take the risk of leaving my religious order. What I learned from Aristotle's work is one of the anchors of this book.

When I left the seminary I was thirty years old and truly a "lost soul." I had advanced degrees in theology, philosophy, and psychology, but such degrees were hard to market. I finally got a job teaching at a Catholic high school but was soon fired for missing work because of my drinking. I was fired from my next two jobs as well. These firings helped me to hit my real bottom, and after an especially bad binge in 1965, I committed myself voluntarily to Austin State Hospital. My commitment required that I be there for only a week, but I was put in Ward 8, which housed people with a variety of psychiatric disorders, including those with severe mental illness. Six of us slept in a room that was about nineteen by twenty-four feet. Alcoholics were despised by this population—we were not considered to be sick enough. I had to be constantly alert to guard against being killed. I left when my seven days were up and entered a twelve-step alcohol recovery program, marrying two years after I sobered up. I pursued sobriety with my usual zealous and polarized passion. I was exemplary, but I could never find moderation. I was either all good or all bad. I worked the alcohol recovery program rigidly for the first nine years and then began having affairs. The first six years of my marriage were wonderful, but I was a covert incest survivor and had a whore/Madonna mentality (which meant you don't have sex with someone you love), and after the first four years of marriage, I became sexually anorexic. I loved my wife, but when it came to genital sex, my body froze. None of this is an excuse for my sexual compulsivity—but coupled with my nine and a half years of abstinence in the seminary was an elaborate denial system that allowed me to justify my sexual behavior. My sexual acting out intensified over a period of six years, and I slowly realized that I had become addicted in a new way.

A PROFOUND LONELINESS

Despite my sexual acting out, I had achieved a modicum of external success. I was making a six-figure income, had a counseling practice with a yearlong waiting list, and was a much sought-after speaker and workshop leader. I did part-time leadership training and stress management for an oil and chemical company, and did one-day workshops for several Fortune 500 companies. Life should have been good—but addiction is a profoundly lonely activity. I was living a lie. My brain engaged in doublethink, one part ravaged with shame and another part basking in the good work of healing I was providing for people. I could heal others but not myself.

I found the beginning of sexual sobriety on August 13, 1981. I found it in a way that still baffles and humbles me today, which I will describe in chapter 5.

However, even in my recovery I remained cut off and felt disconnected from everyone and everything. There was an emptiness in me—a black hole—that held dominion over my life. While I was living according to all the moral laws I knew, I still felt like I was on the outside of life looking in.

I felt no real connection to the schools I had gone to. Even though I had been senior class president in high school, I had little interest in my class and let others organize our reunions. People I had been friends with in the past slipped out of my life.

Sometimes I could hardly remember their names. I lectured at Palmer Episcopal Church in adult theology for twenty years, but after I left Palmer to pursue the challenges created by my PBS television series *Bradshaw on the Family*, I had little contact with the church until recently.

I WAS NOT REALLY ALONE

From the time I sobered up until I stopped my private counseling practice in 1988, nearly four thousand people sought my help with the problems in their lives. Listening to their stories, along with my conversations with friends, made it abundantly clear that I was not alone in my moral confusion. Either people rigidly followed the Bible or held the doctrines of their family religious preference or they floundered. Even those who acted as if they knew the truth about moral goodness were struggling with their marriages, their children, being honest about their taxes, and the specific demands of civic duty; they were horrified by the greed and shamelessness that surrounded them, but did nothing about it.

I heard people say things like "Our child is on drugs and we don't know what to do," "My husband is never home, and when he is at home, he won't talk about anything," "Evil people seem to be making out better than good people," "I can't find a church I feel comfortable in," "I'm struggling with the idea of a loving God," "I don't have any real friends," "I feel lonely and disconnected. I wish I had the absolute faith I had as a child," or "I've accepted Jesus as my personal savior but I can't give up the affair I'm in." Other born-agains were cheating on their taxes or engaged in unethical business deals. The people I knew, counseled, and interacted with were all struggling with the complexity and ambiguity of moral choices.

WHAT HAD GONE WRONG?

My own moral and religious education was rigorous. I remember memorizing the Ten Commandments and the Catholic catechism, and how I was called upon to recite these while a nun held a ruler poised to hit my open palms if I faltered. Once these rules were memorized, it was my duty to obey them without thought or question. In fact, questioning was considered a mark of disobedience and a lack of faith. Good moral behavior was simply a matter of obeying the rules with little or no understanding of many of them. The goal of my childhood moral teaching was to make me virtuous. But this way of teaching moral values, based as it was on blind obedience, did not make me virtuous. Nor did it make my friends or the people I counseled (religious or otherwise) virtuous.

What confused me was that the choices that challenged me as a moral person were often *not* clear and certain. If moral law were a system of absolute rules, there would be no need to deliberate or anguish over what choice was the best for me to make; there would be no need for freedom of choice. But living a good life involved complexity, ambiguity, and risk, and I often found myself puzzled.

QUESTIONS RAISED BY THE MAGNIFICENT MORAL MOMENTS

As the novelist George Eliot says in the quotation at the beginning of this introduction, "The mysterious complexity of our life is not to be embraced by maxims." I can illustrate this mysterious complexity by looking again at the magnificent moral moments with which I started this book. Each one makes a statement about goodness and virtue, but at the same time, each one raises new questions that must be dealt with.

The Fire Department Culture

William Feehan's description of the "fire department culture" underscores the fact that many people have a desire for goodness that transcends material rewards. They have a caring will and an appetite for service; their priority is to help their fellow human beings. But can we say that every person who becomes a firefighter has this caring will? I know some who do not seem to be people of goodwill. The real question is, *how* is this desire and appetite for goodness created? How do we educate people in a way that will nurture and develop a passionate desire for goodness?

Ruby Bridges

Ruby Bridges' strength seems to have come from her religious beliefs. But could those religious beliefs alone sustain this six-year-old girl? One answer is that Ruby was securely attached to her mother, who had a deeply committed religious faith, and both Ruby and her mother were part of a cohesive church community headed by a respected pastor. It was the mutuality of her secure bonding to her mother and her minister that gave Ruby the inner courage and strength to do what she did. Religious faith that begins in secure attachment to beloved source figures is unquestionably a source of moral strength.

But what if those source figures believe in a perfectionist and cruelly punishing God, as Susan Krabacher's mother did, using that belief to abuse Susan? What if people's religious bonding leads them to believe in a holy war that offers them a sure place in heaven if they fly their planes into the Twin Towers and the Pentagon, as the terrorist pilots of September 11, 2001, believed? Can that form of religious bonding be a source of moral goodness? Do we have any objective way to judge what is good or bad religion? Why do so many religions come to believe that their way is the only righteous way?

Maria Montessori

Maria Montessori brought forth the innate intelligence and goodness in the children she taught by creating a special kind of environment. But can environment alone be the source of virtue? The Nazis tried to shape environments that would create a master race—and spawned untold horror and evil. My religious community was dedicated to spiritual development, but it could not contain the spiritual bankruptcy of my addiction. How can we find ways to create the environments that fulfill the promise of Montessori's work?

Conscience and Civil Disobedience

Henry David Thoreau, who refused to pay his poll tax, modeled a conscience that superseded blind obedience to civil law. Hugh Thompson and his comrades also went beyond official duty and military law by intervening at My Lai.

But couldn't we argue that the terrorist pilots of 9/11 were also following their consciences? That they saw America as so sinful, materialistic, and degraded that their consciences demanded taking action against such evil? Thoreau's heirs might say that nonviolence is the solution, but Thompson protected the Vietnamese civilians by directing his crew to shoot any Americans who interfered. Which model should we follow, and when?

Abraham Lincoln

Abraham Lincoln had an ability (now described as emotional intelligence) to inspire and move others to action in order to achieve justice. I could have quoted any one of his famous speeches that played a part in changing the moral history of our country. But the emotional intelligence that Lincoln possessed was also possessed by Hitler, Jim Jones, Charles Manson, and many others who used it to inspire evildoing, cruelty, and murder. What makes emotional intelligence a source of goodness rather than a source of evil?

The Shawshank Redemption

In *The Shawshank Redemption,* Andy Dufresne is an example of the virtue of hope. Dufresne's hope allowed him to endure and triumph over unbelievable odds in order to find his personal redemption. Dufresne was wrongly convicted, but couldn't a guilty prisoner also have an enduring and passionate hope of breaking out of jail? Couldn't hope give him the strength to dig a tunnel to freedom? How do we evaluate what constitutes the *virtue* of hope?

Morrie Schwartz

Morrie Schwartz gained great wisdom from his life experiences. But not everyone uses their experience as a source of wisdom. I recently visited an old, old friend whom I found soured and bitter about his life. He complained about the children he'd raised, suggesting that he would be so much better off financially if he had never had them. He sat across from me drinking one glass of wine after another, angry and resentful. So experience alone is not a reliable moral teacher. What is it that makes one person's experience a source of wisdom and another's a source of despair?

Johnny Pagnini

Johnny Pagnini showed incredible courage in saving a young woman from being raped and probably murdered by two gang members who had kidnapped her. When I asked him how he decided to do what he did, he said that he just did it—he didn't even have to think about it. But Johnny had a family of his own who would have suffered great deprivation had he been killed or injured in a ninety-mile-an-hour auto chase. Johnny also risked the lives of other drivers on the freeway. For most people, the same behavior would have been frivolous and reckless. How can an act of courage for one person be a ruthless, even vicious behavior for another?

Susan Krabacher

Susan Krabacher's choice to devote her life to the poor children in Haiti is a remarkable example of how experiencing evil can motivate us to do good. But when we consider the amount of evil in the world, why aren't more people moved to combat it? We may be sickened by evil, yet still remain apathetic in the face of it. What does it take to move people to virtuous action? And why are people most moved to take action only when there's a terrible crisis? How do we become committed to the long, slow fight to change things for the better?

BACK TO MY ROOTS

In my attempt to answer these many questions, I went back to my early days in the seminary and reviewed my former studies of the Greek ethical tradition that culminated in the work of Aristotle. I also reconnected with the medieval philosopher and theologian Thomas Aquinas. These men had helped me change the direction of my life and shaped my early adult understanding of the mysteries of good and evil, and how the life of virtue can be achieved.

Now, forty-five years later, I realized that when I first studied these great thinkers, I was too immature and lacking in life experience to grasp the depth and grandeur of their thought, even though they did mark a profound turning point in my life. As I reread them, I was amazed at the coherence of their ethical thinking and how it offered real answers to the complex moral questions of today. Aristotle wrote four hundred years before Christ, yet his work anticipates the most recent advances in our understanding of the plasticity of the brain and the part played by intuition and emotion in making moral choices.

It was Aristotle's belief that virtue and human happiness are synonymous. He asserted that we cannot be fully human without developing the inner strengths he called "virtues." Both Aristotle and Thomas Aquinas also believed that at the pinnacle of moral life are the virtues of love and justice, which transcend mere adherence to rules and laws. But these virtues, they said, can be fully developed only when we also develop the skill to make choices based on "lucid and reasonable desire." They believed that this skill was itself a virtue, and they called it prudence or moral wisdom. They saw it as a unique practical intelligence that allows us to discover the best, most caring alternative amid the countless circumstances that are present in every real moral choice. How we can develop this moral intelligence in ourselves and others is one of the cornerstones of this book.

BEYOND THE ANCIENT THINKERS

As stunning and brilliant as their thinking was, Aristotle and Aquinas did not have the benefit of the important new discoveries about human nature that have emerged one after the other in the last 150 years. They did not have the insights we have gained from developmental psychology, such as the critical importance of secure attachment in infancy and how the feeling of shame (which is the foundation for the development of guilt, which governs a good conscience) can be transformed into a toxic shame-based identity that destroys our sense of self and contaminates our moral choices. They did not have the benefit of psychotherapy, which has shown us how childhood neglect and abuse create a wounded "inner child" that can wreak havoc in our intimate relationships. They were ignorant of the neo-Freudian understanding of a strong ego or solid sense of self-esteem, which is a foundation for developing good character. They were not privy to the astounding discoveries in modern neuroscience that have given us new insights about the plasticity of our brains and our potential for excellence. All of these modern discoveries have expanded and deepened their notion of moral intelligence.

I have divided this book into three parts. Part 1 focuses on the nature of moral intelligence. In this part, I'll present more detail on the ancient notion of moral intelligence in Aristotle and Aquinas and also report on some of the modern research and theories that have a direct bearing on how to develop it. For example, research has made it clear that the two hemispheres of the brain *know* in different but complementary ways. Moral intelligence is grounded in our innate moral sentiment, which emerges early in childhood and must be exercised by acting virtuously in order to reach perfection. Moral excellence as the life of virtue is the fruit of integrating both sides of our brain.

In part 2, I suggest some of the preparatory work that is necessary for anyone who is involved in nurturing and developing the moral intelligence of those in their care. We need to nourish and develop *our own* moral intelligence if we are to be models for those we care for. I'll also discuss how unresolved issues from the past can make our lives miserable by distorting our moral choices. I'll present a proven way to resolve our unresolved wounds, hurts, and losses. Finally, I'll suggest a powerful way to solve what Carl Jung called the "ultimate ethical problem."

In part 3, I discuss some new and exciting ways to give our children the best possible foundation for a virtuous and happy life. I'll offer some concrete ways to help you develop your children's moral intelligence. I'll suggest some new ways to help those in your care develop a good conscience and solid moral character.

AN ETHICS FOR OUR TIME

I began working on this book a year before the terrorists' attacks on September 11, 2001. That atrocity was committed by men acting in obedience to a fanatical and polarized religious morality. This is the kind of morality that also produced the Nazi Holocaust, which German theologian Dorothee Sölle described as the product of a "culture of obedience." Those attacks made my decision to write this book far more urgent than I could have imagined.

Obedience and respect for authority are a necessary part of the process of growing up morally, but if we stop there, we become arrested at a developmental stage that predisposes us toward the rigid polarization of rightdoing (good) and wrongdoing (evil).

I believe that our current state of moral uncertainty and confusion offers us an unprecedented opportunity to embrace our ethical responsibility as adults. We *can* develop the inner strengths that will guide us morally no matter how much the world changes around us and no matter what new circumstances we encounter. The ancient philosophers and theologians call these inner strengths *virtues*. As one of the great founding fathers of our country, James Madison, told us: "Is there no virtue among us? If there be not...no form of government can render us secure. To suppose that any form of government will secure liberty and happiness without any form of virtue in the people, is a chimerical idea."

Please join me in my personal journey to make sense out of the complexities and ambiguity of the moral/ethical order. I want to live a virtuous life, and I want you to find a solution to your own moral and ethical dilemmas by using your own moral intelligence and personal faith. Writing this book has helped me, and I hope it will help you. There has never been a time when we had a greater need to call on the "better angels of our nature."

I

THE ANCIENT NOTION OF
THE LIFE OF VIRTUE

All virtues are the qualities that make up our humanity, and in
the virtuous man, humanity and virtue inevitably converge. It is
man's virtue that makes him human.

—Aristotle

Much learning does not teach one to have understanding.

—Heraclitus

"Many who have learned no *logos* [reasoning] live according to
logos."

—Democritus

I remember well my response when my academic advisor told
me I needed to take I. T. Eschmann's course on the sixth book of
the Greek philosopher Aristotle's *Nicomachean Ethics*. Eschmann
taught at the Pontifical Institute of Medieval Studies at the
University of Toronto, which housed some of the most learned
scholars in Greek and medieval culture and philosophy.

My heart sank. I was in my ninth year in the seminary and
couldn't imagine anything more dour and boring than spending a
whole semester on a text called "Intellectual Virtue," and especially with Eschmann, who had rarely been known to smile.
What drudgery!

But as often happens, the course I thought would be the worst
turned out to be the best. Eschmann didn't teach the *Ethics* as a
system of truth that had emerged whole from Aristotle's mind.
Instead he showed us that Aristotle was actively questioning his

own teachers, carrying on a kind of dialogue with the best thinkers of his past. It is in the sixth book of the *Nicomachean Ethics* that Aristotle takes issue with the moral doctrine of his teacher Plato. Why is that so important? Because Plato's thinking has dominated moral thought throughout the centuries. It is the ultimate source of moral doctrines that teach an absolute and unquestioning duty to the law. Even today philosophers are divided in ways that show their Aristotelian or Platonic tendencies.

THE LEGACY OF PLATO AND SOCRATES

Plato's writings recorded the teachings of Socrates, a Greek philosopher who taught that virtue and knowledge were one and the same. In the simplest of terms, Socrates and Plato believed that if you know what virtue is, you will act virtuously. They also taught that people have a duty to obey the law even if it is unjust.

To our knowledge, Socrates did not write a single book. He taught by asking his students a series of questions (we now call this the "Socratic method") that challenged their unexamined beliefs and easy assumptions. Socrates wanted to help the youth of his day think clearly and challenge the status quo in creative and proactive ways. He thought that this method would inevitably lead people to clear, logical, and objective definitions. And once they fully understood ideas such as justice, they would act virtuously.

However, the governing body of Athens saw Socrates as a threat. They believed he was corrupting the youth by rousing them to challenge the existing order. Socrates was ordered to stop his teachings or be put to death. Socrates refused to renounce what he believed to be the truth, but he also refused to disobey the established authority. He was imprisoned and condemned to death.

Socrates' friends and disciples were horrified that the Athenian civil court intended to execute him. They urged Socrates to let them help him escape. However, Socrates refused their help and voluntarily drank the cup of poison hemlock provided by the court.

Socrates' death has been viewed by generations of moralists as one of the great examples of human nobility and courage. Some have even dared to compare the death of Socrates to the death of Jesus.

However, many other moralists believe that Socrates took the love of justice to an extreme that amounted to confusing justice with legality. One should certainly obey and defend the established laws, but not at the expense of justice—especially when an innocent life is at stake. Aristotle himself believed that those who wanted to save Socrates were just to want to make the attempt, even though it was illegal. But what kind of virtue or inner knowledge could guide us in making this distinction?

MY OWN DILEMMA

At the time I took Eschmann's course, I was living in a religious community governed by a strict code of rules and living according to the vows of poverty, chastity (celibacy), and obedience. Holiness and moral rectitude consisted in being obedient to my religious vows and the rules of my community.

In the beginning, I followed the community rules and practiced my vows rigidly. But by the time I took Eschmann's course, my zeal had diminished and I was drinking heavily. I was dismayed by the hypocrisy of a significant number of priests in the community. I had been sexually stalked and fondled by a priest while in high school, and I had been repeatedly propositioned by two other priests after I entered the seminary.

I also realized that I was not the only secret drinker in my religious community. There were several alcoholic priests, including my spiritual director. I was beginning to see that absolute obedience and celibacy were a lifestyle fulfilling for a certain kind of person but not for everyone, and certainly not for most twenty-one-year-old men, which was the average age of those joining this community. Clearly, blind obedience and celibacy did not in themselves make a person virtuous.

My studies in moral philosophy and theology had taught me about the rules and laws of morality. But I did not know how to live virtuously, and neither did many of my teachers.

My course with Eschmann showed me why my earlier moral education and my current lifestyle had failed to help me live a life of excellence. Aristotle's *Ethics* was based on individual liberty, free choice, and concrete *practical* intelligence. It helped me realize that I didn't have to suffer irrationally and dutifully by obeying rules that made no sense to me.

Rules tell us what we should and should not do. They may tell us about virtue, but they do not show us how to be virtuous. Talking about what virtue is and actually being virtuous are miles apart. Blind obedience may be virtuous in certain circumstances, but I would need something more to find my way through the complexities of the real moral world.

ARISTOTLE'S OTHER TEACHERS

Eschmann showed us that the larger context from which the sixth book of the *Nicomachean Ethics* was taken was pre-Socratic. Two of the earliest Greek philosophers were Heraclitus and Democritus. These two philosophers formed a tradition of moral thought that predated Socrates and Plato but was far less well known. These men directly influenced Aristotle and clearly helped him break with the Socratic belief that knowledge and virtue are synonymous and that duty to law is absolute.

Aristotle's first teacher was Heraclitus, whom one scholar has called "the first moralist in the Western world." All that remains of Heraclitus' writings are a number of paradoxical and contradictory fragments. For example, Heraclitus said, "You cannot step into the same river twice, for fresh waters are ever flowing in upon you." In another fragment, he said, "Good and bad are the same." These fragments begin to make sense if they are understood in a moral context.

For example, "Good and bad are the same" points to Heraclitus' understanding that a particular act may be good in one set of circumstances and bad in another. Saving money may be virtuous for one person, while it might amount to hoarding and greed for someone else. Heraclitus' fragments reveal a surprisingly keen grasp of the basic problem in moral science: how can a consistent and abiding norm be established in a realm where incessantly changing circumstances affect human conduct?

"KNOWLEDGE ABOUT" VERSUS "KNOW-HOW"

We know more about Aristotle's other early teacher, Democritus, who envisioned wisdom as doing for the soul what medicine does for the body: "Medical science cures diseases of the body, but wisdom rids the soul of violent emotions."

For Democritus, the purpose of moral knowledge and education is eminently practical. Abstract thinking leads to speculative knowledge. But moral wisdom is directed toward *taking action* and can hardly be grounded on merely speculative knowledge.

Democritus frequently mentions that hard work is necessary to acquire moral wisdom. Example also plays a leading part; we learn by imitating wise and good men. Democritus repeatedly stresses the importance of *good desires*. Character and habit are the basis for the proper direction of one's life. "For those whose character is well ordered, life too is set in order along with it."

Democritus' most famous saying was "Many who have learned no *logos* [reasoning] live according to *logos*." Democritus observed that there were wise leaders and people who were skilled in practical matters who had not studied abstract treatises on morality in order to learn what they knew. They had acquired their wisdom from hard work, experience, good moral models, and the constant practice of goodwill.

Democritus helped Aristotle grasp the difference between speculative and practical knowledge. To Socrates and Plato true knowledge was abstract, eternal, and unchanging. Such a knowledge is speculative, a knowledge *about* behavior. But Democritus' teachings suggested that moral wisdom is *applied* knowledge, the practical know-how that allows its possessor to make ethically sound choices. As Aristotle summed up this distinction: "In regard to virtue, not to know what it is, but to know how to acquire it, that is what is most precious. For we do not want to know what justice is, but to be just."

Aristotle opened a door for me. I *wanted* to be virtuous, but I didn't know *how* to be. I realized that virtue comes from an *entirely different kind of education* than the one I'd had. Becoming virtuous requires more than formal knowledge. It takes years of experience and the good fortune to live in an environment of virtuous people who walk their talk. Learning to be virtuous comes from risking and making mistakes; it also comes from stories about how others struggled toward virtue. Slowly, over a period of time, a person's will is habituated in the direction of desiring to be virtuous and to do virtuous things. The joy of doing them increases a person's desire to do more virtuous acts. Rules may be the scaffold on which we build our own conscience, a framework that supports us until we're ready to stand on our own. But the most important thing is the freedom to choose and learn from our own life experience. This whole process is far more difficult and complicated—but also far more effective and fulfilling—than the simplistic, fearful way I was taught.

HOW THOMAS AQUINAS
CHANGED MY LIFE

While I was taking Eschmann's course, I was also studying the ethics of the thirteenth-century theologian Thomas Aquinas. With Aquinas, we enter a world that has been made radically different because of Christianity. However, it is not as radically different as we might think. To my utter amazement, I found Aquinas embracing Aristotle's ethics as well as many other aspects of Aristotle's work.

Aquinas is a canonized saint of the Catholic Church. He unequivocally believed that the fulfillment of life was to be reunited with God—to experience what he called a "beatific vision." He further believed that once created, each person found the way back to God through Jesus Christ and the grace of God. In view of this, why was he so enamored with Aristotle, whom he called "the Philosopher"?

What Aquinas saw in Aristotle was an affirmation of *human freedom and autonomy*. Aquinas was fully aware that his beliefs in Jesus, God, and grace were matters of faith—they were not knowledge. We humans often have to make our way in this life without certainty. Aquinas believed that humanity had the offer of grace, but that each person was responsible for how he used his powers of reason and choice. Duty is not some childish obedience to biblical or church legalism. Such a duty would demean both God and man. Our human responsibility is founded on free choice.

A VISION OF HUMAN GRANDEUR

Aquinas believed that human nature is grounded in an innate conscience and that all humans have a natural desire for the fulfillment of their life, the desire to achieve human excellence. This achievement, in the final analysis, is what happiness is. Such desire would be useless without the possibility of developing some kind of know-how to achieve it, so our will is grounded in human intelligence. Will is not an arbitrary appetite to be broken, as I had been taught as a child. Instead, Aquinas spoke of the will as an "intellectual appetite" that pushes us in the direction of natural goodness.

Aquinas believed in human grandeur. In the preface to the second part of his *Summa Theologica,* he states that man too, like God, has free will and power over his life. He believed that human beings naturally desire the good but are free to choose. He repudiated any doctrine that described human nature as wanton and therefore in need of an absolute code to keep it in check. But he would also have repudiated any kind of subjective situational morality or moral relativism, or any suggestion that we should just follow our own self-will. *Man, he believed, is governed by the desire for goodness.* He believed with Aristotle that conforming to external rules is not enough because each one of us must be personally present in our decisions. The decisions we make are always ours in a personal way. But we are always bound by the objective order of reality, and also by the inborn intellectual appetite that draws us to goodness. The theme and starting point of Aquinas' ethical thought is that man is an adult, with autonomy and personal responsibility. His will is rooted in his intellectual nature and not in arbitrariness.

For Thomas Aquinas, religion and faith are sources of moral intelligence, but not in the sense that man is a blind, incapacitated sinner who is incapable of being a creative participant in the life of the religion he belongs to and in his own personal moral life.

THE IMPORTANCE OF CONSCIENCE

I remember the day I began studying Aquinas' teaching on conscience. At one point, he asks whether a monk has an obligation to follow his conscience if it comes into conflict with his vows or religious rule. His answer is that the monk must follow his conscience as if it were a divine command. I felt as if Aquinas were speaking directly to me. Suddenly I had permission to accept myself and to listen to my doubts about the absolute religious rule I was living under.

There were many things about my religious rule that I passionately objected to. But these objections had been silenced early on; I was told it was an act of disobedience to question the rules and that I would be asked to leave if I could not follow them. So I obeyed mindlessly, driven by both duty and fear, as did many of my other colleagues. By the time I took Eschmann's course, I wanted to leave the community, but I was still afraid. Studying Aristotle's *Ethics* helped me understand that moral action involves risk, but it was Aquinas' teaching on conscience that solidified my resolve to leave.

A VIRTUE FOR RISK AND DECISION MAKING

Leaving religious life was a choice I had never faced before. There was no book of rules or moral manual to tell me what to do. This was a decision that I would face only once in my lifetime. And, like so many others, it was a decision that had no single right choice.

I had given up almost ten years of my life to study for the priesthood. I wanted those years to mean something. I knew I would be a great disappointment to my family, who saw me as their hero. I was also scared to go back into the world; I had been quite sheltered. I knew the community would give me no help and next to nothing financially. In those days when people left the seminary, they simply disappeared, and there was an unexpressed but inviolable rule of silence about them. There was no way to know how their decision turned out, or to learn from their experience. That has changed in the last twenty years, but the change came too late for me.

All of life is filled with uncertainty, risk, chance, and the unknown. We have to make choices all the time where no proof or certainty is possible. Aristotle saw that we need virtue to guide us in those relative and changing circumstances. We deliberate only when we have a choice to make—in other words, when no proof is possible or adequate; that's when we want to find both good results for our actions and good means to achieve them. Both Aristotle and Aquinas identified the virtue we need when sure knowing is lacking but our conscience or our circumstances demand that we act. Aristotle called that virtue *phronesis*, which means "moral wisdom" in Greek. Aquinas translated it into Latin as *prudentia*, or "prudence."

As I have come to understand it, prudence is the full expression or development of our inborn capacity for moral intelligence. It is conscience in action. I will come back to the virtue of prudence again and again in this book as I explore how we can live lives of moral excellence.

VIRTUE AS STRENGTH

The word *virtue* is a derivative of the Latin word *virtus,* which means both "manliness" and "strength." For Aquinas, the second meaning was dominant. Virtues enhance or perfect our normal powers. Any virtue is performance-enhancing; it gives us added power and inner strength in any situation. For example, the virtue of temperance enhances our willpower.

The Greek word for virtue was *arête,* and it meant "excellence." To be virtuous was to be consistently excellent at doing something. As Will Durant summarized Aristotle's thought in *The Story of Philosophy:* "Excellence is not an act but a habit." And both Aristotle and Aquinas point out that habit is difficult to change.

I was a drinking alcoholic when I first read that, and boy, did I understand it. I had a bad habit I seemingly could not change. Anyone who has had a bad habit knows how true this is. To have the good habits that lead to excellence brings stability and power. Bad habits lead to instability and powerlessness.

The ancient philosophers also referred to virtues as "second natures." In other words, virtues do not arise in us by nature; we are not born with them. Even in the case of moral prodigies, each of us has to work in order to master the virtue or virtues of our choice. Once mastered, however, the virtue becomes a "second nature," a new power that habitually enhances our moral performance.

Great golfers talk about "grooving" their swing, which means that they practice so much that they do not have to think about the mechanics of their swing when they hit the golf ball. Playing a musical instrument well takes years of practice. The solo violinist or pianist plays without having to think about where the fingers need to go. Just so, once a virtue is fully developed, the ethical person does not have to think about it: it has become our "second nature." In the movie *The African Queen*, Katharine Hepburn plays Rose Sayer, a British missionary in a village in German East Africa in 1914. The mission receives its mail and supplies from a coarse Canadian, Charlie Allnutt (played by Humphrey Bogart), who captains the *African Queen*.

The Germans kill Rose's brother and burn down the village. When the *African Queen* arrives, Charlie agrees to take Rose aboard his boat. Rose talks Charlie into taking her to a large lake downriver. It is a perilous journey, and Charlie starts drinking heavily. Rose throws away all his gin bottles, and Charlie begs her, saying it's only human nature to drink. Rose answers in a classic line: "Nature, Mr. Allnutt, is what we are put in this world to rise above." This statement wonderfully illustrates the idea that virtue becomes a "second nature" by overcoming our raw natural appetites.

VIRTUE AS HABITUS

A virtue is not a habit like getting up at a certain time every day or reading before you go to sleep at night. It is not mechanical or routine. In fact, it is the opposite of a mechanical routine. Aquinas called the stuff of virtue a *habitus*. A *habitus* is an inner elevation of our soul that allows us the power to operate in a morally spontaneous way. A *habitus* strengthens our character. It is an inner spiritual strength, an inclination rooted in our spiritual core that moves us toward the achievement of our full humanity, which is also our full human happiness.

We acquire a *habitus* through exercise and use. Over time it becomes our living spiritual armor. Once a *habitus* is formed, it becomes a stable quality, a permanent extension and perfection of the inner self. It is no mere intellectual understanding, and it can't be taught from the outside through instruction.

Just as we develop our muscles and heart through physical exercise, we develop the spiritual strength of virtue through what we do repeatedly.

VIRTUE AS HAPPINESS

Aristotle makes a distinction between two types of actions, depending on their goals or ends. Some ends are different from the actions that produce them. For example, the actions that go into building a house are not ends in themselves. The finished house is the goal.

There are other activities where the purpose is the activity itself. For example, a person may jog and eat nourishing food in order to be healthy—but jogging and eating nourishing food are themselves healthy activities.

Acting virtuously is the second kind of activity. It is not just a way of achieving moral excellence and happiness. For Aristotle, acting virtuously *embodies* excellence and happiness.

What I like about this is that any good act that I do—any act of kindness, generosity, bravery, temperance—*is* a virtuous act. Aristotle says that we have to do virtuous acts repeatedly in order to develop the *habitus* of virtue. (We're not really honest if we're honest only in some situations.) But I can begin to be virtuous at any time.

The underpinning of Aristotle's and Aquinas' understanding of virtue was their belief that everything that exists has a nature or purpose. The purpose of a knife is to cut things. The purpose of a needle is to sew things together. If we try to use a knife to sew things together or use a needle to cut things, both knife and needle become useless.

We humans also have a purpose for existing. When we achieve our purpose for existing, we reach our fulfillment and happiness. Aristotle asked, "Is there one purpose which supersedes all others; one good toward which our actions aim that is not subordinated to any other end—something we pursue for its own sake—something we call the highest good of human behavior?" Aristotle's answer is that it is generally agreed that the highest good is happiness (in Greek, *eudaimonia*), by which he understood habitual human flourishing or being fully human. He writes: "Why should we not call happy the man who exercises his abilities according to the highest standards of virtue and excellence in a context which affords him sufficient resources and not merely for a brief moment, but throughout his life?"

The happy life is the fulfillment of one's nature. So when we act viciously, we are going against our nature, and we diminish our chance to live fully and to flourish. Smoking and overeating are bad habits. Aristotle and Aquinas would call them vices. There are degrees of virtue and there are also degrees of vice. My alcoholism was rooted in certain genetic factors that affected one of the neurotransmitters in my brain, dopamine. Alcoholics Anonymous has said from the beginning that alcoholics have a chemical imbalance. But alcoholism (and all other addictions) are forms of being spiritually bankrupt and morally empty. The twelve steps make this clear. The fourth step asks recovering addicts to take "a searching and fearless moral inventory" of themselves. The eighth and ninth steps are about making amends to the people they have harmed in the course of their addiction. Making amends is one way to repair the addict's character defects. Smoking, overeating, and being addicted to drugs, sex, alcohol, gambling, work, or anything else are ultimately life-threatening and diminish a person's chance for full self-actualization and happiness. For Aristotle, the genuine pursuit of happiness and the virtuous life are one and the same. The realization of one's nature is the virtuous life.

A TASTE OF VIRTUE

To give you a breather from our rather heavy discussion, here are a couple of exercises you can try right away. They will give you a taste of virtue.

Private Acts

In many of the clubs that house twelve-step meetings, there is a flyer that offers practices for building character strength. When I first joined a twelve-step group, the practice I chose asked me to do two good acts each day that no one would ever find out about. As a grandiose addict, for me to do something good without bragging about it was very difficult. I *wanted* the credit.

I started the practice because I desperately needed help. I didn't know how to stop drinking. This practice didn't seem to be about drinking at all, but as it became a daily habit, I was moved by the joy I felt in helping someone in need. At first the helping was a mood-altering experience, but it was surely a better mood alterer than using alcohol. It also allowed me to be more self-nurturing. Alcoholics use alcohol as a form of self-nurturing. The inherent addictive power of alcohol takes away fear, stress, and anxiety.

Doing good acts brings a response of gratitude and when I experienced the gratitude from a person I helped, I felt good about myself. It raised my self-esteem and eased the toxic shame I felt at the core of my identity.

As I remember the joys of helping another, it triggered the desire to help someone else. Soon it became a habit and over many years a *habitus*. As I came to believe that I was a valuable person, I didn't need to drink to feel good about myself.

Preparedness

One of America's great philosophers, William James, was very interested in habits. In *Habit,* written in 1890, he says: "No matter how full a reservoir of *maxims* one may possess, and no matter how good one's *sentiments* may be, if one has not taken advantage of every concrete opportunity to *act,* one's character may remain entirely unaffected for the better." James suggests that small, seemingly unimportant acts, done systematically, can build major strengths.

His prescription: every day or two, do something for no reason other than *you would rather not do it.* You do this because when an urgent situation or catastrophe arises, you will not be as unnerved. You will be able to stand the test. It's like the premiums you pay for fire insurance. The premium does you no good at the time, and you hope you will never have to use the insurance. But if fire does come, having paid your premium will save you from ruin. The same can be said of living your life in general. If you daily deny yourself unnecessary things and are attentive to opportunities to practice virtue, then, says James, "you will stand like a tower when everything rocks around you."

A REALITY I DO NOT LIKE

The twelve steps of Alcoholics Anonymous talk about "character defects." The second step says, "[We] came to believe that a

Power greater than ourselves could restore us to sanity." Being restored to sanity implied I was quasi-insane. That was the reality I didn't like but had to accept. The main virtue I lacked as an addict was prudence. It is the virtue all addicts lack. It is the virtue (or *habitus*) that allows us to choose the mean between two extremes or vices—one of excess and the other of deficiency. Addiction is a disease of extremes. I was either all bad, the teenager getting drunk and going to brothels, or all good, the seminarian kneeling for hours in prayer. I did not know how to find the mean, a moderate course of action. The sum total of all the moral education I had did not teach me how to act wisely. That is why the ancients considered prudence the core or engine of all the other virtues.

ABSTRACT VERSUS PRACTICAL WISDOM

Let me put this another way. Speculative wisdom (what the ancients called *sophia*) is the virtue that allows us to be expert in understanding the nature of justice. Practical wisdom (*phronesis,* prudence or moral intelligence) is the virtue that enables us to be just. A moral philosopher may know everything about justice and still treat his wife and children unjustly. When Erik Erikson was writing his book *Gandhi's Truth,* he realized Gandhi was very hard on his own family. He had intolerance for their imperfections. This bothered Erikson, and he felt compelled to contrast this behavior with Gandhi's philosophy of nonviolence and tolerance. Gandhi's great doctrine was harder to practice at home.

For Aristotle and Thomas Aquinas, prudence as moral wisdom provided an intelligent safeguard against irrational and unjust doctrines. Martin Luther King Jr. refused to obey the unjust laws of segregation due to the dictates of his conscience. His action was civilly disobedient but eminently prudent.

The ancient tradition I'm describing in this chapter saw that one could not be morally virtuous without a governing virtue that was a synthesis of appropriate desires and practical intelligence. They called this ability the virtue of prudence.

ENJOYING, CARING, AND SUFFERING INTELLIGENTLY

Prudence gives blind duty and obedience eyes—vision to find the mean between extremes.

Prudence guides every action toward the virtuous mean. It enables us

- To be brave rather than *cowardly* or *ruthless*
- To be just rather than *dishonest* or *legalistic*
- To be self-controlled or temperate rather than *compulsively controlling* or *impulsive and out of control*
- To take compassionate action in the face of suffering rather than being *self-absorbed* or *weakening and enabling others by doing for them what they could do for themselves*

It's the moral equivalent to having a good ear for music or the ability to find just the right word to express what you mean. The intelligence involved in finding this mean is intuitive. (In chapter 3 I'll refer to it as "felt thought.") It is based in the nondominant hemisphere of the brain—the part of the brain that knows through feelings and desires.

None of this is easy. Aristotle says, "It is hard in each instance to find the mean just as it is difficult to find the center of a circle." He goes on to say: "Anybody can become angry—that is easy, but to be angry with the right person and to the right degree and at the right time and for the right purpose, and in the right way— that is not within everybody's power and is not easy."

Sometimes one of the two extremes is more erroneous than

the other and our experience will help us learn which way to go. Sometimes we won't be able to find the exact mean and we will have to take the next best course, choosing the lesser of the two evils.

Our experience will necessarily be sprinkled with erroneous choices, and we will learn, by means of the pleasure or pain our behavior precipitates, how to discover the mean. It takes time and experience—often failure and suffering—to develop our moral intelligence as the virtue of prudence. But as the French philosopher Andre Comte-Sponville says, "Once we've developed it, we can enjoy, care, and suffer intelligently."

WHERE DOES EMOTION FIT IN?

Aristotle and Aquinas believed that every human faculty—our senses, our body, our will, and our emotions—is imbued with intelligence. Obviously, this goes beyond what today we try to measure on IQ tests. The Harvard psychologist Howard Gardner introduced a theory of multiple intelligences in his book *Frames of Mind*. As any great athlete knows, we have a bodily intelligence (what Gardner calls kinesthetic/somatic intelligence). Sculptors and architects have a kind of spatial intelligence. Great composers and musicians have a musical intelligence.

We also can have interpersonal and intrapsychic intelligence. The combination of these two intelligences has been called "emotional intelligence," and I will have a great deal more to say about this in the chapters that follow.

Aristotle and Aquinas understood that emotion was centrally involved in moral choice. They clearly saw that emotion was imbued with intelligence. They also saw the human will as imbued with intelligence. As I've noted, they referred to the will as an intellectual appetite operating for the fulfillment of our nature. Their ethics is grounded in human desire. The ultimate root of moral intelligence is precisely the will as the life force.

WHY PRUDENCE IS NOT SUBJECTIVE

The gut issues of morality that you and I deal with on a daily basis are not about human action in general, but they have to do with this or that human action in this or that set of circumstances, which we deal with out of our own unique, incomparable personalities. This is what confused me so much in my struggles with morality. I knew rules ad nauseam, but how to apply them was another question. I found that others had the same problem.

This is why Aristotle and Thomas Aquinas believed that mature moral intelligence was about the practical world, where uncertainties and particular circumstances make an exact science impossible. There are no ready-made codes or sets of rules that cover all the ever-changing and unique individual situations that we encounter throughout our lives.

Because ethics cannot be an exact science, *there is a need for virtue to govern particular changing and uncertain situations.* They thought of the virtue of prudence as a kind of "situational conscience." A situational conscience, as we will discuss, has an objectivity about it. It is *not* the same as situational ethics, which is subjective and relative.

PRUDENCE AND INFORMED CONSCIENCE

Prudence cannot be developed without a moral code. Moral action presupposes a code of ethics. But the whole point of having a moral code is to apply it in such a way that we develop the art of living virtuously. A moral code concerns itself first with general principles—universal statements governing moral conduct, such as the Ten Commandments and the Golden Rule. "Thou shall not kill" is accepted by people nearly everywhere as a basic moral precept. This precept is often extended to prohibit the wanton killing of any living thing. But if you are confronted by a burglar inside your home, if that burglar is holding a butcher knife and threatening to kill you if you do not give him what he wants, most moral and legal codes will give you the right to kill your assailant to save your own life.

When a prudent person makes a virtuous choice, the intuition that helps her to ascertain the mean (the action that is neither excessive nor deficient) comes from an objective moral code. There is an interplay between the objective and the personal and circumstantial.

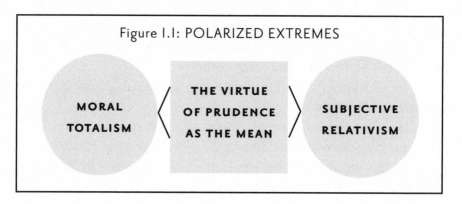

Figure I.I: POLARIZED EXTREMES

MORAL TOTALISM > THE VIRTUE OF PRUDENCE AS THE MEAN > SUBJECTIVE RELATIVISM

Prudence steers a course between our concrete, specific, personal circumstances and our will toward the good, drawing on the emotional intelligence we have developed and the conscience we have put effort into forming. Prudence is our situational conscience, or conscience as applied in the unique, concrete situation a person is facing. The virtue of prudence presupposes:

• An informed conscience based on a person's learned moral code, and tested by experience wherever possible
• The practical ability to grasp the concrete, here-and-now aspects of the unique situation in which a choice must be made
• The unique personality of a person who is choosing (that is, the person's character)

• A right desire or appetite (that is, the person *wants* to do the morally right thing, and has done so frequently in the past)
• A past experience of translating this moral code into action (i.e., a habit of good practical reasoning)

JOHNNY PAGNINI AND ME

For a concrete example of prudence in action, let's go back to the story of Johnny Pagnini, which I presented in the prologue.

Johnny Pagnini was driving down a San Diego freeway when he saw a woman being beaten in the backseat of the car ahead of him. He didn't know that the two men in the car were gang members who intended to rape and kill the woman. Yet Johnny felt the need to act. As he retold the story later, he had no awareness of thinking, *Should I call the police? I have a wife and children, and there's a woman in my car whom I'm taking home from work. In risking my life, I risk leaving my family orphaned and risk my passenger's safety too.*

However, in his subconscious mind there were a number of highly relevant considerations. If he'd had time, he might have told himself: *Two of my brothers are dead, and I vividly remember the excruciating grief my parents suffered because of their death. I can't bear to think of the pain this woman's parents will feel if these thugs kill her. I am in the race car business. I drive race cars and sell them. My passenger is my associate, and she also drives race cars. I am well trained to drive at high speed and maneuver in traffic.*

None of this entered his conscious mind at the moment of his decision to chase after the offenders. The decision, the last practical judgment of prudence that initiates action, was immediate and intuitive—the fruit of all the elements I described above. And for Johnny Pagnini it was a prudent decision.

Each of us can ask ourselves what we would do in such

circumstances. I would have called 911 and reported what was going on and where I was on the San Diego freeway. To do less would be apathetic and uncaring. But as I've said, for me to follow the car for three and a half hours, as Johnny did, would be ruthless and irresponsible.

Johnny Pagnini found himself in an utterly unique situation. His decision was exactly the right one for him. A number of his personal and moral resources meshed in that moment:

- His strong conscience and sense of personal responsibility
- His instinct to love and care for those in need
- His experience with the death of his two brothers
- His daring and skill as a race car driver

All this came together in an act of tremendous virtue.

Johnny Pagnini's decision to follow that car did not stem from a logical judgment based on moral axioms. Such a connection is impossible in changing and novel situations. It came from what Aristotle and Aquinas describe as affective inclination or intuition. The particular kind of intelligence that governed his act was based on affect (feeling) and an intuition related to a sense of union with another human being.

OBJECTIONS TO PRUDENCE

To many people today, a prudent person is an ultraconservative nerd—someone who avoids taking any risks, who always plays it safe and always protects himself. Josef Pieper, a modern commentator on Thomas Aquinas, wrote:

> To the mind of contemporary man...there is no good deed that cannot be imprudent or evil deed that cannot be prudent; rather often he will judge lying and cowardice to be prudent but truthfulness and brave self-denial just as often to be imprudent.

Immanuel Kant, certainly one of the greatest philosophical minds ever known, did not regard prudence as a virtue. He viewed it as nothing more than enlightened or shrewd self-love. Kant, like Socrates, believed in the demands of absolute duty under all conditions no matter what the consequences were. One of his notorious examples asks if you have a right to lie to a murderer who asks if his intended victim is hiding in your house. No, says Kant: "to be truthful ... in all declarations is ... a sacred and unconditionally commanding law of reason that admits of no expediency whatsoever." It is better to turn your friend in than to be derelict in your duty, even if an innocent person's life is at stake. Duty to truth supersedes prudent choice.

This is the kind of absolute reasoning that has become unacceptable to me and to many of us moderns, and it was unacceptable to Aristotle and Aquinas. The Socratic ethics of absolute duty is fertile ground for the emergence of the culture of obedience—the kind that spawned the horror of Nazism and Stalinism and was reenacted by Pol Pot, Slobodan Milosevic, Saddam Hussein, the Taliban, Osama bin Laden, the terrorists of September 11, the white supremacists, and the radical fundamentalists who bomb abortion clinics and kill abortion doctors. The ancient Greek tradition that I've described in this chapter rejected such moral totalism. What is the value of absolute principles if they are detrimental to good sense, common decency, simple humanity, and compassion?

These behaviors take the virtue of obedience to the extreme where it becomes a vice. They expose the potential for evil and inhumanity in an ethics of blind obedience and duty to absolute rule. Millions of people are still suffering and dying because of this blind obedience.

What I gratefully found in Aristotle and Aquinas was a foundation for understanding and developing the kind of applied moral wisdom I've called prudence or moral intelligence. They showed me the way to develop a virtue to replace absolute moral certainty where such certainty is impossible. But the virtue in question was rooted in conscience and developed moral intelligence.

Because moral totalism and cultures of obedience have caused us to be suspicious of any authority that claims to be "the truth," we need to develop the virtue of prudence. Many have resorted to a subjective relativism. But prudence itself is the mean between moral totalism and pure relativism. We desperately need a new model of moral education, and a prudential ethics of virtue fills this need. André Comte-Sponville writes: "We deceive ourselves if we think that prudence is a thing of the past; it is the most modern of our virtues, or rather the virtue that modern times has made the most necessary."

2

NEW DISCOVERIES ABOUT HUMAN NATURE: OUR BIOLOGICAL/ EMOTIONAL GUIDANCE SYSTEM

To know what is good for man we have to know his nature.
—Erich Fromm

Among people, cooperation is just as pronounced among primitive tribes as it is among civilized citizens.... The more people helped each other, the more the community thrived.... It is literally in our nature.

—Matt Ridley

I see affect or feeling as the primary innate biological motivating mechanism, more urgent than drive, deprivation and pleasure, and more urgent even than physical pain. Without its amplification, nothing else matters; and with its amplification, anything can matter.

—Silvan Tomkins

Any neutral observer, and you and I if we could talk rationally, would have to conclude that the state we should aim for is the one in which we are both unselfish.

—Steven Pinker

My recovery from alcoholism demanded that I give up the substances and behaviors that defended me from my feelings of being flawed and defective as a person, what I'll refer to in this chapter as toxic shame. The use of alcohol also allowed me to repress my fear, sadness, anger, and rage. The twelve-step program asks its members to live in a "rigorously honest" way. This meant that if I wanted to get sober, I had to come out of hiding. I had to give up my intellectual façade and let go of my "star, people-pleasing, nice guy" false self. Most of my life I had guarded against being vulnerable. And underneath these masks, there was a true self that I hardly knew. It was astonishing to me that the more I really felt my feelings, the clearer I could think. Slowly I realized that I was making my own choices.

One of the most important recovery rules I learned stated, "We have to act ourselves into a right way of feeling and thinking rather than try to think or feel ourselves into a right way of acting." I slowly realized that this was very close to Aristotle's dictum that we can only become virtuous by acting virtuously. Acting the right way is far more important than knowing the right way to act.

Recovery also demanded that I be part of a community. In the twelve-step group I felt like I belonged for the first time.

I was two years married and five years sober when I went to Rice University to further my studies in psychology, philosophy, and theology. My program included the fields of evolutionary biology and ethics. It was my ethics professor who suggested that I enlarge a term paper that contained some of the insights I will share with you in this chapter; I consider that the long-ago genesis of this book. It was during my doctoral studies that I learned the importance of healthy shame to the development of moral life. During this time I also came to believe that we humans have an innate moral intelligence that is perfected through the development of virtue. Since then, I have been following the many new and exciting discoveries in neuroscience that have filled out the picture of how we come to be moral beings.

THE VOCABULARY OF EMOTIONS:
SILVAN TOMKINS

I grew up being told that emotions were weak. I heard the statement "Don't be so emotional" over and over again. Any expression of anger was punished. Sadness—as in crying for more than a minute or so—was considered very weak, especially for boys. Even joy was curtailed. I especially remember a Saturday night when our whole family was together (quite rare) and we were goofing around, laughing, and acting silly. Suddenly I heard my mom's bellowing voice saying, "I think we have had enough fun for one night," and that was it. Apparently about eight minutes was all she could take.

My recovery experience did not support the belief that feelings were weak. I learned that emotions were what made us alive and that emotions were more important to my real life than logic. As I counseled people, I realized that by simply having them feel their feelings, they could be transformed. When I discovered the work of the psychologist Silvan Tomkins, my belief in the primacy of feelings was validated.

In the early 1960s Tomkins developed a theory of what he called the "affect system" that was truly revolutionary. (An affect is what we commonly call a feeling, although Tomkins used the word much more precisely.) I agree with Donald Nathanson, one of today's leading psychiatrists in the field of affect theory, who says: "That Tomkins did not receive the kind of national or international award that might have saluted appropriately his contribution and its genius is the shame of our era."

THE AFFECT SYSTEM

Most of us learned about the reproductive system, the nervous system, the circulatory system, and the immune system in our high school biology class. The "affect system" that Tomkins identified is just as fundamental. As he said, it is our "primary innate biological motivating mechanism"—the system that gives meaning to our lives and causes us to act on that meaning.

Tomkins' theory traces how our basic biological responses are converted into our most complex emotions. First, a few definitions:

- *Affects* themselves are biological mechanisms that unfold in the body according to precisely written programs. Each of the affects lasts a strictly determined period of time. There is good evidence that these patterns are genetically determined, part of our biological evolution that appeared first in life-forms as primitive as the reptile. We share some affects with other animals.
- The word *feeling* indicates awareness of an affect. Feeling implies the presence of a capacity for knowledge and understanding. The move from affects to feelings involves a leap from biology to psychology.
- *Emotions* require still another level of complexity. Each time an affect is triggered, it happens in the context of some situation, interaction, or scene. As we accumulate experience, affect becomes intertwined with memory. Emotion is the complex combination of a current affect with these memories and with the affects these memories also trigger. Emotion is an affect placed within a script, scene, or story. Whereas affect is biology, and feeling is psychology, emotion is biography.

As Donald Nathanson sums up: "An affect lasts but a few seconds, a feeling only long enough for us to make the flash of recognition, and an emotion as long as we keep finding memories that continue to trigger that affect." So when a person says something like, "I was mad then and I'm still mad," she is remembering the scene that triggered the affect anger, and by remembering the trigger, she once again produces the affect. She feels the anger as if it were happening in the present.

If, as I'm arguing, there is a moral intelligence, then affect is the biological foundation on which it rests. Without affect, there is no emotion, no motivation, and no fuel for the engine of our lives.

A FLASH OF INSIGHT

It was his newborn son that gave Silvan Tomkins his first flash of insight into the affect system. What was it about his infant son that triggered his new awareness? Tomkins' son started crying. While you may be saying, "So what? We've all seen a baby cry," Tomkins saw how amazing it was for his son to cry. His son cried exactly the same way any adult cried, and yet the newborn had no experience and no way of appraising something sorrowful. He was not crying in response to a conscious loss. Unlike an adult, who knows why he's crying, the infant does not know why; he merely cries.

Tomkins had discovered the affect he later called distress, a "hardwired," preprogrammed, genetically determined mechanism that exists in every human at birth. He would subsequently identify eight more affects.

Tomkins divided affects into types or categories and described each with two words that show them on a spectrum, the first word indicating their mildest form and the second representing their most intense presentation. The three types or categories included two positive affects, interest/excitement and enjoyment/pleasure; one neutral affect, surprise/startle; and six negative

affects, distress/anguish, fear/terror, anger/rage, shame/humilia-
tion, and dissmell, and disgust (affects that protect us from toxic
air, water, and food).

The universality of Tomkins' conclusions was later verified by
the cross-cultural studies of psychologists Paul Ekman and
Carroll Izard. They demonstrated that people everywhere in the
world can identify an affect from a simple photograph of a facial
expression. No matter what the culture, people in more than
twenty-one countries recognized the same affect, whether they
were Western or Eastern, literate or (like Ekman's subjects in
New Guinea) preliterate.

While affects are universal, each cuture has its own social
norms, which put emphasis on the expression of certain affects
and curtail expression of others. For example, each affect has a
specific cry or vocalization as well as a specific pattern of breathing. But societies generally do not permit their members to
scream in rage or to cry out in excitement, distress, or terror
whenever or wherever they wish.

Each culture's taboos on certain emotional expressions have
caused some confusion between repressed affect and authentic innate affect. Our country, for example, has been very slow to accept weeping by men. During the 1972 presidential primaries,
Senator Edmund Muskie was viewed as the Democratic front-
runner, but he lost his momentum partly because it was reported
that he broke down and wept as he defended his wife's integrity
and character against a false accusation. His weeping shattered
his image as a strong leader.

AFFECTS MAKE GOOD THINGS BETTER AND BAD THINGS WORSE

Affects intensify or amplify the stimulus that sets them in motion. Tompkins saw that no matter whether it was something his son had seen, heard, smelled, tasted, or remembered that triggered an affect, the experience itself was intensified by the affect. "Affect," says Tompkins, "makes good things better and bad things worse." Whenever we experience any kind of urgent passion, it has been provided by an affect, and the energy of the affect predisposes us to move and take action.

For example, the affect interest makes whatever has caught our attention *very* interesting. Each affect makes us care about different things in different ways. If fear is triggered by something we see, we experience that thing as fearful. But the same stimulus that produces fear in one person may produce enjoyment in another. Children have different temperaments—some are more shy and timid and others are more aggressive. A child's temperament will often determine why the same stimulus (say, a certain kind of toy that makes sounds) might trigger fear in the timid child and interest in the aggressive child.

Before the work of Tomkins, thinking, feeling, and behavior were thought of as three different functions of the brain. Tomkins argued that these distinctions are incorrect. As Donald Nathanson writes: "Not only does affect influence and often control the thinking made possible by the most advanced structures of the new brain (what we call the neocortex), but it is a form of thinking— the action thinking of the old brain."

Another of Tomkins' best interpreters, the psychologist Gershen Kaufman writes: "In Tomkins' view, the primacy blueprint for cognition, decision and action are provided by the affect system." I knew this was true; I had experienced it in my recovery process. The more I owned my feelings, the more I could change my "stinking thinking" and get my "brain out of hock," to use the recovery jargon. Alcohol is a mind-changing chemical, as are all drugs that addicts use. Over years of using, an alcoholic or drug addict's thinking is distorted by the person's defensive denial system. Our feelings are not just a form of thinking; they are essential for making decisions on how to act. As an alcoholic, I tried to solve the problems caused by my drinking by drinking more alcohol. That's what is meant by "stinking thinking" and having your "brain in hock."

Our feelings are the way our minds establish the value and significance of our experiences, the value and significance of an experience is the *meaning* of the experience for the person having it. We simply do not take action on experiences that have no value for us.

Understanding all of this made it clear to me why Aristotle said affective inclination was the source of moral action.

WHAT MAKES US HUMAN?
THE AFFECT OF SHAME

Although we share some affects with creatures as primitive as reptiles, human beings are more than highly evolved animals. "The drives man is born with," writes psychologist Erik Erikson, "are not instincts; . . . [unlike animals', they do not] carry in themselves the patterns of completion." In another place he says, "As an animal, man is nothing. . . . Man's 'inborn instincts' are drive fragments to be assembled . . . during a prolonged childhood."

We humans give up instinctual determinism for freedom, the ability to choose that Aquinas valued so highly. As another psychologist, Erich Fromm, put it, "The price we pay for lack of instinctual determinism is freedom, which brings with it insecurity and tension." Our freedom is part of our human nature, and the essence of our unique human nature lies precisely in those characteristics that are not shared with other animals.

For Tomkins shame is the affect that is most related to our sense of self.

BLUSHING, SHAME, AND CONSCIENCE

In 1839, Dr. Thomas Burgess, a member of the Royal College of Surgeons, published *The Physiology or Mechanism of Blushing*. Burgess' research established for the first time that in addition to light-skinned Europeans, dark-skinned races worldwide also blush; in other words, blushing is a universal human trait. He had identified one biological sign of what Tomkins would later term the "affect system."

Burgess' work became the single most important source for Charles Darwin's study of shame. In *The Expression of the Emotions in Man and Animals,* published in 1872, Darwin asked what it is to be human. He answered, "Blushing is the most peculiar and the most human of all expressions." And the phenomenon of blushing is a manifestation of the affect shame.

The early-twentieth-century Russian philosopher Vladimir Solovyov reiterated Darwin's work placing shame, the mother of the blush, at the heart of his philosophical anthropology and ethics. In *The Justification of the Good,* he writes: "The feeling of shame...is a fact which absolutely distinguishes man from all lower nature...[it] is the true spiritual root of all human good and the distinctive characteristic of man as a moral being." Natural shame, if developed properly, leads to a sense of guilt, and guilt safeguards human conscience. Natural shame is the root of moral intelligence.

As Tomkins points out, shame is innate, a hardwired, genetically determined mechanism, and it operates even before we are consciously aware of it. We need our parents to name the affect shame so that we can recognize it as a feeling.

MY MOST ENLIGHTENING
PSYCHOLOGICAL DISCOVERY

When I wrote my book *Healing the Shame That Binds You* in 1988, I was sharing the most important psychological discovery I had ever made about myself. In naming toxic (unhealthy) shame, I was naming a demon that had almost destroyed my life.

Shame first appears at about eight months. It is usually triggered when a stranger or unfamiliar face intrudes upon us. Suddenly we are exposed, uncovered. A child feels it especially in his face; his self feels as visible and exposed as his face. Blushing actually amplifies the feeling. One feels ashamed of shame. Young children instinctively avert their eyes, look away or down, or hide their faces. Later, however, shame may be manifested as a hostile stare. As a child develops and becomes more aware, shame is experienced as the feeling of embarrassment. Gershen Kaufman puts it this way: "To feel shame is to feel *seen* in a painfully diminished sense.... The self feels exposed both to itself and to anyone else present.... Sudden, unexpected exposure, coupled with binding inner scrutiny, characterizes the essential nature of the affect of shame." Contained in the experience of shame is the piercing awareness of ourselves as fundamentally deficient in some vital way as a human being.

Exposure stops speech, which means that shame is almost incommunicable. However, the experience of shame is stored as an imprint (a scene) in the part of the brain called the amygdala. The amygdala is the brain's sentinel. It operates like an alarm system signaling us that something is new or of interest, or warning us of threat or danger. The feeling of being exposed with no protective boundaries is certainly a threat. It is the job of our caretakers to name the affect of shame for us. And even though shame is an inner torment, it does not have to become a chronically negative internalized state.

Figure 2.1: THE LANGUAGE OF SHAME

DISCRETION (BEFORE AN ACTION)		DISGRACE (AFTER AN ACTION)	
Latin	Pudor Verecundia	Latin	Foedus Macula
Greek	Entrope Aidos	Greek	Aischyne
French	Pudeur	French	Honte
German	Scham	German	Schande

TWO KINDS OF SHAME

The concept of natural shame is hard for English speakers to grasp, because there is only one word for shame in English. Almost every other language has two words for shame (see Figure 2.1). Just as there are two kinds of cholesterol, HDL (good) and LDL (bad), there are two kinds of shame. The first is shame as discretion, from which we develop modesty, guilt as moral shame, awe, reverence, honor, and dignity. The second is shame as disgrace, which is the toxic core of feeling flawed and defective as a human being. While everyone needs a sense of shame, no one need be ashamed.

Figure 2.2: NATURAL SHAME:
THE CORE OF BEING HUMAN

Polarity limits

Permission to make mistakes

Natural boundaries

Adequate amount of shame forms conscience

Morality

Development of identity and intimacy

Contained anger

Sense of dignity and honor

BRINGS A SENSE OF AWE, REVERENCE, MYSTERY

EXPERIENCE OF THE SACRED

Healthy Shame

We are equipped with the affect shame because it safeguards our limits. Tomkins calls shame an auxiliary affect because it monitors our pleasure drive, our sexuality, and our interest (excitement). Natural shame operates as the foundation of our boundary system. It's as a boundary that it serves to cover us and protect us. Natural shame guards against perfectionism.

The great therapist Carl Rogers was once asked what he did to prepare himself to do therapy with someone. He answered (and I'm paraphrasing), "I tell myself that I'm enough. I'm not perfect because perfect would not be enough!" Rogers is saying that he is human, and humans are imperfect. As a human, Rogers was sure he could understand *something* of what his human client's problem was.

Shame keeps us human. It is our permission to be imperfect. It includes failure, mistakes, the need to ask for help, and the full realization of our human finitude. Natural shame also involves the recognition of human nature's *polarity:* We are more than the other animals and we strive to transcend our limits, but because of our freedom of choice, we can become inhuman and dehumanized—a state that makes us less than other animals. Natural shame safeguards our humanity and guides us to find a balance between extremes, and therefore is essential to the virtue of prudence. (See Figure 2.2.)

Whenever we make a mistake, the affect shame is triggered. At that point we need parents who can name the affect, making us conscious of it as a feeling. Since we are feeling the shame in a context, the context is imprinted on our brain as a scene, and it becomes an emotion. If our parents can help us to see that mistakes are normal, that all humans will make them, we will retain the emotion of shame as a positive safeguard for our sense of self. In fact, it can be an occasion for developing optimism—an attitude of learning from life experiences. But if our parents shame us for the mistake, they shame our shame, and it is imprinted as a scene of failure and disgrace.

Healthy shame develops as we experience our personal limits. It helps us learn modesty. As we internalize rules and instructions for good behavior, we feel shame in the context of guilt. One day a child steals another child's toy. His parents talk to him and tell him he must give the toy back. The child's theft is exposed and the feeling of shame now becomes the feeling of guilt, which is moral shame.

We will also experience shame, along with anger, as the protector of our honor, dignity, and self-esteem. Later as we experience our strengths and our limitations, our shame will be the root of the emotion of humility. When we experience life's mysteries, our healthy shame will be experienced as the emotions of awe, reverence, and the numinous (the holy, which simultaneously attracts us, fascinates us, and repels us in fear). Fully mature shame is both the source and safeguard of spirituality, to paraphrase Nietzsche. At its most sophisticated level, shame becomes part of wisdom, putting limits on what is unnecessary and focusing on what is worthwhile.

Toxic Shame

Without a sense of shame, we are shameless. Shamelessness is characterized by a lack of limits or boundaries. When a person becomes shameless, he loses his sense of self-respect and creates defenses that guard his vulnerability. He moves to one or another extreme: either acting invulnerable (perfect), always in control, self-righteous, critical, and blaming, or at the opposite extreme simply giving in and acting out of control, self-deprecating, self-critical, and blaming. (See Figure 2.3, page 73.)

The job of parents is to guard their children and be their children's first boundaries so that they are not uncovered or exposed when they need to be covered. But what happens when a parent is the one uncovering a child who needs to be covered? What if little Susan Krabacher's grandfather, one who is supposed to guard her privacy, violates her sexually, in the very place of her core womanhood? How ghastly that the very one who is to protect you is violating you. All forms of abuse toxically shame children. And because an abuser (say, a sexually abusing grandfather) is acting shamelessly, the abused child must carry the abuser's shame.

Pia Mellody, the therapist who devised our basic treatment program at the Meadows, a treatment center in Wickenburg, Arizona, coined the phrase "carried shame." All abused children

Figure 2.3:
The Polarization of Shame

LESS THAN HUMAN LESS SHAME	THE PERMISSION TO BE HUMAN NATURAL SHAME	MORE THAN HUMAN SHAMELESS
Compulsivity Obsessiveness	Polarity limits	Compulsivity Obsessiveness
Slob/Failure	Permission to make mistakes	Perfectionism
Out of control Gluttony	Natural boundaries	Overcontrolling Self-deprivation
Self-blame	Adequate amount of shame forms conscience	Blame
Intimacy dysfunction	Development of identity and intimacy	Intimacy dysfunction
Passive/Aggressive	Sense of dignity	Rage
Self-judgment		Judgment of others
Despair Hopelessness	Brings a sense of awe, reverence, and modesty	Idolatry Pride

are carrying their abuser's shame. This holds true for any victim of an offender.

Toxic shame also results from emotional abuse. I described how all feelings were shamed in my family. Our needs and wants can also be shamed. Continual shaming results in shame becoming bound to our feelings, needs, and desires, so whenever we feel a feeling, a need, or a want, we feel shame. In dysfunctional families our parents are usually shame-based and they pass their shame on to us. If we don't become aware of it and understand how to embrace our shame, we will pass it on to our children. Toxic shame dominated my life until I began my recovery. Like all addicts, I used what I was addicted to—alcohol and sex—as a way of blunting the pain of my toxic shame.

Cultures of obedience use shaming as a pedagogical tool. Many people think they are teaching children to be moral when in fact they are teaching them toxic shame. They often do it with the best intentions. When parents use shaming as a parenting tool, they are passing on what was done to them. They are not bad; they are misinformed and need new awareness. Toxic shame is a major form of violence in the family, and needs to be stopped.

DEBATES ABOUT HUMAN NATURE

Cultures of obedience see human fallibility as a sign of a fatally flawed or sinful nature. This is used to justify harsh measures to maintain control. Take, for example, Thomas Hobbes, a seventeenth-century English philosopher who has come to personify pessimism about human nature. In his book *Leviathan,* he argued that human beings are essentially selfish and are motivated only by self-interest. Because of our innate selfishness, Hobbes said, rigid laws and a powerful and coercive government are our only protection against perpetual warfare. In a state of nature, he proclaimed, our lives would inevitably be "solitary, poor, nasty, brutish, and short."

However, some of the most respected modern biologists have clearly refuted Hobbes' belief that each living being is only out for its own self-interest. Matt Ridley obtained his doctorate in zoology from Oxford and is now a research fellow of the Institute of Economic Affairs and a trustee of the International Centre for Life. His book *The Origins of Virtue* makes a strong case for the evolution of a human instinct for cooperation. He writes:

> Among people, cooperation is just as pronounced among primitive tribes as it is among civilized citizens.... The more people helped each other, the more the community thrived.... Society works not because we have consciously invented it, but because it is an ancient product of our evolved predispositions. It is literally in our nature.

One of the most compelling arguments for human reciprocity was the failure of Communism. Ridley gives an account of a high-level Communist official who repeatedly refused to use his position to help his wife or any other members of his family, lest he be accused of favoritism. He took this to such an extreme that he would not share his car with his wife on long journeys; she had to walk. He believed that to be nice to your own family was to discriminate against nonrelatives. "He was right," writes Ridley. "Communism would have worked if there were more such men, though it would have been a bleak kind of success." Communist officials constantly proved more corruptible and more nepotistic than democratic ones. The Communist dream was in creating a "new man." Instead it wound up with the old kind—self-interested and connected with his own welfare and the welfare of his family. The family, clan, ethnic group, or province was alive and well. "Communism failed," writes Ridley, "because it failed to change human nature." Human nature works because of self-interest and reciprocity—one good deed does produce another.

Ridley presents a lot of other evidence for reciprocity in human society. We do not have to reason our way to the conclusion that one good deed deserves another, nor do we have to be taught it: "It simply develops within us as we mature." Ridley concludes: "Our frequent use of reciprocity in society may be an inevitable part of our natures."

In *The Descent of Man,* Charles Darwin wrote, "A tribe including many members who, from possessing in a high degree the spirit of patriotism, fidelity, obedience, courage, and sympathy, were always ready to give aid to each other and to sacrifice themselves for the common good, would be victorious over most other tribes; and this would be natural selection."

Some argue that sociobiologist Richard Dawkins' book *The Selfish Gene* shows that cooperation is simply a form of selfishness—I help you out because I've learned that you will probably help me out at a later time when I need help. This seems to be true, but what moved me to help you out in the first place? Robert Trivers, a young biology student at Harvard, wrote a landmark article in 1971 (my first year doing doctoral work at Rice) entitled "The Evolution of Reciprocal Altruism." Trivers argued that baboons are the original archetypes of reciprocal altruism. Male baboons form coalitions and alliances all the time, and they most often ally with other males who have groomed them in the past.

Trivers showed that the source of reciprocal altruism comes from the region of the brain that houses emotions. According to Trivers, a kind of empathy or fellow-feeling initiates the first move in helping a mate. Our simian ancestors have an innate predisposition for altruism: a kind of gratitude moves one baboon to reward another who helped him in the past.

A SHINING EXAMPLE

In his recent book *Social Intelligence,* Daniel Goleman cites an example of altruism in rhesus monkeys that I found incredible. Six monkeys are trained to get food by pulling on chains. A seventh monkey is then placed in full view of the other six and receives a painful shock whenever one of the other monkeys pulls a chain. When the original six see his pain, four of them start pulling a different chain—one that delivers less food but also inflicts no shock on the new monkey. The fifth stops pulling *any* chain for five days, and the sixth for twelve days. In other words, they starve themselves rather than inflict pain on the seventh monkey.

Dawkins' idea of the selfish gene was never intended to imply that we are ruthlessly selfish. In fact, selfish genes are perfectly compatible with acts of selflessness. Parents staying up all night with their sick child may be moved by an evolutionary urge to protect their genes, but it is also a compassionate act. No one would accuse them of being *selfish*. Of course, there are parents who are selfish, but the mother who locks her child in her car while she goes to a bar is hardly honoring her "selfish gene," the evolutionary drive to extend her own DNA.

In most areas of our lives, it is best for the common good if we act compassionately, and we are hardwired to do just that. You and I, not to mention the future of our society and species, are better off if I rescue your two-year-old in the middle of the street and you rescue mine. I am better off if I share my large surplus of food rather than letting you starve while my food rots. We're both better off keeping the peace than we would be if we were constantly at war. The common good of any society is far better served when its people are virtuous.

The evidence clearly points to the fact that humans have an innate predisposition for empathy. Infants and children who have been well nurtured show ample evidence of moral concern. Later on I'll tell you about an infant who atttempted to comfort her weeping mother. Neuroscience may even have located a brain basis for empathy. In chapter 3, I'll discuss the recent discovery of "mirror neurons," specialized cells that allow us to feel what another is feeling. Clearly evolution has designed us in such a way that fairness, kindness, and reciprocal cooperation are part of our innate moral intelligence. Our genes are not containers of instinctual dark selfishness.

Thomas Babington Macaulay, the most popular English historian of the nineteenth century, once suggested that a person's true character could best be measured by what he would do if he knew he would never be found out. An anonymous donor paid for my first two years of college with the simple request that if able, I do the same for someone else later in my life. I'm sure you know many people, as I do, who help others with no possibility of reciprocity. Think of William Freehan and all the other firefighters who gave their lives before, on, and after September 11. Think of all the brave people throughout our history who have given their lives to ensure our freedom. The goodness of our fellows touches our souls and elevates us.

Moral intelligence is clearly part of the design of the human brain, although in childhood it is raw and needs to be developed. Obviously it can be deadened and become dysfunctional, as I will discuss in chapter 3. Our moral intelligence is vulnerable to our illusions. It often confuses morality with legality and conformity, and it has the disastrous habit of too often putting itself on the side of the godly and righteous.

UNIVERSAL MORAL CONCERNS

I recently read a fascinating *New York Times* article entitled "The Moral Instinct," by Steven Pinker, the Johnson Family Professor of Psychology at Harvard University. Just as Tomkins' affects were discovered to be universal, Pinker reports on new evidence for the universality of certain basic moral concerns. The psychologist Jonathan Haidt has synthesized cross-cultural research that anthropologists have conducted everywhere in the world. Despite the many variations in the specifics of how these concerns show up in different groups, five basic themes seem to emerge. Pinker calls them "the primary colors of our moral sense." They are:

- *Not harming others.* It is bad to harm others and good to help them.
- *Being fair.* People should return favors, reward those who are good to them, and punish cheaters.
- *Being loyal to a group.* It's good to share with and support other members of the group and be loyal to the group's norms.
- *Respect legitimate authority.* It is good to defer to legitimate authority and to respect people with high status.
- *Exalting what is pure, clean, and holy.* It is bad to defile, contaminate, and be excessively carnal.

Pinker suggests, for example, that purity, cleanliness, and sanctity are the reason most people would give Mother Teresa the nod for respect and holiness while ignoring Norman Borlaug, the "father of the Green Revolution," who used agricultural science to reduce world hunger. Borlaug may be responsible for saving a billion lives, but Mother Teresa symbolized holiness and purity: "white-clad . . . ascetic and often photographed with the wretched of the earth."

These five themes are rooted in our brains and form the primary fabric of our innate moral intelligence. How they rank in importance differs from culture to culture. Obviously, many people in the world feel little compunction about harming people outside their own group, but the basic categories still hold. Consider respect for legitimate authority. While comedians in the United States treat our political leaders and authority figures as fair game, there are still limits. When singer Sinéad O'Conner tore up a picture of the Pope on *Saturday Night Live,* she was scorned. She was booed off the stage and heckled at other public performances.

More recently, when the Prophet Muhammad was made the subject of a cartoon by a Danish newspaper, many people in the West were astonished by the outrage in the Muslim world, which included threats to kill those involved in producing the cartoon. Similarly, flag burning, incest, disloyalty to one's family or country or religion, gross carnality, pornography, and sexual perversion can trigger disgust and outrage.

All of the five universal moral themes are "gut issues"—they connect directly with our brain's affect system. Harming no one and helping when we can are guarded by empathy, sympathy, and the joy of aiding another. Fairness is guarded by anger. We want murderers, liars, cheaters, traitors, and blasphemers to receive their just punishment—we want them to "get what's coming to them." We feel shame and fear when someone violates the holy and anger when they blaspheme. We may debate all these issues rationally, but our moral intuitions are rooted in our deepest emotions.

WHAT MAKES US UNIQUE: THE TRUE SELF

An extraordinary new position held by some evolutionary psychologists is that the adaptive design of evolution has created something innate in the human psyche that we may call the "true self."

In *The Adaptive Design of the Human Psyche,* psychologists Malcolm Slavin and Daniel Kriegman argue that whatever the environmental pressures to which the individual is forced to adapt, she still possesses and is protected by an inner uniqueness.

Given the same set of external developmental contingencies, no two individuals will experience them or react to them in the same way. While the environment powerfully influences the development of the self, "the social environment *must not* define selfhood beyond certain limits...the environment is not ever a 'neutral' party or wholly an 'ally.'" For example, even in an average good-enough home with average, good-enough parents who are sincerely interested in the child's development, there are limits to their support. Dad and Mom hope that their son or daughter will be interested in most of the things that Dad and Mom consider to be the right things for their children and their children's future. These biases are an inevitable part of the environment into which every human being is born, and they must be dealt with if a person is to survive.

Slavin and Kriegman believe that over sixty-five million years of evolution, we humans have developed inner strengths that prepare each and every one of us to engage in an "extraordinarily complex set of developmental strategies that serve, in part, to defend against having one's interests usurped by others." Such evolved strategies must include motivations that lead one "to maximize the utility of one's ties to others (to use others for one's own vital ends), in addition to simply creating desires for attachment and self differentiation."

Slavin and Kriegman believe that part of our natural evolutionary inheritance is a kind of *intrapsychic intelligence*—the capacity to be alone within ourselves even in the presence of others. In effect, each of us needs a private space that is sufficiently protected from significant others both to survive the inevitable impingements of others and to use our inner strengths to create our self and be a fully functioning part of our culture.

How did the human child evolve the "basic structural, dynamic capacity" to accomplish this task? Given an inevitably biased environment, how would nature design the child's psyche in order to manage and survive such a situation?

A NEW VIEW OF REPRESSION

Freud and his followers emphasized a certain quality of aggressiveness, even a destructive drive in the human psyche. "From an evolutionary perspective," Slavin and Kriegman argue, "the existence of an overriding destructive drive energy . . . would be a costly, unnecessary, and thus unlikely way for natural selection to have designed us."

Slavin and Kriegman believe that there must be an *innate true self* that has a built-in capacity to experience the world in a self-interested manner. When I first read this, I immediately thought of James Hillman's book *The Soul's Code,* which gives copious examples of people's lives that cannot be fully explained by either nature or nurture. The unique self is often hidden in childhood. Mohandas Gandhi was a sickly child, afraid of snakes, ghosts, and the dark; when his true self emerged in adulthood, he stood up to the British army. Robert Perry was a mother's boy, branded a sissy by his peers, who as Admiral Perry discovered the North Pole.

Slavin and Kriegman have made a complete reinterpretation of the Freudian notion of repression, one kind of unconscious mental activity, which we will be discussing next. In Freud's classical presentation of repression, the psyche represses those unaccepted parts of self that do not match parental or cultural expectations. Freud felt that this repressed material was mostly a cauldron of rage and destructiveness.

In contrast, Slavin and Kriegman see repression as a way that the innate and unique human psyche can put aside aspects of itself in order to get the love and attention it needs in order to survive. The parts that are put away are not lost forever. They are pressing to return, and can be held in reserve to be used when the biased environment is no longer a perceived threat. Repression is thus a strategy of the true self. The self puts aside its own individuality in order to get our immediate dependency needs met—even at the expense of our true powers. We do this until such time as it is safe to allow our own self-assertive and self-interested power to emerge to resolve these unmet needs.

For me, one of the greatest living examples of "true self" discovery is Oprah Winfrey. Born to unmarried teen parents, she was raised by her grandmother in her earliest years. When she rejoined her mother, she was molested by relatives and a family friend starting when she was nine years old. After running away in her teens, she had a baby who died shortly after birth. Then she was sent to live with the father who had abandoned her. Yet in high school she was a popular honor student who won a full scholarship to college, and when she cohosted her first local talk show on a Baltimore TV station, her true self emerged. (I was on that show once and saw how powerful she was.) Today she is one of the most powerful women in the world, and she is using that power to help people everywhere. Her true self is shining brightly.

HUMAN NATURE AS CONSTRUCTIVE

Slavin and Kriegman reject any idea of human nature as essentially destructive. They write, "We are biological organisms that have evolved to actualize our own self-interest" and to move toward our own uniqueness. We have from the very beginning "some form of implicit, intuitive capacity to 'know' certain basic givens" about ourselves; we have "a distinct class of motivations that . . . are largely independent of the shaping and regulating influences of the relational world." But at the same time we have an equal need for secure attachment to our mothering source figure. The healthier that attachment is, the more our true self will be able to emerge.

Repression, which is almost always unconscious, allows us to save those parts of our self so that we can reconnect with them when it is safe to do so. How many of us have seen one of our children wind up in a vocation or a direction in their life that we never could have predicted from their childhood? At some point of our life journey, our true self emerges.

As Slavin and Kriegman write, "The true self ultimately stands for *that unique constellation of universal and individual characteristics, the maximization (full actualization) of which is*

known in each individual's experience through a sense of vitality,
aliveness, meshing or fit within a relational context."

The phrase "a sense of vitality, aliveness, meshing or fit" is a
wonderful description of finding the place where we can be ourselves and belong at the same time. It's a feeling of deep happiness. I felt this vitality in my recovery process. During the first
years of my experience in my twelve-step group I felt like I really
belonged to my community of fellow addicts. I felt the same
vitality when I committed myself to do my first PBS series on
family dynamics. Once I made the commitment, I created a space
for all the necessary allies and resources I needed to make it happen. The true self is negotiated and renegotiated throughout our
lives.

THE ORIGIN OF THE FALSE SELF

Since at least as far back as the philosopher Baruch Spinoza in
the seventeenth century we have known that an essential part of
our behavior and mental life is unconscious. The repressed parts
of our true self form one part of our unconscious mind. The parts
of our behavior that are unacceptable to our culture, family, and
religion are repressed. We then internalize the patterns of behavior that *are* acceptable, and these form our false self. Over time,
the false self becomes so familiar that we lose consciousness of
our repressed self.

For example, I had trouble expressing my feelings of anger
most of my life. My family punished any expression of anger, and
my religion taught that anger was one of the seven deadly sins.
Deadly sins were one-way tickets to hell. In order to get this point
across, the nun who taught third grade passed out what she said
were "actual pictures of hell." They showed burned, blackened,
naked bodies ensconced in flames, with anguished and tortured
faces crying out for help. They were terrifying. I wondered where

she got these pictures, and concluded she had been there herself and had come back to torment me.

I repressed my anger for years, pretending to be nice, until at times I just couldn't take it anymore. Then I would explode in rage, dumping every slight and hurt I had repressed for months or years onto others. It was not until I learned how to express anger *prudently*—that is, in a contained and balanced way, that I stopped repressing it and stopped having periodic outbreaks of rage.

We tend to assume that we are only who we think we are consciously. Thinking of myself as only a "nice guy," I had to repress my anger more and more. My anger became a core part of what the psychologist Carl Jung called the "shadow part" of the personality. According to Jung, "Everyone carries a shadow, and the less it is embodied in the individual's conscious life, the blacker and denser it is...it forms an unconscious snag, blocking the most well-meant attempts." The shadow disguises our true self and diminishes the power of the will, therefore limiting freedom.

Our shadow also contains our induced and carried feelings— especially toxic shame. Any feeling that our primary caregiver has suppressed, we carry as our own. My mother was nineteen when she birthed me. She married pregnant and had a lot of shame, rage, and sadness over the state of her life. In my poor attachment to her I carried all her suppressed feelings. I had a devil of a time understanding why I had so much rage until I understood the carried feelings I mentioned earlier.

When we become enmeshed or overly attached to our source figures, we have no identity separate from them. We want them to love us, so whenever they project a feeling on us, we take it on as an identity. Whenever they have rage, shame, or sadness that they are not expressing, we take on those feelings as our own.

In chapter 9, I will discuss the part that our carried shame, anger, wounds, and defenses play in damaging our care for ourselves and others. What we repress appears outside us as some quality in another. We project on others what we can't accept in ourselves.

On a collective level, a great deal of ethnic hate, fear, and condemnation of "the stranger"—those we identify as "not like us"—comes from the parts of ourselves that we fear and are estranged from.

OUR INNER REGULATOR:
EGO AS STRENGTH

I'd like to end this chapter with one final clarification drawn from modern psychology. There is no word that triggers my reactivity more than *selfish*. My mother told me over and over again that I needed to quit being so selfish. My religious education taught me that I was egocentric, selfish, and ruled by my lower nature—my appetites and sex drive. All of this was toxically shaming. Even today, certain areas of New Age spirituality tend to see ego as bad and something to be overcome. An egotist is someone who is self-inflated, vain, arrogant, puffed up. This popular conception of the word *ego* is far from the understanding that I am using in this discussion.

One of my cherished mentors is the psychologist Erik Erikson. When I started teaching high school, I discovered his book *Childhood and Society* and learned about the eight stages of healthy ego development. Erikson was a neo-Freudian and repudiated Freud's teachings on ego. When I'd studied Freud at Rice, his pessimistic views of human nature seemed to validate what I had been taught about ego. But for Erikson, who discussed his break from Freud in *Insight and Responsibility,* ego is an inner monitor of our experience, regulating our drives for pleasure, self-adulation, and sex. A healthy ego guards against a rigidly overbearing conscience. Erikson calls ego "a selective, integrating, coherent and persistent agency central to personality formation." Ego is the guardian of humans' individuality—that is, their indivisibility—and, says Erikson, "the inner 'organ' which makes it possible for man to bind together the two great evolutionary developments, his *inner life* and his *social planning*." A well-formed ego gives us a sense of wholeness, a sense of centrality in time and space and a sense of freedom of choice. Once again, in Erikson's words, "The ego...permits [man] a measure of human balance."

Ego can go astray. We can be thwarted by neglect of our developmental dependency needs and be left with a weak ego. A person with a weak ego lacks the self-efficacy to control his drives and lacks the boundaries to say no and to moderate things (such as drugs, food, and sex) that in excess destroy meaningful experience. Nothing is more damaging to ego development than toxic shaming. Every form of abuse causes damaging shame to the developing child's sense of self.

When our ego is weak, writes Erikson, we often project on the animal world our destructive excesses and conflicts, "comparing, for example, [our] ravenousness with the eating style of dogs, or [our] rage with that of provoked tigers."

What we do not ascribe to animals and are surprised to find in documentaries on the Discovery Channel is that animals in their natural habitat have a certain built-in balance. There is, it seems, a certain restraint and "selective discipline in the life of even the 'wildest' animals," says Erikson, "a built-in regulator which prevents (or 'inhibits') carnivorous excess, inappropriate sexuality, useless rage, and damaging panic, and which permits rest and play along with the readiness to attack when hungry or intruded on."

Animals do stake out and guard their territories, but there are many different species of animals that share environments with a minimum of mutual interference or distraction. Erikson describes the adapted animal as having a kind of "ecological integrity"—a combination of mutual regulation and reciprocal avoidance that safeguards adaptation.

The lack of innate balance is a price we human beings pay for our lack of instinctual determinism. That is why Aristotle warned us that virtue does not come naturally. We can attain a virtue only as the result of a lifetime of hard work.

Prudence cannot be attained without developing a healthy ego. With a strong ego, we are able to find the mean between the two major opposing inclinations that appear at each of the early developmental stages of our life—the one pushing us to be the same as the group and the other pushing us to separate and be our own individual self.

In part 3 of this book, I will discuss how these ego strengths can be built in childhood to become the foundation for strong moral character, and how each stage of our developing ego is the root of a unique virtue.

3

OUR MORAL BRAIN: EMOTION, MIND, FREE CHOICE, AND ATTACHMENT

For if the mysteries of the mind are reducible to physics and chemistry, then "mind is but the babbling of a robot, chained ineluctably to crude causality."
>—Robert Doty, quoted in Jeffrey M. Schwartz and Sharon Begley, *The Mind and the Brain*

Minds without emotions are not really minds at all. They are souls on ice.
>—Joseph LeDoux, *The Emotional Brain*

The mind emerges from the activity of the brain, whose structure and function are directly shaped by interpersonal experience.
>—Daniel J. Siegel, *The Developing Mind*

Willful effort generates a *physical force* that has the power to change how the brain works and even its physical structure.
>—Jeffrey M. Schwartz and Sharon Begley, *The Mind and the Brain*

Bruce D. Perry, M.D., Ph.D., an internationally recognized authority on children in crisis, is the senior fellow at the ChildTrauma Academy in Houston, Texas. In an article called "Incubated in Terror" Perry reports this story:

A fifteen year old boy sees some fancy sneakers he wants. Another child is wearing them—so he pulls a gun and demands them. The younger child, at gunpoint, takes off his shoes and surrenders them. The fifteen year old puts the gun to the child's head, smiles and pulls the trigger. When he is arrested, the officers are chilled by his apparent lack of remorse. Asked whether, if he could turn back the clock, would he do anything differently, he thinks and replies, "I would have cleaned my shoes." His bloody shoes led to his arrest.

He exhibits regret for being caught, an intellectual, cognitive response—but not remorse, an affect. He feels no connection to the pain. He was neglected and humiliated by his primary caretakers when he was young. This fifteen year old murderer literally has emotional retardation. The part of his brain which would have allowed him to feel connected to other human beings and feel something did not develop. Literally, he has "affective blindness." Just as the retarded child has no capacity to ever understand abstract cognitive concepts, this young murderer has no capacity to be connected to other human beings in a healthy way. Experience, or rather lack of critical experiences, resulted in this affective blindness—this emotional retardation.

Perry's work with high-risk children has shown how childhood neglect and trauma change the biology of the brain. His book *The Boy Who Was Raised as a Dog: What Traumatized Children Can Teach Us About Loss, Love, and Healing* sounds the alarm about the disastrous results of inadequate and dysfunctional parenting. It also raises crucial questions about our ultimate responsibility for our actions.

In the book of Genesis, the story of Cain and Abel makes murder the second crime of sinful humanity. Murder is commonplace, yet we know very little about it. What do we know about individual murderers? Could your child or mine become a murderer? Perry compares this fifteen-year-old boy to a retarded child who can never understand abstract concepts. This suggests that his emotional retardation (affective blindness) prevents him from ever being able to develop empathy, the ability to feel another's feeling. If this is true, can we say that this boy has free will? Or can his brain take a new developmental path?

DO WE HAVE FREE WILL?

It seems obvious that at the commonsense level, people live their lives as if they have a mind independent of their brain, and a will that is free and not biologically determined. William James, one of the great psychologists of the late nineteenth century, argued in *The Principles of Psychology* that the ability to fix one's attention "and hold it fast before the mind" was the act that constituted "the essential achievement of will." Only a few years later, however, Freud's emphasis on the unconscious, and his belief that we are driven by the unresolved conflicts of early childhood, sounded the death knell for free will. James rejected this reductive determinism on moral grounds, but he struggled to prove the existence of free will.

For much of the twentieth century, however, academic psychologists, biologists, and cultural anthropologists refused to discuss these concepts, claiming that our mind (consciousness), our emotions, and our will were not valid subjects of scientific research. Science, it was believed, could be concerned only with what was observable and measurable. Behaviorism, which became the dominant psychological movement in the United States, was founded by John B. Watson, who declared that there was no "dividing line between man and brute." It was meaningless, he thought, to talk about "human nature" or to claim that our brain had an innate predisposition toward anything. Instead, Watson and his leading follower, B. F. Skinner, claimed that our behavior can be understood as a response to outside stimuli, and that the human infant could be trained or "conditioned" to become whatever its conditioner wanted. In this model, free will was an illusion.

LEAVE YOUR SOUL AT THE DOOR

I well remember my first psychology class at the University of Toronto. I was a bright-eyed and passionate young seminarian, committed to my new vocation and eager to save the souls of wayward sinners. On the first day of class the first thing my psych professor said was, "Anyone who thinks they have a soul, leave it at the door the next time you come to this class." That shocked me to my bones, but that was the state of psychology in 1956.

In 1971, when I did my doctoral studies at Rice, the psychology department was dominated by behaviorists, and the ethical philosophers we studied were for the most part relativists. Ethical relativism simply means that all values depend on nurture, culture, and environment. There are no moral absolutes. Aquinas' notion of a natural law or an innate predisposition toward goodness was scoffed at.

It is impossible to build an ethics of virtue on such a belief system. If our young murderer had no choice in what he did, how can we punish him? If all violence and crime can be reduced to early childhood abuse, to genes, or to brain damage, we are stuck with biological and psychological reductionism. Both of these isms can be reduced to *materialism,* the belief that the only reality is the physical world. In materialism, consciousness, mind, emotions, and will are not measurable—and hence not real.

But much of materialism seems contradicted by the new data coming from neuroscientific studies of the brain. I do not want to oversimplify here. According to neurobiologist Robert Doty, "The puzzle of how patterns of neuronal activity become transformed into subjective awareness remains the cardinal mystery of human existence." Another way to put this is to ask how mental phenomena (new ideas, free choice, dreams, love songs, poems, novelty, a life of virtue) can emerge from three pounds of grayish, gelatinous tissue encased in the human skull.

Our brains are the most complex organisms in existence. In his book *The Developing Mind*, neuropsychiatrist Daniel J. Siegel states, "The brain has an estimated one hundred billion neurons, which are collectively over two million miles long.... The number of possible 'on-off' patterns of neuronal firing is immense, estimated as a staggering ten times ten one million times (ten to the millionth power)." Such an organism is capable of an almost unimaginable range of activity, and modern research is showing how the mind, emotions, and free will emerge from our amazing brain.

THE BRAIN AND THE ROOTS OF VIOLENCE

There seems to be no doubt that early neglect and trauma have significant, lasting effects that may actually change the brain. Dr. Daniel Siegel, whose expertise includes child and adolescent psychiatry, writes, "Experience early in life may be especially crucial in organizing the way the basic structures of the brain develop ... traumatic experiences at the beginning of life may have more profound effects on the 'deeper' structures of the brain."

Perry concurs: "Experiences which could be tolerated by a 12 year old child can literally destroy an infant (e.g., being untouched for two weeks)."

Yet common sense tells us that most seriously abused children do not become murderers. And some of the serial killers who have been studied do not have neglectful and traumatic childhoods; there are clearly other factors involved.

In the *New York Times* article "The Moral Instinct," which I cited in chapter 2, Steven Pinker points out that many psychopaths (those technically diagnosed with antisocial personality disorder, like our fifteen-year-old murderer) do not seem to have abnormally distressed childhoods. They seem to be affectively blind from birth. These people show moral callousness in early and middle childhood—they chronically lie, bully younger children, torture and kill animals, and fail to develop empathy. In other words, there seems to be some genetic root to violence and lack of empathy.

One researcher has found that many murderers have brain disorders as well as a history of childhood neglect and abuse. In his book *Base Instincts: What Makes Killers Kill,* Dr. Jonathan Pincus, former professor of neurology at Georgetown University School of Medicine, describes his work with his colleague Dr. Dorothy Lewis. In their study of 150 murderers, using PET and MRI scans, they found frontal lobe deficiencies in every case. They concluded: "It is the interaction of childhood abuse with neurologic disturbances and psychiatric illnesses that explains murder."

In Pincus' study, it is not clear which comes first, an upbringing devoid of love and nurturing that causes brain damage, or brain damage that causes children to behave abnormally, which is then worsened by abusive parenting. What is clear is that we must accept that caring for children in their earliest stages of development is the most vital concern any society has to address.

The major source of violence in any culture is the abuse of children. My book *Homecoming* delves deeply into these matters. Much of the violence in the world today is rooted in mentally ill, emotionally disturbed, inadequate parents and out-of-date parenting skills.

The home is still the most dangerous place for women and children. While our entertainment, media, and public policy focus on public and predatory violence, for years I have contended that it is impossible to make any headway in understanding the roots of violence in the community without examining the effects of intrafamilial violence—abuse and neglect—on the development of the child.

IDEOLOGICAL VIOLENCE

The majority of neglected and traumatized children will never become physically violent. Without help from a concerned adult, however, their wounds will result in the death of their spirit rather than their bodies. They will be vulnerable to and set up for another kind of violence—*ideological violence*. People who carry a load of toxic shame and therefore have impaired ego development are easily recruited to cultures of obedience, with their tolerance of child abuse and religious righteousness, and they are ripe for developing racism, sexism, misogyny, idealization of violent heroes, and uncritical nationalism.

Emotional retardation and affect dysfunction also cause tremendous neurotic misery, addiction, chronic low-grade depression, and toxic-shame-based identities. While most people who struggle with these deficits do not perpetrate the kind of physical violence I've described, their lives bear scars that require more than average work and willingness to overcome.

It is only if we fully grasp the dangers of ideological violence, as well as the other forms of violence that result in affect dysregulation, that we can find better ways to ensure for every child an opportunity to develop a normal foundation for moral intelligence. I sincerely hope that this exploration of mature moral intelligence as prudence, the core virtue of all virtues, can help us in developing these new models.

THE BRAIN, WILLPOWER, AND FREE WILL

My excitement about the new studies in neuroscience intensified when I realized that researchers were showing not only how brains are damaged but also how they can be restored. A neuroscientist friend of mine at the University of Texas Medical Center in Galveston sent me a book written by Jeffrey M. Schwartz, M.D., a professor of psychiatry at the UCLA School of Medicine, and award-winning science columnist Sharon Begley. Called *The Mind and the Brain,* it has the subtitle *Neuroplasticity and the Power of Mental Force.* I was fascinated by the phrase "the power of mental force."

Schwartz has done pioneering work on a kind of brain disorder called obsessive-compulsive disorder (OCD). OCD is a neuropsychiatric disease marked by distressing, intrusive, unwanted thoughts (the obsession part) that trigger intense urges to perform ritualistic behaviors (the compulsion part). I have been very interested in OCD myself, because my obsessive sexuality, unlike my alcoholism, seemed to be far more a mental disorder than some kind of chemical disorder. Stopping the first obsessive lust is what must be done to stay sober from sexual compulsivity. Practicing this has kept me sexually healthy for twenty-seven years.

For the OCD patient, obsessive thoughts can focus on almost anything, but they are frequently about cleanliness (fear of touching germs from bodily secretions, especially in public places, leading to repeatedly washing one's hands), about safety (returning several times to be sure the door is locked), or about harming someone else (fearing that you hit someone while driving and repeatedly stopping or going around the block to be sure you did not).

For many years, a major treatment for OCD has been based on techniques of conditioning drawn from behaviorism. In other words, all desired change in behavior can be accomplished by systematically controlling relevant aspects of the patient's environment. The person with obsessive fear of germs from bodily secretions is made to deliberately touch items that might contain germs, beginning with the least fearful (a paper towel dropped on the bathroom floor) to the most feared (a dollop of feces or urine). The person who obsessively looks into his car's rearview mirror to see if he hit someone has the rearview mirror removed from his car. This method is called "exposure and response prevention"—having the patient experience one of his triggers (the exposure part) and keeping them from reacting to the trigger (the response part). During the period after exposure, the patient suffers painful and at times intense anxiety. Over time the patient's anxiety begins to subside and he becomes habituated to the triggers that he fears and obsesses on.

As Schwartz writes, he found this approach somewhat inhumane and techniques such as removing the rearview mirror in the patient's car downright dangerous. He was beginning to realize the impact of quantum physics, which holds that mind and matter are both forms of energy operating at different frequencies. This basically destroys the materialist bias. He was also a student of Buddhist mindfulness, a technique based on more than a millennium of practice and observation. Buddhist mindfulness is essentially a mental exercise that allows practitioners to focus attention in a nonjudgmental way on their own inner reality, thus creating a detached view of the brain's thinking activity. Schwartz thought that if experienced Buddhist practitioners could learn to direct the frontal executive attention network of their brains (which can and has been measured with brain scans), then focused attention must be a kind of mental force. The Buddhist practitioner can attain a state of quiet relaxation and a quieting of the mind's activity so that a kind of "bare attention" is achieved, a clear and single-minded awareness of what actually happens to us and in us at the successive moments of perception.

Mindfulness, Schwartz observed, requires direct willful effort.

He also realized that OCD, though clearly caused by some pathological mechanical brain process, had what is called an "ego-dystonic character." What this means is that when the person with OCD has the obsessive thought, some part of his mind knows, for example, that his hands are not really dirty. This rang true to me. As an alcoholic and sex addict, I clearly knew that I really didn't need a drink or more sex even though I acted on the obsession to drink or have sexual release.

Schwartz believed his patients could learn a practical, self-directed approach that would teach them to use this observing (healthy) part of their brain. He developed a four-step regimen that taught OCD patients to gain insight into the true nature of their imprisoning obsessive thoughts. The four steps instruct the patients to:

1. *Relabel* their obsessive thoughts as symptoms of a disease and false signals
2. *Reattribute* these thoughts by learning to think and say, "This thought reflects a malfunction of my brain, not a real need to wash my hands again"
3. *Refocus* on a constructive behavior, such as "I'll go out to my garden and work" or "I'll read that book I've been wanting to read"
4. *Revalue* the OCD obsessive thought and compulsive behavior, realizing they have no intrinsic value or inherent power

After some extensive work (ten weeks) with OCD patients using the four-step regimen, Schwartz and his colleagues began to see a success rate that exceeded the results of behavior therapy methods and was drug-free. Schwartz's co-therapist, Eda Gorbis, a clinical psychologist, achieved an 80 percent success rate using the four-step method along with a modified form of behavior therapy.

Schwartz used PET scans at the beginning and end of his four-step program. The results were dramatic. His scans showed a dramatic shrinkage in the size of a brain area called the "right caudate nucleus" after the ten-week process. This decrease in size indicated a decrease in the energy circulating between the right caudate, the right orbitofrontal cortex, and the right thalamus. What this means in layman's terms is that a rigid and seemingly automatic process of obsessing on something and feeling compelled to take action rooted in a rigid circular exchange of energy in three parts of the brain had been broken up; a "pattern interruption" had occurred. The key to opening up the brain pattern in the OCD patient, described as "brain lock," had been found. The brain was no longer locked in obsession and compulsivity.

Schwartz was showing that "the adult brain can indeed change...and the mind can change the brain." Here was a crucial example exploding the long-held belief that once the brain reached maturity in late adolescence it cannot be changed. Schwartz's work is an important piece of the growing evidence for the neuroplasticity of the brain. To quote his definition: "*Neuroplasticity* refers to the ability of neurons to forge new connections, to blaze new paths through the cortex, even to assume new roles. In shorthand, neuroplasticity means rewiring of the brain."

It also means that the mind and the brain constantly interact. Schwartz's work clearly establishes the existence, character, and causal efficacy of the will. It shows, as he puts it, that "directed, willed mental activity can clearly and systematically alter brain function; that the exertion of willful effort generates a *physical force* that has the power to change how the brain works and even its physical structure." Using our willpower to exercise free choice to attain virtue is what Aristotle called right appetite, or the exercise of the will toward the good.

These findings are incredibly important for reclaiming virtue. We have free will and can generate our willed mental force to change our habits and actions toward virtuous behavior.

NONGENETIC BRAIN DAMAGE AND IMPAIRED CHOICE

Our will is critical in making virtuous choices, but I want to emphasize again the importance of affect. Yes, we use our reason to make decisions and direct our actions, but it has been found that without feelings we can hardly choose at all.

Dr. Antonio Damasio, of the University of Southern California, has shown convincingly that we cannot make the simplest decision without being influenced by our emotional investment in the alternatives.

In his book *Descartes' Error,* Damasio presents the case of Mr. X, who suffered damage to the orbitofrontal cortex. This is an area right behind the eyes that joins the emotional centers, such as the amygdala, to the thinking part of the brain. After this link was injured, Mr. X was still excellent at logical thinking, but he was baffled by any situation requiring a decision or judgment call—such as what to do when two people couldn't agree on what TV show to watch.

In other cases involving people with damage to the orbitofrontal cortex, Damasio found that they had normal intelligence and an exceptional ability to think abstractly, but had difficulty deciding where they wanted to go out to eat. When presented with a moral dilemma—such as whether it would be okay to steal medicine to save their dying spouse—they could not choose an answer. When the orbitofrontal cortex is damaged, our brains cannot work with our affect system to evaluate alternatives and make a choice. Our choices result from our emotional investment in one alternative rather than another.

LOGIC VERSUS EMOTION

In people whose brains are intact, researchers have come up with ingenious ways to explore the balance of logic and emotion in practical moral decision making. One famous thought experiment, called the Trolley Problem, was devised by moral philosophers Philippa Foot and Judith Jarvis Thomas. A runaway trolley will kill five people unless you flip a switch sending it onto another track, where it will kill only one worker who is repairing the track. Is it moral to flip the switch? Most people interviewed by the researchers said that it's moral to flip the switch. But when the researchers changed the problem so that the only way to stop the trolley is to push a passerby onto the track, most people said it would be immoral to throw another person onto the track.

Notice that, in both cases, five people are saved and one is killed. Considered in purely logical terms, the end result is the same, but people's reactions are quite different, and it was not just a few people who thought this way. As Steven Pinker reported in his *New York Times* article, when the Trolley Problem was adapted for the Internet, most of 200,000 people from a hundred countries around the world, men and women, young and old, of every race, religion, and educational level, came to the same conclusion: they would pull the switch in the first dilemma but would not throw a person onto the track. No one could logically justify their choice. People said that they just knew that throwing another human being to their death was wrong.

In a related study, researchers at Princeton's Center for the Study of Brain, Mind, and Behavior scanned volunteers' brains while they pondered the Trolley Problem and other ethical dilemmas. When subjects were considering throwing the switch, only a brain area for rational calculation was involved. But when they thought of pushing a person onto the track, multiple areas lit up, including those for emotions about other people, mental computation, and conflict.

Jonathan Haidt, the social and cultural psychologist at the University of Virginia who outlined the five universal moral themes I discussed in chapter 2, has also explored these themes using moral dilemmas. He encountered gut-level repugnance when he offered subjects money if they would be involved in certain situations. These situations involved being fair (accepting a TV stolen by a thief from a wealthy family), group loyalty (saying negative things about your country—which you don't believe— on a foreign radio station), and respect for authority (slapping a religious authority in the face—with his permission—as part of a comedy skit). In every case the people asked said they would not do it.

But when he asked if they would accept a TV from a friend who got it free because of a computer error, say something negative about your country (that you don't believe) on a radio show in your own country, or slap a friend in the face (with their permission) as part of a comedy skit, the subjects were okay with these behaviors. Once again their responses to the first set of questions were coughed up by the unconscious emotional brain, although the subjects tried to give reasons for their different answers.

Haidt observes: "We carry out our lives as though our moral judgments are based on reason," but in fact we act on "gut feelings and make up reasons post hoc." And people almost always make gut-level responses when the moral dilemma is related to the five areas of universal moral concern: harming others, fairness, loyalty to community, respect for authority, and purity.

GUT-LEVEL EMOTIONAL MORAL CHOICES

What is this gut-level unconscious emotional knowing? Let me briefly discuss what I have learned about the emotional brain.

For many decades it was accepted that our feelings emanated from a distinct part of the brain called the limbic system, which was described as including structures such as the amygdala, the orbitofrontal cortex, and the anterior cingulate. Today, however, affects, feelings, and emotions are not thought of as limited to exactly defined regions.

Joseph LeDoux, a pioneering brain researcher who heads the Center for Neural Science at New York University, writes: "There may not be one emotional system in the brain, but many." It was his discovery that feeling and cognition (or passion and reason, as the old philosophers would have put it) are inextricably entwined.

In his book *The Emotional Brain*, LeDoux shows convincingly that a large part of our lived experience and many of our choices are unconscious. It is certain that we know a great deal without knowing that we know or what we know. For now, let me suggest that the most significant part of practical moral intelligence is developed from nonverbal sources, coming from our experience and our emotional brain systems. We develop our expertise in making moral choices through a developmental process that is nonanalytic and minimally speculative. Expertise in making moral choices is a kind of intuitive felt thought that is practical. LeDoux writes: "Subjective emotional states, like all other states of consciousness, are best viewed as the end result of information processing occurring unconsciously."

FELT THOUGHT AND MORAL CHOICE

I use the phrase "felt thought" to describe the cognition involved in the gut-level feelings related to moral choice.

We have all experienced the power of music and poetry to move, motivate, and inspire us. Music and poetry are saturated with feeling and intelligence, and I see them as forms of "felt thought," a kind of intuitive knowing that is mediated by our emotions. They impact us through the nondominant hemisphere of our brain, the part of our brain that operates through bodily sensation, imagery, and sound. LeDoux does not use the term "felt thought" to describe this union, but he clearly states that feelings and cognition go together.

The ancient philosophers, especially Thomas Aquinas, believed in this gut-level emotional knowledge and decision making. Aquinas believed that there is an intelligence related to the acquisition of virtue that is independent of abstract logic or science. He referred to this nonverbal intelligence as the root of moral experience. He called it "connatural knowledge," a knowledge that is inborn and shared by all humans. The modern interpreter of Thomas Aquinas, Jacques Maritain, writes:

> Moral experience offers to us the most widespread instance of knowledge through connaturality.... It is in the experiential—not philosophical—knowledge of moral virtues that Thomas Aquinas saw the first and main example of knowledge through inclination or through connaturality. It is through connaturality that moral consciousness attains a kind of knowing—inexpressible in words or notions.

In another place, Maritain explains connatural knowledge as coming from will and emotion, as well as intellect:

> In this knowledge through connaturality the intellect is at play not alone, but together with affective inclination and the disposition of the will.

Connatural knowledge as the nonverbal core of moral intelligence is another way to describe "felt thought." It also captures that "dim knowledge" that Erikson described as drawing us to "the purest leaders who taught the simplest and most inclusive rules for an undivided mankind." It does not seem far-fetched to believe that refusal to deliberately harm others, fairness, being loyal to family and country, respect for authority, and modesty, manners, and purity are the raw innate predispositions of our connatural knowledge—that is, our moral intelligence.

SPLIT-BRAIN RESEARCH AND THE NON-DOMINANT HEMISPHERE OF THE BRAIN

In 1961, Paul Broca, a French physician, anatomist, and anthropologist, reported that injuries to a certain area of the left cerebrum almost invariably produced speech disorders, while injuries to the same area of the right hemisphere did not. It was slowly recognized that the left hemisphere affected language while the right did not. Given the importance of verbal processes in Western culture, scientists assumed that the left was the dominant hemisphere. But the so-called nondominant hemisphere, or right brain, which houses the nonverbal, nonlogical processes, is key to emotion and felt thought.

Philosophers and researchers had long realized that the human brain exhibited different ways of knowing. Intuition is certainly different from a carefully constructed logical argument. Then, in the 1960s, Michael Gazzaniga, working under Nobel laureate Roger Sperry, began to study epilepsy patients whose corpus callosum (the tissue connecting the two sides of the brain) had been surgically severed to control seizures. He discovered that the right and left hemispheres of the brain were like two different, although complementary, minds. When the brain is split, the two sides can no longer communicate with each other. The person can talk only about things that the left hemisphere knows about. If he uses his left hand, which sends touch information to the right hemisphere, to feel an object in a bag, he can recognize the object but he cannot name it. Split-brain research ultimately revealed that the two hemispheres have very different functions, although in their normal state, they function together in a complementary way. Figure 3.1 offers a very simplified comparison of their differences.

Figure 3.1: FUNCTIONS OF THE
TWO HEMISPHERES OF THE BRAIN

LEFT HEMISPHERE	RIGHT HEMISPHERE
1. Specializes in speech and verbal ability	1. Specializes in emotional matters—deals with stress and regulates emotional reactivity
2. Thinks abstractly	2. Thinks emotionally
3. Intellectual	3. Sensual—carries felt sense of self
4. Sequential—logical	4. Intuitive—holistic
5. Time-bound	5. Simultaneous—no sense of time
6. Analytic—technical	6. Spatial (visualizing)
7. Conscious processing	7. Receptive—unconscious processing
8. Reading and writing	8. Symbolic thinking, felt thought (poetry)
9. Abstract categorizing	9. Metaphoric understanding and imagination
10. Verbal memory	10. Experiential memory

TELLING MORE THAN WE CAN KNOW: THE "COGNITIVE UNCONSCIOUS"

In 1977 psychologists Richard Nisbett and Tim Wilson published a paper entitled, "Telling More than We Can Know: Verbal Reports on Mental Processes." Nisbett and Wilson had set up a series of experiments in which people were required to do things and then say why they did what they did. In one study, they lined up several pairs of stockings on the table. Female subjects were then allowed to examine the stockings and to choose which pair they liked best. The women gave all sorts of reasons about their choices, commenting on the texture and sheerness of the stockings. However, unbeknownst to them, the stockings were identical. Nisbett and Wilson showed that people are often mistaken about the internal deliberations that lead them to make choices. Their reported reasons were not true to their internal processes; rather, they were guided by social convention or by what they believed about how they should make choices. In short, they were guessing. The right brain operates automatically and with incredible speed. It allows us to evaluate things in milliseconds. It is certainly at play in making difficult moral decisions that demand we act quickly.

The conclusion from this and other studies is relevant to the question of *moral choice*. The inner workings of important aspects of the mind, including our own understanding of why we do what we do, are not necessarily accessible to the conscious self. Joseph LeDoux comments, "People normally do all sorts of things for reasons they are not consciously aware of." One of the main jobs of consciousness is to keep our life tied together in a coherent story, a self-concept. However, "it seems clear," says LeDoux, "that much of mental life occurs outside of conscious awareness."

THE EARLY PRIMACY OF THE RIGHT BRAIN

We began this chapter with the shocking example of a youngster who killed for a pair of shoes. Conclusions from studies on post-traumatic stress disorder tell us that as little as one catastrophic experience when a person is powerless is enough to change brain chemistry. We also know that many children who are neglected and humiliated do not kill for a pair of shoes.

We do have a fairly clear picture of the psychological dynamic of emotional retardation. It involves an understanding of the early dynamics of attachment and the nondominant hemisphere of the brain.

The right brain is dominant throughout the first three years of life. The left brain becomes fully functional at about three and a half years of age, with the advent of speech. Early interaction between the mother (or any mothering source) and the child is right brain to right brain. The infant's early learning comes through touch, sounds, and images. These are disproportionately stored in the right hemisphere of the brain during the "sensitive period" of brain development, which is crucial for secure attachment or bonding.

SECURE ATTACHMENT: THE DEVELOPING MIND

I've quoted Daniel Siegel previously, but here I'd like to focus on his extraordinary work in explaining how our mind emerges from our physical brain. As he states unequivocally, "There is an entity called the 'mind' that is as real as the heart or the lungs or the brain, though it cannot be seen with or without a microscope."

In his book *The Developing Mind*, Siegel shows how the mind emerges from the activity of the brain, "whose structure and functions are directly shaped by interpersonal experience." It is *human* connections that shape the *neural* connections from which our mind emerges.

Our brains are predisposed toward empathy and social interaction. We are wired to achieve an empathic mutuality with our mother. And the most important precondition for secure attachment is our mother's secure attachment with her own mother. As I've said, no mother can be perfect, but she needs to be free from uncontrolled mental illness or intense neurotic conflict within and outside herself. I will continue to remind you that we have a true self that can overcome the most awful and damaging parenting. Nonetheless, our earliest brain patterns of love and connectedness come from our love story with our mother. In our infancy, feelings are everything, and they will form the foundation of our ability to communicate love and be intimate later in our adult life.

According to Siegel, attachment "is an inborn system in the brain that...motivates an infant to seek proximity to parents (and other primary caregivers) and to establish communication with them." We could describe this inborn system as part of our raw moral intelligence, since secure attachment is the foundation of our moral life. At the most basic evolutionary level, the presence of this innate system improves the chances of an infant's survival. Emotionally, a parent's sensitive response to the child's signals (the activation of an affect) helps to amplify the child's positive affects and modulate their negative ones. In chapter 11, I'll talk about the parent's critical role in naming, mirroring, and validating the child's affects as the way to develop a child's emotional intelligence. "At the level of the mind," writes Siegel, "attachment establishes an interpersonal relationship that helps the immature brain use the mature functions of the parent's brain to organize its own process."

Infants who are securely attached to their parents have the security and courage to venture out and develop relationships with others. Being close to one's attachment figures helps the child to feel there is a safe haven, especially when the child experiences distress. By the age of eight months, children internalize their relationships with their attachment figures, which means that they can evoke their memory (of their faces, smell, voices, taste, touch) even when they are not present. This mental model of security is called a "secure base." They can use this mental map to comfort themselves when they need to do so.

MIRROR NEURONS

Daniel Goleman presents an important new discovery in his book *Social Intelligence:* the existence of mirror neurons in our brains that dispose us to imitate another's behavior. This is why example is so critical for the development of moral intelligence. Mirror neurons are the source of the brain's predisposition for empathy. It is because of mirror neurons that we can feel what another person is feeling. Giacomo Rizzolatti, the Italian neuroscientist who discovered mirror neurons, states that "we can grasp the subjective state of another through feeling rather than thinking." In empathy there is a triggering of the same circuitry between two brains.

Goleman writes, "Mirror neurons ensure that the moment someone sees an emotional expression on your face, they will at once feel the same feeling within themselves." When a child is unwanted and neglected, there is a faulty or traumatized relation with the child's attachment figure. The child's mirror neurons pick up the negative feelings her parent has for her. The child feels shame and cannot internalize a nurturing voice. Distrusting her caretaker's voice, the child cannot internalize the foundations of conscience. Unless some nurturing person comes into her life, the child becomes a shame-based, angry loner, often with an impaired conscience.

Mirror neurons help explain how children are able to learn so much so early on—a quality Montessori calls their "absorbent minds." Mirror neurons help us understand how our innate attachment system is set in motion. Attachment depends on the emotional interaction between mother and child, and without our mirror neurons this emotional dance could not take place. Siegel suggests that these earliest experiences "shape not only what we remember but how we remember. What and how we remember shape our identity and the narrative of our lives."

The mirror neurons in our brains drive our social behavior, and our social behavior shapes our developing mind. Love, the highest virtue, is critical for good relationships, healthy brains, and healthy minds.

TRAUMA AND ATTACHMENT

If you were abused, abandoned, neglected, or used to take care of your source figure's unresolved needs, you built defenses to defend yourself against the very connecting behaviors, such as being taken care of and helping, that form the emotional foundation for moral intelligence. The gifting behaviors that constitute love, such as holding, cooing, and touching—the nonverbal dance of communication that Goleman calls "motherese"—will be missing.

One of the most important neuroscientists who has researched the issues related to secure and traumatic attachment is Allan N. Schore. In his book *Affect Regulation and the Origin of the Self,* Schore presents convincing research showing that early trauma of an interpersonal origin can override genetic, constitutional, social, or psychological resilience factors. Abuse and traumatic attachment especially damage the right or nondominant hemisphere of the brain.

Schore's research provides scientific support for the power

and efficacy of inner child work. For years I wondered why the inner child work I began in 1978 had such impact on people. It was not uncommon to receive testimonials from people five or ten years after they had done a workshop or did the exercises in my book *Homecoming: Reclaiming and Championing Your Inner Child,* attesting that they had had a transforming and life-changing experience.

After reading Schore's work I realized that a large part of the unresolved emotional hurts people carry are largely due to inadequate or traumatic attachment. The wounds are rooted in the right or nondominant hemisphere of the brain. Such wounds cannot be healed with words or the "talking cure," as it is called in therapy. I realized that the exercises used in inner child work—songs, poetry, nondominant-hand letter writing, groups of non-shaming benevolent people who mirror a person's hurt, pain, and shame—appeal to the nondominant hemisphere.

Several of my colleagues and I now believe that all addictions except those to inherently addictive substances are predominantly rooted in traumatic or faulty attachment and that therapy must involve nourishing remedial attachment and feeling work.

Schore has shown clearly that affect (feeling) regulation is the way the self is organized. Repair work involves making available a person's full range of feelings. In short, Allan Schore has completely validated the importance and primacy of the affect system. This is the central theme of this book: the virtue of excellent choosing is based on the habituation of the will toward goodness and the containment and full inclination of the affect system.

THE INFANT STRANGE SITUATION

How do we know whether or not an infant is securely attached? Mary Ainsworth, a professor of developmental psychology at the University of Virginia, collaborated with British psychiatrist John Bowlby to develop a way to actually measure this clinically. The results of this clinical test, called the Infant Strange Situation, have been replicated by hundreds of other researchers throughout the world.

In Ainsworth's study, after a year of observation at home, a mother-infant pair were put in a laboratory setting. During a twenty-minute procedure, the infant was first observed with her mother, then with her mother and a stranger, then with only the stranger, and finally alone for up to three minutes, after which she was reunited with her mother.

This experiment focuses on the infant's response to separation and reunion, and Ainsworth found that the infant's behavior fell into three specific patterns. These patterns were statistically relevant to observation ratings independently performed at home for the year prior to the lab experience.

Most one-year-olds are distressed when they are separated from their mothers. It is the reunion with the mother that helps us measure the infant's degree of attachment. When the mother returned to the child, Mary Ainsworth looked at three points of interest:

• The way the child seeks to be close to the mother
• The ease with which the child can be soothed
• How rapidly the child returns to play

Secure Attachment

What does the child do when the mother returns? A securely attached child is able to use the parent to soothe himself rapidly and return to his innate interest in play and exploration. The child seeks contact immediately and then terminates this closeness once the reconnection has occurred.

In low-risk populations, secure attachment is found in roughly 60 percent of infants.

Avoidant Attachment

In low-risk populations, 20 to 30 percent of infants are avoidantly attached. These infants minimize seeking closeness with their mother. They do not cry when separated from their mother. They squirm or lean out of their mother's arms when picked up. They focus on the environment and want to play with the toys. Parents of avoidantly attached children are emotionally unavailable and unresponsive to their child.

Resistent or Ambivalent Attachment

In low-risk populations, 5 to 15 percent of infants display resistant or ambivalent attachment. These babies are not easily soothed, seem to distrust, and do not readily return to play or exploration. After reunion the infant is not satisfied and remains in a state of anxiety.

Parents in this case are not consistently available, perceptive, or responsive to their child's signals. They tend to project their own state of mind onto their children.

Disorganized/Disoriented Attachment

A fourth pattern, that of the disorganized/disoriented child, was later discovered by Mary Main, a professor at the University of California, Berkeley, and her collaborator Judith Solomon, in their work with high-risk children. Eighty percent of children who suffered parental abuse display this pattern. The disorganized/disoriented infant may turn in circles when the mother returns, or may begin to approach and then avoid the parent; in some instances the infant may enter a frozen, trancelike state or remain motionless.

The parent in this type of attachment shows frightening, frightened, or disoriented communication during the first year of life with their child. It is speculated that these infants have experienced an unsolvable problem in that the parent is the source of the child's fear and is also disorientated, thus making a connected state impossible to achieve.

These classification categories suggest that the inborn attachment system is shaped by interpersonal relationships. They also shape the way the child's mind develops. A child can learn a different attachment pattern for each parent or attachment figure, but without later experiences with a loving, valuing attachment figure, a person's faulty attachment strategies will remain and be a force in shaping future relationships. Secure attachment is unequivocally the ground for developing one's moral and emotional intelligence and therefore the life of virtue.

As Figure 3.1 shows, the right brain plays the primary role in regulating emotions and is crucial in maintaining a unified sense of self. The orbitofrontal cortex works with the affect system to shape the gut-level thinking of the nondominant hemisphere. This is an oversimplification, but it is on the right track. This is what I understand that Silvan Tomkins means when he says that affects are forms of thinking. When the development of our right brain is damaged, we have difficulty managing stress and are prone to hypervigilance and emotional overreaction. Understanding the dynamics of the nondominant hemisphere has vast implications for reforming moral education, which greatly overemphasizes verbal information.

Empathetic mutuality, which is the fruit of healthy attachment, has its early roots in the right brain. When healthy attachment does not occur, one's ability to feel and choose in a functional way is retarded. In the case of our young murderer, his neglect and humiliation at a very early stage of brain development disrupted the attachment process, which in turn disturbed his ability to regulate his emotions and feel empathy or care for another. Both he and his victim are the tragic consequences of a failed nurturing attachment.

EMOTIONS CAN BYPASS THOUGHT AND DISTORT CHOICE

It is now clear to us that feeling can precede thought. One part of the emotional brain, the amygdala, is especially capable of distorting thought processes. If a person has been traumatized, has lived under chronic stress in the past, or is currently under a high level of stress, the amygdala may act like the alarm system we put in our homes to guard against danger. When there is any disturbance similar to the original traumatic event, the alarm is triggered. Over the eons of evolution, this alarm reactivity has had an important survival value. If, for example, an animal was attacked by another animal and survived, whenever any situation related to that attack is sensed, the alarm goes off.

The problem with trigger reactivity is that it is often years out of date. I can experience fear and react with intense rage in a present situation because someone has said something that recalls what my mother used to say to me as a child to shame me—even if I don't consciously recall it or associate it with what is happening now.

Repressed emotion restricts and damages choice. Prudence (right reasoning based on right desire) cannot possibly function when reactive emotion is distorting our reasoning process, especially practical reasoning—reasoning in the here and now. As we will see when we break prudence down into its integral parts, one critical element is what Aquinas called "honest memory" or what I would call effective long-term memory. This means that we need both a kind of rigorous honesty about the past and an authentic presence that allows us to perceive and evaluate the present circumstance with clarity before we act.

Authentic presence means that our judgment is as uncontaminated as possible. I can never resolve this morning's argument with my wife if I am really having a forty-year-old argument with my mother. I have to do the hard work of getting in touch with those past feelings, acknowledging them, and resolving them in some way before I can make honest choices in the present.

In my book *Homecoming,* I use the metaphor of the wounded inner child to symbolize the part of our development that is arrested by abandonment, neglect, and abuse of all kinds. I have done a lot of hard work on myself so that I can be aware when my energy has regressed and I'm feeling and acting like a child. As soon as I realize I'm overreacting, I've learned to take time out. I usually need about twenty minutes to get back to normal after I'm aware of an overreaction (literally an age regression). During that twenty minutes I imagine that I'm talking to a six-year-old boy, and I reassure him that my wife is not my mother. Over time this exercise has greatly reduced my reactivity.

EXCELLENCE AND THE BRAIN

Superior performers who achieve high levels of excellence in their work use their brains differently than the average person. Since excellence is a way to describe virtue (a permanent habitus that forms a new quality in a person's deepest self), I was very intrigued when I found this new research.

In his book *The New Brain,* Richard Restak, a neurologist and neuropsychiatrist, offers more evidence for how willpower— in this case deliberate practice—shapes the brain. In one example, Restak reports on brain scans of chess players, done while they were actually engaged in a game. It showed that grandmasters activate their frontal and parietal cortices—areas known to be involved in long-term memory. Less skilled players, on the other hand, activate their medial temporal lobes—areas of the brain involved in coding new information. The superior player relies on long-term memory to recognize positions and problems and to find solutions. The amateurs were analyzing the moves on a case-by-case basis, trying to figure out the best solutions for problems not previously encountered.

Chess experts have vast amounts of information and experience stored in their long-term memory. Most have spent a minimum of ten years amassing their superior skill, storing in their brains an estimated one hundred thousand or more chunks of chess information (opening moves, end games, and various strategies). Because of this huge reservoir, the top players do not have to think through each move—they almost instantly recognize whole patterns. Masters in other fields show the same kind of brain scans.

Restak highlights another critical factor related to superior performers: they practice far more than others in their field. Studies carried out at a highly regarded music school looked at the behavior of students who achieved concert careers, as contrasted to those who became music teachers. By age twenty, the teachers had put in four thousand hours of practice, while the feature performers had put in an estimated ten thousand hours.

The researcher in this study was Anders Ericsson, a psychologist from Florida State University. Ericsson found the same pattern of intense solitary deliberate practice in superior athletes and mathematicians.

In chapter 1, I wrote about Aristotle's understanding of virtue as an excellence, a moral performance enhancer that is generated by practice and takes years of hard work to perfect. The person of mature virtue makes excellent decisions quite spontaneously, seemingly without thinking, but such mastery of moral behavior is achieved through focused effort and attention. In chapter 6 I'll discuss Aquinas' notion of the integral or essential parts of the virtue of prudence—excellence in moral decision making. One of these integral parts is called *memoria,* which I've translated as "honest memory." I believe that *memoria* may also involve the long-term memory and pattern recognition that come from years of practice and experience in moral behavior.

IMAGES OF HOPE: THE CHILD'S POTENTIAL

Evolutionists describe human beings as "neotonous primates," meaning that compared to other animals, we have an extended childhood and juvenile period of development. It takes the human brain eighteen to twenty-one years to reach maturity. The theory of neotony states that we are intended by nature to maximize, not minimize, the curiosity, creativity, and flexibility of feeling, thinking, and behaving that characterize children. This has conferred tremendous evolutionary advantages on our species, enabling us to survive and adapt to rapidly changing conditions.

Anyone who has ever tried to learn a foreign language or computer skills in middle age finds out quickly what an advantage a younger brain has. Children are capable of learning two or three languages early on, and you would swear that kids today are wired up to the computer from birth. No matter how good we get, we'll never match their seemingly instinctive understanding.

Every child's brain has this kind of extraordinary potential, but it must be nurtured with care. It is also important to remember that our true self has an amazing capacity to adapt to our early environment and emerge later in life when it is safer to express itself.

There do seem to be people who are very damaged. But the research on the plasticity and remapping of the brain gives me great hope. I have worked with over a quarter of a million people in my workshops on healing the inner child. I have received over twenty thousand letters from people in the penitentiary, several on death row. Four men especially touched me. Each was a murderer on death row at San Quentin. They got my book *Homecoming* and did the exercises the book offers. They wrote me monthly letters, and I believed the changes they were making. They never suggested that they be released, but they grieved their own god-awful childhoods. They came to see that they had acted out on innocent people the anger they felt because their own innocence had been taken from them. The memory of these men gives me hope for our fifteen-year-old murderer.

4

THE REVOLUTIONARY DISCOVERY OF THE CHILD'S MORAL INTELLIGENCE

Let us try to learn from children all they have to tell us.
—Anna Freud

[Psychologists] have not seen enough children in their native habitat—homes, schools, playgrounds...[A] young psychologist is very likely to have his head stuffed full of theories of children before he has had a chance to look at any.... [H]e may be so much a prisoner of his theories that he cannot see anything that does not fit into them.
—John Holt

Children come into the world endowed with new energies that could correct the errors of past generations.
—Maria Montessori

On December 22, 1990, Rodolfo Renaldo came home drunk and accused his wife of having an affair. She was sitting in a chair holding four-month-old Raquel. Rodolfo began ranting and raving at his wife and threatened to kill their baby. His wife ran to the bedroom and called 911. When she walked back into the living room, Rodolfo continued to accuse her of infidelity. He got a beer from the refrigerator and continued to rage at his wife. He grabbed the baby and ran to the window. "Come here, woman," he was screaming. "Watch your baby die." Both the police department and the fire department responded to the earlier 911 call. Two police officers, Reeve Ricard and his partner, Dave Decker, crouched behind the door leading to the balcony. Also with them was a fireman, Ron Perlman.

As they later told the story on my TV show *The Bradshaw Difference,* the men got the signal from officers outside that it looked like Rodolfo was about to throw the baby over the edge. The officers rushed the balcony, and Rodolfo lunged forward, dangling the baby over the railing. Reeve grabbed Rodolfo's belt. Dave also got a hand on him. They tried to grab the baby's clothes. "Just for an instant, before I felt I really had the baby, I felt her fall," Reeve said. Suddenly Ron Perlman, the fireman, dove past them all, leaning completely out into the air with one leg up, his left hand stretching out to reach the falling Raquel. Amazingly, Ron snatched the baby. Then, in a move that saved the heroic fireman's life, Reeve grabbed Ron's waist and kept him from falling thirty feet to the ground.

Someone on the ground had videotaped the whole sequence, and we were able to show it to our viewing audience. The show focused on the policemen and the fireman's bravery. But I kept thinking about the innocent child being put through this traumatic event with no way to protect herself, totally at the mercy of the man who was supposed to protect her, her father.

THE PAINFUL HISTORY OF PARENT-CHILD RELATIONSHIPS

Babies like Raquel are still at risk because of the misguided belief that children are their parents' property.

The mistreatment, abuse, and exploitation of children have deep roots in our history. Of all my reading in this area, a book called *Foundations of Psychohistory,* by Lloyd DeMause, summed up this murderous history most concisely. DeMause's opening essay, entitled "The Evolution of Childhood," begins with these words:

The history of childhood is a nightmare from which we have only recently begun to awaken. The further back in history one goes, the lower the level of child care, and the more likely children are to be killed, abandoned, beaten, terrorized, and sexually abused.

I have to report that since I first aired my PBS series *Bradshaw on the Family*, I have received nearly 150,000 letters from individuals describing their childhood experiences. Just when I thought I had read the most awful account of child abuse ever, I'd receive a new letter recounting an even more brutal, violent, and abusive childhood. The devil is in the details, and the details were beyond anything I ever could have imagined. I cannot think of anything DeMause describes in his book that was not in my letters.

DeMause outlines five stages that preceded our modern understanding of more humane ways of caring for children.

Infanticide

The most striking and shocking data presented in DeMause's book concern the worldwide practice of infanticide. In antiquity, DeMause writes, infanticide was common. The historian Polybius blamed the depopulation of Greece on the killing of legitimate children, even by wealthy parents. Ratios of boys to girls in census figures ran four to one. It was rare for a family to spare more than one girl. Illegitimate babies were regularly killed. Christians were considered odd for their opposition to infanticide. Laws against infanticide evolved slowly and were mild until the fourth century.

While DeMause introduces infanticide as the primary mode of controlling children in antiquity, he is careful to note that every one of the stages in the evolution of childhood continues to exist today. Infanticide is still a major evil, especially in many developing countries, because of poverty and cultural preferences that favor boys.

Abandonment

DeMause says that Christians struggled against infanticide, only to replace it with abandonment. The most powerful description of this practice I have read was in anthropologist Sarah Blaffer Hrdy's ironically titled book *Mother Nature*. Hrdy documents the results of placing children in so-called foundling homes. In the eighteenth century, one of the best-known and largest of sixteen such foundling homes in the Grand Duchy of Tuscany was the Innocenti. Of fifteen thousand babies left there between 1755 and 1773, the records show that two-thirds died before reaching their first birthday.

According to Hrdy, foundling homes were in fact an attempt to deal with the disturbing numbers of unwanted infants left along roadsides or in gutters, but in city after city this "solution" proved deadly. Of 1,089 infants admitted to foundling homes in St. Petersburg and Moscow in 1767, 99 percent failed to survive the next year.

I was particularly moved by the passage in which Hrdy expressed her own personal horror as she realized the scale of this demographic catastrophe:

> I still recall the crisp autumn day...when at a conference on abandoned children, the full extent of a phenomenon I had been aware of for years sank in....[As] child abandonment was described, country by country, epoch by epoch...[g]radually it dawned on me that this phenomenon affected not tens of thousands or even hundreds of thousands of infants, as I had long assumed, but millions of babies. I grew increasingly numb. I recall that I had difficulty breathing.

Swaddling and Scare Tactics

When children were not killed or abandoned (to soon die), there is evidence that many parents considered them a nuisance. They were swaddled less for comfort than to control them, to keep them from moving around. Children were considered easy prey for the devil, and some people were afraid they could turn into actual demons. Adults regularly terrorized them with a vast army of ghostlike figures, from the lamia and striga of the ancients, who ate children raw, to the witches of medieval times, who would steal bad children and suck their blood. Nurses often dressed up as monster figures to frighten children to make them stay in bed and make them go to sleep.

Training Little Animals

When parents began to interact more with their children, it was still a common belief that children were more like little animals than human beings. Children were plagued with frequent enemas in order to purge their insides. Parents who could afford wet nurses often sent their infants away to live with them until they were weaned. Many wet nurses did nurture the infants adequately, but just as often they were neglected and abused. Once returned to their parents, the children were treated with love, hate, and fear in bewildering juxtaposition.

Shaming and Corporal Punishment

Slowly parents put an end to prolonged swaddling, wet nurses, and enemas, although remnants of those practices continued to appear. As parents began to toilet-train and discipline their children, the common methods used were shaming and spanking. I grew up with shaming and corporal punishment. I also was psychologically terrorized by threats of damnation and the fires of hell. The belief in original sin necessitated "breaking a child's will" at an early age. Of all the dire consequences of toxic shaming, breaking a child's will is the worst.

THE HELPING MODE

Only in the last sixty years has a new model of child care, which DeMause calls the "helping mode," become widely accepted. The helping mode begins with a belief that the child often knows what it needs at each stage of its life. The helping mode involves the active participation of both parents in the child's daily life. Parents who represent the helping mode are willing to learn from each child's unique and expanding needs. The helping mode requires a high level of emotional maturity on the part of both parents. It also involves a knowledge of the critical importance of the first six years of the child's life.

The evolution of childhood, as Lloyd DeMause describes it, also bears witness to certain abusive psychological ways adults have used children in the past. Children either were the recipient of their parents' unconscious projections of unresolved hurt and anger (projective reaction) or were used by parents to take care of the parents' own needs (reversal reaction). In the latter case, the child acts as the parents' parent. In both cases, the child is being used, and use is abuse.

However, as grim as this seems, the historical evidence also shows that there has always been a third mode, in which some parents empathized with their child's needs and acted to satisfy them. Building on this, the great innovators Maria Montessori and Rudolph Steiner (and to a lesser extent Sigmund Freud) created a new consciousness in the late nineteenth century that prepared the ground for a revolutionary new understanding of a more ethical way to raise our children.

As people such as Montessori and Steiner started observing

children more closely and more scientifically they began to discover "interior patterns" governing the children's lives. The child's mind was seen as "absorbent" and "radiant" and quite different from the adult's mind. But most important, their careful observations answered an often-debated question: whether an innate moral sense or intelligence was part of human nature. The answer was unequivocally yes.

Sigmund Freud was very aware of what he called the child's "radiant intelligence." He slowly came to understand how childhood trauma and abuse could have serious effects on adult behavior, and he posited childhood repression as the major source of character neurosis. His work underscores the importance of childhood as the foundation for character development.

Writing about Freud's contribution to modern thought, Erik Erikson states that it "implies a fundamentally new *ethical orientation of adult man's relationship to childhood:* to his own childhood, now behind and within him; to his own child before him; and to every man's children around him." Here, however, rather than discuss Freud's legacy, I would like to focus on two educators whose life's work was to increase awareness of our true ethical responsibility to children.

RUDOLF STEINER

Rudolf Steiner was born in 1861 in the little Austro-Hungarian town of Kraljevec. As a child he showed an unusual ability for learning, and his parents gave him the best education their means would allow. Steiner helped pay his way through university by tutoring in both scientific and classical subjects, and he was eventually hired to edit the little-known scientific works of the great German philosopher and poet Johann Wolfgang von Goethe. During this period Steiner wrote his earliest philosophical works. He vehemently challenged the prevailing philosophy of Immanuel Kant, especially Kant's absolutist ethical views. His doctoral thesis was later published as a book called *The Philosophy of Freedom,* which became the basis for his theory of education.

In 1919, a prominent Stuttgart industrialist, Emil Moll, invited Steiner to select a "collegium" of teachers to draw up a curriculum for a new school that would offer a free education to the children of his employees. Steiner gathered some of the best teachers he could find and gave them a series of lectures (subsequently published as *Study of Man*) in which he laid the foundation for an approach to education that took children's spirituality and moral intelligence into account. The Free Waldorf School of Stuttgart, named after Moll's Waldorf Astoria Cigarette Company, flourished. Today there are Waldorf schools throughout the world.

Steiner's philosophy of education altered not only the nature of the curriculum but also the way the subjects were presented. The school had no fees. The focus was on the unique dignity of children and was aimed at the release of the creative forces of life inherent in every child. It was these innate powers of the child that the conventional education of Steiner's day had failed to understand.

Steiner believed that the global wars and the chaos of violence and destruction that are so apparent in society are an expression of man's rage and frustration over his repressed natural creativity and spiritual powers.

Steiner was a scientist and an anthropologist. He felt that the evidence for the child's spiritual nature was overwhelming. "The soul," says Steiner, "needs nourishment as well as the body." For Steiner, the environment was crucial. In his model of education, teachers must be free of old biases based on their previous educational experience. Steiner believed that the natural order of the child's physical and psychological development should guide both the subject matter and the way it is taught.

The Change of Teeth

Around the age of six or seven, every child experiences the loss of baby teeth and the eruption of adult teeth as a fascinating, sometimes anxiety-ridden, and important event. Steiner believed that this change of teeth marked a significant developmental turning point.

In Steiner's view the first years of life condition all further developments. During these years, the body, soul, and spirit are one. Mistakes at the early stages entail a string of misfortunes to come. Only as the body is brought to completion does consciousness emerge. The emergence of the adult teeth accompanies this emerging consciousness, in which feelings, will, and thought come together. Prior to this psychological milestone, all formal education is to be avoided. This means that Steiner schools do not teach reading, writing, and arithmetic until the age of the second teeth.

Steiner observed that the young child's mind is unique in that he is able to imitate his environment without any conscious effort. And he insisted that even the preconscious child had a moral character. "His instinctive moral perception at this stage [prior to eruption of the permanent teeth] is every bit as powerful as his sense perception." Thus it is wrong to assume that because the child does not understand, she does not "perceive morally."

Steiner believed that a harsh, discordant, loveless, or even skeptical environment produces a slight freezing and congestion, a prelude to physical or moral weakness in later life, whereas a warm, gentle, loving, and harmonious environment releases moral forces and quickens courage for life in years to come.

The early schooling that Steiner called the "nursery class" set out to provide a right environment, right physical conditioning, right activities, and a right example for imitation. Steiner felt that an attitude of reverence for life should pervade everything.

"The little child," Steiner said, "imbibes the world, where the adult merely reacts to it."

Rigorously Real and Honest

Steiner believed that teachers and parents need to be as rigorously real and honest as their conscious minds are capable of letting them be. Children, he believed, know unconsciously what the source figures are feeling and when they are being dishonest.

This has particular meaning for me, because one of the most important understandings of the impact of parental abuse is what the pioneering therapist Pia Mellody has termed "carried feelings." In the attachment bond, an attunement of feelings between the mothering source and the child takes place, and the young child is especially vulnerable to a parent's or guardian's feelings. My own mother gave birth to me at age eighteen and soon found herself raising three children during the Great Depression and married to an alcoholic. She never expressed the shame and rage she felt (I believe she did not even recognize them in herself), but I carried them for her.

Noise Annoys

Steiner was deeply concerned about small children being exposed to radio and movies because they take the child away from the real experience of the natural world. He felt that the media create a "nervous dependence" and disturb a child's peace of mind. Imagine what he would have said about television and video games.

Play as Work

Steiner discovered in children's play what many later researchers verified: while adults tend to look upon play as meaningless and often use games as a way of keeping a child from bothering them, play is at the center of the young child's development. Steiner commented, "If we were half as devoted and serious in our adult activities as the child is in play, we should be a different order of humanity." Play is work for children, and play activity is precisely the learning the child needs as a preparation for life. Waldorf education at the nursery level emphasizes activities that the child chooses himself.

Awakening the Imagination

Steiner felt that toys should be as simple and unadorned as possible. A doll, for example, should not be the perfect doll you buy at the store, which leaves no room for the child's imaginative powers. Instead, he suggested a rough and ready doll made out of pieces of material or even a table napkin. Such a doll calls out to a child's imagination and stimulates the child's spontaneity.

In a Waldorf nursery school, children role-play many scenes with simple everyday things, such as brooms for horses or chairs arranged as a coach or train. They put on puppet shows, choosing the stories and making their own puppets. Play also includes painting, modeling, cooking, sewing, and building. The children learn nursery rhymes and action songs in two or three languages. They are told simple fairy tales and take part in seasonal festivals.

In all this activity, the emphasis is on the use of imagination as a preparation for life. Steiner insisted that the child should be left in this environment until nature declares the time is ripe for change. Waldorf education teaches us to wait on nature. Nature knows what she is about. The signs are there if we can learn to read them.

Most important of all is Steiner's emphasis on the innate dignity and moral orientation of the child. The focus from the earliest years is on choice, work, experience, and imagination—all essential elements of an education aimed at developing moral intelligence.

MARIA MONTESSORI

One of the magnificent moral moments I presented at the beginning of this book was Maria Montessori's opening of the Casa dei Bambini day care center in a housing project in Rome. Let us note that Montessori opened her school ten years before Steiner opened his. Both Montessori and Steiner were among the major voices in a collective emerging consciousness in the evolution of our understanding of childhood. Montessori herself pointed to psychoanalysis as a precipitating factor in this new awareness. In her book *The Secret of Childhood* she wrote, "If psychoanalysis had not sounded the ocean of the subconscious, it would be difficult to explain how a child's mind could give us a deeper understanding of human problems."

Montessori described her new students as "tearful, frightened children, so timid that I could not get them to speak. Their faces were expressionless, their eyes bewildered.... They were in fact poor, neglected children who had been reared in dark, decrepit homes without anything to stimulate their minds."

As *The Secret of Childhood* recounts, what happened at the Casa dei Bambini brought her a series of surprises that left her "amazed and often incredulous." What she came to believe was that she was making dramatic new discoveries about the nature of the child and childhood development. These discoveries, she felt, would have as deep and lasting an impact on our understanding of human nature as any new scientific discovery. Over the course of several years and after intense observation, Montessori began to formulate a complete philosophy of education and to develop methods of teaching that have lasting significance for moral education as well as intellectual development.

A Personal Note

My own experience with Montessori began when Nancy and I put our son, John junior, into a Montessori school run by two Dominican nuns. John junior was only two years old when he began, and we monitored him closely to be sure we were not jumping the gun. Our friends had reported that their children expressed joy going to this school. My son showed the same enthusiasm; he looked forward to going to school each day. I was also deeply impressed by the orderliness and attention to detail he developed there. (As an adult his organizational skills are amazing.)

During his third year in the program, I read Paula Polk Lillard's book *Montessori: A Modern Approach*. John Holt, an educator I greatly admired, had recommended it as the best introduction to the educator's philosophy, and it helped me to understand many of the things I was observing in my son's behavior, including his autonomy, his creativeness, his willingness to obey, and his respect for property. I later read several of Montessori's major works, and my appreciation of Lillard was confirmed. For the brief summary of Montessori's ideas below, I acknowledge my debt to Lillard's discussion.

The Secret of Childhood

Montessori saw childhood as more than a mere stage to be passed through on the way to adulthood. Childhood, she claimed, is a unique period, an entity unto itself. Adulthood and childhood "are two different forms of human life, going on at the same time and exerting upon one another a reciprocal influence."

Montessori was working more than half a century before the split-brain research I presented in the previous chapter. She understood intuitively that the early life of the child is guided by a holistic, right-brain way of knowing.

The Child as His Own Creator

As a clinician and observer of thousands of children, Montessori concluded that the guiding principle of human development is a personal energy contained within the child. She called this force *horme,* a Greek word for the vital energy that motivates purposeful activity. *Horme* belongs to life in general; it is the source of all evolution. This vital evolutionary force moves the child to grow.

(Steiner believed that the inner urge to movement is the first sign of life, but he simply termed this impulse "one of life's greatest mysteries." Slavin and Kriegman called this life force the "true self," which has its own destiny and agenda.)

In Montessori's words: "The child's psychic life is independent of, precedes and vitalizes every exterior activity."

Even though children are born with a psychic pattern for development that urges them toward maturity, they are not born knowing how to behave to ensure successful development. To survive and thrive, the child needs both freedom and an ordered environment. Children must have the freedom to construct their own personalities through interactions within the safe, adult-monitored boundaries of their environment in order to reach their full developmental potential. To aid in this process during the first six years of life, children are born with what Montessori identified as an "absorbent mind."

The Absorbent Mind

Montessori's book *The Secret of Childhood* is based on meticulous observation of the children at the asylum where she first taught and of the deprived children at the Casa dei Bambini. Later she would write a book entitled *The Absorbent Mind* to expand on her discoveries. The child's absorbent mind, she said, could explain the almost unimaginable changes that take place from the moment of birth through early childhood. The recent discovery of mirror neurons (described in chapter 3), which lead us to imitate the movement of another or give us the impulse to do so, are added proof of Montessori's observation. The absorbent mind is also consistent with modern neuroscience's description of the right brain's nonverbal way of knowing, which registers information automatically, effortlessly, and with great speed below the level of consciousness.

Anyone who pays attention to young children knows that the child's mind is like a sponge and takes in the environment without any detailed formal instruction. Educator John Holt puts it this way in *How Children Fail:*

> Nobody starts off stupid. You have only to watch babies and infants, and think seriously about what all of them learn and do, to see that...they show a style of life, and a desire and ability to learn, that in an older person we might well call genius. Hardly any adult in a thousand, or ten thousand, could in any three years of his life learn as much, grow as much in his understanding of the world around him, as every infant learns and grows in his first three years.

Beginning with nothing, a child is able to absorb unconsciously her environment and to create the mental functions (such as memory and reasoning) necessary for continued development. As Montessori says, "Impressions do not merely enter his mind; they form it. They incarnate themselves in him."

The Sensitive Periods

Montessori also identified a series of "sensitive periods" through which development normally progresses. As Lillard describes them, these are "blocks of time in a child's life when he is absorbed with one characteristic of his environment to the exclusion of all others." In these periods, children obsessively re-peat a task or activity until they master a new function or skill. However, if a child is not allowed to explore these periods fully, it can have lasting and negative effects on the child's psychic ma-turity.

The sensitive periods unfold in this natural progression, Lillard notes: "a need for order in the environment, the use of the hand and tongue, the development of walking, a fascination with minute and detailed objects, and a time of intense social interest."

With the open environment and freedom, the children of the Casa dei Bambini revealed natural laws that were at work within them to direct their psychic development.

First Psychic Law: Work

Montessori observed that the children of the Casa dei Bambini displayed remarkable harmony and contentment after focusing their full attention on work they had freely chosen. Work calmed previous restless or bad behavior, an indication that the act of concentration fulfilled a need within the child and brought him to his normal state. Montessori wrote, "It is certain that the child's aptitude for work represents a vital instinct; for without work his personality cannot organize itself.... Man builds himself through working."

Work is a natural desire of our human nature; when a person fails to find satisfying work, he becomes angry and frustrated. When a child—or any person, for that matter—lives in an envi-ronment that allows him to fulfill his human nature, he achieves what Montessori called "normalization."

As both Steiner and Montessori discovered, the adult's work is different from the child's work. Children work for the joy of the process and feel most gratified when they accomplish tasks by themselves, with no reward expected; adults seek both an end goal and assistance in obtaining it. Children are involved in the second kind of activity that Aristotle described. They are not working to build a house. They are like the people jogging and eating healthy food in which the process is the purpose of their action, to become healthy.

Second Psychic Law: Independence

Montessori wrote: "The child's nature is to aim directly and energetically at functional independence." An inner force guides the child's choices. If this inner force is undermined by coercion, punishment, or an adults' need to function for the child, the child's potential is thwarted. Much of a child's potential is thwarted by generally well-meaning adults. Adults must allow children to move toward independence in order for their personalities to develop to their full potential.

Third Psychic Law: Attention

At a certain stage, a child is able to focus her attention on objects for a prolonged period of time. A child will first direct this attention to objects already familiar to her or those that are instinctually attractive (such as bright, shiny things) but will later expand her attention to previously unknown objects based instead on an intellectual attraction.

Fourth Psychic Law: Will

Montessori passionately confronted the belief that children's natural actions are bound to be disorderly and even violent. For her, disorder and violence were signs of emotional disturbance and suffering, not of "willfullness." Instead, she saw the will as grounded in the previously mentioned universal energy she called *horme*. This evolutionary life force drives a child to act consciously and deliberately in a way that is beneficial to life. This is the beginning of the will.

It is through the development of prolonged attention that a

child's will is then able to form. Because of his new attention span, when a child chooses an activity, he will focus on it completely, limiting his actions and attention to the present task.

It is not moral vision but the inner formation developed by exercising the will that gives a child the strength to control his actions, and this is precisely how the virtue of prudence is formed. Montessori believed that traditional morality "not only denies the child every opportunity for using his will but directly obstructs and inhibits its expression."

I want to explore Montessori's ideas about the development of the will in more detail, because what we believe about willpower is so important to our view of morality.

Montessori identified three phases within the development of the will. The first is independent repetition of a task, through which the child gains a sense of satisfaction and mastery, which in turn stimulates a desire for further mastery. (I believe that this kind of dynamic interplay later produces what I am calling prudence.) Repetition builds a child's self-confidence so long as he is able to perform the task without interference from adults. Lillard makes it clear that for Montessori one of the great dangers in a child's environment is an overfunctioning adult (i.e., an adult who is trying to do for a child what the child can do for herself). Following repetition, a child begins to exert discipline over his actions, choosing to take responsibility for them and thereby forming a sense of pride in his work. Finally, once self-discipline is established, a child develops obedience. The fully developed will is the power to obey, which emerges spontaneously as the child matures.

Montessori found that children readily obey adults except when the adult is violating the instincts that guide the child's development. Children's psyches are innately tuned in such a way that when given freedom in a safe and supportive environment they do not need to be coerced to learn or work. They naturally desire to imitate both adults and older children, which is how they learn to grow up.

This phenomenon of natural obedience is hard for anyone who was raised in an authoritarian, obediential moral system to accept. The suggestion that children will spontaneously and naturally develop obedience seems preposterous to those of us who were taught blind obedience through constant threats of punishment—punishment that was supposed to break our will. I wouldn't believe it if I hadn't seen my son go through precisely these stages.

While Montessori argued that it is our natural obedience that makes social life possible, she found blind obedience abhorrent. She called it an "uncontrolled" form of obedience that can lead to destruction, as in the case of Nazi Germany. Montessori was deeply concerned about discipline based on corporal punishment and demands for blind obedience. She felt that the usual cultural pedagogy of her time assumed that children are unstable, lazy, disorderly, violent, stubborn, and disobedient. She considered this belief about children as an "illness" that could be cured.

What is called the "Montessori method" revolves around the essential point that culture has a "diseased"attitude toward children and does not understand the normal nature of the child. A parent or teacher committed to Montessori principles will gradually find that there is a disappearance of disorder and disharmony and a return to the child's true normalized condition of harmony and peace. Providing the appropriate environment is the crucial issue. A misbehaving child reflects the existence of some need, deprivation, or detrimental influence. "Control the environment and not the child" is a fundamental principle of Montessori education.

In general, the adult personality, with its need for control, its preconceptions, and its unresolved childhood issues, is the most detrimental element in the child's environment.

Montessori observed three stages or levels of obedience in children. At the first level the child obeys sometimes, but not always. At this stage the child's actions are controlled by the life force *(horme)* alone. The stage lasts until the end of the first year.

During the next five years, obedience comes more under the child's conscious control, depending on the developmental level of the child. To carry out an order one must have both the ability to understand it and the ability to carry it out. With two-year-olds, most normal adults know that one has to forbid more or less passionately those disruptive actions that the toddler continues to do. Even after three years of age the child may succeed in obeying a command once, but fail to obey the next time.

Level two is achieved when the child is always able to obey; that is, "his powers are now consolidated and can be directed not only by his own will, but by the will of another." The child can now "absorb another person's wishes and express them in his own behavior." Still, the child does not always obey. This can be due to some unique and idiosyncratic needs of the child or to some delayed inner ability that is not readily apparent.

At level three, the child's obedience turns toward the significant adults whose superiority she feels. Montessori describes it this way: as if the child "had said to himself, 'Here is someone so far above me that she can exert an influence on my mind and make me as clever as she is. She acts inside me!' To feel like this seems to fill the child with joy . . . [it] brings with it a new kind of enthusiasm, and the child becomes anxious and impatient to obey."

For Montessori, such "spontaneous obedience" was a wonderful and incomparable natural development. Observing this phenomenon over and over again, she and her colleagues felt compelled to set up tests in order to verify it. Montessori finally accepted that the will emerges in this way because of the purposeful intention of the life force itself, which impels activities that expand and benefit life. This spontaneous obedience is absolutely necessary for the child's moral, intellectual, and spiritual development.

An Awesome Responsibility

With spontaneous obedience comes a monumental responsibility for the adults who are there for the child. A child at this stage of development can easily be manipulated and indoctrinated. The adult caregiver has a moral obligation to continue to provide an age-appropriate environment and to honor the child's uniqueness, dignity, and personal freedom.

If a child is indoctrinated (we all are to some degree), all is not lost. I certainly was the almost cultlike product of early Catholic education. Being indoctrinated is like being under a spell. For me to break the spell, it took years of experiencing shame and guilt over my failures to be consistently virtuous and over my failures at blind obedience. This is why my discovery of Aristotle's notion of moral know-how or expertise (prudence) and Aquinas' notion of the primacy of conscience was such a liberation for me.

Intelligent obedience is in line with reality. Montessori's conception of will is similar to Aristotle and Aquinas' notion of the will as an intellectual appetite. The will is rooted in intelligence and naturally seeks the fulfillment of our nature. It also resembles Martin Buber's idea of the "grand will," which naturally seeks its destiny and purpose.

Fifth Psychic Law: Intelligence

Although intelligence governs our ability to form an abstract understanding of life, Montessori saw that its primary foundation rested on the child's sense perceptions. Children naturally use all their senses in their first efforts to understand their environment; they need to move, look, touch, taste, smell, and listen. Concepts are grounded in percepts.

One of Montessori's most famous teaching tools is a series of large cards covered with smooth paper on each of which is mounted a letter of the alphabet cut out in fine sandpaper. The children are taught to sound out each letter as they trace the rough surface with the tips of the index and middle fingers. As they trace and sound out the letters over and over again, they learn the movements necessary to form them. They also retain the visual image of the letters. These exercises lead directly to writing and reading.

However, Montessori did not feel that all sensory stimulation was right for a child. Random stimulation, such as watching unguided TV, simply creates what Lillard called "a chaos of mental impressions."

Sixth Psychic Law: Imagination and Creativity

Montessori identified three qualities as essential to the development of the child's imagination and creativity, which Lillard describes as "a remarkable power of attention and concentration which appear almost as a form of meditation; a considerable autonomy and independence of judgment; and an expectant faith that remains open to truth and reality."

Adults often treat a child's imagination as they treat the child in general: as a passive being instead of an active creator of her own life. The adult tries to substitute his imagination for the child's, supplying it with established fairy tales and other fantastic stories, when what truly encourages imagination is freedom for the child to develop her own stories.

Likewise, children need freedom in order to develop creatively. They need to be free to choose their own activities and games, again without the interference of adults, who tend to stifle creative impulses when they try to control a child's choices and activities.

Seventh Psychic Law: Emotions and Spirituality

Long before Silvan Tomkins developed his affect system, Montessori believed that the child has the powers of affect from birth. These affects are first aroused and developed through a loving experience with the mother. Based on this secure attachment, a child's emotional life develops, and he can then form relationships with other people based on an emotional, loving connection.

Lillard states: "To achieve emotional and spiritual maturity, the child must develop not only his internal capacity for love, but also his moral sense." Montessori believed the moral sense (or in my terms, moral intelligence) to be something inborn that then develops over time. The ordered will is a critical part of the development of moral intelligence.

SUMMING UP

Steiner and Montessori agree on the following points:

- There are observable scientific or natural laws governing the inner development of the child.
- Each newborn infant has an innate inner drive to know that moves him to work tirelessly and gives him extraordinary powers of concentration.
- If given the proper stimulus and environment, there is absolutely no need to motivate children.
- The secret of childhood is the secret of life itself. To understand this mystery we have to detach ourselves from our role as all-knowing adults and be humble enough to learn from the child.
- The child has a moral and spiritual nature, but she needs

an ordered, age-appropriate environment in order to develop her imagination and creativity.

- The frustration of the child's freedom, needs, and creative powers are the deepest roots of violence and chaos.
- The most disturbing element in the environment is the
unconscious adult, who projects his own fantasies of
how children should be, tries to control and restrain
them, and does for them what they can do for themselves.
- Misinformed and inept parenting and teaching is like a
disease that creates behavior problems and prevents the
child's normal development.

5

TEN MAJOR SOURCES FROM WHICH MORAL INTELLIGENCE DEVELOPS

Men who love wisdom must be inquirers into very many things indeed.

—Heraclitus

The prudent person is to moral intelligence what the accomplished musician is to musical intelligence, the great athlete is to bodily or kinesthetic intelligence, or the great architect or sculptor is to spatial intelligence. The innate capacity that I focused on in the previous two chapters is only the beginning. It must be developed and shaped if we are to become true "experts" in the moral realm.

Each of the magnificent moral moments that open this book illustrates one or more of the major sources for that development. Over the course of each person's life, all of these sources will play a part in the internalized synthesis that is fully developed moral intelligence—the state of being that Aristotle and Aquinas saw as the virtue of prudence.

I like to use pictures to make abstract and complex material more concrete and understandable. The tree in Figure 5.1 is my way of symbolizing the process by which moral intelligence grows and reaches fruition.

The roots of my tree are the sources from which moral intelligence develops, which I will discuss in this chapter. At the very bottom of the trunk is hope, the rudiments of which are developing during infancy. If an infant achieves a secure attachment with her mothering source, a fundamental sense of trust is established.

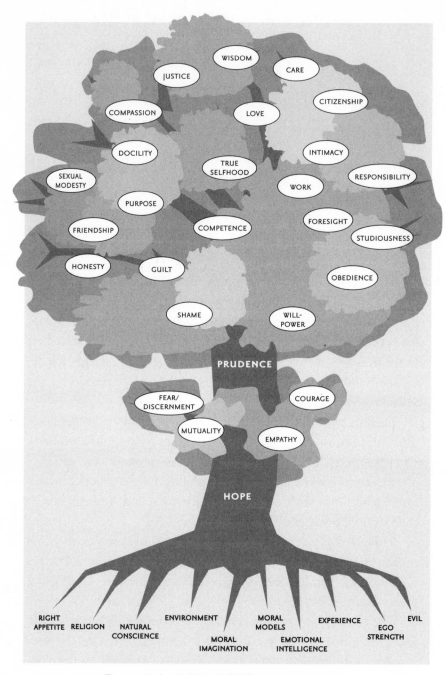

**Figure 5.1: THE ROOTS OF THE TREE
OF MORAL INTELLIGENCE**

This basic trust forms the psychological root of the virtue of hope. Without this foundation, the development of the virtue of prudence will be damaged. The trunk of the tree is the virtue of prudence, which grows stronger and develops branches as our moral intelligence develops. The fruits represent the many other virtues that may emerge at various ages and stages of our lives. The tree has many branches and many fruits, but they are all interconnected. It is an organic whole, a complete life, always growing and expanding.

THE FIRST SOURCE: RIGHT APPETITE OR "GRAND WILL"

The fire department culture that New York first deputy fire commissioner William Feehan described before his own death in the World Trade Center exemplifies right appetite. As Feehan points out, you can't pay people to be willing to risk their lives to save others. That choice is rooted in what Aristotle called a "right desire."

> The origin of action . . . is choice, and that of choice is desire and reasoning, with a view to an end. That is why *choice cannot exist either without reason and intellect or without a moral state;* for good action and its opposite cannot exist without a combination of intellect and character.

Right desire is the energetic fuel of virtuous behavior.

Martin Buber, the Jewish philosopher and theologian, makes a distinction between what he called our "grand will" and our "puny, unfree will." The person who operates out of "grand will" wills with intention as opposed to arbitrary self-will. The grand will moves inevitably in the direction that a person's destiny is calling that individual to fulfill.

In order to understand this statement, think of Slavin and

Kriegman's discussion of the "true self," the part of us that is beyond outside interference and holds the kernel of our destiny and purpose in life.

A Personal Experience of Grand Will

On August 13, 1981, I had a profound experience that proved to be a turning point in my life. My wife and I had a cabin on West Twin Lake in Minnesota, and I used to spend several weeks alone there every summer. One day I was out jogging on the highway. I was especially energized and had run eleven miles. I was making one last lap, running toward a little town named Pequot Lakes, when I looked out to the horizon and clearly saw the face of Christ. It was surrounded by pure white clouds and sunlight. The image came out of nowhere. I hadn't been reading the Bible or thinking about theology or religion. At the same time, I got a clear internal message that told me to do the work I was intended to do, and if I did so, I'd never worry about money again. (Growing up in poverty, I had spent my adult life catastrophizing about finances.)

When I finished my run, I went to our cabin and pondered what had happened. I really didn't know whether I was on an endorphin high or having a spiritual experience. This was a period when I was acting out sexually, and the message hadn't told me to stop. That seemed like a relief at the time.

What I can tell you now is that I ended my sexually compulsive behavior within six months, helped by one of the first Sex and Love Addicts Anonymous groups in Houston, Texas. Within a year of that experience, I began the original pain feeling work that I'll describe in chapter 8, and everything started coming together in my life. People asked me to do a PBS series on the family; others appeared with financial resources to get the show done. That began a TV journey on PBS that lasted ten years. I wrote books on each series, three of which became *New York Times* bestsellers. From 1984 to 1994, I raised millions of dollars for PBS, sold six million books, and was lecturing all over the world. On nineteen occasions during this period, I saw the face of Christ—always when I least expected it.

That vision on the highway in Minnesota was a destiny experience for me. While I heard no audible words, I intuited an internal message that told me to do the work I knew I was intended to do. My grand will was moving me, and as soon as I set my intention to follow it, my destiny as a teacher unfolded. Everything and everyone converged in ways that truly made my work happen.

The "puny unfree will" is controlled by things and instincts. Right appetite is the human will guided by the deep intelligence that flows from the call and destiny of our nature.

Willingness Versus Willfulness

Theologian Gerald May makes a similar distinction in his book *Will and Spirit,* where he speaks of the difference between willingness (right appetite) and willfulness:

> Willingness implies a surrendering of one's self-separateness, an entering-into, an immersion in the deepest processes of life itself. It is a realization that one is already a part of some ultimate cosmic process and it is a commitment to participation in that process. In contrast, willfulness is the setting of oneself apart from the fundamental essence of life in an attempt to master, direct, control, or otherwise manipulate existence.

Because our will is an appetite that is imbued with our intelligence, it can be educated. A finely educated will is what Aristotle called "right desire" or a habituated appetite.

Self-Will Run Riot

When an emotion is cut off from our consciousness and practical thinking, we describe it as uncontained and out of control.

The same is true of the will. When it is not educated and guided by intelligent deliberation and our intention toward the good of human nature, it becomes dissociated. In twelve-step recovery programs such dissociated willfulness is described as self-will run riot.

A dissociated will can destroy our lives and those around us, but recognizing this is not the same as believing that human nature is inherently evil. If the will is evil, we must use coercive and legalistic power to control it. If it is dissociated, we can educate it.

Education of the Will

Leslie Farber, a psychiatrist who wrote an insightful book entitled *The Ways of the Will*, sees the core of many modern problems, including addiction, violence, and immorality, as a failure to develop healthy willpower. Vice is characterized by willing what is unlawful or impossible. Willpower must be modified by true limits (natural shame) and a healthy resolution of early developmental dependency needs.

To develop right appetite, the will that leads us toward good, we have to practice self-control and get in the habit of doing small virtuous acts. It feels joyful to help a friend or do an act of bravery. Habituation of the will requires doing virtuous behaviors habitually. The more we serve, care for others, and refuse to lie, the more we experience the joy of virtuous acts and the more we want to do those virtuous things. Over time, virtuous behavior becomes internalized and we do virtuous acts almost without thinking. Our will habitually seeks the good. Our appetite is right.

THE SECOND SOURCE: RELIGION, THE AUTHORITY OF A HIGHER POWER

Nothing has more moral authority for us as children than the precepts of our parents, who represent our first experience of a higher power. Clinical psychology has established that until approximately age four, children deify their parents. Mom and Dad are "god and goddess"—they know everything and are the all-powerful source of delight or pain. The psychologist James Masterson calls this "the illusion of omnipotence." Then at age four, if they are developing healthily, children begin to see their parents' limitations; they experience natural shame, their own and their parents'. Children's energy shifts to what I like to call "parentalizing the deity"—which means they project onto someone called God the all-knowing, all-powerful magic their parents formerly possessed.

Ruby Bridges

Six-year-old Ruby Bridges had internalized a sense of safety because she had a strong, religious mother and belonged to a church where the minister was also a powerful voice of security. Both her mother and the minister taught her the Bible as God's word and assured her of God's protection and love. Children are in special need of some source of absolute security because of their fundamental powerlessness. Children find it natural and comforting to believe in God. All humans have an innate survival need in childhood that moves them to attach themselves to a source of trust and safety.

Most healthy human adults also believe in some kind of higher power. Some adults may not think of their higher power belief system as God, and many do not belong to a specific religion, yet we want to believe that something shapes our lives, even if it is the god of chance or chaos. The Lutheran theologian Paul Tillich believed that a person's ultimate concern was equivalent to their higher power. All humans have attachment needs, and all normal humans have a natural sense of shame, understood as modesty, awe, and reverence. Natural shame lets us know that we are limited and that there is something or someone greater than ourselves: natural shame is the source and safeguard of spirituality.

There is a difference between religion and spirituality. In the words of Alla Renée Bozarth: "Religion is a faith system outside of oneself to which one belongs in solidarity with others. Spirituality is a meaning system within oneself that belongs to the realm of personal, original, and inward experience." They overlap, and true religion engenders spirituality. Rigid and authoritarian religion, on the other hand, often crushes spirituality. When a religion fails to engender spirituality, it becomes religiosity and often takes the form of a totalistic system.

Human beings' first moral developmental task is to experience a fundamental trust in their primary source figure. It is from their basic trust and attachment to a parent, or surrogate parents, that children unquestioningly accept their source figure's religious beliefs, whatever they may be.

Basic trust leads to the formation of a primal sense of hope. Trust and hope are essential if we are to develop our innate moral intelligence. Religion offers a powerful source of hope. Each of us needs to go through the first stage of obedience to an absolute source of authority, which has its prescribed good behaviors and concomitant consequences if they are not adhered to. As we mature, this natural sense of obedience blossoms into inner strength.

A Sustaining Faith

In his book *Legacy of the Heart,* Wayne Muller recounts a story told by the American Buddhist teacher Jack Kornfield:

> [He went] with Maha Gosananda, a respected Cambodian monk, into the refugee camps where thousands of Cambodians had fled the terrible holocaust conducted by Pol Pot. Every family had lost children, spouses, and parents...their homes and temples had been destroyed. Maha Gosananda announced to the refugees that there would be a Buddhist ceremony the next day, and all who wished to come would be welcome.

Since Buddhism had been desecrated by Pol Pot, people were curious if anyone would go. The next day, over ten thousand refugees converged [to participate]. . . . Maha Gosananda sat for some time in silence on a platform in front of the crowd. Then he began chanting the invocations that begin the Buddhist ceremony, and people started weeping. They had been through so much sorrow, so much difficulty, that just to hear the sound of those familiar words again was precious. . . .

[Next he] began to repeat this verse from the *Dhammapada,* a sacred Buddhist scripture:

> Hatred never ceases by hatred;
> But by love alone is healed.
> This is an ancient and eternal law.

Over and over Maha Gosananda chanted this verse . . . [and] one by one, thousands of voices joined together in unison.

These people who had been oppressed, made homeless, aggrieved, wounded and crushed by pain still desired the goodness of peaceful compassion, love, and forgiveness. Their love and Buddhist practice had become what Aquinas described as a habitus, a quality of their soul. When their holy leader arrived and offered to lead them in a service, they welcomed him. Their appetites were right; they exercised a goodness that had become a part of their very being. Their willingness was part of their habituated appetite and their grand will. Their religion was the secure base that sustained them.

THIRD SOURCE: NATURAL CONSCIENCE

Mother Teresa once wrote:

There is a natural conscience in every human being to know right from wrong. I deal with thousands who are Christians and non-Christians and you can see such a conscience at work in their lives.

One of my magnificent moral moments is the story of Colburn, Thompson, and Andreotta at My Lai, who courageously followed their conscience and risked their lives to oppose the authority of Lieutenant Calley. Another model of conscience is Henry David Thoreau, whose convictions pushed him to stand up against the U.S. government. Thoreau impresses me because, despite my conscious convictions, I still find it hard to express my dissent when I'm with a majority who are speaking in a racist or chauvinistic way. Fear of rejection keeps me silent.

Thompson and Thoreau clearly show us that the sting of conscience is not limited to our feelings of discomfort when we have done something wrong. Conscience also makes us uncomfortable when we fail to honor our true self and act according to our highest ideals. Erik Erikson speaks of a "generative guilt" that appears when we fail to become the person we know we can be or when we fail to stand up for our own values.

An Extraordinary Conscience

Our own innate need for secure attachment and our natural desire for cooperation are evidence of our natural conscience. The lives of moral prodigies provide us with more dramatic evidence of an innate moral giftedness, or what theologian Richard Rubenstein called in his book *After Auschwitz* an "instinct for righteousness."

One of the true moral prodigies of our time was Agnes Gonxha Bojaxhiu, otherwise known as Mother Teresa. The story of her life is the story of an extraordinary conscience in action.

Agnes was born on April 16, 1910, in Skopje, the capital of the Republic of Macedonia, and it was clear very early that she possessed an extraordinary moral giftedness. Although her family was well-off, her brother Lazar tells of her frequent visits to a poor widow who lived with her malnourished children in a dark and dirty room. She also had an unusual interest in reading about missionaries and the lives of saints.

In her late teens, Agnes joined the Sisters of Loreto, a group of nuns based in Ireland whose mission was to teach in India. She later said her vocation came in a moment of clarity regarding the future. This was her first calling. She believed it had come from God.

In the convent, Agnes took the name Teresa, after Saint Thérèsa of Lisieux. After her training, she was made principal of St. Mary's School in Calcutta. Sister Teresa became Mother Teresa.

It was on her way to a retreat in Darjeeling in 1946 that Mother Teresa had "a day of inspiration," a second calling, one that would attract the attention of the entire world. As she later explained, "I clearly felt a call within my calling. The message was very clear. I had to leave the convent and consecrate myself to helping the poor by living among them."

This was no easy decision, and there were huge barriers formed by her initial vows. She was asking for "exclaustration"—the right to leave her convent and do a work not associated with her religious order. It was unheard of, but no matter what her struggle or need was, she found a way to get it done. Perhaps it was a case of a will made powerful by aligning with "grand will" and matched with unusual powers of persistence and leadership?

Mother Teresa knew what to do without ever taking any formal courses in leadership. She knew how to make things happen, how to inspire, how to get others involved. She knew this simply and decisively.

The philosopher Jacques Maritain says that we know the natural law through the inclination of innate conscience and not by rational reflection. He writes: "Thus it is that men [and women]...are unable to give account of and rationally to justify their most fundamental moral beliefs." This may be the answer to the mystery of how Mother Teresa got from Skopje to the gutters of Calcutta.

Since Mother Teresa's death, it has also come to light that at times she felt herself painfully distant from God. That actually reassures me, because faith is not knowledge. The theologian Paul Tillich felt that without doubt, one's faith is not really strong. Faith would not be faith if it had the certainty of knowledge.

FOURTH SOURCE: ENVIRONMENT

The great French naturalist Jean-Henri Fabre was called the "Homer of the insects" because of the wealth of information he gave the world about insects and because his method of study was revolutionary. Fabre did not take insects into the laboratory in order to experiment with them. His method was to let the insects be free and live in the environment most suited to them. He was careful not to let his presence interfere with their natural functions and mode of living. He was patient, allowing the insects to reveal their secrets to him.

Maria Montessori and her seemingly miraculous transformation of the children in her Casa dei Bambini represents, for me, the power of the environment to develop moral intelligence. I discovered in reading about her that Montessori drew on the work of the biologists of her time—including Darwin, Mendel, and Fabre—to support her theories. Her experimental school was based on years of study and observation of children. She saw them as free and exuberant. In her actual observations, as opposed to preconceived notions of how children should behave, she adopted Fabre's method of noninterference, creating an environment that was best suited to the child's natural freedom. Montessori's method was based on "freedom in a prepared environment." Freedom is one of the defining characteristics of moral choice, and without choice virtue is impossible.

One Mile Apart

In *The Moral Life of Children,* Robert Coles tells about a boy named Hank. Hank lived in New Orleans about a mile from Ruby Bridges and attended the school to which Ruby was escorted daily by federal marshals.

Coles interviewed a great number of the white children during that time, but seven-year-old Hank stood out because of his obsession with Ruby Bridges. He couldn't figure out what made her tick, and that bothered him. Hank told Coles that Ruby was crazy for continuing to come to school. But at the same time, Coles got the feeling that Hank was impressed by her—almost against his will. Hank's father was an embittered militant segregationist, a constant heckler of Ruby, and a member of the Ku Klux Klan.

Hank's father was encased in prejudice, envy, resentment, and a despairing and powerless egoism. Hank's father and Ruby Bridges' mother both used the Bible to teach their children. For Ruby's mother, the Bible was a source of strength and compassion. She passed that strength to Ruby, who smiled at and prayed for her oppressors. Hank's father, on the other hand, loved to read aloud from the book of Exodus—particularly the twenty-first chapter, which incorporates the ancient *lex talionis* (the law of retaliation, as in "an eye for an eye"), and especially the part about the treatment of slaves by their masters. Hank heard his father preach revenge; he heard him use the Bible to justify his hatred of blacks and his desire to have them deported to Africa.

Ruby and Hank lived only a mile from each other, but their moral environments could not have been further apart. Later, when Coles interviewed Hank in his early teen years, Hank had become more combative, more outspoken, ready to beat everyone up—more like his father.

Ruby went one way; Hank went another. Coles writes that Hank was persuaded not only by his family life, but by the "fate" that comes, finally, to mean a given set of experiences in a region, a neighborhood, a school, a workplace.

THE FIFTH SOURCE: MORAL IMAGINATION

Perhaps the least explored but one of the most critically important sources of moral intelligence is our moral imagination. Magnificent moral moments, such as the scene I described from *The Shawshank Redemption,* stir our imagination and move us to act virtuously.

Imagination has a potential power that goes beyond logic or reason. It is closer to the practical intellect. Imagination brings life to the particular—particular scenes with particular characters. In doing so, it moves the heart.

This ability to bring a scene to life, to create a story with cause and effect, is critical when we are faced with a difficult choice. We must envision each alternative and imagine as fully as we can the consequences of choosing one rather than another.

Imagination is also the core of mature empathy, the capacity to put ourselves into someone else's shoes, to experience their reality and feelings. As the poet Percy Bysshe Shelley argued so eloquently in *A Defence of Poetry:* "A man, to be greatly good, must imagine intensely and comprehensively; he must put himself in the place of another and of many others; the pains and pleasures of his species must become his own. The great instrument of moral good is the imagination."

Like all human faculties, imagination can also be a source of evil. The Nazis' fantasy of a master race was a horrible example of imagination gone awry, bringing suffering and death to untold millions, including the six million Jews who died in the Holocaust.

Dead Poets Society

A few years ago I had a powerful cleansing moral experience watching another movie, *Dead Poets Society.* In that Academy Award–winning film, Robin Williams plays the role of Mr.

Keating, a new teacher at an elite, very traditional boys' prep school, which he himself attended as a student. On the first day of English class, Keating has the boys rip out the introduction to their poetry textbook. Instead of reading an arid analysis of types of meter and verse, he wants the boys to plunge into the poetry and experience it for themselves. He encourages them to write their own poetry.

The class soon discovers that when Keating was a student, he belonged to what was called the "Dead Poets Society"—a group of boys who would get together and share poetry for the sheer love of it. Some members of Keating's class decide to form their own Dead Poets Society. They meet secretly at night to read and share poetry.

The kids love Keating's class. It is spontaneous, upbeat, experiential and creative. The administration, however, is not as enthusiastic. Keating does not quite fit the rigid, ordered, obediential environment of the elite school that caters to wealthy parental benefactors. One of the boys in the Dead Poets Society decides he does not want to go to college to study pre-med, as his father insists that he do. When he informs his father that he wants to be an actor, the father orders his son to continue along the path that the father has decided on. After their confrontation the boy commits suicide. Looking for a scapegoat, the school administration blames the entire tragedy on Keating and fires him.

After he is fired, Keating goes to his classroom to get his coat and books. The new teacher, a stodgy, rigid authoritarian, is reading aloud the introduction that Keating had the students tear out of the book. It is a very dramatic moment. The boys are caught between their love of Keating and the way he opened their minds and hearts, on one hand, and their fear of the new teacher, on the other. As Keating quietly starts to walk out, one boy jumps on his desk and begins to recite "O Captain! My Captain!" the beautiful poem written by Walt Whitman after Lincoln was assassinated. The teacher is furious and threatens to expel the boy. Then one by one, each boy stands on his desk and recites, "O

Captain! My Captain!" At the end they are all standing in tribute to their fallen hero, Keating.

When I saw this movie, I was extremely emotional all the way through it. The last scene sent me into deep sobs. I've seen the movie three times, and each time I have the same reaction.

This movie touched an unresolved part of my own moral experience. When I left the seminary I was hired by an elite Catholic high school, to teach the seniors religion. The students were rebellious and angry about the authoritarian indoctrination the school was subjecting them to. They were made to wear jackets and ties, and it was not uncommon to see students kneeling in the hall to have their sideburns shaved.

I was angry at my own rigid seminary indoctrination and felt that there were creative ways to teach religious truths and moral values by challenging the students imaginatively. I had them read Dostoyevsky's *Crime and Punishment,* a novel that is emotionally engaging and explicit about the power of conscience. I had them see movies that powerfully involved them in moral dilemmas that we later discussed together. The students became avidly involved in my religion classes.

After a few months I was visited by the mother of one of my students. I had called her in order to warn her that her son had a serious drinking problem. She was irate and denied that her son had a problem. The budding alcoholic's mother was a leader in a conservative group that was already upset about my teaching methods, and now they began a campaign to have me fired. The Jesuit principal and many of the teachers were on my side, but no one would go up against the Bishop of the diocese, who refused to say the traditional Mass of the Holy Spirit to start the school year as long as I was there. I was fired.

I had a wife and a baby on the way. I was frightened and unsure of how I would make it financially. My own shame and guilt stimulated my internal critic, which was filled with voices from my authoritarian Catholic childhood. I felt morally confused. My students had seemed genuinely excited about moral and religious issues, but the voices in my head were accusing me of projecting my own rebellion onto my students.

I never really resolved this dilemma or grieved my loss. Years later, *Dead Poets Society* helped me see the whole situation objectively and acknowledge the injustice done to me. I felt power and vindication. My weeping was coming from a deep well of sorrow and self-respect. Nothing else could have helped me the way this movie did. This is the power of moral imagination.

SIXTH SOURCE: MORAL MODELS

By refusing to pay his poll tax, Henry David Thoreau modeled the courage to stand alone against an unjust system of government. His willingness to act on his beliefs helped to inspire two of the great liberation movements of the twentieth century. Both Gandhi and Martin Luther King Jr. read Thoreau's essay "Civil Disobedience."

"What you do speaks so loud that I cannot hear what you say," said Ralph Waldo Emerson, who was a friend and mentor of Henry David Thoreau. More than two thousand years earlier the Greek moralist Heraclitus said, "It is not the oath that makes us believe the man, but the man the oath." These voices point us to a significant source of moral intelligence.

The people who raise us, teach us, coach us, boss us, and preach to us are integral parts of our life experience. Example is almost always more important than sermonizing or being bombarded by precepts and rules. The tradition of the Greek philosophers Democritus and Heraclitus saw moral behavior as more important than moral knowledge. Aristotle constantly urged his students to find good, prudent men and women and watch how they lived their lives. This is why Aristotle exhorts us to listen to "the unproven sayings and opinions of experienced and older people as much as we attend to the demonstrations of philosophers."

My Changing Models

I found that growth demanded that I be willing to change gurus or teachers and move on to others. I've always had Jesus in my moral mirror, but not in the way I often hear people talk about Him. I chose Jesus in a very simple way, based on the three gospel stories that modern biblical scholars believe come closest to the actual words of Jesus. One is the story of the prodigal son. I could really identify with that one. Another is the story of the shepherd and the lost sheep. Knowing that no reasonable shepherd would leave his entire flock to go after one sheep makes the story all the more powerful. The last story is about the businessman who paid everybody full wages, even those who came to work late in the day. All three comprise Jesus' theology, and all three have Jesus revealing to us that His Father loves us beyond reason, and beyond any deserving.

For me this is all I need: pure unconditional love and forgiveness from my higher power. This is the highest virtue, that which makes us truly godlike. As far as I'm concerned, true religion is simply *love*. I'm in no way putting down the people who go to church or the rituals each religion uses. I had to go through five distinct stages to arrive at this conscious contact with unconditional love.

Stage one: Find a mentor to be your role model, and change whatever harmful pattern your life is in. Nothing changes until something changes.

Stage two: Find a program (religious community, twelve-step group, therapist, or therapy group) to help you stop going astray. For me, my first mentor was my twelve-step sponsor.

Stage three: Find a therapist who can guide you through your original pain work—your deep feeling work.

Stage four: Find workshops, books, or a therapist to help you learn the developmental tasks you did not learn growing up. A therapist could be a coach or mentor here.

Stage five: Find a spiritual master—it could be your religion's founder or some other spiritual master—as a mentor for working a spiritual program.

I started with my grandfather, who was the only male in my life. He loved me a great deal and he was a man of loyalty to his Catholic faith, totally responsible and committed to his wife and family. He was also a man of virtuous moderation. I believe that the image of my grandfather's goodness moved me to do something about my drinking. I couldn't really look him in the eye until I stopped drinking.

But I needed a twelve-step sponsor for the first three years of my sobriety. I found a professor (I was a professor too) named Francis who was tough on me but just what I needed to get the program. One day he told me that I might be too smart to make the simple twelve-step program work. He was challenging my intellectual elitism. And sure enough, I fell off the wagon and wound up in Austin State Hospital. I kept thinking about what he'd said about being too smart. I thought about the slogan "Keep it simple, stupid," and that was the day I began my forty-three years of uninterrupted sobriety.

After my bout with sexual addiction, I realized there was something deeper that I was not getting to. I called my problem addictiveness, and realized that my childhood abandonment, neglect, chronic distress, and shaming had left deep wounds that were ungrieved. I needed a new model and a new teacher. I found him in a therapist named George Daugherty, whom I will describe shortly.

I did three years of heavy feeling work, like what I'll describe in chapter 8, and grieved the core of my unresolved pain, which before had been the black hole I could not seem to fill. The black hole was the root of my addictions. I put the cork on the bottle and stopped drinking, but the unresolved grief was still there as painful shame. I needed to grieve it.

After George, I needed someone to guide me in learning social skills—things such as emotional containment and learning how to set good personal boundaries (express anger respectfully, be able to say no to people). I needed to become aware of my needs, learn how to ask for what I needed, and learn how to nurture myself. The models I used for these parts of the journey were workshop leaders and books, especially books on assertiveness and boundary building. This journey of skill building is always in progress, but as I began to feel good about myself and learn how to get my needs for human connection met, my spiritual needs began to emerge.

The unconditional love and forgiveness of God as a father, revealed by Jesus, was always in the background. But to accept that unconditional love was overwhelming at first. As I've worked on being virtuous and finding more and more wholeness, I began to accept that healing love. But not without struggle and doubt.

I came to believe that it's up to each of us to find a spiritual program that is uniquely our own, not one we've been coerced by fear to accept, but a program that keeps us growing spiritually.

In recent years I've found that Asian spirituality has deepened my understanding of virtue. Asian spiritual masters have helped me grasp Heraclitus' belief that reality is constituted by polarity. Everything is intrinsically related to its opposite. Life leads to death; night follows day; there is no joy without sorrow, no sound without silence, no good that can be polarized and separated from evil. The spiritual life is about accepting these polarities and living with the tension of these opposites.

Prudence is the virtue that allows us to choose well in synthesizing opposites. As the engine of all the virtues, prudence allows us to truly live in reality and subdues our tendency toward polarized righteousness.

The Therapist as Moral Model

George Daugherty had a reputation for fierce honesty and integrity. The therapist friend who recommended him told me, "Don't go to him if you are not prepared to be confronted about any part of your phoniness. He will also confront you morally." I felt I needed such a person. By the time I sought out George I was well known locally and considered to be one of the best counselors around. I'm not saying this to be grandiose, only to explain that I was intimidating to the previous therapist I'd seen.

From my first visit to George, it was obvious that he was not intimidated. At one point, I mentioned "my ministry." He stopped me and asked what I thought my ministry was and if I thought it was special. I hemmed and hawed until he interrupted me with a laser-beam-like statement. "What you do is a job," he said. "It is different from what most people do, but it is not special in the sense that it makes you any better than anyone else." I've never forgotten that confrontation. To me it was a model of honesty and love.

George also once interrupted me as I talked about how bad my childhood was. He instructed me to say "Suffering is ordinary" as many times as I could remember to say it over the following week. It took me a while to understand what this was all about. When I first repeated the phrase, I felt myself getting angrier and angrier. My anger lasted for days until I realized how attached I was to "my" suffering. I had made it into an identity. As long as it was an identity, I could not grieve my unresolved pain. This kept me stuck in the past.

George could also be tender, validating, and encouraging. He knew just the right time to be confrontational and just the right time to be nurturing.

For me, George embodied prudence. He was a gifted therapist and a deeply moral man. He taught me some great and pivotal lessons that literally changed the direction of my life. When I think about George, I think about the words of the poet-philosopher Paul Claudel, who wrote:

> There is a deep mystery and an infinite source of tragedy that we are the condition of salvation one for the other—that we alone carry within ourselves the key to the soul of such and such of our brothers and sisters who can be saved by us and at our expense.

George had done his own suffering; though he never shared it with me, I knew what it was. He died rather young—and, I think, tragically.

SEVENTH SOURCE: EMOTIONAL INTELLIGENCE

In selecting the magnificent moral moments to include in this book, I chose Abraham Lincoln as my example of mature emotional intelligence. He could move people's minds and hearts in such a way that they were compelled to take action. Leadership and motivation are highly developed stages of emotional intelligence. Our greatest and most noble leaders are people of unusual emotional intelligence.

Although Lincoln had to teach himself to read and write and was gangly and a bit awkward, he had a great gift of oratory and emotional intelligence. He was a great debater and an excellent lawyer. Greatness emerges when ordinary people respond to challenge and adversity in an extraordinary way. Who could have predicted, looking at his austere beginnings, that he was the man called by fate, destiny, and God to face the greatest challenge in the history of our democratic way of life? He accepted that challenge with his awesome emotional intelligence and went on to greatness. He was able to use his own emotions in a way that triggered others' emotions and moved them to take steps to save the "last best hope of earth."

Is Emotional Intelligence the Same as Moral Intelligence?

In 1990, two research psychologists, Peter Salovey and John D. Mayer, first proposed a model that they called "emotional intelligence." Their work was later popularized by Daniel Goleman in his bestselling book *Emotional Intelligence*.

According to Salovey and Mayer, emotionally intelligent people are aware of cues within themselves that signal the presence of an affect or emotion. They can name the affect they are having and can differentiate their feeling from thought, desire, or fantasy. They can soothe themselves with their own positive emotional scenes and can use their emotional scenes as a source of self-motivation. All of these abilities flow from their *intrapsychic intelligence*.

Emotionally intelligent people also have *interpersonal intelligence*. They can establish rapport. They can make contact with others and resolve conflicts and differences when they arise. This gives them the ability to get along with others and, when appropriate, be intimate with them. At its highest level, it gives them the ability to move others to action.

Certainly, a high level of emotional intelligence is a crucial element in our ability to act virtuously. Emotion must be consciously contained in order to fuel good choices. Contained emotion is not apathy or neutrality. It is emotion that is operating under the guidance of intelligence, as opposed to reactive, impulsive, unconstrained emotion. This involves using the intelligence that resides in the nondominant right hemisphere of the brain, the "felt thought" that I described in chapter 3, as well as the logical intelligence of the dominant left hemisphere.

The difference between emotional and moral intelligence is that emotional intelligence is neutral and can be used for good or ill. Martin Luther King Jr. used his emotional intelligence to motivate millions of people to campaign nonviolently. Hitler used his emotional intelligence to motivate his fellow countrymen to kill millions of people.

The primary aim of moral intelligence is to become skilled in making moral and ethical decisions and acting on them. But to attain expertise in choosing well, we need a high level of emotional intelligence. Both Aristotle and Aquinas declared that emotion, or "affective inclination," was the major factor in making a moral choice and moving into action. Antonio Damasio's neuroscientific studies as well as the Yale studies I spoke of in chapter 3 have looked inside the brain to validate the primacy of emotion in making choices. Being as fully aware of our emotions as possible is an essential part of the process of developing the expertise I'm calling moral intelligence.

The Problem of Blocked Emotions

When a person has blocked emotions, she is not able to use the intelligence of the emotional, nondominant hemisphere of the brain. Blocked emotions distort our ability to choose well. We cannot motivate others emotionally unless we are in touch with our own feelings. When I'm aware of my feelings, I can use them for self-soothing and self-motivation. And when I am aware of what I'm feeling and can name the feeling, I have a foundation for developing my emotional intelligence.

Shame Binds

For many years I avoided venturing out to investigate anything really new because my emotions were bound in shame. (I've discussed this at more length in the revised edition of my book *Healing the Shame That Binds You*.) Choosing a new experience meant that I ran the risk of being exposed. With a shame-based identity, I felt flawed and defective deep down, even though I had strong façades to cover up my fear of exposure. This has cost me a great deal in terms of the richness of choice and experience in my life.

Getting in touch with my emotions by grieving the unresolved pain of the past has allowed me to feel my feelings in the present. I'm now making choices that are truly my own. I'm willing to risk and make mistakes because that is part of my perfectly imperfect self.

To have your feelings bound by shame is to live a narrow and guarded existence. Life becomes a lonely, defensive maneuver, and courageous choosing and moral excellence are largely shut off from you.

All of our feelings are necessary in order to have a full moral life. Emotional intelligence is a critical companion of moral intelligence. Self-restraint is the fruit of learning to contain emotional impulsivity, and empathy is the emotion that lies at the core of altruism and compassion. We cannot develop our moral intelligence fully without also developing our emotional intelligence.

In chapter 11 I will have more to say about emotional intelligence and about the developmental stages that foster it. The education of our emotions is new territory, and we have lots to learn about how to go about it.

EIGHTH SOURCE: EXPERIENCE

Morrie Schwartz was a man of wisdom. He was a professor and academician, but the insights and love he shared with his former student Mitch Albom seemed to come directly from his life experience, not from book learning. Morrie was a professor and a master teacher. His ability went far beyond book learning. Morrie taught Mitch and all of us with his dying.

I was deeply moved by Morrie. Perhaps you saw the movie *Tuesdays with Morrie* or read the book. It was a great solace for me in grieving my mother's death to remember that death ends a life but not a relationship. Millions of other people have also found their particular life dilemmas clarified by Morrie's wisdom.

Your experience is yours alone, and it's potentially full of wisdom. You've done things you never knew you could do, and you probably have many more surprises to come. But experience is mere rote events unless you are open and alive to what it can teach. "Someone who is not allowed to feel can't learn from experience," says Alice Miller in her book *The Untouched Key*. When we can't feel, nothing really matters. And as Silvan Tomkins points out, with feeling, anything can matter. Experience is an opportunity to grow and learn. What we do with our experience is what counts. But why was experience a great teacher for Morrie and not for my old friend who was bitter, depressed, and resentful about his children and his life? I'm not sure of the answer. My brother Richard, who has great moments of wisdom, once said, "The meaning of life is life."

Morrie loved to dance. In the movie *Tuesdays with Morrie*, we learn that Morrie had a regular day when he went dancing. He danced whether he had a partner or not. It seemed clear that Morrie loved life, and dancing is one of the great expressions of life. The philosopher Friedrich Nietzsche wrote in a letter to a friend, "I could only believe in a God who dances." When a person loves life, he is open to all experiences. He looks for the wonder in everything, and he finds it.

I think of my depressed, angry, and resentful friend. I remember spending the night at his house in my early adolescence. His mother was depressed, angry, and bitter. Everything she said was negative. His father was a mystery, seldom there. My friend told me his father was very cruel to his mother. I remember thinking how awful their marriage must be. When I visited my old friend, he told me they had not changed and they were still together and as miserable as ever.

He said he never saw them anymore and that they had never taken an interest in his family. It seems pretty clear that his parents did not think that life was joyful. One of the great differences between those who learn from experience and those who don't is that those who learn from experience are optimistic and are open to the wonder and mystery in everything.

The psychologist Martin E. P. Seligman wrote a book called *The Optimistic Child,* which presents a program to safeguard children against pessimism and depression. Seligman's program builds resilience and self-esteem.

Essentially Seligman suggests that "pessimism is a theory of reality." Children learn this theory from their parents, teachers, preachers, or the media. They then recycle it to their own children. Certainly pessimism is not inborn. In fact we are born with interest and the desire for pleasure and joy. The natural child is full of joy—"born comrade of bird, beast, and tree" and "elated explorer of each sense," as Christopher Morley expressed it.

As the rhyme says, "The optimist sees the doughnut, the pessimist sees the hole." But to learn from experience means that we have to fail. We can learn that failure and mistakes are our teachers, building blocks for feeling good. To love life, we must accept the reality that joy and sorrow, success and failure, good times and bad times are all part of an existence. In the movie *Shadowlands,* Anthony Hopkins, playing C. S. Lewis, says, "The joy we are having now is the pain we had back then and the pain we feel now is the joy we had back then, that's the deal." The deal of reality, if we are willing to accept it, is that joy and sorrow are inexplicably intertwined. In the film *Zorba the Greek,* when Zorba's well-calculated conveyer system collapses, he dances! Zorba understands that failure, suffering, and death are ordinary. They happen just as often as success, joy, and new life happen.

In our lives each experience is a lesson. Optimism is the core of the virtue of hope. The basic trust that results from secure attachment is the root of hope and optimism.

Optimism is a virtue itself. When an optimist meets with failure, she can accept it as part of the deal and look for what she did wrong or for the wisdom her failure can teach her.

Aristotle insisted experience is crucial to the development of virtue. We learn to be virtuous by acting virtuously. It takes time and experience to get the practical knowledge and skill that give us the ability to choose virtuously. While the acquiring of virtue is different from the acquiring of athletic skills, there is some similarity. Think of any skill you have. Remember learning to ride a bicycle—how awkward you were at first, how many times you fell and started over? Most of us don't remember when that skill became internalized. Once something is internalized, we no longer even have to think about it. The same is true for driving a car, playing tennis, or learning to ski. Once you know how, you can still do it years later. It has become second nature to you. In the case of moral virtue, once you have internalized it, it becomes part of your character.

When you are virtuous, you do the right thing with very little thought. For example, you don't have to think twice about whether you'll return the wallet you found or not pass along gossip or not blame somebody else for something you did. But you certainly still have to think through complex situations, such as whether or not you will give money to your unemployed adult child. You need all your experience to figure out the variables of this particular person, this particular situation, your motivation, the possible results, and so on.

NINTH SOURCE: CHARACTER

I was clicking the TV remote one day some years ago when I happened upon the evangelist Billy Graham, who was speaking at one of his revivals.

I stopped clicking and started to listen. Almost immediately tears came to my eyes, and in a matter of minutes I was weeping. I remembered the first time I'd heard Graham speak, some fifty-seven years earlier in Rice Stadium. I was ten years old at the time, and I was so moved by his charismatic presence I almost went up to be saved. My Catholic family would have been horrified.

As I reflected on why I was weeping, I realized that for more than half a century Billy Graham had been leading revivals, and for all those years he'd pretty much preached the same thing the same way. Whether or not you agree with everything he says, no one can argue about Graham's fidelity to his faith, his public commitment, and his intense belief in Jesus Christ. And no one can argue about his moral character.

Whatever else character is, it is distinguished by continuity and commitment to acting on one's beliefs and values. Graham prizes and cherishes his beliefs and publicly proclaims them whenever it is appropriate to do so. This invisible source of personal consistency gives him a deep structure of stability and power.

As a child, Billy Graham had energy that today might make him a candidate for Ritalin. In college, he was often smitten with girls, "kissing until my mouth was chapped," he said. But he never engaged in premarital sex: "God kept me clean." Perhaps it was God, but it may also have been Graham's temperance, his powerful sense of self-discipline, the kind that people of strong ego and powerful self-efficacy possess. Graham's life has been free of any scandal. He has always been just and conservative about his financial rewards.

Watching him on TV fifty-seven years after I first heard him preach, I was moved by the force of Billy Graham's character. His hair was completely white and the wrinkles of age surrounded his eyes, but the fire and energy were still in his voice. *Here is a good man,* I thought, *doing for the umpteenth time what he believes in. Here is a man of virtue.*

Johnny Pagnini

Strong ego is often a mark of character. That is why I included Johnny Pagnini in my magnificent moral moments. Ralph Waldo Emerson said, "Character is higher than intellect," and Johnny Pagnini embodied for me ego strength and character. His bravery was unusually powerful. In my interview with him, I was moved by his matter-of-factness and humility. I also used Johnny Pagnini's story because he represented someone who was an ordinary guy. Billy Graham may be known all over the world, but Pagnini had a reputation of bringing peace to his neighborhood and of refusing to be intimidated by the gangs that lived around him. Many people testified to his overall strength of character.

I need the model of ordinary people who do extraordinary things to move me to risk being extraordinary in my own unique way.

TENTH SOURCE: EVIL

The Susan Krabacher story in the prologue shows how an experience of evil can motivate us to take virtuous action. But hundreds of thousands of people, perhaps millions, witness similar suffering, have the means to help, and yet do nothing. From the account in her book, it seems as though the vow she made to God as a child was her motivating force to help fight the evil she saw before her. At first she escaped her horrible abuse by using her sexuality to be valued (many incest survivors go this way). But Susan had a deeper calling from her grand will.

In the face of evil, humans have always resorted to denial as a coping mechanism. Some might say children suffer everywhere and nothing can be done; some might blame the suffering in Haiti on the idolatry of voodoo; some blame all evil on the devil and say that God will root it out; some think that prayer alone will eliminate evil. Holding on to concepts such as the devil forces us to conceive our moral spiritual life as a struggle between two polarized extremes, two forces which are outside ourselves, thus diminishing our personal responsibility to do something about it.

Evil is real and it has been intensified in the twentieth century by two world wars, Nazism, Stalinism, the genocidal regime of the Khmer Rouge in Cambodia, and murderous ethnic cleansing in many parts of the world. These reigns of evil form what has been called a collective shadow, and we have seen repeatedly how many people choose to remain naive and unconscious in the face of such evils.

"To deny that evil is a permanent affliction of humankind," say Connie Zweig and Jeremiah Abrams in *Meeting the Shadow,* "is perhaps the most dangerous kind of thinking." By denying evil, he says, humans have heaped evil on the world. Historically, great misfortunes have resulted as humans, blinded by the full reality of evil and thinking they were doing good, have dispensed miseries far worse than the evil they thought to eradicate. I once heard John Sanford, the great Jungian psychoanalyst and Episcopal theologian, say, "Deliver me from people who want to 'do good'—because in their zeal they overlook the impact their good is doing to individuals and the ultimate consequences of their actions." The Crusades during the Middle Ages and the Vietnam War are examples that come to mind.

"We must beware of thinking of good and evil as absolute opposites," writes Carl Jung. Good and evil are halves of a paradoxical whole. Each represents a judgment, and we cannot pretend to know exactly what is good and what is evil. Totalistic moral systems, especially religious ones, are villains of polarization. They try to divide life into us (the good) and them (the bad).

My part in their creation of good or evil depends on free will. Goodness depends on sound ethical judgment, which, as Jung points out (as did Aristotle long ago), is not black and white. Good and evil are not polarized absolutes but depend for their existence on the choices we make. This is why we so urgently need the virtue of prudence.

Susan Krabacher was moved to fight evil by the emotional horror of seeing babies dying of starvation. Evil motivates us to develop our moral intelligence, and as strange as it seems, without evil there would be no need for goodness and virtue.

6

MORAL INTELLIGENCE IN ACTION: DOING THE RIGHT THING

Morality is not sufficient for virtue; virtue also requires intelligence and lucidity.

—André Comte-Sponville

Moralities sooner or later outlive themselves, ethics never.

—Erik Erickson

Morality without ethical maturity is dangerous.

—Spinoza

Our moral life is born when the attachment bond is established. The empathic mutuality that grows from the attachment bond is the foundation for the Golden Rule.

Anyone who had a secure figure who genuinely cared for them most of the time, who stroked them physically and verbally, who gave them their time and attention, and also allowed them to have their uniqueness and their need to separate and do things for themselves, was given a deep sense of hope and trust in themselves and in others. Secure attachment gives an infant the feeling that she is lovable and can expect love from others. From the feelings of being lovable come the beginnings of genuine caring, which is the root of the virtues of love and justice.

In chapter 3 I mentioned Daniel Goleman's description of the proto-conversation that goes on between the mother and her baby. The mother must clearly initiate the action. She smiles, talks baby talk, and makes tender facial expressions, and the baby's mirror neurons kick in. These interactions take place in seconds. Coleman calls the mother's gaze, her coos, her tone of voice, and her touch "motherese." As communication is synchronized, an empathic mutuality is established. The infant's brain is predisposed to participate in this duet, and from it the child actualizes her own ability to be empathetic with others. If the mother is needy and has been dysfunctionally attached to her own mother, she will be impeded in doing her part to initiate the process.

GENUINE CARING

I love this statement by philosopher Milton Mayeroff, which describes how genuine caring makes us *at home in the world.*

> Through caring for certain others, by serving them through caring, a man lives the meaning of his own life. In the sense in which a man can ever be said to be at home in the world, he is at home not through dominating, or explaining, or appreciating, but through caring and being cared for.

This statement grabbed me deeply. I felt my loneliness and longing to be cared for. True caring comes through the interchange of feelings. It cannot come from being lectured to or from domineering correction. Some parents who were neglected in their own childhoods demand that their own children have a level of maturity far beyond their age. I have heard physically abusing parents of infants and young children say, "I told him [a one-year-old] five times to be quiet," or "I explained what I'd do if she kept on crying." In both cases the child was physically hit. I'll never forget a sexually offending father who whacked his four-year-old, saying, "She was laying a guilt trip on me."

Mayeroff is describing a state of being. Caring is the most

human way of being in the world. Deep empathic caring is a description of love and compassion; it flows from our connectedness with ourselves.

When we genuinely love and care for ourselves, we cannot help loving others too and wanting their rights preserved in justice, because they share our humanity and have value in themselves, just as we do. One good test of our care for another is this: are we doing everything in our power to help them achieve their own self-actualization?

As our mutuality is nourished during each stage of our interpersonal growth, our caring becomes an empathic desire to experience others from the inside, to walk in their shoes, to see things from their point of view, and to grasp their uniqueness.

Genuine caring for and connectedness with ourselves and others create the foundation for developing all our known virtues. Temperance, honesty, hope, self-love, self-esteem, industriousness, and thrift are virtuous ways we love and care for ourselves. Justice, charity, courage, compassion, responsibility, kindness, and generosity are virtuous ways we care for and become connected to others. Prudence is the engine and governing virtue of them all.

In the remainder of this chapter, I will explore how prudence develops from a secure base of attachment, producing the many skills that contribute to mature moral intelligence. Finally, I will return again to the core of love with which I began.

THE LIFE OF VIRTUE IS A PROCESS

The maturing of moral intelligence is a complex process, with many influences shaping it along the way. We may even develop moral intelligence without secure attachment and the achievement of mutual trust and care in infancy, though it takes grace and good fortune to find a secure attachment figure later in our development. When I recognized that I was an avoidantly attached child and that I feared commitment and intimacy, I had to do some intense grief work and experiment with trust in order to stop choosing attachment figures who could not give me the nurturing that I needed. The inner work is necessary for us to be able to recognize that possible attachment figure when he or she comes along. I can attest to the fact that remedial work can be done. When mutual secure attachment is achieved, trust and mutual caring are the roots of the virtue of hope. A feeling of hope is the safeguard that allows our affects of interest, curiosity, and pleasure to emerge.

Each of the child's first small acts of trust involves the primitive hope that the other (Mom, Dad, the world) is friendly and trustworthy. You can see this clearly in a baby who is learning to walk. As the child steps out, he is not only strengthening his muscles and balance but also learning how to be hopeful. And when the child has hope and trusts his source figure, he is willing to venture out and explore the world in spite of his fears. This interest and curiosity form the beginning of courage.

As a child takes these small steps (and is nurtured and rewarded for them) he feels joy, and his hopefulness and courage are again reinforced. The occasional crash landing teaches a useful polarity: the child also learns that certain things are to be feared. Their fear and pain are primary lessons in caution and discernment.

With trust, care, hope, courage, and discernment, a child is able to heed the inner movement of the life force that pushes her toward separation and autonomy. The affect anger is one way the child experiences separation. But anger must be tempered by healthy shame, which puts limits on the child's autonomy. Out of the crisis of autonomy versus shame, willpower emerges. Willpower is the root of temperance and helps a child to find a balance between willfulness and the freedom that demands limits.

I hope it's becoming clear that virtues such as care, hope, courage, and temperance develop in an interactive way with prudence. Prudence embodies the practical knowing of how to be caring, hopeful, courageous, and temperate. By *being* virtuous, a person learns *how* to be virtuous.

Let's follow a toddler as she moves into a larger space and continues the journey of self-discovery. As the child grows she is taught manners and civility. She learns the family's rules. Having a degree of temperance allows the child to become more focused and self-disciplined. Gender identity emerges as an issue of self-discovery. As some degree of gender identity is achieved, the child develops a sense of purpose related to her gender identity. Curiosity is tempered by modesty.

CONSCIENCE

External Conscience and Guilt

Guilt develops from the affect shame, as well as from the rules of an environment that models manners, caring for others, respect, politeness, individual freedom, and responsibility. Guilt as moral shame is the guardian of a child's "external conscience." External conscience is made up of the parental commands, the limits of the environment, and the rules and laws a child internalizes.

At first the external conscience is very rigid, and obedience to it resembles the spontaneous obedience Montessori describes. This early state of morality is often described as the morality of constraint.

Anyone who's ever lived with a preschooler also knows that these are stormy years, when a child struggles with frustration, with parental limits, and with her own uncontained emotions.

Through meeting and surmounting these early crises (which involve trial, error, and consequences) the child is learning to be prudent—that is, learning how to attach to someone in a caring way, how to hope and trust, how to be courageous, how to be temperate and purposeful, and how to heed the voice of guilt.

In a good-enough average family, children move on to the early school years and learn how to be respectful of structure, rules, and authority and how to care for and cooperate with others. In addition, they develop a sense of competence. As they play games at school and in the neighborhood they learn how to be honest and to play fair. This period marks a softening of the morality of restraint and is the beginning of a morality of cooperation. In adolescence, they will learn how to be a loyal and faithful friend; they learn about themselves and their sexuality, and they continue to negotiate and renegotiate their awareness of their true self.

Internal Conscience

In middle and later adolescence, children begin to sift through the external voices of their parents, teachers, and religious influences and critically evaluate them against their own experiences. They begin to formulate their own internal conscience. This internal conscience builds upon the still, quiet voice of the raw conscience we develop early on. It is imperative that each person make his conscience his own. It is not finished, nor fully informed, but it is his own. Those who have been indoctrinated in a totalistic religion, a culture of obedience, cannot make this crucial step in moral maturity. The absolutism and rigidity of their culture of obedience's rules have them arrested in fear at an earlier age of development. I will discuss this movement from external to internal conscience later in the book. The adult years bring the challenge of maturing ethical responsibility—learning how to commit to another in a faithful love, how to negotiate a career, and how to care *for* others in a widening circle: one's children, one's creativity, one's neighbors, the strangers who are not like us. I will be discussing these issues more thoroughly in chapter 10.

As each crisis is resolved and the root virtues are formed, the child's, the adolescent's, the adult's moral intelligence is being perfected. Each root of virtue a person acquires forms a foundation for the development of prudence.

WHAT MAKES PRUDENCE WORK

For most of us, the virtue of prudence is not fully mature and operative until middle adulthood. In chapter 5, I discussed the major influences—or roots—from which it is formed. Now I want to go back to my ancient sources to give you a more expansive and concrete picture of how mature prudence works.

In his *Summa Theologica,* Aquinas presents what he called the "integral parts" of prudence. I'll list them first, and then explore each one in turn.

Aquinas' first five integral parts focus on the general qualities of mind that prepare us to make prudent (morally intelligent) choices. They are:

- The humility that moves a person to seek advice and predisposes her to new learning (he called this *docilitas*).
- The insight that comes from an informed conscience (he called this *intellectus*).
- A rigorous, honest long-term memory that allows us to use our past experiences correctly in the present situation (he called this *memoria*). In chapter 3 I wrote about long-term memory as being one major source of those people who perform in excellent and extraordinary ways. I'm sure Aquinas would embrace the findings of neuroscience in this respect. An honest long-term memory of

one's behavior in the past would certainly help clarify present choices. Such clarity about the past allows one to be authentically present and to remember what works and what led to failure.

- The intuitive ability to find the exact mean or balance between extremes (he called this *solertia*).
- Deftness, sagacity, or expertise in practical reasoning (he called this *ratio*).

Aquinas' next three parts focus on the practical judgments that shape our decision to take a particular action:

- Foresight, the ability to evaluate the future consequences of one's choice (he called this *providentia*).
- Circumspection, the ability to consider all the facts surrounding the choice to be made (he called this *circumspecto*).
- Precaution, the awareness that even seeming good choices may have a hidden potential for evil, and the willingness to probe these possible consequences (he called this *cautio*).

As you can see, these last three abilities require a realistic imagination, because we can never know for certain everything about the present and future.

Aquinas, like Aristotle, understood that virtue exists not only in the intellect and will but also in the emotions. This was a crucial insight, but we now have a much richer understanding of the indispensable role that emotion plays in choice and judgment—and, indeed, how affect is a form of thinking. Based on the modern neuroscience that I surveyed in chapters 2 and 3, I have added three new integral parts to Aquinas' list. Thanks to researchers such as Tomkins, Damasio, Siegel, and LeDoux, we have a better understanding of how emotions are essential to judgment and choice, indeed, how affect is a form of thinking.

• Contained emotion. This involves the guidance of the orbitofrontal lobe, which safeguards overreaction.

• Healthy shame as modesty. Modesty is a conscious feeling of shame that guards us against being grandiose. It also monitors excessive pleasure and unbound interest. Shame as modesty keeps us from going beyond our own boundaries and prevents us from violating another's boundaries. Shame as modesty expands to humility. Knowing our limits and being in touch with our true humanity is an essential part of fully mature prudence.

• Ego strength as willpower. Willpower is the mental force that rests upon focused attention. Will as concentrated mental force can literally change our brains, as we saw in the work of Jeffrey Schwartz.

As I go along, I'll provide some real-life personal examples. I also challenge you to come up with your own example or examples for each item. When we think about it, we are all pretty much experts on this stuff.

The Humility That Moves Us to Seek New Learning (Docilitas)

Even Michael Jordan, arguably the best basketball player who has ever played the game, needed a coach. In any area of skill and know-how, being open and willing to learn more is an essential feature of excellence. Aquinas' humility, or *docilitas,* is not just the willingness to learn; it is the desire to find new teachers who can take us beyond where we are now, and humbly ask for their help. It is, in the broadest sense, the desire to be a better and better person.

In chapter 5 I talked about the importance of being open to changing moral models for the purpose of continued growth and to become a more virtuous person. Let me add a few details to that story.

For the first three years of my sobriety, my twelve-step sponsor was a necessary part of my recovery from alcoholism. He taught me the humility to follow the twelve steps and not try to improve on them. I have deep gratitude for his help. But there came a point when he could not take me where I needed to go in order to grow. I was acting out sexually, and he believed that had nothing to do with abstinence from alcohol. That is when I sought the help of a therapist to do the grief work related to my childhood abuses. After several years of this work, I became deeply vulnerable, stopped resenting my parents, and had no more tears to cry. But I did need to learn the living skills I had not learned because of childhood neglect. I read two books on assertive skills and did a workshop using a book entitled *Your Perfect Right* by Robert Alberti and Michael Emmons. This course helped me immensely. Finally, as I developed my ego strength, I felt the urge to expand and grow spiritually, and I sought to consciously live my Jesus theology and keep a conscious contact moving to a more intense consciousness. I needed another spiritual master to begin to work on my spiritual growth. I discovered Henri Nouwen and learned seven meditation techniques. I tried each one for a period of time until I found the one I felt I could go the deepest with. This I practice to this day. My life has been a series of endings and beginnings, and each stage demanded my being willing to leave one teacher and seek a new one to learn from.

The Insight of Informed Conscience (Intellectus)

I've spoken of our innate human conscience—the inner urge that, from our first breath, disposes us to desire life and avoid what denies life. This urge is a part of our true self. Aquinas and the philosophers of his time described this innate urge or desire as *synderesis,* which they defined as a basic urge in all humans to do good and avoid evil.

The medieval philosophers Bonaventure and Albert the Great argued that history makes it clear that wherever humans have existed, they developed laws and taboos. The defined good of one group of people may seem bizarre to later generations. For example, the Assyrian practice of making horrible examples of their conquests, such as destroying whole cities, impaling the enemy king for public display, and decapitating whole armies, was part of the Assyrian code of laws. They thought their laws were good. We find them barbaric. And yet the Assyrians operated under the rule of law.

Laws and morality evolve. While some elements of this ancient punitiveness remain today in certain parts of the world, the laws in the code of Hammurabi, the Magna Carta, and the evolving laws of democracy as expressed in the French and American constitutions show a continuing modification of cruel, vengeful, and punitive practices. Steven Pinker quotes the anthropologist Donald E. Brown's list of human universal moral concepts and emotions stemming from our innate moral sense. They include a distinction between right and wrong, empathy, fairness, proscription of murder and rape, redress of wrongs, admiration of generosity, sanctions for wrongs against the community, and taboos.

The intelligence that Thomas Aquinas saw as integral to prudence is twofold. First, it is the knowledge of general moral principles such as the five I describe in chapter 2: harm no one and help those in need, fairness, loyalty to the community, respect for authority, and purity. These universals certainly encompass the Golden Rule, which operates as the major premise of prudent judgment. And second, it is the knowledge derived from the experience of applying these general principles to the changing and practical matters that make up the world of choice. The latter knowledge is practical and intuitive. It is developed with time and experience, and it gives us an intuitive, hands-on understanding of general moral principles.

Conscience takes time to develop, and we cannot expect it to be fully mature until the thinking part of our brains is fully developed in our late teens. (I'll talk more about the development of conscience in chapter 12.) Our word *conscience* is derived from the Latin *con* (with) and *scientia* (knowledge or information). A person with a mature conscience has experienced enough of life to have internalized the teachings he has been given by his religion, spiritual tradition, and elders. Even though we experience conscience as an inner voice whose promptings come from deep within us, it attains a kind of objectivity because it is informed by our emotion and intelligence and all that we have learned about right and wrong. We have briefly discussed how conscience evolves as our consciousness evolves. Our forefathers who believed in slavery had an erroneous conscience. A lazy person may have a lax conscience; because she is not willing to study the necessary data on global warming, she may continue to pollute the environment.

Honest Memory: Being Fully Present (Memoria)

I'm interpreting Aquinas' notion of *memoria* as long-term honest memory in a way akin to the example of a master chess player who remembers thousands of moves and strategies. Prudence is the excellent state of our raw moral intelligence. A prudent person remembers her successes and failures and is honest about interpreting her past.

For me, the most personal and most important meaning of this part of prudence is a rigorous honesty in relation to one's past. This kind of honesty is necessary if we are to be fully present in any situation we are in. Otherwise it's likely that our thinking will be contaminated by unfinished or unresolved grief or pain, distorting our ability to deliberate objectively.

Let me give you an example of this. I have struggled with weight all my life. I go through periods of being in good shape, exercising, monitoring my sugar and fat intake, and feeling exhilarated.

But then there are times, especially when I am on the road giving lectures or workshops, when I make a decision that is in opposition to my goal of good health and staying in shape. I'll be ordering room service, and the voice on the phone will say, "So how about some dessert?" This is the crucial moment. The right response is "No, thanks," but instead I nonchalantly say, "Well, what have you got?" Recently the order taker answered, "One of the biggest and most delicious banana splits in the country!" I heard myself saying, "I'll take one!"

The voices from my past, the ones demanding to be soothed with a sweet treat, were screaming at me. The last banana split I ate not only was a complete violation of my prescribed diet (I have coronary artery disease) but was the beginning of a slip that cost me about fifteen pounds. I've tried to laugh this off, but the fact is that the binge eating that followed my slip is contributing to my death. Eating a banana split is a moral choice for me.

This is a good example of how emotions can go awry and take over our choice in an unhealthy way. As a recovering addict, I've come to realize how much my addictions were a way for me to engage in self-soothing. As a child I did not develop my emotional intelligence, which when developed can be used as a source of self-soothing. In the banana-split story, my need for self-soothing simply took over and bypassed my adult thinking. Had I used the emotional intelligence that I have been developing, I could have gotten in touch with a memory, a scene of my finishing a nice workout. With that image I could get in touch with the feeling of satisfaction and joy that come after a good workout, and I could have used that feeling to soothe myself. As a child I cried when the ice cream truck came around because we didn't have money to buy ice cream. I could imagine my grown self coming into that scene and talking to that little boy. I could tell him about the great restaurant my wife, Karen, and I had plans to go to when I got home. I could tell him we can go to the beach at our condo or swimming in the swimming pool. Even getting in touch with the exhilaration I feel when I've exercised can be consoling. This doesn't work all the time, but it does a lot of the time.

Excellence in Practical Reasoning (Ratio)

The part of prudence that Aquinas called *ratio* is the good use of practical reasoning in applying the general dictates of conscience to a particular moral choice. Practical reasoning involves the know-how learned from observing respected moral models, from images embedded in moral imagination, from emotional intelligence, from a habit of goodwill, and from the experience a person has had in choosing. The more we have the freedom to experiment and choose alternatives that achieve outcomes that will bring good to ourselves, as well as good to others, the more we will learn how to think and choose in the particular circumstances that surround any moral choice. As with any practical skill, a mistake can be a great teacher.

The best example of excellence in practical reasoning that I know of is the work of the renowned therapist Milton Erickson. Erickson has been universally acknowledged as a man of genuine humility and love for the people who came to him for help. He is the embodiment of the virtue of prudence. He believed less in any theory of therapy and more in helping his clients learn. In their book *Phoenix,* Erickson students David Gordon and Maribeth Meyers-Anderson sum up his belief:

> Each [person] is an individual. There are no two people alike. No two people understand the same sentence the same way. So in dealing with people you try not to fit them to your concept of what they should be...you should try to discover what their concept of themselves happens to be.

Erickson was brilliant when it came to identifying and utilizing people's unique underlying patterns of behavior in order to effect change in their lives. Here is one story from his case files.

A man about 80 pounds overweight entered and said, "I am a retired policeman—medically retired. I drink too much, smoke too much and eat too much...I have emphysema and high blood pressure. I like to jog but I can't...the best I can do is walk. Can you help me?"

I said, "All right. Where do you buy your cigarettes?"

He said, "There's a handy little grocery store around the corner from where I live."

"How do you buy your cigarettes?"

"Usually three cartons at a time."

I said, "Who does your cooking?"

He said, "I'm a bachelor...I usually do my own."

"And where do you shop?"

He replied, "At a handy little grocery store around the corner."

"Where do you eat out when you don't do your own cooking?"

"At a very nice restaurant around the corner."

I said, "Now the liquor?"

"There's a handy little liquor store around the corner."

I said, "Now your therapy isn't going to require very much. You can do all the smoking you want...buy your cigarettes one package at a time by walking to the other side of town to get the package. As for doing your own cooking, well you haven't much to do, just shop three times a day. Buy enough for only one meal, but no leftovers. As for dining out, there are a lot of good restaurants a mile or two away—that'll give you a chance to walk. As for your drinking...I see no objection to your drinking. There are some excellent bars a mile away. Get your first drink in one bar, your second drink in a bar a mile away and you'll be in excellent shape before very long." He left the office swearing at me in the most eloquent fashion.

Now why would I treat him that way? He was a retired policeman...he knew what discipline was and it was entirely a matter of discipline.

About a month later, a new patient came in and said, "A friend of mine referred me to you. My friend is a retired policeman. He said you were the only psychiatrist who knows what he is talking about."

The ex-policeman's problems involved lots of content: smoking, drinking, obesity, emphysema, and high blood pressure. What Erickson recognized was that the pattern of behavior that supported all of these problems was the same. Whatever the ex-policeman wanted, he obtained with the least expenditure of energy. Erickson didn't get speculative with him. He didn't discuss why he smoked, drank, or overate. He knew the ex-policeman would have intellectual justifications for these behaviors. Erickson didn't moralize or medicalize the man's problems or tell him he was killing himself. Instead he built his therapeutic plan on the man's strengths. He utilized the ex-policeman's disciplined background, his subculture, in a way that automatically moderated his intake of food, alcohol, and cigarettes and simultaneously gave him the exercise he needed to retune his body. This is practical reasoning at its best.

The Intuitive Ability to Find the Mean Between Extremes (Solertia)

Aquinas got the notion of *solertia* from Aristotle, who defined it as "a faculty of hitting upon the middle term instantly." All choices involve polarity, the presence of two (or more) alternatives. To be prudent we must have both the ability to tolerate ambiguity and the ability not to fall into polarization and extremes. *Solertia* is a readiness of mind, a kind of quickness to see what the balanced thing to do is when faced with a particular choice. The prudent person can make a quick and just practical decision.

Being unable to discover the mean, to come up with a balanced response, is a major defect of all addictive personalities. People with money addictions either hoard money (become addicted to deprivation) or overspend wantonly and become chronic debtors. Eating disorders are polarized between starving (anorexia) and bingeing. Every addiction is marked by the inner dynamics of polarization.

A time-honored example of *solertia* is the biblical story of King Solomon and the two women who come to him in a dispute over the ownership of a baby. Each claims to be the mother of the child. Solomon immediately suggests an extreme polarization. He calls for a sword and proposes that the baby be cut in half so that each woman can have her share. When one of the women cries out in horror and says she would rather give up the baby than let him be harmed, Solomon awards her the child. He does this knowing that the baby's real mother would refuse to let her child be hurt.

Such practical ingenuity becomes ingrained as our prudence develops. Once the virtue is truly second nature, we can often choose the mean without thinking.

Circumspection (Circumspectio)

Since prudence deals with concrete situations that contain many combinations of circumstances, it is necessary to have the ability to evaluate the circumstances accurately. Our term *circumspection* comes from the Latin words that literally mean "to look all around." It is the ability to survey the whole situation.

Great quarterbacks are masters of circumspection. If you're a football fan, you know that a quarterback can change a play when he comes to the line of scrimmage, because he's surveyed the whole defensive team and spotted a weakness. This kind of circumspection calls for acute and lightning-fast sensory perceptions and pattern recognition built up by long experience. Committing to action based on such well-developed skills is an act of prudence.

Often a person's extreme beliefs contaminate his concrete,

sensory-based ability to look at facts; his absolutizing beliefs actually cause him to disconnect from reality.

Any form of addiction embodies a failure in circumspection, a failure to see facts. I once counseled a couple in which the husband was an acting-out sex addict. The wife was in a state of severe depression. As she spoke, I noticed him looking at his watch and fidgeting in his chair. He even had what looked to me like a smug grin on his face. What was obvious was his failure to empathize with his wife's pain.

I later learned that this man's mother had shamed him as a child and made unending demands for his love. His father had abandoned him. His mother was also sexually seductive; she made him sleep in the same bed with her until he was thirteen years old and often walked around the house nude.

When a child is abused in these ways, he develops ego defenses that operate like trance states. (I described these in my book *Creating Love*.) All of us are capable of not seeing what we see (a seductive mother) and not hearing what we hear (a harping, shaming mother's voice). We can visually and auditorily dissociate and numb out and in effect be no longer present.

My adulterous client was acting out his rage at his mother by using one woman after another in his affairs and punishing his wife for what his mother had done to him. Although he had a job that required rigid attention to detail, he was blind to the excruciating pain he was causing his wife, and also to other possible consequences of his adultery, such as the impact it would have on their children.

The childhood abuse this man suffered is no excuse for his behavior. He needed some serious long-term therapy. He was emotionally blinded by his wound and was unable to see the circumstances around him. He was also lacking in *memoria*, the ability to be truly present when he was interacting with his wife.

Foresight (<u>Providentia</u>)

Foresight is necessary when we come to make our final decision in a concrete situation—the inner command to take this particular action rather than another. The Latin word *providentia* has a double meaning in English: it means both "looking into the future" and "providing for." The prudent person provides for herself by looking ahead. This requires imagining the outcome of her choices.

Let's take a break from the heavy stuff and talk about the three little pigs. One built a house of straw and the second built a house of sticks, but the third pig had the foresight to build her house out of brick. It probably took a lot longer to build the brick house, but she was looking ahead and providing for herself. You probably remember what happened—the wicked wolf was able to destroy the houses built of sticks and straw and devour the inhabitants, but as much as he huffed and puffed, he could not blow down the house of bricks.

Foresight is an extraordinary and creative ability. It involves the use of one's *realistic imagination*. The Jewish theologian Martin Buber made an important distinction between a realistic imagination and a fantastic imagination. The first has to do with what is true, with facts and real possibilities. The fantastic imagination produces an unrealistic and often grandiose fantasy that can encompass a person's life.

I once counseled a daughter of a clergyman who spent most of his time with the poor and homeless, so much so that he abandoned his wife and family. His daughter had rebelled against his neglect, acting out her anger by using drugs and getting into trouble with the law. When he came to see me, I sensed a supercilious air of piety about him. He had a fantasy of himself as a saintly pastor, but he seemed anything but saintly to me. He referred to his daughter as "the whore of Babylon." My assessment was that he was so taken up with his fantasy of saintliness he could not see that he was neglecting his wife and children. They were just as much his moral responsibility as the poor and homeless. I never got through to him because he was so caught up in the unreality of his fantastic imagination about his ministry.

There were many things this minister failed to provide his family, including his time, his presence, and his emotional support. He was so caught up in the accolades he was receiving that he was unable to see that he was destroying his future relationship with his daughter.

Foresight is grounded in reality and is at the same time creative, looking at real alternatives that lead to a good outcome. It involves the ability to be very objective and uncontaminated in regard to the future. There is much that is unknown in any act of choice, and no one can ordain the future. But the little pig that built her house with bricks came close to it.

There is growing evidence of the impact of abuse and trauma on the frontal lobes of the brain—the part of the neocortex (the thinking brain) that has the ability to "futurize." Many adults who grew up in alcoholic, sexually addicted, emotionally abusive, or otherwise battering families seem to be arrested at various childhood developmental stages. Their frontal lobes have not fully matured. Unless treated, these developmental deficits will seriously affect their ability to have foresight and therefore their ability to act with prudence.

My own pain over my abandonment and abuse left a deep sorrow that seemed insatiable. This formed the template for my addictions, which gave me a false kind of nourishment. There were a few times when I felt completely helpless and considered ending it all. But I went on, sobering up, doing my original pain therapy, and stopping my unbridled compulsivity. My true self moved in the direction of another of my major sorrows, the loss of a stable family and home. My first PBS series was on functional and dysfunctional families. Growing up, I never had a real home, being moved among relatives' houses; I slept on a rollaway bed at times and shared a bed with my brother at others. But in the middle 1990s, at the height of my PBS career, I had one home, two ranches, and four king-size beds. Our brain has an amazing plasticity. Don't ever give up. Our wisdom often flows from our wounds.

Carefulness or Precaution (Cautio)

The word *cautio* does not mean being cautious in the sense of timorous, small-minded self-preservation. It is more akin to what is meant by the word *precaution*. Aquinas describes the prudent person who has developed carefulness *(cautio)* as "one who is wise as a serpent and guileless as a dove." *Cautio* for Aquinas is a balance, including both openness to life and realism about the snares that lie in wait for us. We can be both wise *and* trusting, avoiding the polarized traps of cynicism on one hand and gullibility on the other.

For Aquinas, carefulness or precaution is the quality that enables the prudent person to anticipate and avoid evils that are in some way mixed with good.

At one point in my career, I was invited to do the feature interview in *Playboy* magazine. At that time the *Playboy* interview was highly prestigious. Excellent writers were assigned to conduct it, and the list of past interviewees was distinguished, including President Jimmy Carter and the Reverend Martin Luther King Jr. Some of my friends suggested that my ideas would reach an audience who might otherwise not read my books, and that doing the interview might achieve some good. I also wanted the worldwide publicity I would get from it.

But there was another side to the story. At the time, I was in a group with men who were dealing with sexual addiction—some whose drug of choice was masturbation with pornography. One man I counseled had lost his wife and family because of this addiction. He spent hours locked in his workroom masturbating, and he spent money the family needed on phone sex and buying pornographic books and magazines.

All sex addicts have severe problems with connectedness and

intimacy. Their pornographic sex partners are literally images on a piece of paper—or, these days, on their computer screen.

My personal experience with people who had this problem, my belief that *Playboy* diluted its soft pornography with its intellectual content, my sadness and pain over the people I knew whose lives were ruined by self-sex and pornography (many of whom had begun their habits with *Playboy*), my utter repugnance at pictures of Hugh Hefner running around in his red pajamas—all these considerations led me to my decision to turn down the interview. I know this was a prudent decision for me. The *Playboy* interview may have been good for Jimmy Carter, but it was mixed with evil for me. I finally decided that whatever good might come out of doing it, the harm it might cause was greater.

Contained Emotion

When Aristotle speaks of being angry with the right person, to the right degree, at the right time, and for the right purpose, he is talking about contained emotion—in this case, anger. We now know that the ability to contain any powerful emotion depends on specific aspects of brain development that I discussed in chapter 3. Rather than having an automatic, knee-jerk amygdala reaction—an explosion of rage straight out of the limbic system—the emotional impulses are moderated by the neocortex. We are able to think before we act. This ability is shaped in the brain from toddlerhood on—for instance, when we constantly urge children to "use their words" rather than shrieking and hitting.

We also contain our emotions when we express them appropriately rather than repressing them. People often repress their anger and then let it out at inappropriate times. Unfortunately, parents shame their children's emotions and cause them to repress them. Containment integrates emotion and thought; repression causes a child to numb out. Numbing out sets a child up for addiction, because once a person is numbed out, one of the ways she can feel is with her addiction.

For example, Agnes was very angry because her husband, Jack, brought his mother on the first vacation they took, a year after they were married. But she believed a good wife shouldn't criticize her husband, so she never discussed it with him. Four years later Jack was late for dinner. He had been late for dinner many times before, but on this occasion, Agnes blew her stack. She began a litany of hurts, reminding her husband about taking his mother on their vacation four years earlier. Agnes' anger is uncontained and inappropriate.

I'll expand on this discussion of contained emotion in chapter 12.

Shame as Modesty

I briefly discussed shame as modesty in chapter 2. Let me add a little to that discussion. Shame is the feeling that lets us know we have gone too far. Shame lets us know that we are fallible and prone to make mistakes, that we don't know it all. This helps us develop the modesty that keeps us from the kind of arrogance and absolutism that sabotage moral decision making. One major character defect that many addicts have is grandiosity (in moral terms, pride). I had to either be the best of the best or the best of the worst. Recovering alcoholics tell their stories in front of the group as part of their recovery. This offers a person the opportunity to share their shameful behavior associated with drinking. This allows others who are still hiding underneath their shame a chance to see that they are not alone or hopeless.

In the beginning I so desperately wanted to belong that I greatly exaggerated how bad my drinking was. My story was an excessively passionate "drunkalogue." This was an attempt to make me the best drunk of all (a reverse grandiosity). The ethically moral person is very aware that all moral decisions have an air of mystery surrounding them. No one knows *the* truth. That is simply not possible for us human beings. Modesty leads to humility.

Contained Willpower

To choose well one needs to develop willpower. Willpower is a rudimentary ego strength that starts to develop roughly between the age of six months and three and a half years. We strengthen and develop our willpower as we mature and make choices. Willpower becomes our grand will as we grow in virtue and maturity. In our fully prudent acts and as an integral part of the virtue of prudence, our willpower is one with our destiny and life purpose.

If the developmental stage of willpower is not resolved well, our future ethical life will be drastically impoverished. People without a developed will become slaves to the will of authority, to the whims of the significant people in their lives, or to their own willfulness.

Healthy willpower in itself is a virtue. It is the core of the virtue of temperance. Willpower emerges from a crisis in which willfulness and disciplined limits are synthesized. Like our emotional powers, it is contained. We slowly learn that there is no real freedom without limits.

Willpower is the ability to find a healthy balance between lack of control and overcontrol. Willpower is the key to delaying gratification and to controlling our impulses in the service of achieving a goal. Willpower does not just restrain us. It drives us forward. And if it's not contained, we can just walk all over others to get what we want. A lot of people admire that kind of bullish willpower, and sometimes it is lifesaving. When your two-year-old is wandering into a busy street, it is not the moment for discussing a time-out or have a democratic council meeting. You probably need to yell and rush out and physically pick up your child.

Willpower is the integral part of prudence that allows us to balance the polarities of holding on and letting go, of giving and receiving.

Lance Armstrong won the Tour de France *seven* times. Armstrong's personal story—his recovery from cancer—and the race itself are extraordinary demonstrations of willpower. However, the race is not simply about endurance, and winning does not entail simply having the willpower to ride the fastest for the longest period of time. The Tour de France requires team strategy. Armstrong had to be willing to let others on his team pace his speed. He had to know where he could let up and come in third or fourth in a particular stage of the race without sacrificing his final standing. The Tour de France is an amazingly complex event, and the key to winning is using willpower in a contained way.

I hope it is clear to you that what makes prudence work is far more dependent on practical know-how than on theoretical ethical science. Cultures of obedience want absolutes. Moralists want unvarying rules, and what I have just shown is how poorly this matches with the actual experience of making moral choices in particular situations. My failure to live up to certain unchanging rules that had to be fitted to new, uncertain, and changing situations caused me a lot of the toxic guilt and moral confusion I suffered for the first forty years of my life.

Moralists underrate their resistance to finding guidelines that take into account changing circumstances in particular concrete situations, and they overrate the power of the possibility of scientific accomplishment in moral affairs. Prudence as fully mature moral intelligence gives us the ability we need to deal with particular choices that must be made in concrete, particular, ever-changing circumstances.

PRACTICE: THE BEST PERFORMANCE CHANGER

Our discussion of the brains of superior performers makes it clear that if you want to be excellent at any endeavor, you will have to remember the lessons that your experiences give you and then be committed to practice passionately. At one tournament Tiger Woods, the world's number one golfer, played very poorly (for him). After the round he went to the driving range and practiced for three hours. The next day, in match play, he birdied twelve of twenty holes. People who have achieved excellence in any intelligence do so by making an intense commitment to practice. Virtue is an excellence that becomes a *habitus* through habitual action.

I'll never forget spending a day with the late singer John Denver at a unique experimental ranch in Santa Fe, New Mexico, created by Charles and Beth Miller; entrepreneurs who have helped many people, including me, and espoused many causes. Their ranch, called Sol y Sombra, operated off solar energy and was an ecological system in microcosm that could be used as a model for other small communities.

As a committed environmentalist, Denver had volunteered his time to do a fund-raising event for Beth and Charles. What amazed me was how he prepared for the evening performance at Sol y Sombra. Shortly after lunch, he met with the people running the sound system and started practicing his songs. For three hours, he went over every detail.

Here was an accomplished artist who had just finished a very successful tour of Japan, preparing energetically for what would be a crowd of possibly sixty people. What I learned that day was how dedicated to practice this superb artist was. This story is told over and over again: greatness and excellence take practice, dedication, and commitment. Prudence in action is also the fruit of commitment and practice.

HOW CAN WE BE SURE WE'VE CHOSEN WISELY?

How can we be sure we've chosen wisely? I had an acquaintance who was the heir to a considerable estate. One day he got the upsetting report that his grandfather had used questionable means of making his money and that my acquaintance might not be the legitimate owner of the estate. He did a considerable amount of research and could not find any document or other evidence suggesting that anyone else was entitled to his grandfather's estate. I think most would agree that my acquaintance had a right to conclude, "I am entitled to keep this estate." Justice is satisfied and his judgment to keep the estate is certain because his goodwill led him to research the issue for over two years. He also told me he would give up the estate if new evidence should appear. His judgment was both certain and uncertain. His decision was in accord with a right appetite (his will directed toward the good), but there is a chance, however slim, that some new evidence will turn up. In this case, and in most cases of human choice, the last judgment leading to action always falls short of absolute certainty.

The issues of truth and certainty are quite different in the practical world of our everyday decisions than in the abstract world of speculation. The truth of practical judgment is not one of logical analysis but one of the desire of a right appetite or habituated will and emotional intelligence. Speculative truth consists of conformity with an unquestioned set of real facts. Practical truth is the result of our intellect being in conformity with the demands of an honest will and in conformity to the inclination of a right desire and contained emotion. As I will outline in part 3, we can educate both our will and our emotions. There you will clearly see that contained will and emotion are anything but whims or unbridled subjectivity.

When we do something based on our good exercise of will

and honest intentions, it could still turn out to be disastrous. But as long as our choice is based on an honest desire to do the right thing, it attains the level of practical truth because of an honest will—doing our best to know the facts through long-term honest memory, modesty, conscience, foresight, circumspection, and carefulness. When these elements are present, there is normally a high level of agreement with the facts and a high degree of success.

A person of right desire may be contaminated by unconscious and unresolved emotional issues or because of his overly exaggerated belief system. A good example of this is the case of General George Patton, who believed in winning at any cost and who soiled his reputation by slapping a shell-shocked soldier because the soldier was crying.

Unresolved emotions and unconscious anger may distort a person's judgment even though his or her intentions and desires are honest. I have written much about this in my other books, which describe parental abuses that are unintentional.

So how can we know for sure if we've made a truthful moral choice? I'd answer by saying that truth in the practical world must be understood in the context of the nondominant hemisphere of the brain. The nondominant hemisphere (the right brain) is the seat of intuitive and emotional intelligence. It operates in the realm of "felt thought" and deals with images, sounds, symbols, and the intelligence that informs emotion and volition (the will). The judgments of prudence attain truth in the moral order when they are in agreement with right desire. Aristotle and Aquinas agreed that truth in the moral order is determined by the truth of the affective inclination that leads to choice. The affective inclination in question would be the result of experience, conscience, emotional literacy, and the grand will. In other words, the affective inclination in question would be the fruit of probably years of hard work. At the point of the choice, the educated emotion might even be operating unconsciously.

I smoked for some thirty years. Over time I became aware of all of the logical reasons to quit smoking, but those did not convince me to stop. One day I'd had enough. I *wanted* to quit and I did. The whole thing that determined my choice was desire and emotion. There was no logical reason to stop when I did.

I sobered up forty-three years ago. My dad was a severe alcoholic, and I experienced a great deal of emotional pain in my childhood over his drinking. The last thing one would expect was for me to start drinking...but I did. I started at an early age and was in trouble from the start. I had a hundred reasons to quit—early blackouts (forms of amnesia), disgraceful behaviors, and scandals when I was a seminarian studying to be a Catholic priest. I had five hundred conversations with people urging me to quit drinking. But none of those led me to quit. One day I just wanted to stop, and I did. I cannot give you any reasons why I stopped when I did.

"Seeing the light" comes from an emotional and volitional intelligence within us. One day I saw the light and quit smoking. One day I saw the light and joined a twelve-step group for alcoholism. One day I had a profound spiritual experience—the vision of Christ as I ran—that seemingly had no relation to sexual compulsivity, but six months later I ended that addiction for good.

ETHICAL MATURITY AND MORALITY

Ethical maturity is not the same as legality or morality. Many believe that the real problem of today is due not to the demise of morality but to a confusion between what is legal, what is moral, and what is ethical. There are many companies and individuals who avoid paying U.S. taxes by putting their money in offshore corporations. It is legal to do so, and many equate legality with morality. But is it ethical? Big corporations often find legal but unethical ways to manipulate their accounting of profits to make them more appealing to those buying their stock. The fat cats of Enron and Tyco, with their yachts, numerous vacation homes, and six-thousand-dollar shower curtains are unethical men, even though in some cases they may not have broken any laws. They claim that they are good and moral, and they love to say they did not know what was going on. No man of ethical character would succumb to such a cop-out. Top executives were paid exorbitant amounts of money to oversee what was going on. Their innocent ignorance cost thousands the pensions they had spent their lives accumulating.

Duty and Virtue

Duty and virtue are not the same thing. Duty is a constraint, and virtue is a freedom. Certainly both are necessary in the large view of things. The relationship of morality (duty) and virtue (ethics) is complementary. They are symmetrical rather than identical. For example, the *more* one is generous, the less generosity seems like a duty or constraint.

Perhaps the best example of the difference between morality (duty) and ethical maturity is the virtue of love. Love that is a commanded duty is no longer love. But as we reach the pinnacle of moral intelligence and live the life of virtue, our ethical maturity is rooted in the virtue of love. True, authentic, virtuous love takes us to a place beyond the rigid moral distinctions of good and evil.

Morality Replaces Our Lack of Love

We need so many moral laws only because we do not love. As André Comte-Sponville says, "Duty...*obliges us to do that which we would do simply out of love, if in fact we loved.*" The human condition seems to point to the fact that we do not love enough. Because of this, we spawn never-ending moral laws in such a way that we polarize good and evil.

Goodness, as a moral absolute, is dangerous because it does

not own its own shadow, because our attachment to the principle of being good supersedes our care and concern for the individuals who have to suffer for our goodness, and because we get so engrossed in our intention to be good that we can't be bothered with the consequences. I mentioned the clergyman whose obsession with being good caused him to neglect his own family. He wasn't the only one.

Ethical Maturity Is Beyond Good and Bad

Ethical maturity transcends morality and its polarization of good and bad. Those who feel constrained to do good are not true carriers of the virtue of love. Love is not a command; it is an ideal of holiness.

The philosopher André Comte-Sponville writes, "Duty is a constraint (a 'yoke,' says Kant); it is a sadness, whereas love is joyous spontaneity." What I do out of love does not come from a feeling of constraint or duty. This is why love is beyond the nitpicking good and evil of moral systems and why it is relatively absent in cultures of obedience.

Comte-Sponville writes, "We all know that some of our most patently ethical experiences have nothing to do with morality, not because they go against it but because they simply have no need of its obligations." The whole matter comes down to this: "Morality does not proscribe love; instead, it asks us to perform out of duty the very same action that, if we loved, we would have accomplished for love alone."

Morality is not to be spurned. Morality is born of attachment and mutuality; it teaches us politeness and respect for laws, and moves us toward love. This is why we can love morality and moral laws, austere and burdensome though they may be.

Love Is Ethical Maturity

Again Comte-Sponville: "Must we also love love? . . . If we do not, then morality can do nothing for us. Without this love of love we are lost." Dostoyevsky said, "Hell is the inability to love." Hell, the inability to love is damnation in the here and now. We have to either love love, or love nothing. Without love, what virtues would remain?

What is done out of the true virtue of love is done, as Nietzsche said, "beyond good and evil." Augustine, the great theologian, agreed. "Love God and do what you wish," he said. The acts of love that morality prescribes as duty will have already been done through love, if there is love. This line of thinking calls to the very best angels of your nature. Maybe only a few will reach this level of excellence, but the ideal is there.

RENEWING PRUDENCE

Developing prudence, the governing virtue of love, is difficult. All of us like certainty; however, the virtuous life occurs in particular, concrete, and changing circumstances. Emotion and volition are amorphous and unpredictable in relation to moral science or the strict laws of obedience upon which much of our current moral training rests. Often a prudent person has to fight his way in solitude amidst puzzled companions who say they cannot understand why the person is doing what he is doing. Our companions may not have had our experiences or heard the different drummer we hear. Each of us has a reservoir of resources from which the know-how to make the choices we are making comes from. Yves Simon writes, "Inasmuch as the ultimate practical judgment admits of no logical connection with any rational premises, it is, strictly speaking, incommunicable."

Prudence fell out of favor long ago. But renewing it is an urgent task. You know how good it feels to help someone, to do small acts of kindness, to be generous, compassionate, and patient. I am finding that small virtuous acts bring me great joy. And I know that I'm developing prudence with every small act. I often miss good opportunities to practice virtue. But I know that the more I do, the stronger my prudence will become. And the stronger it becomes, the more I do small acts of love and virtue. The more I do, the more I want to do. I urge you to join me on this journey. Virtue stems from the better angels of our nature and is the endeavor that most gives us our dignity.

Part 2

Developing Your Moral Intelligence

INTRODUCTION

THE OXYGEN MASK PRINCIPLE

I would be so happy, if only I were happy!
—Woody Allen

Lying to ourselves is more deeply ingrained than lying to others.
—Fyodor Dostoyevsky

We know we have found our bliss when we cannot think of anything else we would rather be doing with our lives.
—Joseph Campbell

The cabin attendant tells us at the beginning of every airline flight that "in the event of a loss of cabin pressure an oxygen mask will drop from the compartment above." If we are traveling with a child, we are told to put our own oxygen mask on first, and then to help the child.

The same principle holds true for developing the moral intelligence of those in our care. *If we are not pursuing the life of virtue ourselves, there is no way we can teach it to others.* In chapter 7, I will attempt to show you why the moral pedagogy many of us were raised with has serious limitations. This statement is not intended as a judgment on our parents or on the teachers, religious or secular, who instructed us. I believe that in most cases they had the best intentions. But in the same way that the founding fathers could, in good conscience, own other human beings as slaves, many of our parents believed that they owned their children and used a primitive pedagogy that aimed at breaking their children's wills. They believed that spanking was their God-given duty, and many people still do.

In the work that I do with adults who were abused as children, I tell the participants that their caregivers', teachers', coaches', or preachers' *intentions* are not relevant. It does not matter how sincere their conscience was. A sincere conscience can be ethically immature and erroneous. The impact of the abuse that a child suffers in being chronically shamed or spanked (in many cases beaten) is in no way diminished because the "discipline" is justified by erroneous beliefs. Abuse is abuse.

In chapter 4 I summarized Lloyd DeMause's analysis of the two basic kinds of parental acting out: (1) the "projective reaction," where the parent does to her child what she wanted to do to her own parents as retaliation for being abused. Many parents hit their children because their parents hit them. (2) The "reversal reaction," where the wounded child in the parent wants his child or children to do for him what his own parents never did. If your parents rarely told you they loved you, you may demand that your own children constantly express their love to you. These two types of parenting operate unconsciously, which certainly diminishes the parent's culpability. But this unconsciousness in no way diminishes what is done to the child.

A SEARCHING AND FEARLESS MORAL INVENTORY

If we want to stop these abusive cycles of unconscious parenting—and teaching, ministering, coaching, and bossing—each of us needs to take a searching and fearless inventory of our own childhood. This kind of examination demands work and a willingness to be rigorously honest with ourselves.

People who did not endure childhood abuse find the accounts

of it hard to believe or accuse me of exaggerating. But I stand on my experience.

As I said in chapter 4, since I first presented information on various kinds of dysfunctional families and child abuse on PBS in 1985, I have received over 150,000 letters from people describing their own childhood abuse. I've also received over 20,000 letters from men and women who are incarcerated in prison who shared with me that because of my books and the PBS series, they have come to a better understanding of what caused them to lead a life of crime. Many of them realized that they were acting out on innocent people the repressed rage they experienced as innocent children toward their abusive caretakers. I continue to be shocked by the childhood cruelty these letters reveal.

I've also done my workshops on the wounded inner child (a metaphor I use to describe the abused child) in every major city in the Western Hemisphere. More than 250,000 people have attended my workshops. As I mentioned before, many of the descriptions of abuse that come up in the workshops are brutal and shocking.

This problem is by no means limited to American families. My book *Homecoming: Reclaiming and Healing the Inner Child* has been translated into more than twenty languages. I have worked with Irish, English, Spanish, Australian, Canadian, Japanese, Norwegian, Danish, Finnish, and Russian therapists who find my work relevant to their country's styles of abusive parenting.

I'm reporting this to give the reader some idea of my experience in dealing with the immense problem of child abuse. Cultures of obedience are still dominant in many nations, as well as in individual groups of various kinds. They are fostering moral totalism and actually hindering the development of moral intelligence in their members.

The most common way abuse is kept alive is that parents, teachers, and clergy reenact the abuse they experienced on children in the ways DeMause has described.

Any caretaker who is acting out either a projective or reversal reaction (and we often act out both, either at different times or the same time) is not authentically present to the ones in his or her care. The unresolved wounds from the past keep a person blocked in the past. This causes the person to live a guarded life, defended against the threats of past pain. Unresolved abuse blocks the emotional energy necessary for *healthy choosing*. Since good choice is the essence of prudence, a person cannot develop the virtue of prudence until their emotions are available to them.

In chapters 8 and 9, I'll describe the method that I've been using for the last twenty-five years to heal these blockages. The ability to be intimate and connected is a crucial thing in developing moral intelligence. It is difficult to connect with someone who is not real and truly present. Some of you may have to consider changing if you want to be there for your spouse, children, students, congregants, patients, and friends.

7

NEW WINE IN OLD WINESKINS: WHEN THE SOLUTION BECOMES THE PROBLEM

We are the last generation of an old age and the first generation
of a new age.

—Alvin and Heidi Toffler

Do not believe in what you have heard; do not believe in traditions because they have been handed down for many generations...do not believe merely in the authority of your teachers
and elders. After observation and analysis, when it agrees with
reason and is conducive to the good and benefit of one and all,
then accept it and live up to it.

—Buddha, *Kalama Sutra*

Raised to their extremes, all virtues become vices.

—Judith M. Bardwick

Neither is new wine put into old wineskins; if it is, the skins
burst, and the wine is spilled and the skins are destroyed. But
new wine is put into fresh wineskins and both are preserved.

—Matthew 9:17

We're living in a time not only characterized by a war against
terrorism but also in which we are bombarded hourly with bad
news about the moral fiber of our society: children murdering
other children, high school teens killing their schoolmates, violent
pedophiles abducting and raping or killing children, an epidemic

of domestic violence and financial greed. We are witnessing scandals in the church, police departments, trusted corporations, and with our political leaders, and an unhealthy pattern of sexual acting out that could easily be termed a plague.

In times like these, we want someone or something to blame. The solution I hear most frequently is that we need to return to the past.

RETURNING TO THE PAST

As you've already seen, I return to the past quite a bit in this book, but we have to be specific about what past we are returning to. The Synod of 1679 was a gathering of Puritan clergy in Boston. Their published list of sins included teenage pregnancy, drug abuse, frivolous lawsuits, greed and excessive profit taking, and women in lewd clothing. Worst of all, the family was breaking down—there was a complete loss of discipline. Not much has changed in the general categories of domestic problems in the past two hundred years.

The terrorist bombings on September 11, 2001, are another powerful reminder of the dangers of returning to the past in a simplistic way. The dominant model of traditional morality is patriarchal, authoritarian, and obediential; it demands absolute adherence to the rules handed down by the heads of the family and of society. Is this not exactly the kind of moral system that has spawned terrorism? A return to this type of moral system will not alleviate our current difficulties or help us develop moral intelligence.

In fact, such a regressive attempt will actually intensify and worsen today's problems. Developing moral intelligence was not a clear issue in the past because morality was not thought of as intelligence. It was viewed as a duty, an act of obeying rules. In certain contexts, obedience to duty can be virtuous, but there is certainly no moral intelligence in the wanton and cowardly taking of innocent lives in the name of obedience to any authority, especially the authority of God.

The problems we face today call us to constantly challenge our sense of moral rectitude. Aristotle wrote a brilliant ethics, yet he agreed with the consensus of his day that some humans are born to be slaves. He believed that slavery was natural. Today we hold unequivocally that Aristotle was wrong.

Our founding fathers, the creators of the United States Constitution and the Bill of Rights, were mostly slave owners. I'm not accusing them of being bad men. I'm demonstrating that not all moral truths are absolutes and that some of our forefathers' beliefs were immoral in the light of our present consciousness.

We are currently at another historic turning point, a time when we must look critically at the moral and ethical guidelines that were called into question in the twentieth century. We need a vision of how an ethics of virtue differs from the kind of obediential morality that can spawn a culture of obedience.

I cannot overstress the value of reading a book such as Stephanie Coontz's *The Way We Never Were: American Families and the Nostalgia Trap*. Coontz is a professor of history and family studies at Evergreen State College in Olympia, Washington. Her well-researched book is a real challenge to people who glibly talk about "traditional values" without being specific about what these values were and the historical context in which they existed. Even worse, the ideas people claim as "traditional values" cannot be verified historically. Part of the subtitle to Coontz's book, "the Nostalgia Trap," suggests that we imagine and long for more idyllic times and treat our fantasies as if they were true.

If we are going to live the life of virtue and model it for our children, we will have to update our own vision of moral intelligence and be guided by a moral model somewhat different from the one we grew up with.

HOW THE SOLUTION BECOMES THE PROBLEM

In family systems theory, when a family has a problem or experiences distress, the solution that is chosen is all-important. If an inadequate solution is chosen, the harder the family tries to make it work, the worse the problem will become. The more the family tries to change, the more it stays the same. The solution becomes the problem.

Let's say Mom gets hooked on prescription drugs. She begins to neglect her responsibilities and becomes lethargic and severely depressed. In order to deal with this situation, Dad calls a meeting with the children and assigns them many of Mom's responsibilities. Dad also tells the children to be more loving and to make no demands on their mother. He further tells them not to talk about Mom's problems, to be careful not to disturb her when she is sleeping during the day, and above all, not to discuss her situation with neighbors, friends, or relatives.

The children respond willingly and do all they can to relieve their mother of her normal responsibilities. The family considers this a loving way to treat her. But Mother's condition slowly worsens and she becomes even more lethargic and less functional, primarily because the family is overfunctioning and taking on her responsibilities. The father believes he is treating his spouse with loving care—*but his solution is making the problem worse.*

The same dynamics apply to trying to solve today's problem by appealing to the patriarchal, authoritarian obediential morality of the past. The world we live in today is significantly different from the world of fifty years ago and radically different from the world of patriarchal families of the past centuries.

OBEDIENCE AS A VIRTUE

Thomas Aquinas was a Dominican monk who took a permanent vow of obedience, yet he stated frequently that conscience is a higher law than obedience. He made it clear that a truly virtuous act must be grounded in liberty, that it cannot be solely based on an external rule. In other words, there must be a personal presence and choice in every act of obedience if the act is to be considered virtuous.

Children learn to respect authority when they experience loving and nurturing guides (father, mother, teachers) who firmly protect them by setting and helping them to understand good boundaries.

Boundaries are necessary for a child's security. Children who are indulged and not given firm guidelines feel insecure, overly dependent, frightened, and angry. They will often act out this fearfulness in misbehavior.

When good boundaries are internalized, they give us the inner stability and discipline that enable us to be effective and virtuous adults.

A Culture of Obedience

The virtue of obedience is essential to the full development of moral intelligence. Yet, taken to an extreme, it can generate evil. The twentieth century created several cultures of obedience that demonstrate this all too clearly.

Hitler's Germany, Stalin's Russia, and Osama bin Laden's fundamentalist terrorist affiliates magnify such large-scale politicized cultures of obedience and bring us awareness of how certain religions and smaller social units, especially families, can transform the virtue of obedience into an extreme. In such cases, the virtue of obedience is transformed into a cultlike adherence through what has been called the "language of nonthought."

Critical thinking is prohibited and replaced by highly simplistic and oft-repeated dictums or slogans, which slowly hypnotize people into submission to the authority figure or figures who guide them.

Fundamentalist religions are replete with simplistic slogans. From fundamentalist Christians, we sometimes hear phrases like "It's all in the Bible" or "Jesus is the answer" repeated without any attempt to explain their meaning in the context of the actual situation being discussed. Muslim fundamentalists in turn have their own versions of absolutized beliefs and the slogans that express them.

A culture of obedience represses all emotions except fear. It especially represses anger, or redirects it against approved "enemies." When emotions are repressed, they do not go away. They are acted out against others (especially anger) or "acted in" against oneself in depression, self-negation, suicide, and the chronic suicide of drug addiction. The depressed and self-negating person is a ripe target for absolutist authoritarian dogma.

How Cultures of Obedience Destroy Moral Imagination

Cultures of obedience leave a narrow place for the work of moral imagination. Moral imagination is crucial for the development of moral intelligence in three ways. First, we find in stories, biblical parables and symbols, movies, novels, and TV shows moral models that inspire us and provide guidance. Second, we need imagination to envision alternatives, consequences, and future outcomes of moral choices. Third, without imagination we cannot develop four of the integral parts of prudence: foresight, precaution, circumspection, and good practical reasoning.

THE POISONOUS PEDAGOGY

Alice Miller has described authoritarian child rearing, which is the lifeblood of cultures of obedience, as "the poisonous pedagogy." A poisonous pedagogy ostensibly pertains to raising children but unconsciously caters to the needs of the adult. These needs are:

- To pass on to others the shame one had to endure as a child
- To find an outlet for repressed emotions
- For self-defense (i.e., the need to idealize or villainize one's childhood and one's parents by either dogmatically applying the parents' rules to one's own children or totally rejecting one's parents and having no rules at all)
- To eliminate the fear of the helplessness and vulnerability the adult sees in his child and has repressed in himself and dares not let surface
- To take revenge for the pain the adult suffered as a child

The poisonous pedagogy also imparts to the child unproven or false information that has been passed down for several generations. For example, I was taught that tenderness or doting on a child was harmful; a high degree of self-esteem is harmful; anger, dislike, and hatred can be done away with by forbidding them; strong feelings are harmful; and severity and coldness toughen you up to face life.

A culture of obedience breeds physical child abuse and wife battering. Children are considered their parents' property and wives are considered their husband's property. In a culture of obedience, children have no legal rights and no one to advocate for them.

Sexual abuse of children is more common than anyone ever could have imagined. The impact of incest, molestation, and covert sexual abuse is most often life-damaging and always causes suffering. The belief that parents own their children and have unbounded rights over them sets up an environment for sexual abuse.

The sad fact is that many of our parents were brought up in this poisonous pedagogy, and since they had no means of bringing their unconscious abuse to awareness, they could not treat us any differently. *Awareness is the only way out of this vicious multigenerational cycle.*

DE-SELFMENT

I've come to describe the impact of strict obediential morality as *de-selfment*. With no mind, will, needs, or feelings of one's own, it's hard to have a self. The only self you can have is the one projected on you and expected of you, that is, the family-authorized way of behaving, which later becomes the culture of obedience's way of behaving.

One of the most destructive results of de-selfment is that the victim most often feels as though what's happening is her fault and feels shame and guilt for even talking about it.

People who have been slowly and systematically de-selfed tend to dismiss any expression of child abuse as self-pitying. The adults who ridicule those who take child abuse dead seriously were ridiculed as children and never had their own pain validated. In *The Drama of the Gifted Child,* Alice Miller writes: "Those who were mistreated at the hands of the authorities can no longer feel, and regard their abuse as children as normal."

BEYOND MERE OBEDIENCE

The brilliant German theologian Dorothee Sölle wrote a book entitled *Beyond Mere Obedience.* In it she asks: "Is it possible to think about morality and use the word obedience as if the Holocaust has not happened?" She suggests that moral or theological concepts cannot be divorced from their history. "If the concept of obedience was used by idealistic young Nazis to commit the greatest crime in the history of my people, then one has to reflect on what was wrong with this concept."

In the West, cultures of obedience are associated with monarchy (the divine right of kings), patriarchy, religious patriarchy, and the literalist's interpretation of biblical texts. In that context, the pillars of a culture of obedience rest on:

- The acceptance of a superior power, which controls our destiny and excludes self-determination
- Subjection to the rule of this power, which needs no moral legitimization in love or justice, but is identified with the will of God
- A deep-rooted pessimism about humans, who are seen as prone to selfishness and evil

In a culture of obedience, the chief virtue is blind obedience, and self-sacrifice is at its center. In a religious culture of obedience, God's power is far more important than God's justice, love, and nurturing righteousness.

What happened in Germany, on a collective scale, was partly rooted in the rigidity of the German family. Religion justified the power of authority as coming from God. The ultimate authority figure must be obeyed no matter what. The person in authority will have to answer to God if he or she is corrupt or evil.

As Sölle reminds us, Hitler may have been answering to God, but that is little solace for his six million Jewish victims.

TOTALISM AS A NATURAL TENDENCY

The blame for totalitarian states or for what is called "totalism" does not rest solely with patriarchy and obediential morality. The potential for wholeness is rooted in human nature. When

· people cannot develop in a way that allows them to achieve wholeness, they turn to forms of totalism. As the term implies, totalism offers a total, nonambiguous, certain solution to all human problems. We will always be vulnerable to totalistic solutions, because life will always be insecure and problematic. In fact, the appeal of totalism is one of the strongest arguments for developing moral intelligence and building a life of virtue. Only then will we have the inner strength to stand by our conscience and defend our own chosen values.

A culture of obedience is a political system in which the question "Why?" is forbidden. In a culture of obedience, an obedient person is a reactor who is required to sacrifice critical reason, personal choice, and spontaneity—that is, his moral intelligence. Dorothee Sölle sees the culture of obedience as the primary reason that morality has been cut off from an ethics of virtue. It is also the essence of the fundamentalist Muslim's justification for terrorism and "holy war."

VIOLENCE AGAINST WOMEN

There are horrific costs to women living in a culture of obedience. *Time* magazine did a shocking exposé of the treatment of women under fundamentalist Islam. In one graphic picture, Zarghona, a fifteen-year-old girl, lies in a Peshawar shelter after being burned by her father-in-law, who said that she had not cleaned her husband's clothes properly.

During the Taliban regime in Afghanistan, all schooling was forbidden to girls over age eight. This kind of prohibition is how cultures of obedience continue from generation to generation. They are closed systems, crushing their constituents' minds and wills, leaving them without a self. These violations of human rights are not limited to the Taliban. In Iran, the legal age of marriage for women is nine. A verse in the Koran, very similar to the Christian Bible's text attributed to St. Paul, says that women are to be completely submissive to their husbands. In Islam, men are admonished to beat an insubordinate wife. Wife beating is so prevalent in the Muslim world that social workers who assist battered women in Egypt spend much of their time trying to convince victims that their husbands' violent acts are unacceptable.

In our country, wife battering and brutality against children still go on at an alarming rate. Our American forms of female subjugation, especially in recent history, may not be so dramatically heinous, but the rights of women have been slow to evolve. Women in America now have law on their side, but the behavior and psychology of battered women are slower to change.

WHEN OBEDIENCE MAKES SENSE

Obedience makes sense when a person has a solid sense of self-worth and accepts a system of laws that are consistent with the person's value system. People are capable of incredible devotion and self-sacrifice, and these acts tend to inspire awe no matter what the context. But people who lack solid selfhood obey out of fear or substitute the collective self (their church, their company) for the self they do not have. A mother caring for her newborn obeys her duty as a mother by getting little to no sleep because of her love for her child. Her act of obedience is probably not even conscious. However, except in the military, acts of self-sacrifice, self-denial, and suffering that are expressed simply because they are demanded by others are most often senseless and produce nothing.

BLIND OBEDIENCE AND MORAL INTELLIGENCE

Throughout the whole history of monarchial, patriarchal, and matriarchal dominance, the concept of obedience has been focused on the practical technique and manner of obedience, to the exclusion of all objective content. It is not what people do obediently but how rapidly, how punctually, how joyfully they obey. The less one reflects on what is demanded, the more significant the act of obedience. Put another way, blind obedience requires no real intelligence.

This book is about developing practical moral reasoning and conscience. The virtue of obedience can be helpful in that development, but a culture of obedience—based on power and subjugation rather than on love, the mutuality of power, justice, and care—fears equality and ultimately fosters violence, war, and death. A culture of obedience is intrinsically incapable of fostering moral intelligence and virtue.

Obediential morality is hard to change because its abuses were mostly unintentional. The lie involved in it is repressed and unconscious. We tend to consider what we grew up believing to be normal. Corporal punishment (spanking) is a good example. Humiliating and shaming were also thought to be an effective pedagogical tool.

Traditional patriarchal obediential morality is too dangerous to be a solution to our problems of today. It is, in fact, unquestionably a partial creator of the problems of today.

The New Testament warns against putting new wine in old wineskins, stating unequivocally that it will not work. The world of today is vastly different from any historical precedent. In the United States, there are many different ethnic groups and religions. The information revolution, the Internet, the mapping of the genetic code, cloning, stem-cell research, and terrorism are the potential creators—or, alternatively, the evil specters—of a new age.

We need an ethics of virtue, and that kind of ethics can only be nurtured in an educational environment quite different from the one many of us grew up in. Those of us raised in a culture of obedience must be willing to change. This is no easy task.

Figure 7.1 offers you a comparison of the essential differences between an obediential morality spawned by a culture of obedience and an ethics of virtue grounded in prudence as mature

Figure 7.1: BEYOND A CULTURE OF OBEDIENCE TO AN "ETHICS OF VIRTUE"

CULTURE OF OBEDIENCE (OBEDIENTIAL)	VIRTUE OF OBEDIENCE (PRUDENTIAL)
Rationalism Speculative intelligence	Emotional intelligence Practical intelligence
Patriarchal—male chauvinism Monarchical Totalitarian	Equality of sexes Democratic Interdependence
Extrinsic Outer-directed Defocuses inner self De-selfment	Intrinsic Inner-directed Nurtures inner life True self
Blind obedience Duty Preventive Reactive Rigid Unimaginative	Informed conscience Habituated will—includes virtue of obedience Inventive Proactive Flexible Imaginative
Freedom as doing your duty	Freedom as inner spontaneity within the pull of goodness
Fear-based Punishment Justice	Courage-based Consequences Love (care), justice, mercy
Toxic shame	Healthy shame, modesty

CULTURE OF OBEDIENCE (OBEDIENTIAL)	VIRTUE OF OBEDIENCE (PRUDENTIAL)
Love as giving up self	Love as gaining of selfhood or self-actualization
Emotions are weak	Emotions are essential to choosing
Heroic, perfectionistic	Nonheroic, courage to be imperfect
Righteous and judgmental	Compassionate and nonjudgmental
Polarized	Polarity

moral intelligence. This chart sums up much of the discussion in part 1 of this book.

A few comparisons need expanding on.

Freedom as doing your duty	Freedom as inner spontaneity within the pull of goodness

There really is no freedom in a culture of obedience. Freedom simply means obeying the rules. You are free in such a system to rebel, but in order to do so you need a strong will, which very few have. Rebellion entails the possibility of severe consequences: loss of freedom, imprisonment, or even death. Freedom rooted in spontaneity is not anomie or lawlessness. It is freedom that flows from the inner laws of our nature, especially our desire for caring, mutuality, and cooperation.

A virtuous person is drawn to the good and, having once tasted it, wants and desires it. An ethics of virtue is based on the courage to risk making mistakes and the courage to be human or imperfect. Patriarchal obediential morality operates out of the fear of punishment and seeks control and certainty.

Heroic, perfectionistic	Nonheroic, courage to be imperfect

The philosopher/psychologist Ernest Becker's book *The Denial of Death* makes a superb argument against what he terms "perfectionistic heroic ethics." In Figure 7.1, you can see that I've contrasted perfectionistic heroic ethics with nonheroic ethics and included Alfred Adler's phrase "the courage to be imperfect."

Becker's thesis is that our moral heroic perfectionistic systems are all in some way related to our fear and/or denial of death. Heroic perfectionistic moral systems honor those who have faced and escaped death or who have died for a noble cause. Such people are genuine heroes, but heroism is certainly not limited to them. Ordinary life, with all of its stresses, reversals of fortune, and suffering, also calls on our courage. Millions of people go to their death having faced and sustained their lives in the face of tremendous odds. Their commitment to life, love, and responsibility may not be honored as heroic, but their kind of subtle heroism defines a life of true virtue.

Righteous and judgmental	Compassionate and nonjudgmental

Righteousness and judgment can be shameless behaviors because no one is perfectly righteous. Right now, "legitimate authorities" in our own country say it's okay to torture prisoners and hold people without a trial. Does the fact that we're a democracy make this okay? Thoreau, where are you now?

OUR TRUE SELF

The first step many of us must take if we are to reach ethical maturity is to recover from the de-selfment imposed by the culture of obedience and reconnect with our true self—including our human imperfection.

Cultures of obedience and many systems of moralistic perfection (including the one some of us grew up in) are basically inhuman because they attempt to be more than human. They foster a kind of morality which is polarized and overidentified with goodness as an inhuman demand. The Episcopal priest John Sanford writes: "If we strive to be only good and perfect, we become hateful; for too much of the vital energy within is being denied. For this reason there are few people more dangerous in life than those who set out to do good."

I call the process of reowning our true self the "recovery of innocence." The reunion with my true self does not, in itself, make me prudent or ethically mature, but it is the only ground from which I can become truly virtuous or ethically mature. I cannot be virtuous without belonging to myself.

I can be a good moral person without having a true self. I can follow and obey the civil and moral laws with a false self. I can obey them because I fear punishment and because I get rewarded for obeying. This is certainly not all bad. It's likely that some of this kind of motivation is involved in most people's moral life. But being a moral person without having a true self cannot lead one to ethical maturity.

I'd like to urge you to move beyond a narrow definition of morality. Is it possible that we can do good because we love what is good and want to do it for its own sake? Can we be vir-

tuous because we believe it is the only true way to human fulfillment, thriving, happiness, and bliss? Can we learn to recognize,
acknowledge, and contain the parts of our nature that can harm
ourselves and others? I feel hopeful in answering yes when I see
the natural goodness that people exhibit in times of crisis.

THE PROCESS OF RECOVERING OUR INNOCENCE

My model for recovering innocence involves two major
stages. In the first, we strengthen our character by grieving the
past and finishing it. This releases the energy that we have been
using to hold on to our defenses, resentments, and hurts.
Finishing the past helps us to become authentically present, and it
helps us move from impulsive, reactive behavior to proactive personal freedom and choice.

In the second stage (which I will discuss in chapter 9), we up-
grade our conscience through rigorous honesty. This stage involves recognizing and owning the parts of ourselves that we feel
ashamed of or that have been shamed by others. At this stage, we
also embrace lost parts of our true self that we had to repress long
ago, and we discover strengths and capabilities that we did not
know we had. Recovering our innocence can lead us to a revolutionary transformation whereby we embrace our true self with
unconditional self-love.

As a child, I was repeatedly told to be strong. Once your feelings and needs are numbed out, you can feel invulnerable. You
can do awful things to yourself and others once you stop feeling.
In *For Your Own Good,* Alice Miller quotes Hitler's chilling
statement of his educational aims:

> My pedagogy is hard. What is weak must be hammered away. In
> my fortresses of the Teutonic Order a young generation will

grow up before which the world will tremble. I want the young to be violent, domineering, undismayed, cruel. . . . They must be able to bear pain. There must be nothing weak or gentle about them. The free, splendid beast of prey must once again flash from their eyes.

The consequences of this kind of strength are written in blood. Today we need a new kind of strength, one that is founded on right desire and which leads to the inner strength that fuels the life of virtue.

8

RECOVERING YOUR INNOCENCE: AUTHENTIC PRESENCE AND EMANCIPATING YOUR WILL

History, despite its wrenching pain
Cannot be unlived, but if faced
With courage, need not be lived again.
>—Maya Angelou

We are healed of suffering
only by experiencing it to the full.
>—Marcel Proust

Being alone with unbearable emotions
is at the root of psychopathology.
>—Diana Fosha

During a counseling session, Maxine speaks softly of her frustration over Tom's lack of presence in their family life.

Tom interrupts, exclaiming, "I was home from Friday afternoon until Monday morning. What the hell does it take?"

"You hardly spoke to me or the children," replies Maxine. "You worked on legal briefs all day Saturday and watched football Sunday afternoon."

"Didn't we go to a Sunday brunch at the country club? Do you realize what it costs to be a member of that club so you and the kids can swim and play tennis?" Tom snaps back.

This nondialogue goes on until I stop it. I address Tom, telling him that his need to be more financially successful than his father (which he had discussed obsessively in earlier sessions) was ruining his relationship with his wife and children. I warn him that if he loses his wife and children he'll have nothing, since his father is dead. And even if his father were alive, without his family he'd have nothing but money.

Tom's father had been an autocratic patriarch who equated financial success with manliness and happiness. He shamed Tom endlessly for any shortcomings he fancied would block Tom's financial career. Now, twenty years later, Tom's reactions to his wife's urgent requests for his presence were dominated by these unresolved issues with his father. Because all his energy was focused on this unresolved material from the past, he was truly present only when he was working. He was not present in his family, and his frozen emotions from the past blocked his ability to make effective decisions in his current situation. He was reactive rather than proactive.

Tom also lacked foresight. He was unable to see the future consequences of his behavior. He could not see that his sons were growing up with an emotionally absent father who never made time for them. He could not envision the vapid emptiness he and his wife would experience once his children were grown up. He couldn't see that he was modeling work and responsibility only as a means to make money. Tom was dedicated, persistent, and determined, but only to his law firm and its success, which was also his success. He rarely expressed words of love or care for his wife and children.

Tom had no way to model virtue for his children.

ESCAPING THE TRAP OF THE FALSE SELF

Tom had a brash demeanor. He was articulate and spoke in strident, almost warlike phrases. He seemed to have no sense of vulnerability. This brash demeanor was Tom's false self. Fortunately, Tom hung in there with me as his counselor. I had drawn a line in the sand. I told Tom he had to do some intensive feeling work, the kind I do in my inner-child workshops, the kind offered at the Meadows in Wickenburg, Arizona.

The deep feeling work is useful for everyone. The majority may not need residential treatment, but because we are all born into a biased culture and bear the conscious and unconscious projections of our parents' expectations, I've never met anyone who could not benefit from the kind of grief work I'm going to describe in this chapter.

Each of us responds to those projections and biases in our own unique way. If you were born to good-enough parents and grew up in a good-enough environment, you may be able to find your true self with greater ease. If you were born to neglectful or abusive parents or into a pathological environment, you have probably developed a false self. This false self is related to the kind of abuse and the degree of that abuse that you experienced. But it is also related to your innate temperament as well as to your own unique true self's sense of destiny.

For some, working on their insatiability and shame will be a lifelong process. I am one of those people, and while I can genuinely say I'm happy and grateful for all the wonders and grace in my life, the judging voices, dull pain, and emptiness still reappear from time to time.

Mysterious Exceptions

There are those who seem to be mysterious exceptions, people who seem to have escaped the intense impact of their pathological environments. I agree with psychologists who say that we need to study and learn from them. *The Invulnerable Child*, edited by E. James Anthony and Bertram J. Cohler, offers many examples of people whose true self has been strong enough to overcome every kind of biased environment.

James Hillman's book *The Soul's Code* also gives ample evidence that some people have defied any logical or psychological analysis of the expected consequences of their abuse. The adaptations that many of us developed in order to survive have served as our most important skills. This is something we do not want to forget. It has often been said that our wisdom is in our wounds. Our courage and our virtuous strengths are often precisely the products of our suffering.

Healing Insatiability

Insatiability is the great enemy of the life of virtue, because insatiability has no limits, polarity, or balance. Insatiability and ungrieved wounds block us from developing many of the integral parts of prudence I discussed in chapter 6. Insatiability is the root of all forms of addictiveness. Addicts seldom have a single addiction. Tom is addicted to making money, but he is also what has been described as an "avoidance addict." He fears intimacy and finds ways to avoid being intimate with his wife or children.

The good news is that we can heal our addictiveness. I have personally stopped three insatiable patterns all rooted in my ungrieved wounds. I'm still building good boundaries and growing in prudence. And I'm no longer chronically fantasizing about an unrealistic future. As the actor playing C. S. Lewis in *Shadowlands* says, "I don't want to be someplace else anymore, not waiting for anything, not looking around the next corner or the next hill. Here, now, that's enough." To live virtuously requires that we live authentically in the present.

Healing our unresolved wounds not only frees us, it enables us to care more effectively for our children. As Maria Montessori observed:

> Misbehavior and disorder in children most often reflects in some way the adult parent or teachers' own detrimental patterns of unresolved inner drama, repressed pain or emotional distress from childhood.

Or as Carl Jung stated: "The most damaging thing to children is the unlived lives of their parents."

More Effective Ways of Caring

One of the greatest gifts we can give our children is to do the work of discovering our own true self. Many of us need to find the "normalized child" within ourselves—our true self. Montessori, Steiner, and others made it clear that our presuppositions about children (and human nature in general) have been quite diseased in the past. As long as we hold such erroneous beliefs, they guide the way that we attempt to form our children's moral intelligence. We also carry these diseased beliefs about ourselves.

I've often said that they give Jack-in-the-Box employees more training and knowledge than we give prospective parents. Raising children is an immensely difficult task. It may be the hardest job you're ever going to do. I'll underscore again that some ineffective parenting is unconscious. Bad parents are not necessarily bad people (although some are); they are more often immature and unaware. When my children were growing up, I didn't recognize some of the damaging things that I was doing to them. In many areas, I simply didn't know how to parent them. No one is blaming you or me. This is too serious an issue for us to engage in blame games. If you love your children, you'll want to investigate what I'm saying and the material I've gathered here, change the ways you may be unconsciously hurting them.

THE ORIGINAL PAIN PROCESS

It's quite frightening to grow up and leave home, and it's especially terrifying if you're unhealthily emotionally attached to your family of origin. If you have been abused or enmeshed, you have no solid sense of self. Being unable to separate in the past, you've failed to develop a strong ego. And no one wants you to go, especially the family members you're enmeshed with. Abuse enmeshes you with your abuser. So separation is about grieving—but it is also about reconnecting with your own life.

Some people live their whole life and never know who they really are. What a tragedy. I want to be a catalyst in helping you save the only life you can save—your own. I want to help you find the underlying cause of that insatiable inner self that keeps looking to be filled. I want you to know that the insatiability cannot be filled—it has to be grieved. Grieving restores you to your innocence. Grief is the healing feeling. Grief finishes things and lets you begin anew. Grieving allows us to reconnect with the vitality, spontaneity, exuberance, and resiliency that is every child's birthright. That child is still living within us, waiting to come forth. We need the energy of our natural child, his or her curiosity, industry, and openness to learning. These qualities need to be maximized to make us fit for life.

In what follows I'll describe the method that I've been using for the last twenty-eight years, and I'll explain how this process helps to restore us to "authentic presence" and gives us the ability to make our own conscious choices. It takes us from reaction to proaction and allows us to reconnect with our feelings and our vulnerability. When we recover our innocence we can begin to repair our character defects and make morally intelligent choices. We will also have to face the fact that some of our disowned or detested parts of ourselves are really and truly ourselves. Discovering this can bring us to wholeness.

RECOVERY OF INNOCENCE, PART I: ORIGINAL PAIN PROCESS

If you choose to do this work, I can guarantee you nothing. It will work best if you take it with all the seriousness you can muster. The process I will offer you now has helped hundreds of thousands of people over the last twenty-eight years. It is similar to the most groundbreaking work that is now being used in the treatment of trauma victims.

I believe that there are many more people who are trauma victims than the technical clinical definition tends to include. I had a father who abandoned us and a mom who toxically shamed my sister, brother, and me throughout our childhood. Abandonment and years of toxic shaming can have the same impact as a major catastrophic event. A single catastrophic event can permanently change our brain chemistry, but so can repeated or chronic experiences, even if they seem on the surface to be less traumatic than, say, a car crash. Any form of chronic shaming or criticism could be catastrophic to a child. I personally have all the major symptoms of post-traumatic stress disorder (PTSD).

My experience makes it clear that there are no quick fixes, and for those who were raised in a pathological environment, healing generally requires a longer time than we would like. So beware of the infomercial tapes. Beware of the cognitive therapists who imply that they can talk a person out of traumatic hurts and abuses or who say things like "Deal with it—we all had tough childhoods." Beware of those who want to shame the very process of dealing with childhood abuse and trauma.

Yes, there are people who make an identity out of their victimization and cannot finish their grief. Remember that my own therapist told me to repeat, "Suffering is ordinary" over and over again. But many people are just downright afraid of doing grief work. Going into childhood pain is frightening, especially for people who've been guarding against their vulnerability for most of their life—people like the lawyer Tom, whom I described earlier.

The process I'm about to describe works with any kind of painful loss. In the case of childhood pain and loss, it requires some careful guidelines and boundaries and must be done in a context of safety. I have never done an intensive "inner child" workshop without a number of licensed therapists present. The therapists provide an envelope of safety. In fact, no one will let their guard down and allow themselves to be vulnerable unless they feel safe. I give people complete freedom to go only as far as they feel safe in going.

If you feel that you would like to work on some unresolved issues from the past as you read this book, let me suggest two important boundaries for you. First, if you are presently working with a licensed therapist, discuss this chapter with him or her. Be sure your therapist has read about the process and feels comfortable that you are doing it. Second, do not do grief work by yourself. If you are moved to begin this work, be sure to find someone with whom you feel safe. If you begin the work and feel unexpected fear or terror, stop immediately.

STEP ONE: FIND A BENEVOLENT WITNESS

A benevolent witness is there to be your support person and to give you sensory-based feedback. You will also be his or her benevolent witness. In the workshop we work in groups of six. If you can find more than one person who will commit to do the whole process with you, that would be great. The best scenario would be to work with five other people and hire a therapist to mediate the process.

The benevolent witness is a mirroring resource who commits to being nonshaming. The witness's job is to validate or legitimize your feelings. Most of us had source figures who did not know how to be present for us when we were experiencing strong feelings. In fact, most of us were taught that the kind and compassionate thing to do when a person experienced grief was to take the grieving person out of their feelings.

Let's say you are crying about your dad, who abandoned you. In the old model, you may be reminded about the uncle who took you to the movies and gave you presents. Or you may be shamed— what did you suffer compared to Romanian orphans or the starving children all over the world? You may be told that God especially loves you to send you such pain. I could go on and on, but the point is that an attempt is being made to distract you from your feelings.

In the old model of patriarchal obedience, feelings were considered weak, and when you had them they were illegitimized. I can remember being asked, "Why are you crying? There's nothing to cry about." Or I was told how much worse my mother's pain was than mine. My pain was trivialized or discounted.

Benevolent witnesses allow you to have your feelings without being shamed or made to feel guilty for having them.

STEP TWO: WRITE OUT A SCRIPT OR SCENE

In discussing Silvan Tomkins' work in chapter 2, I mentioned that when an affect is named and made conscious, it becomes a feeling. Feelings take place in a context or situation. Once the feeling is embodied in a situation, it becomes an emotion. The situation that embodies the feeling is called an "emotion." The situation in which an emotion is embedded becomes imprinted on your brain as a scene, or as Tomkins called them, "scripts." Over time, similar scripts link together in our brains, so one scene or script may trigger another scene or script. If I am experiencing the emotion of hurt or sadness, for example, it may trigger several other scenes or scripts from my past.

I encourage people to write out the most dominant scene related to their childhood hurt or trauma that they can safely handle. When it is a question of severe incest or trauma, I would absolutely forbid a person from working on such a scene without a therapist or therapy group. Sometimes people have to work with less painful memories for some time before they feel safe enough to approach the major trauma.

Writing is essential. It has been clinically tested and proven to be a way to focus emotions. The more detail you can put in the scene you write, and the more specific and concrete you can be—the more you can touch, see, smell, hear, and taste—the better. Detail elicits emotion. I once heard the contract serial killer Richard "Iceman" Kuklinski being interviewed on television. He spoke about his father, Stanley, repeatedly beating his mother, himself, and his brother. Then he said very matter-of-factly that one day Stanley killed his brother, Florian, and made the family act as if it were an accident. That detail made me gasp in horror.

STEP THREE: READING THE SCENE

Once you've written your scene, you and your benevolent witness or witnesses take turns reading your scene to each other. Be prepared for a powerful affective response. This response has to do with looking at the faces of our witnesses. The primal scene in our life was looking into our mother's eyes. Ideally she mirrored back our being with total and unconditional acceptance. Reading our scene and looking into the face of another is powerful. That is why it is important for the benevolent witness or witnesses to look directly at the person reading his or her scene.

STEP FOUR: RESPONDING AS A BENEVOLENT WITNESS

The benevolent witness or witnesses need to respond in one of two ways. The first and easiest way is simply to tell you, the reader of the scene, what they were feeling as you read your scene. They probably felt several feelings in sequence. For example, they might say: "As you began to read I felt sad [mad, afraid], and then as you read I felt mad [afraid, sad]," and so on. The important thing is for the benevolent witnesses to stay with what they are feeling and not get into any kind of questioning, analysis, or rescue operation.

This is difficult for many people if the reader of the scene starts expressing strong emotion, especially sadness. I warn people to refrain from hugging a person who is crying unless that person has asked to be hugged. It's okay to ask your partner if he would like a hug or if there's anything you can do for him. But unsolicited hugging is usually about the person giving the hug and much less about the person crying. If you, as the benevolent witness, have your own unresolved sadness about the issue in question, the other person's crying can get very uncomfortable for you. Giving the crying person a hug becomes a way for you to deflect your own emotional pain. You may think you are offering help, but you are really trying to help yourself. Most people are not aware of this.

For example, parents often try to stop their children from crying or having intense emotions because their child's emotion either triggers the parent's unresolved emotion or causes the parent pain because they don't want their child to be unhappy. Say little Billy asks Mom for a bicycle and says that two other kids on the block just got new bikes. Mom feels bad because she doesn't have the money to buy Billy a new bike. Mom says no. When Billy starts crying, Mom tries to shut him up because it is painful to her.

Defusing Our Defenses

The group's feeling feedback can be enormously helpful to the person whose strong defenses usually keep him from connecting with his own feelings. We defend our hurt and painful feelings by using two primary defenses. One is called "dissociation." When a person dissociates, he imaginatively goes away and focuses on something else.

Another defense is called "projective identification." When we use the defense of projective identification, we project our feelings on another. If we are caretakers, those in our care take on our feelings as if they were their own. When I project my shame onto my children, they take it on as their identity.

Dissociation and projective identification keep us out of touch with our own painful emotions and therefore out of touch with our true self. This exercise helps you connect with your real feelings. For example, if you have dissociated from your pain, when several other people tell you that they were feeling angry when you read your scene, it can help you reconnect with your anger.

Observing Versus Mental Evaluating

The second kind of feedback is called "observing" or sensory-based feedback. Most witnesses find this much more difficult than reporting their feelings. The key here is to use your eyes and your ears to watch and listen to the process the reader is going through, and to avoid interpreting, fantasizing about, or evaluating what the reader has said. Simply describe what you see and hear, focusing on the person's body movements, vocal stress, or other behavior. For example, after a person reads her scene, I might say, "I saw your facial muscles grow taut. I saw you clench your teeth, and I heard your voice become louder. You talked faster and more stridently. Your lips looked pursed at the end."

It's important to stop there. The goal of the exercise is mirroring and validating. Most of us have a hard time saying only what we see and hear. We often use language to avoid feelings. We do this by going into the dominant hemisphere of the brain, which uses evaluative rather than descriptive language. The goal of this exercise is to mirror back the person's feelings without interpreting them. Interpretation involves imagining what's going on inside the person reading her scene, and it runs the risk of subjective distortion from your own projected feelings.

STEP FIVE: FEELING THE FEELINGS OF GRIEF

The next stage of this process may go on for a long time after the workshop. The grief process has been studied a great deal since Freud first wrote his paper "Mourning and Melancholia." Both Freud and, much later, Dr. Elisabeth Kübler-Ross, who worked with people who were dying—people who were literally grieving for themselves—discovered that grieving involves a whole range of complex emotions. Freud called this process "grief work"—the work that the psyche does in separating from the object of loss.

Grief usually begins with shock, followed by denial. When someone dies we often say something like, "Oh no, not Bob. I saw him two weeks ago." It takes time to work through the denial, which usually involves minimizing and rationalizing.

I once counseled a couple whose four-year-old son had died in a boating accident. The husband was almost inconsolable, but his wife began to give an elaborate explanation of how their son was an "old soul" and only needed to live for four years. She was quite rational, using the philosophy of transmigration of souls to deal with her boy's death. Her philosophical explanation was a form of denial. Then the denial broke down and so did she.

Anger will often, but not always, come next in the grief process, followed by hurt (sadness), depression, then guilt or remorse (if only we had spent more time with our little boy). Loneliness emerges as the full reality of separation sets in. Finally comes acceptance, usually signaled by more interest in life. This process does not always follow neat, tidy stages. A person can be angry for a few months and then pop back into minimizing or depression. Sometimes people get stuck or frozen in a stage.

Psychologists Monica McGoldrick and Randy Gerson in their book *Genograms in Family Assessment* give an example of fear and grief in the family of the novelists Charlotte, Emily, and Anne

Brontë. After the early death of their mother, the family was frozen in time. Nothing was changed or painted in the house for the next thirty years. The siblings fused together. Only Charlotte left home for more than a brief period. Two older sisters who had died in childhood developed their fatal illnesses when they left home to go to boarding school. Charlotte died at thirty-eight, the same age as her mother at the time of death. Their brother, Bramwell, had an illicit affair with a mothering figure seventeen years older than he. Emily, Anne, and Bramwell all died within a nine-month period.

When I was growing up children were not helped in grieving, and for a long time it was believed (erroneously) that children didn't grieve. When my mother divorced my father, my sister, brother, and I knew nothing of it until it was final. My mother announced it to me as I was heading out for baseball practice. I wept all the way to practice and all the way home. It was not mentioned again. A week later my grandfather called to ask me how my poor mother was doing. He said nothing about our grief. Most of us carry some unresolved grief from childhood.

The length of time people grieve can vary quite considerably. An adult working on unresolved childhood pain may need several years to do the grief work. This is why, ideally, it's best if we can resolve our painful unfinished issues before our own children are born. This is usually not possible, however. In many cases, these issues don't emerge until after we get married, although they will definitely show up then. Sometimes unresolved issues emerge when our child reaches the age at which we experienced our own abuse or trauma. For my PBS special on family secrets, we had a therapist interview several participants prior to the show. One woman told the therapist that she had no memories of her grandfather's incest and a neighbor's molestation until she had her first child, a daughter. One day as she stared at her beautiful innocent baby girl, the memories started coming back. She had been violated when she herself was an innocent little girl.

The grief work allows us to finish the business from the past.

Grief is often referred to as the healing feeling. The energy that we previously used to guard against the pain is released and reintegrated into our life. We no longer unconsciously need to reenact the hurt, pain, or trauma, and we are free to be present to reality. Our false self is no longer necessary to defend against our hurt and pain. When the past is resolved, our true self can emerge.

FINISHING THE PAST

Rigorous honesty, the *memoria* Aquinas named as an integral part of prudence, allows us to accurately remember how we chose in the past, which gives us the ability to be authentically present. Our energy is no longer blocked and congealed in the past. We develop circumspection, the ability to see what is truly going on around us. We also develop the foresight to evaluate the possible consequences of our choices.

Resolving the unresolved issues from the past also allows us to use our emotions in a fresh way. We no longer need to control our emotions by dissociating, projecting, or repressing them. I've often said that we either have our emotions or they have us. When they are frozen in the past we overreact or react in other inappropriate ways. This is one of the most destructive ways that choice is distorted. We cannot develop the virtue of prudence when our emotions are blocked or uncontained.

GRIEF WORK AND THE BRAIN

I had been leading groups in the grief work for more than twenty years when I became aware of the new studies about the brain that I discussed in part 1. I can still feel the excitement of that discovery. I knew the grief work changed people's lives. But now I knew how and why. There is sound evidence that putting the painful scene into words, by writing and reading it, helps to bring the imprinted memory under the control of the prefrontal cortex, the thinking part of the brain. It also remaps the imprint of the scene in the amygdala.

As I explained in chapter 3, hurt and trauma are recorded primarily in the part of the emotional brain called the amygdala. The more intense the trauma, the more it sensitizes the amygdala. This is true even if we do not currently remember the event. When something happens that recalls that unresolved memory, the amygdala responds in a hair-trigger manner, bypassing the thinking brain. We can be overtaken by emotions and actions that are shocking even to ourselves. This is why past trauma is so disruptive to choice. Anything that resembles the original event can set off the neural hijacking mechanism. Ordinary events can be perceived as emergencies. In essence, the unresolved issue has become an acquired fear.

Brain researcher Joseph LeDoux makes a distinction between an "emotional memory" and the "memory of an emotion." The troublesome or traumatic scene is the container of emotional memory. Any emotion can be and often is unconscious. Shame scenes and traumatic events are especially likely to be repressed and to exist as emotional memories. If you and I share a fun time together and feel a sense of joy about it, I will retain that joy as the memory of an emotion. The memory of an emotion is a much more conscious event.

When we write out the amygdala scene in a safe environment and reexperience it with a benevolent witness or witnesses, the alarm is reduced to a manageable tone. The emotional memory becomes available to the thinking part of the brain and can slowly become the memory of an emotion, allowing some emotional containment to take place. When this happens the emotions connected with the trauma do not have control over us; we have control over them. Once we can talk about the emotional wound in a safe and caring environment, we become present to ourselves, and then the grief work can begin.

BECOMING PRESENT TO YOUR CHILDREN

Children need parents who are real and authentically present. Once you have become present to yourself, you can listen to your children. You can see them as they are, with minimal projected fantasy. Montessori's principle of observation suggests that children will reveal their uniqueness to their parents if the parents are available to receive it. This is impossible without contact and presence.

Parents who are authentically present also have a far better chance of intimacy with each other. Parental intimacy is a crucial issue for children. When husbands and wives work out their family-of-origin issues, they minimize their projections on each other. But if childhood issues are unresolved, there are always two contracts going on in a marriage: the adult-to-adult marriage and the wounded-child-to-wounded-child marriage. The latter is what devastates many relationships. Doing original pain grief work is the single most dramatic intervention I've discovered for helping marriages. In *The Drama of the Gifted Child* Alice Miller says, "Mourning leads to an intrapsychic structural transformation and not simply to new forms of interaction with present partners." In other words, the grief work is not putting new wine in old bottles, like so much traditional therapy. It allows us a fresh start.

Children need the support and structure of a solid functional marriage to help them form a good conscience, and they also need their parents to model intimacy for them. As an eight-year-old girl named Clare once told me, "I feel good and beautiful when my mom and dad are loving each other."

9

ENCOUNTERS WITH THE DARK SIDE: OWNING YOUR SHADOW

This thing of darkness, I acknowledge mine.

—Shakespeare, *The Tempest*

If only it were all so simple! If only there were evil people...and it were necessary only to separate them from the rest of us and destroy them. But the line dividing good and evil cuts through the heart of every human being. And who is willing to destroy a piece of his own heart?

—Aleksandr Solzhenitsyn

Judge not, that you be not judged. For with the judgment you pronounce you will be judged.... Why do you see the speck that is in your brother's eye, but do not notice the log that is in your own eye?

—Matthew 7:1–3

Once we've dealt with our unresolved grief and moved out of reactiveness and dysfunctional choosing, we can begin to live in a proactive and authentically present way. Now, however, we must confront the second major obstacle that keeps us from recovering our innocence: our dishonesty with ourselves. This includes the unconscious dishonesty that comes from years of repressing our toxic shame and the things we detest about ourselves. It includes the ways we are consciously in denial about our phoniness, hypocrisy, and secret behaviors (lies, sexual stuff, cheating, etc.). It also includes the repression of the true self.

At some point along the road toward ethical maturity, we must become rigorously honest with ourselves. And then we must embrace all the parts of ourselves with forgiveness and compassion. This is the road that leads to a fully informed and functional conscience.

TO HEAL TOXIC SHAME WE MUST EMBRACE IT

Toxic shame is the feeling that something is wrong with me. It is the feeling that I am flawed and defective as a human being. The deeper the toxic shame, the more I feel that I don't deserve to exist. If something is basically wrong with me, if my real self is defective, then I must only display behaviors that are or were acceptable to my source figures and that meet the norms and expectations of my culture. Everything else about me must be hidden.

As I explained in chapter 2, healthy shame is the foundation of morality; it lets us know that we are limited and are capable of wrongdoing. But all of us also carry some degree of toxic shame, and we pay a heavy price for it. It takes a lot of energy to play the accepted roles and act out the adapted scripts we are given to live by, while we repress and hide our true self. The parts of ourselves that we disown and hide make up our shadow, and the more we focus on the light (the accepted parts of ourselves) the darker the shadow becomes. In the words of Carl Jung: "Everyone carries a shadow, and the less it is embodied in the individual's conscious life, the blacker and denser it is." Jung believed that confronting one's shadow was the highest moral act because it involves the strongest commitment to rigorous self-honesty. Self-honesty is an ethical challenge because it involves recognizing and owning our individual failures, weaknesses, and wrongdoing, along with the deceptions that make up our false self.

In doing so, we will discover that there are also many positive and unrealized parts of ourselves in the shadow, parts of our true self and our natural talents that we have repressed. Jung often spoke of the "gold" in the shadow.

SHADOW WORK AND PRUDENCE

Owning our shadow takes us beyond the polarization between personal good and evil, the either-or that makes us either angel or devil, more than human or less than human. It permits an intrapsychic integration that allows us to reach a fuller self, closer to our true self. *Making the shadow conscious is a precondition of prudence.* We cannot be truly prudent without an informed conscience, and we cannot have an honest functional conscience until we acknowledge both our strengths and our weaknesses.

We spend huge amounts of energy keeping our demons—the disowned, detested parts of ourselves—out of consciousness. When we disown and reject parts of ourselves, it forces us to overidentify with the parts of ourselves that we, or others, find acceptable. Because we overidentify with our so-called good side, we become polarized and rigid about that part of ourselves.

We also spend immense amounts of energy trying to prove to others and ourselves how good and righteous we are. One way we keep our disowned and detestable parts unconscious is to project them on others and see in them what we refuse to see in ourselves. We want the light of holiness around our heads. Projection is an unconscious (involuntary) transfer of our own unacknowledged traits and behaviors onto others. This allows us to believe that we are the soul of niceness while the people around us are seething with hostility, or that we ask nothing for ourselves while others are takers and manipulators.

CONFRONTING OUR SWAMP CREATURES

Fifteen hundred years ago an anonymous poet set down the old English tale *Beowulf*. If you saw the recent movie version with Angelina Jolie, you probably weren't thinking about its symbolism. But I like to use the story as a way to describe shadow work. *Beowulf* can be read as a man's descent into his unconscious in order to confront his demons and recover the most disowned and vulnerable parts of himself.

As *Beowulf* begins, the court of King Hrothgar of Denmark is under attack by a diabolical swamp creature named Grendel. (Our toxically shamed parts often feel like diabolical swamp creatures.) Grendel appears at night and fights off Hrothgar's best warriors. He tears men and women limb from limb and carries their remains back to the swamp.

Then Beowulf arrives—a mercenary warrior prince who offers his services to foreign kings. Hrothgar agrees to give Beowulf half his kingdom if he can conquer Grendel. (Each of us must struggle with and engage our demons if we are to achieve ethical maturity. Despite its loathsomeness, this creature Grendel has humanlike aspects.)

That night, Beowulf waits for Grendel. He carries no sword because Grendel cannot be killed with a weapon. (We have no weapons for our psychic demons.) After a ferocious battle, Grendel is defeated, and one of his limbs is displayed to the kingdom. Beowulf receives his rewards and his honor.

Beowulf's honor is short-lived, however, because the very next night something else comes out of the swamp, a creature even more terrible and destructive: Grendel's mother. (The problem has not been solved. We must not only engage and destroy the thing we fear—or embrace and integrate it—but also get to the source of our fear, the very thing that's given birth to the terror.)

Grendel's mother is symbolic of the deeper work that many of us have to do. My deeper work had to do with what I called "original pain work" in my book *Homecoming*. Until this work is confronted, there can be no peace. When I put the cork in the bottle and stopped drinking, I thought I had it made. I still felt the loneliness, but everything on the outside went well for quite a while. Then I began my sexual compulsivity. When I reached my bottom six years later, my therapist said I had to deal with my father and mother issues. I had kept my abandonment feelings repressed for years. I didn't even know what being my mother's surrogate spouse meant or that I had experienced covert incest. All of that had to be dealt with if I wanted to cure my addictiveness. Carl Jung called this work "legitimate suffering." It takes a great deal of energy to keep our unresolved grief repressed, and many people, perhaps the majority, appease this as long as they can. They refuse to confront their own vulnerability and shame. There is an enormous cost for this refusal.

After some deliberation, Beowulf decides he must go to the swamp and plunge into the depths where Grendel's mother lives. Everyone is aghast. Of all the great Danish warriors of Beowulf's day—no matter the heights of their manhood—none would contemplate descending into the dark waters to wrestle with Grendel's mother.

Beowulf will not be deterred. He heads for the swamp. The description of the swamp is frightening. The waters are dark and "infested with all kinds of reptiles. There were writhing sea-dragons and monsters slouching on slopes by the cliff."

King Hrothgar's wife, Queen Weatheow, says of Beowulf, "He admits to his weaknesses and in the admitting they became strengths." Beowulf tells the self-righteous Unferth, one of Hrothgar's warriors, that things are not black or white. He implies that when we admit to our weaknesses, they become strengths.

Beowulf's Leap into the Dark Waters

Beowulf leaps into the water and sinks to the bottom where Grendel's mother waits for him. He battles her for a long time and they struggle into her den and Beowulf sees a sword hanging on the wall. He breaks the chain that holds it, and with a sudden blow kills Grendel's mother. Beowulf's final grasping of the luminous sword represents the need we have for grace and virtues to help us. In legend and myth the act of killing signals a deeper kind of integration.

Integration

When Beowulf kills Grendel and Grendel's mother he has become Grendel and Grendel's mother. They represent his own demons, and monsters and strengths. As poet David Whyte says in *The Heart Aroused,* "Beowulf has wrestled with his interior and exterior monsters to the point where he admits them as himself."

This is exactly what happens when we own our disowned parts. We become them and they become us. The reowning is an absolutely essential ethical act.

WHOLENESS AND PROJECTION

One of Jung's most famous declarations is "I'd rather be whole than good." Owning all of ourselves (the good with the bad) brings us to a state of wholeness.

We need to strive for wholeness because when I can accept and love all of me, I can accept and love all of you. Being whole and accepting my own selfishness and vulnerabilities helps me to stop projecting the unaccepted parts of myself on my children (through projective reaction and reversal reaction) as well as on my spouse, friends, and above all strangers—those who are either unlike me or like me in ways that I refuse to accept in myself.

Projections are unconscious, but they are usually dishonest and dangerous. In chapter 4 I discussed how parents' projections damage their children. When tracking projections, the thing to pay attention to is energy. It takes a lot of energy to keep some undesirable part of myself out of consciousness. It is as if I have built a dam around some part of my energy in order to contain it.

The more we fail to achieve the wholeness that leads to ethical maturity, the more our projections become the hatred, blame, judgments, and criticisms that we put on others. The fact that projections are unconscious and involuntary does not make them benign. They are *more* dangerous because they are unconscious. *Projections are the most malignant part of a culture of obedience and the basic root of fanaticism.* Deceit is part of survival. We concealed our true self in order to get our needs met. Over the years our deceit becomes unconscious. This may be what Dostoyevsky meant when he said "that lying to ourselves is more deeply ingrained than lying to others."

"WOE TO THEM WHO SPEAK OF GOD"

Accepting our most disliked, despised, rejected parts is equivalent to loving every part of ourselves. Many people find it hard to accept their most unattractive and despised parts primarily because we have been taught to accept only our polarized, righteous "good" self. Because totalistic religious beliefs set up their followers to overidentify themselves with goodness and righteousness, these believers have trouble accepting their own shadow, sin, and selfishness. Paradoxically, overidentification with goodness is one of the primary causes of human evil, as it creates the fanatical polarization that sets up the opposition between us, "the good," and them, "the bad."

When Augustine warned, "Woe to them who speak of God,"

he was naming the dangerous temptation that comes from the belief that a certain religious or moral doctrine is the one truth, and that it brings its possessor a unique salvation. When such a belief is totalistic, anyone who believes differently is considered wrong, bad, unsaved, or whatever other negative term one might use to describe them.

Osama bin Laden felt righteous in killing innocent Americans. His surrogate killers flew their jet-fuel-loaded "missiles" into the World Trade Center and the Pentagon for the glory of Allah and their sure reward of heaven. The Christian Crusades against the Arabs were extraordinary acts of aggression based on the claim that "our God is the only true God." The sadistic and wanton destruction of human life, committed in the name of goodness, holiness, religion, and God, is one of the ultimate paradoxes of our moral history.

The Bible says that no one has ever seen God and lived to talk about it. The ancient Hebrews were loath even to speak the name of God. Augustine says:

> Have we spoken or announced anything worthy of God? Rather I feel that I have done nothing but wish to speak: if I have spoken, I have not said what I wished to say. Whence do I know this, except because God is ineffable?...For God, although nothing worthy may be spoken at Him, has accepted the tribute of the human voice and wished us to take joy in praising Him with our words.

He seems to be saying that we will always fall short in trying to speak of God. Shame as modesty keeps us from getting carried away. We certainly know the love we have for God, but we have to use symbols and analogy, which go beyond words. The revelations of holy books (books that the faithful believe are divinely inspired) are always subjectively interpreted. Even our best scholars endlessly debate the meaning of passages in Holy Scripture. Any totalistic moral system or fundamentalist religious belief rests upon a lie: that *they*—the saved, enlightened or chosen ones—*know* who God is and what God teaches and wills for us. In my view, people claim absolute certainty because they can't handle the tension that true faith demands. St. Paul says "We see through a glass darkly."

The Christian Jungian analyst Fritz Kunkel once said, "In a showdown, God is always on the side of the shadow, not the righteous self." The shadow never lies; it tells it like it is. It is the false self that lies, trying to impress others or to be accepted.

Our most realistic possibility of a life of virtue and true happiness comes from accepting that all of reality is polarity. This is a truth philosophers have taught for millennia. As the poet and philosopher Lao Tsu reminds us in the *Tao Te Ching:*

> Difficult and easy complement each other.
> Long and short contrast each other.
> Front and back follow one another.

There could not be light without darkness, nor sound without silence, nor good without bad.

Integrating our polarities leads to self-compassion, the ability to accept ourselves completely without any reservations, denials, delusions, or excuses. We are fallible and full of ambiguity. Without wholeness and self-compassion, our choices will always be tainted by our personal lies, unconscious dishonesty, and self-aversion. Once we're willing to embrace our shame—to dive down into the murky swamp to fight Grendel's mother—we have the opportunity to begin our quest for wholeness. The path to wholeness is not easy. I identify with St. Paul's statement in his letter to the Romans (Romans 7:18–19): "I can will what is right, but I cannot do it. For I do not do the good I want, but the evil I do not want is what I do." Goodness and holiness (wholeness) is a journey with smooth moments of joy and other times when things come apart. Yet it is worth it, because the journey to achieve wholeness is itself virtuous, just as doing exercise to be healthy is part of being healthy. While a fully developed conscience embodies the integration of all our polarities, such a conscience would still be a human conscience and subject to imperfection. That is why Aquinas thought precaution and foresight were crucial elements in the virtue of prudence. I've often thought I was acting virtuously, yet what I did turned out badly.

OWNING, NOT CONDONING

Let me be clear: owning our dark side does not mean that we condone our undesired and unacceptable parts, and it doesn't mean that we will act on their impulses and directives. It means that the more we are aware of them and embrace them completely as part of our selves, the less chance they will take over our lives. The more I overidentify with righteousness, the less aware I am of my own potential for evil. Whatever evil I'm willing to own and be aware of immensely reduces my chances of acting it out.

RECOVERY OF INNOCENCE, PART 2: DOING OUR SHADOW WORK

To enter into the dark region of our psyche is an act of courage and honesty. We cannot fully develop our inborn capacity for moral intelligence without taking the feared journey of self-confrontation. The illusions of a "righteous" false self are very comforting. But a righteous false self is dangerous. As the psychologist Harriet Lerner points out, "We can be no more honest with others than we are with ourselves."

Our inner work is always private, unique to us, and can never be fully displayed. We cannot show others exactly how we slew our monsters. What is potent and good in the inner world will not translate in an exact way to the outer world. For this reason,

I warn you to be careful of books and people who give you exercises for doing shame reduction (shadow work)—even the exercises I offer here or in my book *Healing the Shame That Binds You.* Each of us has his own calling, hears the beat of his own drummer, and has his own sense of destiny. There are no techniques or exercise that will help everyone, and for some people such exercises may be no help at all. With that warning, here are a few you may want to try.

Exercise I: What's Obvious to Your Loved Ones

One of the simplest ways to recognize a part of yourself that you refuse to own is to listen to those who love you. As the Jungian scholar John Sanford once wrote: "Our shadow personality is often obvious to others, but unknown to us." My family has helped me a lot in owning some parts of my shadow. I remember my son confronting me about my obsessive need to work and make money. I went into a tirade about how my working and making good money allowed him to have all the things I never had. For days afterward, I obsessed about what my son had said, and my anger lingered on.

One of the telltale signs of unconscious shadow material is intensity and energy. This is a clear sign that something unconscious is being exposed. Slowly I realized how terrified I was about money. We had no money growing up. So here I was, fifty years old and catastrophizing about scarcity and loss. The fear was irrational, and it was driving me and consuming my life. Worst of all, it was robbing me of my time with my son. Owning it was not easy.

Exercise 2: People You Dislike

Here's another very simple way to track down your disowned shadow parts. Make a list of five people you dislike. Maybe you've even wondered why they annoy you so much—there's just something about them that gets under your skin. They can be acquaintances, neighbors, people at work, movie stars, or TV personalities. Beside each person's name write an adjective for the character trait that sums up your disdain—something about their behavior. Here's a sample list:

- Joe Smith—egomaniac
- Marilyn Trainer—verbal and boring
- Phil Lubwig—constantly trying to get me to promote his work
- Jim Lamberti—apathetic and a total conformist
- Suzy Salido—a 50-year-old cheerleader, always joyous and positive

Now imagine that each of these character traits is a disowned part of yourself. It takes a lot of energy to keep these parts out of consciousness. They are like huge inflated balls that you are trying to keep under water. Ask yourself these questions about everyone on your list: "How can this person be my teacher? How can I learn about parts of myself that I am overidentified with by accepting these people I disdain? How would it change my life if I owned some of their behavior?" Now imagine that you can ask each disliked person what he or she thinks about you. Listen carefully.

When I go through this exercise I learn from Joe that I'm very egocentric; I just cover it up by playing humble pie. So I decide to acknowledge and talk about my achievements at times. I feel much more balanced doing this.

Marilyn helps me see how much I talk—a criticism several close friends have gently given me. I decide to spend several evenings just listening to other people. I'm surprised to discover how connected I feel with the people I really listen to and validate.

Why am I so annoyed when Phil pushes me to promote his books and get him lecture jobs? Is it because I'm reluctant to promote myself or my own books? I believe in them; I spent years writing them. Why am I ashamed to promote them? I decide to mention my books whenever I'm lecturing on a subject where it is appropriate, and to cite my ideas when they're relevant to a question.

Jim helps me to see that I need to identify situations where I can be a follower. I decide to take a course on a subject I know nothing about. I don't have to be passive or apathetic, but I don't have to be the star or the leader, either. I can be a real student and follow the teacher's instructions.

Suzy bugs me because I have a hard time expressing joy and excitement. I decide to let myself lighten up and be more spontaneous. She also bugs me because sometimes I force myself to be positive when I really want to express anger or disappointment.

In each case, my dislike for the person is based on my own issues. Embracing each issue and changing my behavior in small ways adds real balance to my life. I like myself for trying these new behaviors.

Exercise 3: The Banquet Feast with Myself

An exercise that has been powerful for me was inspired by a poem by Derek Walcott. It's called "Love After Love."

> The time will come
> When, with elation,
> You will greet yourself arriving
> At your own door, in your own mirror,
> And each will smile at the other's welcome,

And say, sit here. Eat.
You will love again the stranger who was your self.
Give wine. Give bread. Give back your heart
To itself, to the stranger who has loved you

All your life, whom you ignored . . . .

Sit. Feast on your life.

Today I will imagine that I am having a feast with myself. Of course, I've invited all the parts of myself that I value the most. Some are the grandiose parts that I've used to cover up my deep inner sense of being flawed and defective. But mostly they are parts of myself that I really like. As I sit at my banquet table, I see my outgoing good guy that most people seem to enjoy. I see my writer self, the one that's written three *New York Times* best-sellers. I see the generous me, the one who gives people gifts. I see the good athlete sitting at the table with his college write-ups, especially the one about the game he won single-handedly.

By now you've probably had enough of these fine figures. After all my guests are seated, I imagine looking out a large window in my dining room and seeing faces looking in. They are the uninvited ones.

I see the young seminarian who cheated on several theology tests while studying to be a Catholic priest. He's lonely and full of shame because I've rejected him for so long.

Then I see the guy who compulsively masturbated while he was supposed to be living a celibate life. I turn away—I don't want to even acknowledge his presence. When I look again, I see the guy who gossips about his friends.

I also see a guy who acts so nice and pretends to like everyone but who does not really like a lot of the people he says he does. He talks about them behind their back or he makes internal judgments about them.

I could go on, but I think you get the point. These people represent parts of me that I don't want to accept. And yet if I exclude them from the table, this is not really my banquet. How can I eat and drink with a joyous heart while those rejected souls are peering through the windows? This is my feast; I need to have all of me at the table if I am to find happiness.

Then I remember that there may be other parts so repressed that I'm completely out of touch with them. Over the years, these rejected parts have become like hungry dogs in the basement. They are angry and lonely; they come out as projections of hatred or moral judgments on others. They form the core of my shame and self-hatred.

Tonight I soften my heart and go to the door. I invite each of my disliked or even repulsive parts to my banquet table. I imagine that they are dressed in ways that embody my disdain. I have a moment of fear as they enter, these ragged, dirty, shame-faced people.

When all are assembled, I talk to each of these disliked guests. I imagine that I see each one as my own frightened or insecure child. I imagine that I am each one's parent. How can I be a better parent to them? How will I take each one back into my life?

Everyone at the table is part of me. If I want to be whole, I need to love and forgive them all. This acceptance may mean feeling the shame and guilt that I've avoided. Owning those parts has helped me to make amends. It has moved me to change the behaviors I dislike. And it has made me less judgmental and more forgiving toward others.

Finally, the more I have owned them, the less they are real options in my life. And the more I understand them and embrace them, the more I can forgive myself.

I urge you to do this exercise yourself.

All kinds of virtues flow from this restoration of wholeness. We stop judging, criticizing, and blaming others. We start allowing our self-love and self-compassion to overflow in love and compassion for others, especially strangers—the ones who are not like me. Out of the well of self-love, innocence, and self-compassion come mercy, kindness, tolerance, and forgiveness of self and others.

In many ways, nonjudgment is the most beautiful fruit that flows from self-compassion. To be rigorously honest with oneself is the best way to stop judging others. It is clear to me that the more I accept my own flawed humanity, the more I accept the shame that is part of being human. All of us are limited, make mistakes, are disappointed in life, and experience the need for help. Healthy shame gives me *permission to be human.*

Exercise 4: Your Positive Shadow

Each of us has a true self that holds the positive powers and talents we were born with and makes us the unique, unrepeatable people we are. The true self can come as a sudden awareness as we do the grief work I discussed in the last chapter. Or it can emerge as we are confronted with crises and challenges we never expected. But it is usually discovered slowly in the course of our normal life cycle.

Here is an exercise to help you look at your positive shadow. Make a list of five people whom you genuinely admire. Perhaps you want to be like them. Or perhaps you feel you couldn't be like them, that you don't have the strengths or talents they have. Beside each person's name, write down the quality or qualities that make them stand out for you.

Close your eyes and spend a few minutes breathing deeply. Now focus on each person in turn. See their face, their eyes, their clothes. If you have trouble seeing them, imagine hearing them, as if you were having a friendly chat with them. If there are celebrities on your list, don't let yourself be intimidated by them. They are human beings just like you. They have their own joys and sorrows. They may be struggling in their relationships or have problems similar to yours. Focus on their humanity rather than on some extraordinary talent they have. Or if you think of their talent, just imagine the hours and days and years they've spent in practice to develop their special skills.

Once you have them in focus, imagine what really attracts you to them and think of a time in your life when you acted in a similar way. What you did may not have been as dramatic, but it had the same human quality.

When I did this exercise, I focused on baseball great Mark McGwire. Of course, I deeply admire McGwire's record of seventy home runs in 1998; he was one of the greatest home run hitters of all time. But what else? I admire McGwire's caring for his team and his lack of animosity during his famous home run contest with Sammy Sosa. I admire his love for his son and how Mark had the boy with him when he broke Roger Maris' record. I also admire how he honored Maris, the man who had broken Babe Ruth's home run record thirty-seven years earlier. On the day McGwire expected to top him, he invited Maris' family to the ballpark and paid tribute to them and to Maris.

Finally, I admired how McGwire ended his career. He stayed on for two years after he broke the record, playing with injuries most of the time. Then Barry Bonds broke McGwire's record, and McGwire treated Bonds with honor and respect. He decided that rather than come back for another season, working on his worn-out knees and bad back, he would retire. Many a man would want to fight to get the record back, but McGwire knew when it was time to call it quits. There's a time to go on and a time to stop with dignity. McGwire chose the latter.

Today both McGwire and Bonds have been accused of using performance-enhancing drugs, but I can still be inspired by the qualities McGwire has demonstrated for so many years. And I can commit to bringing these qualities into my life in my own way.

Pause and think about the five people on your list. The plain fact is that I couldn't admire Mark McGwire or you couldn't admire whomever it is you are working on if you didn't have an element of those qualities within yourself.

I can think about specific times in my own life when I showed humility, team spirit, love for my child, or care for another's success. These qualities are part of my true self. Go down your own list and do the exercise with each person you admire. At the end, make a list of the positive human qualities that you may not be owning. Make a commitment that you will start owning and living these qualities in your own way.

Often our positive qualities are harder for us to acknowledge than our negative parts. Perhaps you were shamed as a child any time you mentioned something you did well. You were told, in effect, that you should never look at your own talents and achievements, and so you feel ashamed when you honor your strengths.

This is entirely wrong. You need to be as aware of your strengths as you are of your weaknesses.

To recover our innocence and self-compassion we need to reconnect with and nourish the true self; this is our unique incarnation in this world. You've never existed before and will never exist again. No one can or will express the unique way of being human that you manifest. You are the only copy left of a book in the library. When you die, the book you are will be gone forever. That's why we need to know and love you. Give everyone around you that chance.

10

CARING FOR YOURSELF AND CARING FOR OTHERS: YOUR TWO CAREERS

The price of greatness is responsibility...a free society can only be created and maintained by citizens who are conscious of their obligations as well as their rights.

—Winston Churchill

For the first time in human history, virtue is a condition of effective work.

—Alvin and Heidi Toffler

He who has power over others can't empower himself. He who clings to his work will create nothing that endures.

—Tao Te Ching

I tell thee Love is Nature's second sun,
Causing a spring of virtues where he shines...
For Love informs them as the sun doth colors...
O! 'tis the paradise! the heaven of earth!

—George Chapman

I can vividly remember how terrified I felt standing on the corner of Lamar and Main in downtown Houston one busy Monday morning. I was twenty years old, I had completed two years of college, and I was absolutely overwhelmed at the thought of my future. Men in fine suits and women with shopping bags passed me by, each hurrying somewhere. I imagined they had jobs, money, cars, homes, and spouses. I wondered how all that happened. I had walked into the world of adulthood, but

I felt bewildered as to where or how to begin. I stood at the beginning of my first career—the career of developing the virtues of responsibility, love, and work.

LEAVING HOME

I have been an avid student of the psychologist Erik Erikson for forty years, and I still find his developmental chart, entitled "The Eight Ages of Man" (first presented in his book *Childhood and Society*), very useful, although I now notice a distinct male bias in his work. In what follows, I've adapted Erikson's core insight: that moral and psychological development requires us to face and resolve a series of crises. A life cycle crisis is a period of increased vulnerability and at the same time an opportunity filled with urgency and potential for new inner development. The first five stages cover childhood and adolescence. Each stage involves a synthesis of two polarities that forge an ego strength allowing a person to know her own potentials as well as her limitations.

Adulthood is the time for the full flowering of a virtuous life. Either we develop the virtues necessary for each stage of adulthood or we succumb to various degrees of apathy or out-and-out vices. Either we develop intimacy in a committed love relationship or we succumb to the isolation that comes with love and sex addiction or have anger at the opposite sex that destroys intimacy. Either we develop a meaningful livelihood or we succumb to laziness, work addiction, the greed of money addiction, or the pride that keeps us from staying committed to any one job because we believe we're better than the job.

In midlife we need to develop generativity, a kind of productivity that involves care and compassion, or we succumb to various degrees of self-absorbed greed, pride, and gluttony. Finally, either we come to the full self-acceptance that leads to wisdom or we despair and are filled with regrets, envy, hatred of others, and loss of faith.

These crises—and the suffering that goes with them—are the ordinary way we develop a virtuous life.

Early adulthood is about leaving home, leaving our family of origin, and making our way in the wider world. The first major crisis that occurs during these years requires us to work out an intimate relationship with a new attachment figure. Intimacy demands time and therefore the responsible working out of a long-term commitment to another person and to the new family that we create together, or, if we decide to be single, the ability to establish a network of friendships and a feeling of connectedness with a community.

The second crisis focuses on finding and sustaining a meaningful livelihood, one that is balanced by the demands of love (family), health, and recreation. A meaningful and satisfying livelihood—that is, a productive and self-actualizing vocation—also means coming to terms with our culture's dominant success myth, which defines success in terms of physical beauty, athleticism, winning at almost any cost, and acquiring money and property. I do not believe that any person can develop a virtuous life unless he's come to terms with the meaning of money in his life.

I call the resolution of these two crises your first career.

What Is at Stake

As Figure 10.1 shows, the moral outcome of the first crisis is the virtue of love. The outcome of the second crisis is the virtue of work, which is really a collection of virtues, including patience, perseverance, self-discipline, and industriousness.

The grave danger that nonresolution of the first crisis entails is isolation, disconnectedness, or codependent enmeshment. Many people, especially folks like me who were avoidantly attached, feel disconnected, find engulfing relationships, have fears of full commitment, and like to isolate themselves. In codependent enmeshment, the two people fail to self-actualize. Instead, they replace their incomplete selves with the strengths of their partner.

Figure 10.1: YOUR FIRST CAREER

The ability to respond to the needs for finding a new secure attachment figure (a committed love relationship) and a meaningful form of work.

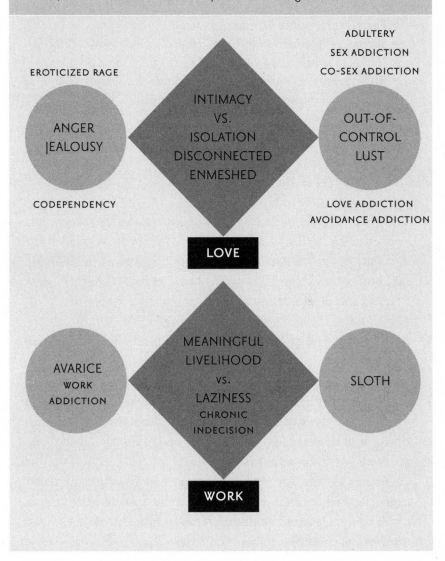

The members of a codependent couple utterly depend on each other like two people in a canoe, in which each person's life balance and direction are dependent on the movement of the other.

The grave danger that noncompletion of the second crisis entails is one of the following:

- Laziness, avoidance of work
- Staying at the first job one gets for one's whole work life because of the fear of taking a new risk
- Moving from one job to the next because of a grandiose and unrealistic fantasy of striking it rich or because a person believes they are above any job they take
- Work and money addiction

Venturing into Adulthood

The day I stood on the corner of Lamar and Main, I was facing my first career. I had just finished two years of pre-med at the University of St. Thomas, a small Catholic university in Houston, and I had realized that I did not really want to be a doctor. I was confused and afraid. Being afraid was not unusual for me. I had been afraid as far back as I could remember.

I didn't know what a healthy relationship with a woman looked like, much less how to achieve one. I had begun frequenting brothels at age thirteen, but I had never engaged in sex with the "nice" girls I dated. I had been violated sexually in childhood and molested by a Catholic priest in high school. My father abandoned me early on, and I had a fragile male identity fostered primarily by my mother's anger at men.

Despite all this, the stirrings of nature were telling me that I needed to find a bond of love with some special woman that would serve as a new, secure base from which I could create my own family and find a meaningful career. But I had no idea how that was going to happen, and marriage and family seemed like an overwhelming responsibility.

My resolution of this first crisis was to join the congregation of St. Basil, a teaching order of Catholic priests.

The nuns in Catholic elementary school and several priests at my Catholic high school had suggested that I had a "vocation," a special calling to be a priest, and I began to think they were right. In many ways I hated the lifestyle I was living. I frequently slipped into a church and spent quiet time thinking about a life devoted to caring for and helping others. During periods of sobriety, I felt attracted to a holy life. When I decided I wanted to be a priest, I was willing to give up my sexuality and devote my life to God.

Joining the congregation demanded that I take vows of celibacy, poverty, and obedience. The vow of poverty meant that all money and property were owned by the community. The community, however, would take care of all my individual financial needs.

I now realize that this was a perfect resolution for the two life cycle crises of the first career of adulthood. Celibacy meant I could avoid all the thorny problems involved in love, sex, and intimacy, and poverty solved the problem of finding a meaningful livelihood. However, I was consciously dedicated to these two vows until I left the Basilian order, and it was years before I recognized how many problems they solved for me.

As my life has unfolded, I've found that I really did want the priestly life of educating and caring for others, but I certainly did not want to be celibate or renounce ownership of worldly goods. As I've said before, I'm speaking only for myself. I have several colleagues, priests and nuns, who do seem to be well suited for religious life.

When I left the Basilians at age thirty-one, I had no clothes, car, place to live, or money. After ten years, the Basilians gave me the hearty sum of $400 to make my way back into the world. All of my old friends were married, had children, and were doing pretty well financially. I was overwhelmed, a true lost soul.

To this day I can only point to a higher power that helped me through this period of my life. I cannot explain to you how I made it. Did I mention that I didn't know how to drive and that I had a serious drinking problem?

I did have one ego strength and a fairly well-formed virtue going for me: I was a indefatigable worker. I had always done the things I set my mind to do, and when I decided to do something, I did it all the way. I had begun working when I was ten years old, and I had taken care of myself financially until I entered the seminary.

Nonetheless, as I mentioned in the introduction, getting a job was not easy at the age of thirty-one. My degrees in philosophy, psychology, and theology were not very marketable, and my drinking cost me the first three jobs I did get.

When I finally sobered up, I was able to work steadily. However, I lost my best job—teaching religion at Strake Jesuit High School—after I'd been sober for two years. I mentioned this earlier when I talked about my unusual emotional response to the movie *Dead Poets Society*.

I now know that losing that job was one of the best things that ever happened to me. When I was fired I was newly married with my son on the way, and the weight of responsibility forced me to begin to create work for myself. My wife at the time, Nancy, and I put our noses to the grindstone and began to create our own family.

We were very much in love and overjoyed with our new son, and our first six years together were truly wonderful. Both of us, however, brought a lot of baggage into the marriage, which contributed to its ultimate breakup. I had never worked on my childhood abandonment and abuse issues. My "love map" (which I'll explain later) led me to a partner who had her own issues of abandonment and abuse. We had both grown up in highly dysfunctional families.

Nancy had two children from a previous marriage, and that was an added responsibility. Blended families are commonplace today, but they still pose their own set of new problems for both the parents and the children. I'm happy to say that I still have deeply loving relationships with both my stepchildren.

And as I've said, I was terrified about money. I had grown up dirt poor and everything in my childhood revolved around money. I lived in a state of constant fear about not having enough money to take care of my family.

Like my ex-wife and me, most people discover the impact of pathological environments and the kinds of issues they create as they begin to deal with courtship, sex, attachment, marriage, responsibility, and work.

When we marry, early childhood wounds and damaged developmental dependency needs emerge in issues such as

- Boundary problems
- The inability to resolve conflicts
- The noncontainment of emotions (especially anger)
- Communication problems
- If we have children, lack of parenting skills
- Sexual problems

These issues are huge and plagued me every step of the way during my first marriage. This is one reason I urge people to do the kind of work I've described in the last two chapters. I found that I needed to resolve these issues before I could develop the virtue of love.

LOVE

Love has universally been thought of as the highest virtue, but it is difficult to define for the same reason that words cannot fully describe the flavor of an orange. Love flows primarily from the nondominant hemisphere of our brain. This is why we have always called on poets and songwriters to celebrate it. But love also involves practical knowledge; it is more about *doing* than about speaking pretty words.

Love has a power that hints at the mysterious core of our longing. Many would say that love touches the divine. This is why I've said that the highest form of love, agape, certainly transcends morality, because when we love we voluntarily undertake the very same actions that morality asks us to do out of duty.

Of course, most love offers us only glimmers of the transcendence I've just described. We may say we "love" an animal, an antique, a piece of jewelry, or a certain sport. Being "in love"— the love most poets and songwriters describe—is *eros*. The love of friends or of our fellow human beings is called "filial love," or *philia* in Greek. There is another love that exists between people of unequal power, like the love that exists between parents and their children. The word for caring love between adults is *agape* (from the Greek; it is *caritas* in Latin, the root of our word *charity*). Agape begins with the love of God, and then, by extension, becomes descriptive of deeply committed love among humans.

Eros

The most influential ancient work on love is Plato's *Symposium*. The scene is set at a banquet at the poet Agathon's house, where six of his friends have gathered to celebrate his success at a poetry competition. The topic of conversation is love (eros). Each person gives a speech or tells a story defining eros, but the two great stars of the occasion are Socrates and Aristophanes.

Socrates tells those present that all he knows about love he owes to a woman, Diotima, whose words he is relating. Diotima taught Socrates that love is always about desire and lacking. Erotic love is not completeness but incompleteness. It is not fulfillment but all-consuming want. Eros never rests; it is always on the move, always yearning. The love of eros is a love of bounteous suffering, a strange commingling of joy and anguish.

Aristophanes' discourse is the most often cited—probably because it is what we may most want to believe about romantic love, that our passion can guide us to wholeness and bliss. The god Zeus, he explains, was jealous of humans' original wholeness and power—so jealous that he split us in half, leaving us in a state of incompleteness and longing. We were left to wander the world looking for our other half, longing to reunite with our soul mate.

Here it is, the fairy-tale notion of romantic love, where we merge into utter oneness with our beloved. Aristophanes' myth also suggests that we have only one true love, our single other half. Love is thus exclusive and permanent. Problems in love simply mean we have not found our soul mate.

It is startling to see how this romantic fiction has survived to this very day. Thanks to the research of anthropologists, biologists, chemists, psychologists, and neuroscientists, we're beginning to get a picture of why this myth prevails. It has lasted because it is grounded in the actual biological experiences of lust and attraction, which we commonly refer to as "being in love."

New Insights into Eros

Anthropologists William Jankowiak and Edward Fischer have found evidence of romantic love in at least 147 of the 166 cultures they studied. Romantic love (eros) is not an invention of the Western mind; it is a universal phenomenon—one that stretches across cultures and is fueled by our evolutionary need to procreate and preserve our genes.

Two important researchers have helped me greatly in understanding the difference between falling in love (eros) and love as agape (the virtuous work that goes into the creation of lasting love between two people). The first is anthropologist Helen Fisher, author of *Anatomy of Love: The Natural History of*

Monogamy, Adultery and Divorce, who examines romantic love. The second is psychologist John Gottman, author of *Why Marriages Succeed or Fail,* who is a leading authority on long-term love.

Eros, the Chemical Bath

According to Helen Fisher, it is now pretty clearly understood why eros produces the sensation of being swept away and why we feel that the person we lust after or are attracted to is someone we *must* have, someone who completes us.

These feelings of euphoria and being swept away are the result of our brains being flooded with chemicals. Many of the substances swamping the brain are chemical cousins of amphetamines. They include dopamine, norepinephrine, and especially phenylethylamine (PEA).

The PEA/dopamine cocktail, as I like to call it, explains why lovers can talk for hours on end, make love endlessly, show inordinate generosity, and act in other ways that are atypical for them. PEA elevates both lovers' testosterone levels. Even people whose sex drive is very low may experience intense desire when they are "in love." During the in-love period sexual behavior creates amazing oceanic feelings of wholeness in both partners. Mother Nature wants babies, and she gives us the chemical equipment driving us to mate and procreate.

The Power of Lust

I see our natural biological drives as necessary for the continuance of the human race. In itself, lust is not bad. It is integral to human courtship. But as religious philosophers and theologians have taught for centuries, nature—the hardwired biological drive that emerges in adolescence as part of our awakened sexuality—must be moderated by our higher feeling system and by our ability to reason. Here is an opportunity for a lot of work. Practicing modesty, respect, and responsibility builds virtue—temperance in a new context. Those who can enjoy their lust while recognizing it as a biologically determined drive, and who can keep it in check and not let it take hold of their lives, have achieved a high level of intimacy and sexual maturity.

In the sixth century, when Pope Gregory the Great developed a list of seven deadly sins, lust was at the head of the list. These sins served as a classification of the normal perils of the soul in the ordinary and everyday conditions of our life, and I cannot envision the two careers I'm describing in this chapter without including the grave dangers that arise as we face each of the crises of adult life. Here, in the first crisis of love, the "deadly sins" of anger, envy, and lust can each cause us to fall short and in some cases even destroy a marriage.

Lust, the craving for sexual satisfaction, is one basic element in our instinctual drive for love. The trouble arises, according to Fisher, because lust is a separate affect program from attraction and attachment. This is why we can be in a love relationship with someone, with high intensity and attachment, and still lust for someone else.

At its worst, lust can become a full-fledged addiction. In my mind, addiction is a state of being that dehumanizes us. The classic definition of sin as "missing the mark" has the same meaning as dehumanization when we let lust take over. It becomes our obsessive goal, and obsessive lust is like an idol that dehumanizes us. Many people who have been abused, neglected, abandoned, and enmeshed turn to lust and the euphoria of being "in love" as a way to soothe themselves. Today there are thousands of sex and love addiction programs around the country, and people in them have no doubt that both being "in love" and having a craving for orgasm can be full-fledged addictions. There are also many programs for codependents of sex addicts.

Addiction as Moral Bankruptcy

In fact, all of the deadly sins are embroiled in addiction. St. Augustine once said, "Sin is the punishment for sin." As I've described, I attempted to solve the problems caused by my drinking by drinking more. Thus St. Augustine can say, "Betrayal of self and betrayal of others is the substance of sin." Sin is the destruction of one's self as well as the destruction of one's relationships with others. Addictions, like sin, are forms of spiritual bankruptcy.

I'm well aware of the medical model of substance addiction, especially alcoholism. I'm sure I have the chemical predisposition for alcoholism, which means that my brain's system of dopamine and dopamine receptors is awry. It is generally believed that this chemical predisposition is transmitted primarily from father to son. But I have several alcoholic friends whose sons have not become alcoholics, so genes are by no means the whole story.

But alcoholics are considered to be spiritually bankrupt, and you can't be spiritually bankrupt without being morally bankrupt. The fourth step in the twelve-step asks us to take a fearless moral inventory. Later steps ask us to make a list of those we have harmed and to make amends whenever it is possible to do so.

There is also the mystery of moral choice I underscored in chapter 6. Why do any of us quit using addictive substances when we do? Some say it's the level of pain. But I had been in far more intense pain several times before I finally quit. If substance addictions are only chemical diseases, then it's hard to imagine a person just stopping without some chemical reinforcement.

Certainly some people have quit because of interventions and others because they've been in extensive treatment programs. Still, there is a final *choice* that every addict must make. That choice is a moral and spiritual one.

I hate moralizing and I detest TV evangelists ranting about sin. But there is sin and immorality. It has to do with missing the mark as a healthy, fully functioning moral and spiritual human being. Substance abusers, love addicts, gambling addicts, sex addicts, and food addicts are not fully functioning moral and spiritual beings.

The twelve steps take us to a moral and spiritual awakening. I think we need some of the more pungent language of virtue and vice, spiritual well-being and sinfulness. It is far more cutting for me to say that I lived in adultery for six years than to say that I acted out sexually or was sexually compulsive for six years.

Some of the so-called old timers in AA (most with fewer years of sobriety than I have) act like rigid moral dictators when they sponsor new people. The last thing I want is for twelve-step groups to become citadels denouncing sinners. Still, it is true that when I was at the height of my alcoholism and sexual compulsivity, I was dehumanizing myself, missing the mark, and a sinner.

Our nature is so rich and intricate that it can go terribly wrong. Our human freedom gives us the potential for making decisions that do not necessarily enhance our humanity. We can become dehumanized and live sinfully. As one gives in to lust over and over and acts on it, one becomes isolated from any true kind of intimacy. It is in the fruit of this choice that lust can be seen as one of the seven deadly sins. Sex or love addicts are deeply isolated and lonely people. They have lost their identity or, better said, they have *internalized* the lust so that they do not have lust, their lust has them. They've become *identified* with it.

Attraction

Lust is a sexual attraction, but as the work of Helen Fisher has made clear, we are now learning that lust is not the only reason one person is attracted to another. Studies have shown that symmetry (roundness, waist-to-hip ratio, the regularity of a handsome or beautiful face), scent, power, status, and what is called "familiar love" play a role in attraction.

One of the most powerful of these elements is "familiar love"—a kind of subliminal guide to the ideal partner. Researcher

John Money of Johns Hopkins University calls this our "love map," and it can either help us or sabotage us in our search for love. Our love map is drawn from the experiences of our childhood, the things we liked or found enticing and exciting about our parents and other people. If we liked the way one of our parents laughed or told a joke, or the cadence of their voice, meeting someone with similar behavioral traits can stimulate our attraction program. Also, *anything* with a strong emotional charge helps create the map—even abject terror. All the experiences and associated emotions gathered while growing up are imprinted in the brain's circuitry by adolescence. While no partner meets every requirement, meeting a person with a significant number of matches can stoke the fires of love.

Familiar love is imprinted in early brain development, which is why it can be very dangerous for those whose childhood was marked by abandonment, abuse, and enmeshment. Quite often, the hyperventilating attraction between two people can be rooted in the most destructive parts of their familiar love. Children in dysfunctional families hunger for love. Love is more important than food. Nature abhors a vacuum. When we have been deprived of love we need it and seek to find it again. Unfortunately, our love maps guide us toward people who resemble the attachment figures we wanted to love us. The wounded child in us wants to make everything come out right. This sets us up for what is described as the "compulsion to repeat." This compulsion to repeat explains why we keep trying to get love from the same stone, rather than going to someone who can actually give it—or even being turned off by someone who can give it.

This is why adults who were abused as children often pick partners who abuse them, and why children of alcoholics often marry alcoholics. Those who bear these emotional scars and have emotional hungers for love have lost the ability to choose well; they have developmental deficits. Just as the damaged brain I discussed in chapter 3 cuts off feeling and the ability to choose, so also those of us who numbed out in childhood often make very poor choices in our adult lives. Children of alcoholics can marry alcoholics even if the person seems to them like a normal social drinker when they first get together. They can marry abusers who come over as protective and deliciously possessive, and so on. They have a gullibility that causes poor choices for mates. When a person has several bad relationships, then it's easy to become terrified of trusting one's own feelings. In *Homecoming,* I've outlined a program that heals developmental deficits, allows people to break this kind of vicious relationship cycle, and shows them how to build the boundaries that help them to make better choices.

The Highs Don't Last

Whether you're in love and getting married or having an affair, the PEA highs don't last forever. This is why passionate romantic love is short-lived. As with any amphetamine, the body builds up a tolerance to PEA, and over time it takes more and more of the substance to produce love's mind-altering high. This is why "love addicts" or "attraction junkies" often jump frantically from affair to affair or relationship to relationship. They move on as soon as the first rush of infatuation fades.

For married couples, the challenge comes when the PEA runs out after the first two or three years. This means the euphoria is ending and the hard work of committed love must begin. Especially aggravating in many marriages is the return to normal testosterone levels. Although this is true for both men and women, baseline levels are usually lower in women than in men. Often males are bewildered that their beloved, who used to make love until dawn, often initiating the lovemaking, can now go for weeks or months without responding sexually.

This discrepancy in desire is an enormous letdown and is the cause of much marital discord, but it can be worked out if both partners understand what is happening and both are willing to make compromises. Developing the virtue of love requires the willingness to seek out information and the habituated will needed to be patient, negotiate well, and respect each other's differences, especially in such a sensitive area as sexual desire.

THE FIRST CRISIS IN YOUR FIRST CAREER: INTIMACY VERSUS ISOLATION OR ENMESHMENT

Being "in love" is *not* love, nor is it true intimacy. But being in love has a real purpose. Its mysterious power frees you from the mundane and routine busyness of your life. In *The Soul of Sex,* Thomas Moore writes, "Being in love moves you to experience your 'soul' life, in which passion and imagination are far deeper than the world of pragmatism."

Intimate love takes many years to create, and it requires us to work on many major issues, including:

- Good self-identity
- Self-disclosure—being willing to be vulnerable and to share in a rigorously honest way
- Emotional containment—a key skill for emotional intelligence
- The ability to express one's needs clearly
- The ability to listen
- The ongoing disclosure of positive love messages
- Friendship with one's partner
- Admiring one's partner
- Being able to support your partner's values when they differ from your own
- Having a spiritual connection
- Nurturing each other's growth and self-actualization
- Continuing to touch and hold each other both sensually and sexually
- Modesty and healthy shame

Developing these elements of the virtue of love requires time, kindness, patience, and, for many, instruction.

Intimacy can truly occur only between equals. The old patriarchal model of marriage that guided many of our parents was not a contract between equals. This is why many of us need help in the form of instruction and information.

When I married for the first time at age thirty-five, I didn't have any idea how to connect and be intimate. I had never seen a deeply intimate marriage. I went to workshops, got therapeutic help, and read books in my attempt to learn. My wounds from the past, primarily engulfment, also set me up to avoid intimacy. Being "in love" a lot and having many sex partners are ways to *avoid* intimacy. This was true for me. Most love and sex addicts know nothing about love or sex.

Even the healthiest people have to deal with the issues of intimacy I've described. Those with rigid, false self-defenses, deep wounds, and emotional illiteracy are at a grave disadvantage. Nature's pull is simply to establish a biological connection. As therapist Pat Love puts it, Mother Nature wants us to "meet, mate and procreate." Nature also moves us to seek people with DNA that's very different from our own. This gives our offspring a biological advantage and adds diversity to the evolutionary process. But nature does not give a hoot if we're compatible with the partner we're "in love" with. And compatibility is one of the most important issues in long-term love and intimacy.

Being "in love" is a bona fide altered state of consciousness, an ecstatic prelude to true love, a state of bliss that discounts differences and incompatibilities. In that state, we are given a first taste of agape, and we glimpse a mirror image of the intimate bond that we may develop, through commitment and hard work, in the years ahead. *Work* is the operative word.

Attachment

What takes people beyond the crisis and power struggles of the early years of marriage? Helen Fisher identifies this drive as attachment. Attachment, she says in *The Anatomy of Love,* is "humankind's most eloquent, most complex and sophisticated desire" and "the ornate commitment to another's living soul." Attachment is rooted in the earliest bond between the mothering source and the child. Failure in this early bond is one of the major factors in relationship dysfunction.

The need for attachment remains with us all our lives. One's lover is chosen in an act of attachment and affiliation. In friendships and partnerships, young adults become the nurturing parents of each other. In reasonably functional people or people who have done some of the grief work resolving their original pain issues and some of the skill building related to their developmental deficits, then it is their freely chosen decision that bonds two people in a more intense level of love, the love that moves people to marriage and long-term commitment. Many children from dysfunctional families who have done no remedial work will be distorted in their choice of mates. If they marry, they will have to work especially hard to remedy their past issues. Yet if both partners with dysfunctional pasts are willing to ask for help, their marriage can itself be the psychotherapy by which they work out their past family-of-origin issues.

Let me repeat, however, that the three systems I've been describing—lust, attraction, and attachment—are independent of one another, and each has its own discrete neural circuitry and neurotransmitters. There is a considerable tension between the human drive to pair and the restlessness that tends to accompany long-term relationships.

It helps to remember that long-term marriages are a relatively new phenomenon. In the historical past, when early death was commonplace, it is estimated that marriages averaged twelve years. The exigencies of sheer survival were also far more demanding in marriages two hundred or even one hundred years ago; partners were bound by necessity. We need to consider this when we look at today's divorce rates, remarriage patterns, and the frequency of adultery. In spite of the great human drive to bond, we are not really well suited biologically for long-term pair bonding.

The Virtue of Love Sustains Marriage

I mentioned earlier that the work of John Gottman, a psychologist at the University of Washington, has been a key to my understanding of long-term love. Gottman has put in years of study to determine the way good-enough average couples go about the business of staying married.

Here's one of his striking conclusions: many marital problems never get fully resolved, even in long-term happy marriages. Gottman cites many researchers who have come to this realization. The plethora of books on love, marriage, and relationships is also evidence that there are ongoing problems that are not being resolved by religious teachings or psychotherapy. People simply have to learn to accept the differences between them, find ways to express them respectfully, and then focus on the parts of marriage that work. The longer I'm with my wife, the more my love includes her idiosyncrasies (even ones that bug me at times). They make up her uniqueness; at times I think they are cute. Having fun and having a good sense of humor are also important for long-term love. This know-how of the virtue of love is rooted in emotional intelligence, not in rational calculation or IQ. It seems as though people who happily persevere come to recognize what is worth fighting over and what isn't, an understanding that's rooted in the wisdom of the virtue of prudence. After counseling some eight hundred couples, I found that those who see the larger intentions of their relationship create a context around their annoyances and disagreements. The larger intention can be their religious faith in the sacredness of marriage, their belief in having happy and healthy children who embrace long-cherished values, or the desire for a strong family that contributes to their society's well-being.

The virtue of love is the ability to sustain commitment and the persistence and determination to work out livable solutions. Gottman says that the essence of a good relationship is the ability to "argue well." Do your arguments go round and round and end in unresolved anger? Does the same argument come up over and over again without a satisfactory solution for either of you? Does one of you always give in and resent it? Couples in effective marriages argue in several different ways, but they come to some resolution, often a compromise. And finally, do you have the realistic expectation that you are *never* going to agree on everything and—as the new studies show—many of your marriage problems will never get fully resolved?

The virtue of love allows each partner to know and love himself or herself. As I've described, knowing and loving yourself involves rigorous honesty and the ability to accept your own shortcomings and faults. This unconditional positive regard for yourself reduces your negative judgments and also the likelihood that you will project your own shortcomings onto your partner. With virtuous love, differences are not right or wrong, they are just different. Over time, you may even come to see that your partner's difference is exactly what makes him or her a unique, unrepeatable person.

Virtuous love requires more than poetry. Real love means keeping the vows and promises you have made to each other. It means the willingness to change, being open to getting help if necessary. It means helping your partner when you don't feel like it and being strong when your partner needs support. Real love demands being honest (merciful and respectful) about your true feelings. It means taking care of your own and at times your partner's needs. It means energetically nurturing the needs of your relationship.

Virtuous love also requires you to take full responsibility for your own wounds. Unresolved wounds will keep you from communicating effectively and honestly. They operate unconsciously and cause reactions rather than choices. As you resolve these wounds, you will find that emotional containment becomes easier, and so does intimacy.

Learning these skills is part of a virtuous commitment to work on marital conflicts. The virtue of love says, "We can work it out no matter what"—with one important qualification: it is not virtuous to stay in a relationship where you are being abused, you've sought help, and yet the abuse continues. Battered partners (mostly women) often become bonded to their abuser, and they need therapeutic help. I have also counseled couples where the wife or husband is having an affair. After I tell them it is impossible to continue their therapy unless they end the affair, they refuse to do so. I end the counseling with such a couple and strongly suggest that the partner who is not having an affair seriously consider leaving such a marriage, where the vows are being flagrantly scorned.

I'd like to end this section with a quotation from an interview with Gottman in the *Milton H. Erickson Foundation Newsletter*. Asked for the key to a successful marriage, Gottman describes virtuous behavior without ever using the word *virtue*. He tells the interviewer:

The answer is not complicated.... What I call "the masters of marriage" are individuals who are being kind to one another. They may raise difficult issues, but they also soften them in a very considerate way. They frequently express appreciation. They communicate respect and love every day in numerous small ways ... they communicate greater interest ... and scan the environment, looking for opportunities to say "thank you."

When I read this, I immediately thought of the words of St. Paul in 1 Corinthians 13:4–7:

> Love is patient and kind; love is not jealous or boastful; it is not arrogant or rude; it is not irritable or resentful; it does not rejoice at wrong, but rejoices in the right. Love bears all things, believes all things, hopes all things, endures all things.

THE SECOND CRISIS IN YOUR FIRST CAREER: A MEANINGFUL LIVELIHOOD VERSUS LAZINESS, CHRONIC INDECISION, GREED

After leaving home, we not only need a new intimate attachment figure, we need a job.

The second crisis that I had to face (as did many of the couples I worked with during my twenty-five years of counseling) centered around establishing a meaningful livelihood.

The only male in my family who modeled job success was my grandfather. His advice was to find a job and stay with it. He had gone to work at the Southern Pacific Railroad as an office boy and worked himself up the ladder to become the auditor of the railroad. He was traumatized during the Great Depression, although he didn't lose his job; he was a very fearful person and lived in a constant state of fear that another depression would come. In the light of his circumstances, he had done very well, but "stick with the first job you get" is not necessarily a good strategy for finding a meaningful livelihood, unless you really love that job.

Elements of a Meaningful Livelihood

A meaningful livelihood implies that I have enough money to provide for myself and/or my family and that my work is acceptable to my sense of worth. A meaningful livelihood would ideally need to support my personal growth—maybe not at first, but the job would have the potential for me to learn and grow. My workplace would provide a community that I feel connected with and have a sense of loyalty to. My bosses, supervisors, the owners of the company, and/or the board of directors would care about me and my future well-being; this might entail a good health care plan and a reasonable pension plan. A meaningful job would also give me more and more independence and responsibility.

Virtue as a Condition for Work

As Alvin and Heidi Toffler point out in their book *Creating a New Civilization,* the information age, along with its dazzling technology, has radically changed the nature of work since my grandfather signed on at the Southern Pacific. In this new world of work, a meaningful livelihood would involve a high level of individuality, creativity, and autonomy; one would need a highly developed emotional intelligence, especially the ability to self-motivate and be a team player. All of these attributes are inner strengths. This is why the Tofflers can say that "for the first time in human history, virtue is a condition of effective work." This new world of work is the most urgent practical reason we need a new approach to moral education, with prudence as its leading virtue.

Work as a Virtue

Seeing work as a virtue means that it can be an integral part of a person's development. Work has been considered a Christian virtue, but in the new world of work, it transcends the Christian idea of the daily grind and perseverance under almost all circumstances. The new possibility of people being "knowledge workers" and creators opens up a larger opportunity for individuals to create their own unique sense of spirituality.

The virtue of work builds upon the earlier development of virtues such as temperance or self-discipline, industriousness, perseverance, courage, and patience. It requires us to have the knowledge or skills appropriate to the job. It asks us to develop our character, our sense of identity, and our own unique style. People who have developed the virtue of work have their own style no matter how mediocre their job might seem to others. No one is condemned to mediocrity, although many may succumb to conformity and apathy. That is the tragedy. It is a mistake to identify a meaningful livelihood with a specific kind of job. For the virtue of work, any job will do. It's how you do it that counts.

I can remember Mr. Caston, Bubba Jones, and Joe Jackson from my childhood. Mr. Caston ran the neighborhood drugstore and was the neighborhood pharmacist. He gave us candy if we caught his eye when our parents weren't looking. My mom trusted his knowledge of medicine far more than our doctor's. Several times he suggested over-the-counter medicines that worked better than what the doctor had prescribed. Above all, Mr. Caston was a happy man. He always had a big smile, and I felt at home in his drugstore. Bubba Jones ran the produce department at a grocery store where I worked when I was twelve. He was raw and coarse, but he washed lettuce, celery, and tomatoes with gentle care. He was known to have the best produce in town, and he was extremely proud of it. Joe Jackson was our mailman, the soul of reliability. I used to watch him on cold rainy days and marvel that he was still smiling and good-natured. He had a special way he wrapped the mail on rainy days. He seemed to love his job, and everyone loved him in return.

With the virtue of work people transcend questions of status and prestige. As James Hillman says in *The Soul's Code*, "There is no mediocrity of soul. The two terms do not converge. They come from different territories. 'Soul' is singular and specific; 'mediocrity' sizes you up according to social statistics—norms, curves, data, comparisons." I know people who keep moving from job to job. They seem to always think the job they have is not good enough for them. There is an element of pride in these people; they have an inordinate "sense of themselves." I believe that real self-development comes from working wholeheartedly at the job you have, learning whatever there is to learn. You may want to move on at some point, but chronic indecision is a vice found in many people who wind up as failures.

Routine

I hear a lot of people (especially youth) complain about routine. The jobs I had that required punching the clock every day taught me a lot. The virtue of work requires perseverance, which is itself a virtue. Perseverance is the product of self-discipline, which is a necessary strength we need to overcome apathy and laziness.

The novelist Flannery O'Connor expressed it well in a letter to a friend. "Time," she says, "is very dangerous without a rigid routine.... Routine is a condition of survival." For me routine is a crucial element of work. My addictive tendencies and my laziness do not like routine, but without it I get lost. For me, routine is a guardian—it does not have to be rigid, but it has to exist for me to work well.

My addictions were so destructive because they lacked boundaries. We need boundaries because they give us structure. Imagine traveling over a long bridge with no guardrails. I frequently quote an anonymous writer who said, "Of all the masks of freedom, discipline and structure are the most mysterious." Freedom is impossible without limits. Without limits it becomes chaotic.

One of the most notable models of the virtue of perseverance is the former Baltimore Orioles baseball player Cal Ripken. On September 6, 1995, Ripken played in his 2,131st consecutive game, surpassing Lou Gehrig's hallowed record, which no one had believed would ever be broken.

Ripken's streak began in his first full season in the major leagues and continued as he played in every game year after year. Ripken represented the ideal of the reliable working person who shows up every day on time and scorns sick leave (in Ripken's case, frequently ignoring injuries that would have disabled most of his teammates).

There probably are many hardworking men and women who can match or even trump Ripken's commitment and dogged perseverance, but his work ethic stands out even in a sport that relies on each member of the team being counted on to do his job every day. There are great individual players, but everyone acknowledges that the league champions are always a well-oiled team where every member can count on every other one.

Ripken's father was his ideal. He once said, "I don't know if I could put my approach into words, but if I did I'm sure it would sound like my dad's, something like, 'Nothing's worth doing halfway.' I heard my dad say those words and I witnessed him living his life by them." Ripken also embodied them in a memorable way.

Laziness and Chronic Indecision

Laziness and chronic indecision are potent enemies of the virtue of work. All of us have an inclination toward laziness. It may be the way we embody the law of entropy—that a certain amount of energy is always unavailable for doing work. Being lazy is there from the beginning, from not brushing your teeth to not doing the tasks required by your allowance. Children who are overindulged and excused from responsibility learn that they don't have to delay gratification or do things they don't want to do. This can become a vicious habit and is probably the core enemy of the development of any virtue, not just the virtue of work. The old Christian moralists called laziness the "sin of sloth."

Laziness is not the same as taking time off. The new work culture of the technological age goes to the opposite extreme and seems to demand that we work incessantly and that we be always available by e-mail or cell phone. And some people feel scared and guilty if they take time off. Some people become addicted to work. Work addiction is not fulfilling and has life-damaging consequences, such as having no time for your children or your spouse. Many work addicts wind up in divorce court. Some down time is *needed* in our lives. The connotation of the word *recreation* is that it helps revitalize us. Vacation can be a way to be creative and allows us to go back to work with new vigor. Paradoxically, true work addicts work more and more but achieve less and less. They get burned out and do not really enjoy their work. Finding a meaningful livelihood will be characterized by some degree of enjoyment.

Taking down time is qualitatively different from laziness or sloth. The people I had contact with that I would call slothful were of two kinds. One kind stayed at the job they had out of fear. They hated their job but were too lazy to improve themselves. The other type worked enough to get by for a while, then would quit their job until they had to work again. When people internalize sloth, their whole life will be damaged by it. Slothful people often envy and are angry at others who are more successful than they. They seem to wallow in envy and anger, but never do anything about it.

The virtue of work requires courage. To create a meaningful livelihood a person needs to be willing to stick with a job that offers potential for learning. My grandfather's advice to stay with one job is okay for some people, but there are jobs that can be spiritually stifling. I know people who have risked moving on to new jobs. Some made less money but found a new freedom and enjoyment in their work. I'm not supposing that any particular job is wrong; I'm saying any job is dangerous when it stifles a person's spirit. I know doctors, lawyers, and rich CEOs whose spirit has been stifled by their work. They shared their pain with me during many hours of counseling.

I remember Irma, a friend of my mother's. She hated her job from the first day she went to work until she retired forty-five years later. Irma had some form of rheumatoid arthritis, and at times it crippled her so severely that she had to take sick leave. Her sick leaves would sometimes last four to five weeks. When she retired with an ending pay of $2.42 an hour (after four and a half decades) her arthritis got radically better. I always thought there was an emotional element to Irma's illness. The rage she felt toward her job (which she expressed only mildly) was taking its toll on her body. Her body was revolting against a job that was killing her spirit. Irma is a tragic example of fearful conformity.

Greed and Avarice

The second deadly sin that haunts the world of work is the greed that fuels avarice. Greed is the virus that haunts our society and turns work and money into sources of spiritual bankruptcy. Greed becomes the deadly sin of avarice, the unending and insatiable need to make more and more money and acquire more and more things.

The culture of the America I grew up in made youthful beauty, athleticism, winning, and the accumulation of wealth and property the marks of success. This idea of success is really equivalent to an idealization of physical narcissism, materialism, and unending greed. I believe this ideal is so polarized that it has created its own shadow in the eating disorders that plague our society. These are directly related to heart disease, diabetes, and other ailments. If I can't be handsome, athletic, or rich, I'll live in a shameful way and be just the opposite.

Our cultural success myth not only makes money an obsession for the haves but dominates the lives of the have-nots. I grew up thinking and worrying about money all the time. I also had great prejudice toward the rich. I believed that a rich person could not possibly be virtuous or good. Yet obsessing about money and catastrophizing about losing everything I had were my ghostly companions. No matter how far down the value scale I placed money and those who had it, I lived with a burning desire to acquire money. I believed money, not virtue, was my door to happiness.

By the time of my life-changing experience on the highway in Minnesota, I had compromised my work life with jobs I should never have taken. In 1982 Carol Burnett had asked me to run the Palmer Drug Abuse Program in Los Angeles. This job took me away from my family for more than two months a year, but I wanted the money and prestige it offered. I already had a full-time counseling practice with an enormous waiting list. I sometimes counseled over sixty hours a week. That was insanity. In 1978 I was offered a job as the director of human resources at a newly formed oil company. I was also asked to be on the board of directors of this company. I knew nothing about the oil business, but I took the job because the founder and president of the company promised to make me rich. I took consultant jobs at two other companies, one an oil company and the other a chemical plant. Keeping all these balls in the air was also a form of insanity. I was stressed to the gills even as I led company workshops on stress management.

As I described in chapter 5, the voice I heard on the highway promised that if I did the work I knew how to do, I would be freed from my anxieties over money.

I wasn't sure exactly what any of this meant, but I couldn't get the experience off my mind. Soon afterward, I not only stopped my sexual compulsivity but did the deepest personal psychotherapy I had ever done. With my therapist George Daugherty at the helm, I did the grief work I described in chapter 8.

From 1985 on, money came to me like manna from heaven. I

bought antiques, a fine car, a ranch in Montana, and later a ranch in Cat Springs, Texas. But I gradually came to see that in itself, money did not bring me happiness. My first realization of money's impotence came a year and a half after my divorce. Making money was not the direct cause of my divorce, but my fearful obsession with money over the years certainly contributed to it. In my loneliness, I contrasted the joys of love, family life, and friendship with my now affluent lifestyle. When I ran across a quotation that said "Happy is harder than money," I knew it was true beyond a shadow of a doubt. I also had counseled many miserable millionaires, including a number of movie and TV stars, and I saw in their lives that money and fame do not bring the inner peace that characterizes happiness. That was when I really began to ask the moral questions I outlined at the beginning of this book.

Before I get carried away and start sounding too righteous, let me say that having money is not bad, and having it as the fruit of a life of perseverance and hard work is something I am surely proud of. Money in itself cannot make a person vicious or virtuous. The unbridled accumulation of money is like an unending pregnancy. Yet money is important. The multimillionaire J. Paul Getty once jokingly said, "The meek will inherit the earth, but not its mineral rights!" Some balance is needed.

So how can a person find a virtuous way to understand money? How can making money and having money be a source of self-actualization and spiritual growth?

Money as a Source of Spiritual Energy

What I have found important is that I have control over my money rather than letting my money control me. The Bible does not say money is the root of all evil; it says the *obsession* with money can cause great evil. TV evangelists certainly use the Bible and religion to promise people money, wealth, and happiness.

Some of these very preachers are being investigated for their own greed and opulent lifestyles. I don't know if God wants you to be rich, but certainly He must want you to have a decent life. Money has the same potential as lust—a huge energy that can be used for good or ill.

We do have to be careful of the many TV evangelists and non-denominational church leaders who justify their affluence with biblical arguments. With few exceptions, these people seem to be completely delusional. The tithing schemes they use to bilk their congregations are comical to any person with moral intelligence.

We need money to provide for ourselves and our families so that we can have a decent life. Everyone deserves to live above the terrible stress of not knowing if you can feed and house yourself and the people you love tomorrow, next week, or next month. Money can also enhance personal freedom and self-esteem. I'm proud of the perseverance that took me from being a "lost soul" to living above the stress.

I no longer *have* to work, but I do not want to stop working because a meaningful livelihood means more than money. My vocation, my life purpose, is to be a teacher and helper. Teaching flows from my grand will. I continue to be a teacher and helper through my writings, workshops, and lectures. I can work for enjoyment, and money is no longer the issue that determines what jobs I do.

But I had my own important discovery about money: I got the idea of money as spiritual energy. I found how living above the stress of just making ends meet allowed me the freedom to do many things that I wanted to do. I stopped catastrophizing about money. I had the freedom to travel and pursue spiritual learning. The virtuous use of money as spiritual energy took me out of myself. I have been given great blessings, and money has been one way to show my gratitude. The beginning of my sobriety started at the Houston Council on Alcoholism, and I was able to give them a substantial gift. PBS gave me a chance to present material that has helped hundreds of thousands of people, and I am committed to help them financially. I gave to the elementary and high schools that had given me scholarships because I didn't have money to pay the tuition. I honored the man who paid for my first two years of college by helping another young man. I am outlining these things to show that charitable giving is one of the meanings of money as spiritual energy. The joy that has come to me in being able to return the love that was given to me is almost beyond words. Money as a source of spiritual energy allows me the time to connect to my true self, my soul.

"Let go and let God" is a slogan in every AA club. It was *only* when I trusted my spiritual experience and completely gave up trying to control and manipulate my way into becoming rich that I in fact made a lot of money. Let me be plain: I'm not saying that letting go of your puny will and ego control are new techniques for making money. I'm saying that letting go and letting God worked for me. Letting go did not mean becoming passive. I had no logical explanation for the success I was having. I chose to understand it as grace; grace is a gift, and you can't really earn a gift. But it did not mean I should stop doing what I knew how to do well. It gives me joy to work as a teacher and writer.

I could only create what I wanted when I was willing to let go of my fearful, puny will, which tried to control what cannot be controlled. This puny will is directed by a weak ego and a lack of character. Refusing to trust God, we try to control everyone and everything. We have to let go of conscious ego control in order to access a larger level of consciousness. We have to let go of our false pride, another of the deadly sins. If we are willing to let go, we move into the focused energy of our grand will. It is only then that we find our lives rooted in an interconnected unity with all life. At that level you may not even care about making money.

As Thomas Carlyle wrote, "Blessed is he who has found his work."

RAISING THE BAR OF CONSCIOUSNESS: YOUR SECOND CAREER

Albert Schweitzer once wrote:

> Often people say, "I would like to do some good in the world. But with so many responsibilities at home and in business... there is no chance for my life to mean anything." This is a common and dangerous error.... No matter how busy one is, any human being can assert his personality by seizing every opportunity for spiritual activity.

Albert Schweitzer was one of the great moral and ethical models of the twentieth century. By age thirty he was an acclaimed biographer, a first-rate theologian, and a distinguished musician. He decided to change careers and study medicine in order to devote his life to helping the sick and poor in Africa. This career for the spirit I call your second job.

While most people will not choose as dramatic and all-embracing a life change as Schweitzer did, all of us will come to a point, most often in later adulthood, where we seriously question the moral and spiritual meaning of our lives.

The great Florentine poet Dante Alighieri engaged our moral imagination in his famous poem *The Divine Comedy*. The first part of this poetic allegory, called *Inferno*, describes Dante's descent into hell. At the midpoint in his life, Dante says, he discovered he had strayed from the true way of his spiritual and religious life and entered into a dark wood. It was the eve of Good Friday 1300. He was in a painful state of emotional suffering. He wrote: "So bitter is it, death is little more."

When the sun came up the next morning, he woke up hopeful, prepared to climb the mount of joy. But his hope turned into fear when he found himself blocked by the three beasts of worldliness: the leopard of malice and fraud, the lion of violence and ambition, and the she-wolf of incontinence.

In terror, Dante is driven back into the wood and begins to feel despair. Thus, he began his journey into the dark pit, hell, where he encounters every kind of vice and sin. Suddenly the shape of the poet Virgil comes to his aid, explaining that he represents human reason and has been sent to lead Dante out of error by another path. Virgil tells him that he will lead him as far as he is capable of going (the limits of reason) and then turn him over to another guide, the lady Beatrice, the revelation of divine love.

Dante's descent into hell is a metaphor for the crisis in his soul at the midpoint in his life, which forces him to take a searching inventory of his own personal moral life and compels him to look at his life in a more rigorously honest way. Dante has to face his own finitude, his personal delusions, and his own personal evil.

Like Dante, most of us come to a point where certain essential questions intrude into our consciousness. These essential questions seriously disrupt the "suspended doubt" that most people live in for the first half of their lives. Suspended doubt results from the fact that most of us are too busy growing up or taking on our early adult responsibilities to ponder ultimate questions. But no maturing person keeps the ball of suspended doubt in the air forever. A day comes when we cannot avoid the ultimate questions that relate to the meaning of life in general and our own lives in particular.

In Figure 10.1 I've outlined the two crises of our first adult career. Our second career shown in Figure 10.2, also involves two crises, the first of which is triggered by something that ruptures the world of suspended doubt.

Figure 10.2: YOUR SECOND CAREER

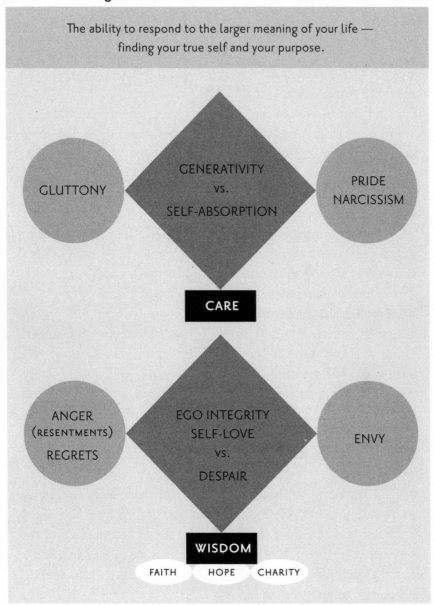

The ability to respond to the larger meaning of your life —
finding your true self and your purpose.

GLUTTONY

GENERATIVITY
vs.
SELF-ABSORPTION

PRIDE
NARCISSISM

CARE

ANGER
(RESENTMENTS)
REGRETS

EGO INTEGRITY
SELF-LOVE
vs.
DESPAIR

ENVY

WISDOM

FAITH   HOPE   CHARITY

THE FIRST CRISIS OF YOUR SECOND CAREER: THE RUPTURE OF "SUSPENDED DOUBT"

The philosopher Alfred Schutz wrote a great deal about our everyday, commonsense view of the world. He described it as the world of "suspended doubt."

Our first career takes place in this world of suspended doubt, meaning a world unruffled by any questioning of the ultimate meaning or purpose of our lives. We take society's accepted "consensus reality" for granted.

Our second career begins when our suspended doubt is ruptured. At that point in our lives, we begin to look for the larger meaning and purpose for our lives. We move inward in order to ponder and meditate on why we are here and how we can make a difference. We are challenged to find our larger spiritual home, our unique place in the family of humankind.

The first crisis of this second career results from the tension between generativity and self-absorption. To be generative means being able to produce or create; the literal meaning refers to offspring of whatever sort. To be generative in midlife means going beyond the limited confines of my particular life, going beyond duty and morality. Achieving generativity requires finding a balance between my own primary relationships, family and self-interests, and the needs of others understood as the larger family of humankind.

If I leave this crisis unresolved, I run the risk of becoming more and more selfish, self-absorbed, and cut off from the larger community. I run the risk of a former friend of mine who says he's made his fortune and the hell with everyone else. He has become grossly obese and has an unending desire to accumulate property and goods of all kinds.

The second crisis asks us to come to terms with aging and death. It is often triggered by some aspect of failing health. Mine began after I had quadruple bypass surgery. Erikson describes this crisis as "ego integrity versus despair." During this crisis, a person has to come to grips with the meaning of his whole life in the face of death. I had to decide if my whole life was okay and acceptable in spite of my addictions and failures.

To resolve this crisis, a person has to get beyond self-condemnation and regrets. Achieving ego integrity means we totally accept and value ourselves. We realize that we are now the elders and have a lot more to contribute to life.

The moral fruits of our second career are the virtues of care, compassion, love of God (or whatever we call our higher power), gratitude, kindness, and wisdom.

The Genesis of Your Second Career

When I was forty-one my youthful vigor, with its unconscious images of immortality, was suddenly ruptured by the death of my father and two of my high school friends. By that point in my life, I had been betrayed by someone, experienced failures, and felt disillusioned in some of my fantasies about how life was supposed to unfold. I was working frantically, but I had achieved no inner peace or sense of security.

Our second career usually begins in midlife, when we realize that life is much more difficult and painful than we had thought. The fragile nature of reality hits us in the eye. Our vulnerability calls us to question the meaning of life.

Entertaining deep philosophical questions can be threatening or confusing, and looking back, I see that I blew these questions off and became more selfish and self-absorbed. Questions that scare us can make us cling to the certainties we already have or cause us to dull our consciousness with overwork, distracting activities, or mood-altering drugs. Some people seek apathy when their suspended doubt is ruptured. Others take refuge in their religious faith, turning it into a sacred certainty that must not be questioned. They become more rigid and closed in their thinking.

The death of my father and high school friends weakened my faith and moral beliefs, but I was too scared either to leave my faith or to accept the challenge of facing my vulnerability.

As I buried my father, I began a sexual affair, which triggered a series of behaviors dominated by compulsive sex. I concomitantly began working compulsively in the almost insane way I described earlier.

Life Transitions

The philosopher Ralph Waldo Emerson once said, "Not in his goals but in his transitions man is great." The impact of my spiritual experience on the highway in Minnesota ended my sexual addiction, and my therapy revitalized me. I prayed for forgiveness. I acknowledged my vulnerability when I did my grief work. I learned about families as systems and how families become dysfunctional. In the light of my alcoholic family dysfunction, I realized that my choices had been quite predictable—I wasn't crazy or evil. This was a major breakthrough for me. I slowly began to see that sharing this new knowledge could help others as it had helped me. I knew what I had to do. I wanted to share my discoveries with others. At first I didn't know that this sharing was part of the work the voice had told me to do. I gradually began to see that it was. I also realized that this was the work of my true self. It was safe now for my true self to emerge.

In 1984 I made a ten-part series called *Bradshaw on the Family* with KUHT, the PBS station in Houston. That series was later shown on every PBS station in the United States. Five more series and six books followed, touching the lives of countless people.

I had worked hard prior to 1985, but my work was not generative. It was obsessive and self-absorbed, the work of my false self, an attempt to quell my deep fears about money and insecurity. My new work took me around the world. By 1987, I was in a place of spontaneity and flow, beyond anything I had ever known. I simply *received* the celebrityhood and money that came with it. I rarely thought about being a public figure or making money. I was moved when I received thousands of thank-you letters each month. The letters also expressed a level of pain I had no idea that so many people were in. I realize that my own suffering and pain had a meaning beyond myself. Sharing my own story as honestly as I knew how created a generative energy that was helping countless other people. I realized that my true self's purpose was to be a teacher and nurturer of other people. In a way I had become the priest I set out to be at age twenty-one.

Erikson's Seventh Stage: Generativity Versus Self-Absorption or Stagnation

Without realizing what was happening in the early stages of my work at PBS, I had entered fully into what Erik Erikson described as the seventh life cycle crisis. Erikson views this crisis as a choice between generativity, understood as a caring for the larger life around me, and self-absorption or stagnation. Generativity is a larger kind of caring and creating and goes beyond being on our own, making a living, marrying, creating a family, and caring for our children. It urges us to find the fuller purpose of our lives and to live it. For most, generativity may resemble what you've already been doing, only now you see your life with an expanded consciousness. Your work or vocation, no matter what it is, takes on the larger purpose of enhancing the quality of life for everyone.

Care and Generativity

For Erikson the virtue of *care* is the result of the seventh psychosocial adult stage, solid selfhood. Erikson sees care as our human calling and self-absorption as the stagnation of a person's life. Self-absorption is the core of the sin of pride, and it is often accompanied by gluttony. The people I know who seem to have chosen self-absorption at this stage of their lives are gluttonous not just for food but also for pleasure of every kind. They treat themselves like their own spoiled brat.

For people who already know about caring, especially women, generativity may involve developing a more generous caring for themselves. This may involve pursuing a new career that taps into parts of the self they have not previously actualized. My wife, Karen, is a good example of this. In her early twenties, she had to raise her child alone. She was able to form her own company, and for twenty years she was a highly successful commercial real estate developer and broker. However, she always wanted to be an artist, and now she has become a serious student of metalsmithing and jewelry making and is creating beautiful and unique jewelry.

For many people, finding a love partner, creating a family, and parenthood are what Erikson calls their "prime generative encounters." However, generativity in stage seven goes beyond parenthood. Erikson writes, "Man *needs* to teach, not only for the sake of those who need to be taught, and not only for the fulfillment of his identity." Every mature adult needs to teach, and every generation depends on its teaching adults. The virtue that is needed is *care,* which is a sense of responsibility, arousing out of our love or kindness, accompanied by painstaking and watchful attention.

Caring goes beyond the love of one person or one family to the love of all living things. Caring is the state of being that Milton Mayeroff described in his superb little book called *On Caring,* which I quoted earlier:

> Through caring for certain others, by serving them through caring, a man lives the meaning of his own life. In the sense in which a person can ever be said to be at home in the world, he is home not through dominating, or explaining, or appreciating, but through caring and being cared for.

He sees that care is an orientation of character, an attitude of largesse by which a person is related to herself and the world as a whole.

As I've grown older and dealt with life's larger questions I've realized my limitations. I have enough money, and I know I can't save the world. I want to assume the responsibility of being a good elder and that means modeling good boundaries. Erikson writes about generativity as needing to be needed. Without that sense of being needed we can, he says, succumb to "the moral deformation of self-absorption" in which we become our own "infant and pet." Erikson's description exactly fits many of the CEOs who have been indicted recently. In contrast, Bill Gates, Warren Buffett, and Oprah Winfrey are examples of wealthy people who are using their wealth in extraordinarily generous and generative ways.

Deepening Spirituality

The aloneness of midlife and the vivid awareness of suffering, evil, and death demand our attention and reflection. It is here that a true religious faith can be the most powerful resource we have. If we've read the philosophers and spiritual masters, we are aware that no one knows the ultimate meaning of life and that life is a complex of inexorable opposites: birth and death, good and evil, happiness and misery. As Carl Jung said:

> We are not even sure that one will prevail against the other, that good will overcome evil...Life is a battleground. It always has been, and always will be; and if it were not so, existence would come to an end.

The complexity and mystery of moral choice and the responsibility of ethical life make it clear that there is no human security. Once we fully understand this we enter the true realm of spirituality and the choice of faith. Faith is a choice—a leap, if you will.

True faith can come only when there is no absolute knowledge and no human security. In experiencing our vulnerability and powerlessness, we are in the arena where true faith is possible. We can fully come to God only with a "broken and contrite heart," as the psalmist says.

THE SECOND CRISIS OF YOUR SECOND CAREER: ENCOUNTERING MORTALITY

Just when I thought I had everything in order, the roof fell in. Life is like that.

I had been experiencing some shortness of breath, which I thought was my childhood asthma acting up. But it got progressively worse, until one day lifting my bag into the overhead compartment on an airplane caused me to feel as though I had just done forty push-ups. On March 9, 1998, I went under the knife for quadruple bypass surgery.

Feeling helpless in the face of coronary artery disease, knowing that my chest had been sawed open and my heart taken out of my body, I could not avoid the realization of my vulnerability. My life seemed so short. I had to ask what seemed like the most essential questions: What is the personal meaning of my life in the face of my inevitable death? Is there really a God? Is there life after death? It forced me to deal with my self-reflections, my regrets, and at times my feelings of despair. I asked God whether my life was over or if there was more life to live, new valleys to explore, new contributions to be made. I became more and more depressed as I groped with these questions.

The signs of aging didn't help my depression. One day I looked at how withered the skin on my legs and arms had become. I had not noticed this before. It seemed like it happened overnight. I saw hair growing out of my ears and my nose. My knees started hurting. I had been a fine athlete, jogging forty miles a week for the last twenty years, and now I found it difficult to walk very far.

The second crisis that occurs during our second career is triggered by our awareness of aging and of the inevitability and imminence of our own death. For me, the second crisis was ushered in by my quadruple bypass heart surgery.

Belonging to Oneself: Ego Integrity Versus Despair

Erik Erikson describes the "ego chill" that comes with this second crisis of your second adult career. (In Erikson's model, it is the eighth stage of the human life cycle.) Ego chill is the imagined experience of your own death, your own naughtness. In the face of that, you have to decide what your life has meant and what you will do with the life you have left. We have to accept and belong to our self. Erikson describes belonging to oneself as ego integrity and views the eighth and last developmental task in life as the achievement of wisdom.

Just like the other adult crises, this eighth crisis is an either/or. Can we own our ego integrity, or will we succumb to despair? If the challenge is resolved well, it can lead to full ethical maturity and wisdom. But it may be the toughest fight of our life. We face a crucial choice: succumb to apathy or some form of obsessive activity or addiction in order to deny the grief we feel about the end of our own life, or find that we can still grow and that we still have something important to offer. Are we willing to accept the role of eldership and do what we can to continue being generative, but most importantly just focus on being a model for others? This last crisis comes down to our presence, who we are, rather than what we still have the power to accomplish. A prime example—the one I set up in the prologue—is Morrie Schwartz. He is certainly a model for the next generation.

In an essay called "Faith and Doubt," the theologian Romano Guardini says this about aging:

> Persons who once seemed indispensable die. One after another disappears—parents, teachers, onetime superiors first, contemporaries next. One has the feeling that a former generation has come to an end and that the following, one's own, is beginning to crumble. Many enterprises one has seen collapse.... One has lived to see the end of trends and fashions and standards of values. Concepts of what is right and fitting that had appeared unshakable and part of existence have lost their validity.... Reality then becomes questionable.... Reality engages the will in what is at the moment to be sought, done, mastered.

Despair

Some people don't seem to accept that they have a new developmental task to deal with. They are bitter, angry, and envious, resenting their past and thinking everyone got the breaks but them. Caught in the jail of their arrogance and anger, they fail to learn what their life experience could teach them. And beneath their bitterness is despair. The man or woman who has internalized despair is bitter. Guardini comments, "Those who despair become addicted to 'transitoriness'; everything is *now*...having their special chair, controlling the conversation, refusing to listen to anyone, demanding to have the last word in any discussion." This addiction to transitoriness is a way to avoid the past or the future, where suffering, death, and "that undiscovered country from which no traveler returns," as Shakespeare put it, puzzle the will.

Guardini adds, "Wisdom comes when the whole comes into view." Once we know that absolute security is an illusion, we need faith in God, whatever you understand the word to mean. And having faith means taking a risk.

Resolution of Depression

I cannot tell anyone else how to deal with this crisis. My friend Thomas Moore, the author of one of the finest books I've ever read, *The Care of the Soul,* sent me the manuscript before the book was published, and what he said there about depression was surprising and helpful to me. Moore suggests that we embrace our depression and go deeply into it. (He is not talking about clear medical conditions such as bipolar disorder, which can be helped by medications, but about the depression that is simply part of living.) Depression is grief taken to the extreme. All of us must grieve. To live well is to grieve well, as life itself is a prolonged farewell.

Moore helped me grasp that there was potential power in my depression. No one understands the full breadth and depth of the mystery of life. Our soul (our true self) has intentions and necessities we do not fully grasp. Depression bubbles up from the depth of the soul. It is a "soul symptom." Embracing this symptom led me to an understanding of the deeper intentions of my true self. My depression was asking me to do something I had never truly done—to look deeply into the *meaning* of my personal life and my personal death. I came to see that my life is unique and unrepeatable. I discovered that everything that has happened to me, everything I have learned along the way, is part of a woven fabric that I am creating and that I am responsible for. All of it is necessary. This realization gave me power because I felt wholeness and reconciliation. Accepting myself and my one and only unique life with unconditional love is the moral achievement of ego integrity.

Ego Integrity and Wisdom

For Erikson, ego integrity means "a new, different love of one's own parents, free of the wish that they should have been different, and an acceptance of the fact that one's life is one's own responsibility." That text resonated in me. I had worked hard to resolve my issues with my parents. As I entered this last developmental crisis both my parents had died. During my soul-searching I came to a complete and unconditional forgiveness of them. I saw them in their own tragic circumstances. My father never had a male figure in his life. He had been totally abandoned by his father. My mother had a very faulty attachment with her mother, who was bedridden the first two years of my mother's life. My mother had my older sister at age eighteen and was shamed by her rigid Catholic family. All in all, I found a deep compassion for my parents and a gratitude for the gift of my life.

The virtue that flows from the resolution of this last life cycle is wisdom. The virtue of wisdom is the fruit of a new and expanded consciousness as the whole comes into view. We know what is important in life and what is not worth worrying about. We are conscious of choosing well in terms of time and energy.

This wisdom is both speculative and practical. Its speculative side offers enlightenment, actualizing the beautiful childlike traits we all carry inside ourselves—playfulness, tolerance, love, curiosity, spontaneity, resilience, and above all faith in God. Its practical side is fully developed prudence, the ability to make the right choice at the right time for the right reason.

THE WATER OF YOUR BELONGING

Slavin and Kriegman comment that the characteristics of the "true self" are "vitality, aliveness, meshing or fit within a relational context." The greatest fruit of wisdom is that as I come to belong to myself I learn who, what, and which ways of living make me most alive.

I once heard an audiotape of the poet David Whyte reading and discussing a poem by Rilke entitled "The Swan." Rilke contrasts the swan on dry land and in the water. Swans walk awkwardly, almost comically, when they are on dry land. But when they enter the water, they move effortlessly and gracefully. They are carried along as if they were one with the water itself.

In our eldership, we can ask ourselves, "What is the water in my life? What is the work that I like to do or the lifestyle that I like to live that simply in the doing gives my life beauty and grace? Who are the people I love to work with? Who are the people with whom I can be myself, who give me a greater sense of who I am? What brings me alive and tells me that I'm home—that this is the place where I belong?"

The water of your life is where you have the most energy and vitality. Your true self—your soul—has moved you toward this water all of your life.

Your true self does not care whether you've lived up to someone else's expectations. What it wants to know is, "Did you love fully and live your own life? Did you belong to yourself?" For myself I would add, "Did you use your God-given freedom? Did you find your way of being a unique incarnation? Have you followed your grand will?"

My true self, my soul, my grand will is where I feel alive, where I have the most energy, and where I seem to belong. I now do the work that brings me alive. I hang out with the people I feel uninhibited with, the people I feel at home with. I want to teach until the day I die. That is my calling.

Part 3

Nurturing the Moral Intelligence of Those in Our Care

INTRODUCTION

EVERY SMALL ACT OF VIRTUE

New opinions are always suspected, and usually opposed, without any other reason but because they are not common.

—John Locke

The renewal of society will come when we can imagine it differently and when we are ready, like artists, to take on the actual work of creating new forms.

—M. C. Richards

All beings are owners of their karma. Whatever volitional actions they do, good or evil, of those they shall become the heir.

—Gotama Buddha

The educator John Holt in his book *How Children Learn* talks about the fallacy of saying things like "I'm learning to play the cello." He points out that if I decide I want to play the cello, I simply begin. Obviously in the beginning I will not play very well. But the important point is, the day I want to play the cello I am playing the cello.

We hold the strange idea that when we begin to learn an art there are two different processes: learning to play the cello and playing the cello. This belief is nonsense, says Holt. We learn to do something by doing it.

Aristotle understood this long ago and applied this insight to the attainment of virtue. He taught that every small act of virtue strengthens our virtuousness. An education that aims at the formation of virtue rests on this simple instruction. Our children, students, religious congregations, athletes, employees, and citizens can only learn *how* to be virtuous by *doing* acts of virtue.

I can't give you a detailed formula for developing the moral intelligence of those in your care. I can tell you that every time they perform an act of kindness, every time they overcome their fear and take a healthy risk, every time they help a friend, they are being virtuous. Encouraging and validating such behavior helps to create a virtuous person. The one thing you can do that will surely impact the people you are responsible to and for is to be a living example of the kind of virtuous person you want them to be.

THE GOOD PERSON AS THE RULE

Aristotle saw the virtuous person "as the rule and measure of human action." In essence, Aristotle said that if you want to know how to be virtuous, go find a virtuous person and watch to see what he does and how he does it.

Unless you are virtuous, your words will be hollow and unconvincing, and even if you are virtuous, those in your care may not necessarily turn out to be virtuous in the exact way you expected. What is virtuous for one person may not be for another. I will never chase gang members down a freeway, as Johnny Pagnini did. But Pagnini will never help a traumatically abused incest survivor work through their pains, as I have done.

Every person's uniqueness—the thing that makes me who I am and you who you are—is a complex mixture of an inner calling and a particular set of outer circumstances. As parents, teachers, ministers, coaches, and bosses, we can be part of the outer environment. But we must remember that everyone has a true self and a personal uniqueness.

MY ANGEL AND YOURS

Some call the urgings of our true self our soul. James Hillman, following Plato, suggests that each of us has been assigned a helper (*daimon* in Greek) that moves us toward our life purpose. Christians call this helper our guardian angel.

I'm personally convinced that some strange force entered my life and caused me to move in a direction that created a radical change, which has taken me to heights I could never have imagined. On December 11, 1965, I was in a locked ward in Austin State Hospital. That was my first moment of grace. On that day, my soul, perhaps pushed by my angel, offered me a moment of intense emotional resolve that led me to stop drinking alcohol. A second encounter with my helper occurred on the highway in Minnesota. I encourage you to consider that a higher power or powers are at work in our lives. It seems right to keep reminding ourselves and those in our care that our lives are more mysterious than anyone can fully comprehend. As a teacher, this reality keeps me from thinking that I can do things that I really can't do, and it softens my overburdening sense of responsibility to do more than I can do.

A unique personal calling is sometimes easier to see in the famous or in the tragic. It is harder to see in the schoolteacher, the book editor, the single mom struggling to raise her children, the plumber, the butcher, the mailman and others whose lives get little press. Sometimes we do not see the ordinary person's extraordinariness until there is a calamity or crisis. Hillman writes, "The outstanding figures make human the general idea that all lives have an exceptional component that has not been accounted for by the usual psychological and biological theories."

It is the utter uniqueness of each human being that makes an absolutist or dogmatic ethics of virtue impossible. Even though I will make some general and specific suggestions for an education that helps develop moral intelligence, no one's moral and ethical life can be reduced to a system.

One evening while watching *Larry King Live,* I heard Paul McCartney, the former Beatle, say that he heard the song "Yesterday" in a dream. He also said that at the time he hardly knew anything about writing or reading music. McCartney's musical angel was at work in his dream. I believe that every one of us has a helper. We may not recognize our helper's interventions, because we may be looking in the wrong places. My moments of grace were very dramatic. That fits my personality. Your and your child's angel may help in less dramatic ways. James Hillman has shown that many extraordinary people grow up in stark conflict with their parents. So don't fall prey to the belief that you are solely responsible for your child's destiny. If you're so disposed, believe in your own unique helper; if you're a believer, trust in God as you understand God.

11

THE INFANT WHO SOOTHED HER SOBBING MOM: THE BUILDING BLOCKS OF EMOTIONAL INTELLIGENCE

It stands to reason that the key skills of emotional intelligence each have critical periods extending over several years in childhood. Each period represents a window for helping that child instill beneficial emotional habits.

—Daniel Goleman

In 1987, I made an instructional videotape on codependency entitled *It's Not My Problem*. During the filming, a young mother started to sob as she described how her cocaine-addicted husband had abandoned her, leaving her penniless with their three-month-old infant. She was holding the infant while she spoke. We were all amazed when the baby began to sob and pat her mother's face in an attempt to soothe her.

The infant clearly seemed to have some understanding that her mother was in distress. But how?

ATTACHMENT, MUTUALITY, AND MORAL INTELLIGENCE

Anyone who has ever looked in on a nursery full of newborn babies knows that when one baby starts to cry, it can trigger crying in all the other babies. This innate capacity for empathy is the foundation for the attachment bond and the first building block of moral intelligence.

For this inborn capacity to develop, however, it is essential that the infant experience a basic trust in a person who provides a secure base. The caretaker need not be the biological mother or father, and there can even be several caretakers, but the *same* people need to be there for the child day in and day out. Every infant needs the feeling that he will not be abandoned. The attachment bond is the result of an intuitive alignment between the brain of the mother (or mothering source) and the brain of the child, a wordless dialogue between right hemisphere and right hemisphere.

The nursing child stares constantly at the mother's face. It is the sight of her face that provides continuity. The mutual gaze of mother and child is the primal scene, the source that sets the affect system in motion. And it is sight that will later motivate the child's desire to reach for animate and inanimate objects and to begin to explore the world.

Figure 11.1 gives you a visual overview of the building blocks of emotional intelligence. It shows that emotional intelligence includes two different but related parts: intrapsychic intelligence, or how we manage our inner emotional life, and interpersonal intelligence, or how we handle our social relationships. Both of these strengths develop in age-appropriate ways. We don't expect a three-year-old to handle the distress of social rejection the same way a ten-year-old could deal with it. But with the exception of the attachment bond, which creates our secure base, I'm not suggesting emotional intelligence always develops in predictable steps. In fact, most of us probably grew into whatever emotional intelligence we have in a more incidental way. I'm simply trying to provide a map for parents and caregivers—and for everyone who feels they have gaps in their own development. This chapter covers the early years, while the last four steps are discussed in chapter 14.

Figure 11.1:
THE BUILDING BLOCKS OF EMOTIONAL INTELLIGENCE

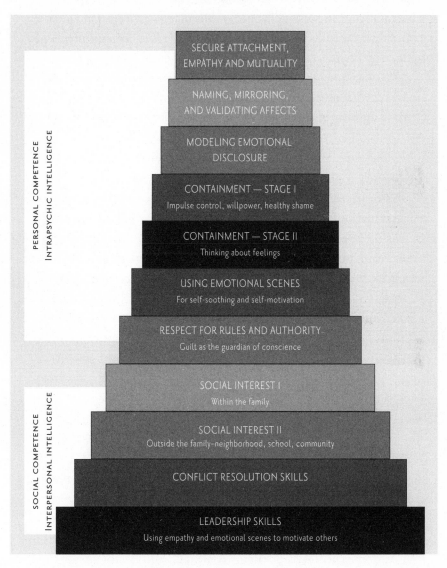

Educating the Emotions

I'd like to emphasize that in starting with the emotions, I'm presenting a radical change in our approach to moral education. I know of no system of ethics that is built on the foundation of emotional and social intelligence. It has taken modern brain science centuries to help us fully understand the primacy of emotional intelligence as the foundation of the life of virtue.

We must educate our emotions for three reasons: (1) our emotions are the primary motivators in our lives; (2) we cannot make choices without the evaluative function of our emotions (or what Aristotle called "affective inclination"); and (3) the last practical judgment that precedes any virtuous act depends on emotional intelligence.

Without our feelings, nothing really matters. I cannot imagine a life where nothing is interesting, enjoyable, or surprising. The nurturing of our affect system is the basis of all subsequent emotional and intellectual growth. The development of our emotional intelligence is clearly our most fundamental education.

My family, as I've told you, thought emotions were weak, and I was chided for having them. When our emotions are shamed, we numb out. And just as people with the kind of brain damage that shuts off their emotions cannot make the simplest choice, those who are numbed out emotionally have trouble choosing. Each time I had an emotion, it was shamed. Soon all my emotions were bound in shame. Shame was no longer just an emotion; it was my identity. You can see the awful moral dilemma that patriarchal cultures of obedience create for their members. A shame-based person is set up to obey an absolute and totalistic system of morality and the leaders who teach such systems. Because such systems demand emotional repression, it's little wonder that some members of totalistic cultures of obedience will blindly follow leaders who instruct them to attack, kill, or torture people who do not believe as they do.

YOUR FIRST LOVE RELATIONSHIP: THE EXPERIENCE OF EMPATHY

When we resonate with another person's positive feelings, it feels good. When a mother is focused on her infant's affect, she is unintentionally swept up into its contagious quality—whether it's distress or joy. And if she purposely imitates her child's facial expression, she will instantly experience the same affect. This imitative and contagious quality of affect is the foundation of empathy, the communicative interchange whereby we learn to share and understand each other's emotions.

Psychiatrist Karl Stern describes how attachment grows from the simplest actions:

> Communication comes first from what mother does, the way she picks [the infant] up and puts him down, how she carries him, feeds and diapers him, bathes him and covers him up. Contact with her body, with her warmth and softness, her nearness, the smell of her and the music she makes with her voice—all these mean everything to [the infant], while words mean nothing.

In this intimate back-and-forth, the mother and baby are responding to each other moment by moment. All future communication is based on this exchange.

Exercise: Gross Body Mirroring

Emotional synchronicity happens in milliseconds, which means that we cannot *not* communicate at the emotional level. However, there are also more conscious ways to deepen empathy. This exercise calls for you to mirror another person's facial expression, breathing patterns, and body posture. With an infant it may be impossible to mirror body posture, but imitating the baby's facial expression and breathing will usually take you into the child's experience. When you're communicating with older children, squat down to their level to mirror them.

As a counselor, I was taught to mirror my clients' body posture, breathing, and facial expressions during my sessions with them. It was amazing how often I could identify and validate their feelings by doing this. Now I understand that my mirror neurons were doing the work; I was simply facilitating them. Try this with others and see if you don't experience their feelings more intensely. The person you are mirroring seldom notices what you are doing because she is absorbed by the content of her own words or of yours. I urge you to use this exercise as a tool of loving connection, not as a gimmick to manipulate someone.

PARENTS' UNRESOLVED NEEDS

To be prepared for parenting, a mother and father need to have addressed their own unresolved dependency needs as far as they are capable of doing. Doing your own family-of-origin grief work and shadow work is great preparation for parenthood, because it will help you not to pass your unconscious wounds on to your baby. Many conscious, dutiful parents pass on their unresolved or suppressed emotional issues to their children, and my intention is not to blame them. However, once we understand the dynamics of covert dysfunctional bonding and "carried feelings," we have a moral obligation to our children to do something about it.

This interaction begins even before birth. The Jungian analyst Marion Woodman writes: "When the mother is not at home in her own body she cannot joyously interact with her unborn child nor triumph in its actual birth." And if the mother lacks the authentic presence I described in chapter 6 as an important part of prudence, the infant will carry her sense of loss or any other unresolved feelings, including shame, anger, and fear. This is baggage a child should not have to deal with.

THE ROOTS OF POLARITY
AND POLARIZATION

If all goes well, the reciprocal feeling between the infant and the mother creates a mutual bond of connectedness, the secure base the infant relies on as he ventures out to explore life. This secure base also forms an optimistic and trusting foundation for further moral development.

One of the first developmental challenges the infant must meet is the achievement of what is called "object constancy." This is so basic to our sense of the world that it's hard to grasp that we had to learn it. What it means is that by about ten months of age, the infant can maintain an internal image of his mother when she leaves the room. He can use that image to soothe himself, and when she reappears, he realizes that the face coming closer to him is the same face that previously vanished through the door.

Recognizing that the mother who comes back is the same mother who leaves, or that big mother (leaning over his crib) is the same as little mother (across the room), extends to an important emotional realization: there is the pleasurable mother (good mother) who is readily available with milk, touching, and holding, and there is also the irritating mother (bad mother) who does not immediately respond to the infant's needs. But "good mother" and "bad mother" are not two separate and polarized objects, as the infant initially experiences them; they are one and the same person.

As a child matures, the polarity of good and bad will also be extended to himself. The child intuitively knows: "Just as my mother is both good and bad, so also I am both good and bad." This intuitive understanding of polarity is the foundation for our later discovery of the virtuous mean of prudence.

If the affective bond is not created and object constancy is not achieved, the child maintains a polarized image of the mother and will have a difficult time experiencing anyone or anything but in a polarized way. People will be all good or all bad, true believers or absolute enemies. This is one of the hallmarks of moral totalism.

To be human is to be both good and bad. We humans are perfectly imperfect. What all forms of moral totalism and religious fundamentalism lack is the polarity that points to the vulnerability of our humanity.

Infants are utterly dependent on their parents, and their parents are their first experience of what seems to them godlike power. The psychiatrist James Masterson called this "the illusion of omnipotence." This illusion is gradually replaced as the child sees the parents' flaws and weaknesses and learns that the parents themselves rely on a higher power. The parents model a belief in something or someone greater than themselves. This gives their child a new sense of security.

RELIGION AND THE VIRTUE OF HOPE

Erik Erikson sees the ego strength of hope emerging out of the first year and a half of life. In order for infants to develop a basic sense of trust, they need to attach and bond to a mothering source and develop empathy and mutuality. This makes attachment, mutuality, and empathy the foundation of hope. All of the rest of the virtues will build on this bedrock of hope.

There is no question in my mind that the best environment for developing hope includes source figures who believe in a higher power and who embrace a moral and/or religious code that offers an optimistic vision of our personal destiny. Each of us needs to feel that our life has meaning and purpose beyond what any limited, finite mind can comprehend.

It also helps greatly if our source figures belong to a community that shares a similar belief system. Belonging to such a community creates a sense of solidarity in the face of the unknown mysteries and immensity of life.

As Erikson writes:

The parental faith which supports the trust emerging in the new-born has throughout history sought its institutional safeguard (and, on occasion, found its greatest enemy) in organized religion. Trust born of care is, in fact, the touchstone of the *actuality* of a given religion. All religions have in common the periodical childlike surrender to a Provider or providers who dispense earthly fortune as well as spiritual health.

MUTUALITY AND THE GOLDEN RULE

When mutuality is truly achieved, it serves as the blueprint for the fundamental rule that every organized religion holds in one form or another, at least for its own members: the Golden Rule.

We can see this mutuality at work from the earliest days of parenting. As the child goes through each developmental stage, the caregiving parent has an opportunity to work through each of his or her own unmet developmental dependency needs. One of the great benefits of marriage and parenting is not that adults produce children but that children produce adults. They are partners at each stage of development. As Erikson points out, caregivers can activate strengths *"appropriate to* [their] *age, stage, and condition,"* related to their own developmental deficits, even as they activate in their children strengths appropriate to their developmental age. When we overreact to something our child is doing at a certain age and stage, this is a real clue that the child is triggering an unmet need we had at the same developmental stage. I had my autonomy and boundary needs shamed and repressed as a toddler, and while my son's autonomy needs were well met in the Montessori environment, I've had lots of trouble handling other people's toddlers. I have been helped and blessed to see my daughter parent my toddler grandchildren in a non-shaming way. Understood in this way, the Golden Rule is at work in the formation of human personality.

NAMING, MIRRORING, AND VALIDATING AFFECTS

We can help children become conscious of their affects by naming or labeling them. As affects are labeled, they become feelings, and since we experience feelings in a context that is internalized as a scene, they become emotions we experience as uniquely our own.

Even before the child learns to speak well—at about three and a half years—it is helpful to say things like, "Oh, you are really mad [sad, scared]" or "You don't like that smell [taste]." The child's absorbent mind will register these labels and use them later.

Another important way we can help our children develop their emotional life is by the kind of mirroring I described above. Looking into their caregiver's eyes is the first and most important way children become aware of having a separate self. When we mirror their facial expressions, especially as they experience their affects, we help them know themselves as separate from us.

Validation involves both labeling and mirroring, but it is a little more sophisticated. Validation is a kind of feedback that fosters self-confidence in the one receiving it. Three-year-old Susie comes to her mother in tears, hardly able to speak. Her five-year-old brother has taken her doll out of her baby buggy and taunted her by throwing the doll onto the ground.

As Susie's mother gets the whole picture, she says, "You were taking your doll for a ride in her baby buggy and your brother Bobby came up and stole your doll and threw her to the ground. You ran in here to tell me about it. I can see and hear that you're crying and I can imagine how sad you feel." (You probably never heard anyone talk like this. But you can learn to do it. It is a skill of emotional intelligence. It takes practice.) Susie's mother ends by asking, "Would you like me to hug and hold you?"

Susie's affect is being named, and the whole scene is being described and validated. In this way, Susie is being helped to connect with the reality of her experience. Why is this so important?

Because parents who believe feelings are weak and irrelevant discount and invalidate their children's feelings. Telling a child she has no reason to feel sad or mad is an invalidation. This is crazy making, for the child or for anyone.

I can remember waking up one night at 3:00 A.M. and feeling scared, lonely, and abandoned. I was about five years old. My parents were having a loud party downstairs. I walked down the stairs and told them I was scared and lonely. My father said, "No, you're not! Look at all the people in the house. How could you be scared and lonely? Go back to bed." I remember going back to bed, thinking, *There must be something wrong with me. I could have sworn I was scared and lonely!* Any child whose feelings are continually discounted and invalidated feels more and more that there must be something wrong with him.

MODELING EMOTIONAL DISCLOSURE

Children learn by imitation. Long before he can speak, a child's absorbent mind is taking in all his parents' behaviors. I remember being startled when I heard my four-and-a-half-year-old son say to one of his friends, "Shit, that's a damn shame." I looked at my wife and said, "Where did he learn that?" She just nodded in my direction. Our children even pick up habits we thought were secrets known only to ourselves. In my book *Family Secrets,* I made it clear that there are really no toxic shame secrets in families. What children do not consciously register, they may act out. I had a male client who was absolutely shocked when he found a stash of pornography in his fourteen-year-old son's closet. This man, an elder in his church, had his own stash of pornographic films and books hidden behind a private lake house. His son knew about his pornography habit at some intuitive level and was already acting out his father's secret at age fourteen.

The power of modeling can work for us when we use it consciously, and one way we can help our children's emotional development is to express our own emotions as fully and clearly as possible. (Of course, this skill is important in marital intimacy and in business relationships as well.) Please note that disclosing your emotions fully and clearly does not include shouting, cursing, or screaming. The more we learn to contain our emotions, the better we can express them.

Emotions are affects embodied in a scene, and skill in using emotional scenes is part of emotional intelligence. Positive emotional scenes are important tools for self-soothing, self-motivating, and motivating others, but negative scenes can be powerful motivators, as well.

For example, expressing anger to his three- and five-year-old sons, Dad might say, "I was tired after a long day's work and when I came home tonight I saw your new skateboards lying in the front yard. I was angry. I've told you how important it is to take care of your skateboards and put them behind the fence. I feel sad that you boys don't listen to me and I'm angry at you."

There's absolutely nothing wrong with parents expressing anger to their children when they *are* angry. Feelings that parents do not express are picked up by their children. In the example above, the father stays focused on the sensory details that he interpreted as carelessness. He is careful to use self-responsible statements such as "I feel sad" and "I'm angry." He does not use "you" messages, adjectives that demean his sons ("irresponsible"), or shaming ("You don't deserve nice new skateboards"). Leaving toys out is, after all, quite common for three-year-olds and is not uncommon for five-year-olds. The father has no need to shame his sons. He is modeling the self-disclosure of his emotions and setting a strong boundary for his sons.

When parents readily express their emotions, their children learn how to express their own. Their children also are clear as to what is going on beneath Mom and Dad's skin.

I frequently wondered what my mother was feeling as I was growing up. She had repressed her own feelings for so long she really didn't know what she felt. I now know she was enraged over the state of her own life. Her rage came out in sickness and my sister, brother, and I carried it throughout our early lives.

FEAR

Children have fear as an innate affect. Some children are more temperamentally fearful than others. Initially there are only a few things that naturally activate fear, such as loud noises and loss of support (although many toddlers love to be tossed into the air and caught). However, most of the fear that curtails and discourages children is taught or acquired.

Educator John Holt describes how his daughter Lisa learned to be afraid of bugs. At first she showed no fear of crawling or flying things. She was curious about them and wanted to pick them up. "One day," Holt writes, "a twelve-year-old friend of her older sister came to visit. Lisa was in the room with the two older girls, when the visitor saw a spider in a corner. She began to scream hysterically, and kept on until they got her out of the room and killed the spider. Since then, Lisa has been afraid of all bugs." Some spiders are dangerous, and a child who lives where there are dangerous species needs to be taught to avoid them. But the twelve-year-old's phobic reaction was disabling—for herself and, by contagion, for Lisa.

Children raised by fearful parents learn to be fearful. My mother and grandmother were survivors of traumatic abuse. They were hypervigilant. I have struggled to develop the virtue of courage. The problem is that early fears are programmed into the nonthinking part of the brain, and the earlier this happens the more magnified our fears seem to be. I cannot remember a day of my childhood when I was not afraid.

Fearful and anxious parents and teachers can destroy young children's courage to learn. They do so by making them afraid of not doing what other people want, of not pleasing adults. They also make them afraid of failing. They often create fear by shaming and threatening physical punishment. And even when they don't create children's fears, they use whatever fears their children already have to manipulate and control them. Cultures of obedience use fear to control their subjects.

Courage and Discernment

In killing their interest and curiosity, we rob children of opportunities to develop their courage. Overcoming natural fears at this stage plants the root of the virtue of courage. *Courage is action in the face of fear.* At the same time, a child needs to learn that some things are dangerous. It is at this exploratory stage that we can learn *fear as a form of discernment.* There are physical dangers in the child's world, such as electrical wall outlets, hot irons, poisonous bathroom cleaners. There are also people and situations that are dangerous. Gavin De Becker wrote a book called *The Gift of Fear.* De Becker heads a security firm that protects celebrities and politicians, and his expertise is to spot dangers that his clients might not be aware of. He teaches discernment.

Healthy fear and risk are the first roots of the virtue of courage. As a child acts courageously, she learns how to deliberate well in situations where a mean must be discovered between healthy exploration and recklessness.

Prudence deals with and presupposes uncertainty, risk, chance, and the unknown. Prudence is being formed each time we choose to take a risk with discerning fear.

CONTAINING FEELINGS

Healthy attachment, parental mirroring, labeling, validating, and modeling disclosure of emotions—these create the basis for emotional intelligence. But we also need to know how to contain our emotions. Aristotle's statement about expressing anger to the right person at the right time for the right reasons and in the right way is a description of containment. Containment is the way we learn to relate to our emotions so they serve us and make us effective in the world, rather than harming ourselves and others. The first stage of containment involves willpower, the mental force we discussed in chapter 3. Exercising willpower is like exercising our muscles to make ourselves stronger.

Containment of emotions develops in two stages. The willpower stage begins during the toddler period, from about eighteen months to the middle of the fourth year. The second stage begins during the development of the left hemisphere of the brain and of the area right beind the eyes called the orbitofrontal cortex. Now the child begins to talk fluently, think more logically, ask "Why?" repeatedly, and make deductions about sensory data.

Stage I: Impulse Control, Willpower, and Healthy Shame

Toddlers are explorers. As great innovative educators such as Steiner and Montessori pointed out, children are constantly learning and seeking to learn. The affect interest is the engine that moves them to learn and grow. Once children have mastered something, it is no longer as interesting to them, and they move on to the next item that strikes their fancy. These interests are not random, but follow the needs of the sensitive periods I outlined in chapter 4.

The child's desires are the first manifestation of the child's *will*. This period of development is often referred to as psychological or second birth because the child is beginning to separate from the parental bond and wants to do things his own way and feel a sense of autonomy.

When a child's needs are getting met, he will not have to enter into many power struggles and tantrums in order to achieve his individuality. The children who chronically create power struggles do so either because they are being projected on by the adults who are overfunctioning for them, their self-esteem has been damaged because too much has been expected of them, or their need for autonomy has been blocked. The most devastating projections come from parents raised in families dominated by cultures of obedience, where the breaking of the child's will is considered an educational goal.

The Toddler's Energy

After a preliminary exploration of the environment, the toddler comes on like a locomotive, touching, tasting, holding, and dropping everything in his wake. Just as toddlers are learning how to control and balance their muscles, they are also learning how to use the power of their will. They are learning how to hold on and let go, and the process is utterly fascinating to them. Think of the first time you learned to ride a bicycle; you wanted to do it over and over again. Discovering the power to hold on and let go occurs during a sensitive period for muscle control with the hands. We could say that toddlers "work out" all day.

The emergence of will is a way children separate and test their limits. During this period, the affect of anger is intensely activated and children begin to say "No," "I won't," and "It's mine." These are statements that establish boundaries. Children act oppositionally at this stage, but they are still attached to their parents.

I saw a little toddler in the airport recently. She was struggling to make her mother let go of her hand. "No hold hands," she said, and then pranced a few steps in front of her mother. Suddenly, realizing she was on her own, separated from her attachment figure, she stopped and looked back to be sure her mother was coming.

Our parents or guardians represent our secure base. As our

life progresses, we gently leave them behind but always keep them in view. Later we find friends, lovers, and spouses as our new attachment figures. We will always need to be cared for and to care for someone special.

Autonomy

From eighteen months to three and a half years, a child needs to develop a sense of autonomy that is balanced by a healthy sense of shame understood as limits. *Autonomy* is a broader term than *willpower*. Saying "No," "I won't," and "It's mine," gives the child the sense "I am me," apart from her earliest identification with her source figure. There are reasonable and safe ways to set up the environment so that children can have what is theirs. They can also be offered numerous choices that allow them to say no. (Instead of saying, "I want you to wear your blue socks today," for example, a mother can hold up two or three suitable pairs and let the child choose.) There are myriad situations where the child's saying no is not a big deal. Just like you and me, our children want to do things their own way. Part of controlling the environment is presenting age-appropriate choices to children.

One of the greatest errors we can make as parents is to do for our children what they can do for themselves. By invalidating their efforts, we cripple them. We deny them the opportunity and the self-esteem that comes from doing something new, something they've never done before.

Anger and Rage

Even the most even-tempered babies can turn into stormy toddlers. It helps to remember that anger is an affect that protects one's personal boundaries. Our anger is our strength. Anger says, "You've stepped on my toes! You've violated my limits!" Or in the case of two-year-olds, "You've stopped me from getting a need met," or "I'm angry because you are setting limits." Some anger is simply testing. Two-year-olds know what they want, but they do not yet know what their limits are. And because they have not learned how to contain their anger—and in fact don't yet have the brain development to do so—they often resort to rage to get their way.

The child's will can be broken by means of corporal punishment, coercion, or shaming, but in the long run this kind of training will backfire, as I will discuss in chapter 13. Impulse control and the ability to delay gratification are a necessary part of moral education, but moral intelligence is destroyed by crushing a child's will. The will is the agent of choice. How can one develop prudence without being able to choose? The will needs to be educated, not destroyed. In fact, the ego strength of willpower is what *enables* us to control our impulses and delay gratification. Without this ego strength, we can easily become weak-willed, willful, or wanton.

Healthy Shame

Developing healthy shame is an essential part of the development of emotional and moral intelligence. Healthy shame is called an "affect auxiliary." It puts limits on the affects of excitement, curiosity, enjoyment, and pleasure. It also keeps us grounded in reality, helping us to know our limits as perfectly imperfect human beings. As I discussed in chapter 2, healthy shame gives us permission to be human. If it is developed well, shame becomes a sense of guilt that can be defined as "moral shame." Without a sense of moral shame, we cannot develop a conscience. Willpower and healthy shame together are the two roots of the virtue of temperance.

The Freedom to Be Virtuous

To love our children we must practice the virtue of love. The goal of love is to empower them. When we hover over them and put ourselves in control, they are robbed of their willpower. Our need for control has to do with our own shame, fears, and insecurities.

When we give up control and refuse to project our wishes or needs on our children, we give them the liberty to be virtuous. As Aristotle asserted about all practical learning, the way we learn to do the things we don't yet know how to do is by doing them. Children often make mistakes and do things wrong, but their mistakes are one of the most powerful ways they learn. Think of your own learning: driving a car, typing, using a computer or the Internet. You learned by making mistakes. But in families that embody the principles of a culture of obedience, the rules of operation are perfectionism, control, criticism, and zero tolerance. Children are punished for mistakes.

Mistakes are an essential part of human experience. An airplane flies in a continual process of deviation and course correction; a .300 hitter in baseball fails more than two out of three times. When I fish, I pick an area and cast my lure from one side to the other. If I get one strike in twelve casts, I'll catch a boatload of fish. The child with a developed sense of will learns what is expected of him and what is beyond his limits. A young child is often defeated, but learns from his defeats.

Temper Tantrums

Parents often dread the temper tantrums of the toddler period. While I don't want to minimize this problem, in many instances it does not have to occur. My own son never had a temper tantrum, nor was he ever a discipline problem. My spouse and I put him in a Montessori school at two and a half, with the clearly defined agreement that if he disliked the school, we would take him out. I realized that, having had my own will broken at an early age, I was starting to treat him the same way I had been treated. I knew it was wrong, so I opted for Montessori.

At the time, I did not know a great deal about the Montessori method, and when I read about Maria Montessori's idea of "normalization," I was quite skeptical. Those of us who had our wills broken at an early age have a hard time being around toddlers. It is difficult for us to believe what can happen when children are allowed to function in an environment that is suited to their inborn powers and predispositions. Montessori herself was amazed at "their feeling for order, the choice of tasks which appeared to correspond to their inner needs, their indifference to rewards and punishment, their understanding and love of silence, their sense of dignity, the spontaneous discipline."

Yet I saw this happen with my child. As I wrote in chapter 4, I became convinced that the features of a normalized child are constant, universal tendencies—they are the "natural laws" that should form the basis of education.

Dealing with a Tantrum

If your child does have a tantrum, you can respond in a way that helps him learn containment. Pick the child up and take him to the most private place you can find. Hold him tightly against your chest, make as much eye contact as possible and speak in a firm, unwavering voice. Tell the child that his behavior is unacceptable and that you expect him to calm down. If he continues, repeat this statement several times. You can tell him that a consequence or time-out will be decided later, if you like. But do not threaten, bargain, cajole, or offer any reward for stopping the tantrum. This firm holding communicates that you are in charge. Keeping your voice firm and consistent makes it clear that you mean business.

In some cases, it's helpful to distinguish between a manipulative tantrum and a falling-apart tantrum, where an exhausted or frightened child really doesn't have the resources to pull himself together. In the latter case, imposing consequences or a time-out later is likely to be ineffective. The holding itself provides a needed time-out. The parent simply has to be the "container" until the child is able to contain himself.

Environment as Boundary

Children this age need limits on doing things their own way, but the environment is a much more effective limit than power struggles with parents. We cannot develop willpower and temperance without external boundaries. Parental discipline provides these boundaries and guidelines. Our word *discipline* comes from the Latin meaning "to learn." It's primary meaning is not punishment as many people believe.

Educator John Holt suggests that parents of children in the exploratory stage (eight months to three years) keep within the toddler's reach only objects that are cheap and durable—we shouldn't have to worry if the child breaks them. He suggests that ordinary household objects make good presents—an eggbeater, a saucepan, a flashlight. Children can also learn the right way to handle objects. Montessori showed that very little children could easily be taught to take care of things and move them without breaking them.

What we want to do is encourage the child's curiosity and confidence. This is how the virtue of courage develops.

In *The Secret of Childhood,* Montessori wrote, "The environment must be a living one, arranged by an adult who is prepared for his mission. It is in this that our conception differs both from that of the world, in which the adult does everything for the child, and from the passive environment in which the adult abandons the child to himself."

In the Montessori planned environment, children regularly exert their will by choosing from a wide variety of goal-directed activities and materials. Children select objects that interest them and perform a task with that object over and over again. They are self-directed and unencumbered by the distraction and interference of ordinary adult teaching. Such individual liberty allows a child to develop the power of decision making as a routine aspect of their daily activity. I know of no better preparation for the habituated appetite that is essential to the wise choosing, which itself is central to the virtue of prudence.

Montessori believed that when a child's disruptive behaviors continue for an extended period, it is either because of the caretaker's unresolved issues or because the child is trying to tell us that some great need of hers is not being met. Often a child's reaction is disruptive because she is fighting for her life. Montessori found that when the environment was changed so that everything was suitable to the child's age and growth and obstacles to the child's development were removed, the disruptive behavior disappeared.

As amazing as it seems, touch, taste, and exploration are absolutely essential for the development of intelligence in general and moral intelligence in particular. Without objects to touch and hold, the neurological structures of perceiving and thinking cannot develop. Touching and holding are also the root experiences of caring, nurturing, and compassion. Moral virtue is being formed in this second sensitive period of human unfolding. Kind words and gentle touches have their roots in this earliest phase of life.

Stage 2: Thinking About Feelings

From age three and a half to seven, the child is gradually learning to contain his emotions. Containing emotions depends on our ability to recognize and think about an emotion before impulsively acting on it. In chapter 9, I described a remedial process for reducing reactions and moving to proaction. We would not have to worry about remedial work if we had learned to contain our emotions as children. The impulse control I spoke of earlier is the basic foundation for containment.

Mature containment is an intrapsychic process in which emotion, a right-brain, holistic form of knowing, is differentiated from the more linear, logical thinking of the left brain. It is the product of both sides of our brain working in unison, and it cannot occur until the left hemisphere of the brain comes online, beginning between ages two and three and continuing into early adulthood.

What does it mean to reflect on a feeling before responding to it? Let's take anger as an example. Many people have trouble containing anger primarily because it has been so forbidden and punished by rigid parenting based on blind obedience. When anger is forbidden, it does not go away. It can reappear as passive-aggressive behavior—as when we "forget" to do something very important to the person we're angry with or "accidentally" destroy something that person values. A passive-aggressive person may also use malicious gossip as a release of anger. Some people store up their anger and blow up when they have enough hurts or affronts to feel justified at being angry.

It is not just repressed anger that comes out in a disguised way. All repressed feelings are stored as repressed energy. When the person carrying the stored emotion (say, sadness) reaches a threshold, he "loses it," meaning that the emotion overtakes him; it has him, he doesn't have it. People say things like, "I don't know what came over me today, but I started crying uncontrollably when my coworker told me she was going to divorce her husband." This person had a lot of repressed sadness and her friend's announcement of her divorce triggered it.

Containment allows a person to experience emotion in a way that allows the left brain (the logical thinking brain) to be involved. Containment is a prerequisite for healthy decision making. We cannot deliberate objectively on the alternatives that surround a prospective choice if we are flooded with undifferentiated feelings.

Instead of scolding children, spanking them, or shaming their feelings, parents and caregivers can teach children how to contain their feelings, both by modeling containment themselves and by using time-outs to encourage their children to think about their feelings.

The Time-Out

I first experienced time-outs when my seven-months-pregnant daughter modeled them with my grandson, who was four and a half at the time and in perpetual motion. She visited me for four days one summer, and my grandson wore me out in about three hours every day. I was ready to get away and be quiet. But I stuck it out and was truly amazed at how my daughter handled things. I never once wanted to interfere (quite unusual for an overfunctioning caretaker type).

Here's what happened: My wife and I have a baby rabbit named Oreo. My grandson loved to hold the rabbit, but when Oreo was put down, she began hopping and my grandson couldn't help getting excited and chasing her, which posed some danger to the rabbit. During the course of the rabbit chase he was given two firm time-outs: once for being slightly out of control, and the second for saying something angrily to his mom when she told him to slow down.

When my grandson sassed my daughter, she spoke firmly but without yelling. She simply said, "That hurt my feelings. You take a time-out, think about it, and apologize." After about a minute, an almost inaudible apology came out. This was not acceptable to my daughter. She had him continue the time-out. After another 60 seconds, a strong apology came forth, and my grandson was off and playing.

My daughter and son-in-law have continued to use the time-out quite effectively as my grandson has grown older. It is a real joy to watch. My grandson has had serious medical problems since birth, and early on I feared he would be overprotected and indulged, but that has not been the case at all.

The time-out works in two ways. First, it is a time (60 seconds plus) for a child to quiet down and gain control. The purpose is to learn impulse control and to break up a negative or escalating behavior pattern. It gets the child's attention. It is best to have the child go to another room. The second purpose of the time-out is to teach the essential skill of emotional containment. In the years from about three and a half to seven, the child acquires the basic brain ability to think about feelings and to put some brakes on impulsiveness. But this skill is developed only by repeated practice. It also depends on feelings having been labeled and disclosed in a good-enough attachment bond.

My daughter modeled contained anger when she told my grandson he had hurt her feelings and that she wanted an apology. She never shamed him. She stayed within her own skin, saying, "When you speak like that to me and stick out your tongue, I feel hurt and angry and I want an apology." My grandson can learn to contain and express his anger by imitating my daughter's modeling. Our anger is the affect that allows us to set limits in relation to others; it is a boundary that allows us to protect ourselves. It is also the passionate fuel we use to fight for change and address wrongdoings.

Validation and Containment

A parent can also talk a child through an emotion by first mirroring or validating it and then by making thoughtful suggestions. Consider the following scenario with my friend David and his son Tom.

Playing basketball in his driveway with three older friends, nine-year-old Tommy is shoved, falls on the cement, and skins his knee. Tommy rushes into the house to get his baseball bat so he can hit the guy who shoved him. Tommy's father intercepts him and tells him to sit down. The father speaks in a firm voice, asking Tommy to talk about what happened. As Tommy speaks, his father repeats the story and mirrors the tone of Tommy's voice, the speed at which he is talking, and even pretends that he's clenching a baseball bat in the same way Tommy is. He says, "I can see and hear how angry you are." His father is mirroring and validating Tommy's anger—at this point without any judgment. Slowly, as his emotional state is validated, Tommy starts to calm down. This may take five minutes or more.

The father then suggests that he and Tommy *think* about

choices he has other than hitting his friend with the baseball bat. Finally Tommy decides he still wants to play and that he will tell his friend how angry he felt about being shoved. If the friend does it again, Tommy will tell him to go home.

Tommy's feelings have been validated, he has thought about what happened, and he has decided on a plan of action. His father acted as a facilitator in helping Tommy contain his feelings.

Many of you may think the scene I've described is unrealistic. I respectfully suggest this may be because your own intense emotions were ignored, shamed, or punished, and no one modeled this kind of response.

USING EMOTIONAL SCENES FOR SELF-SOOTHING AND SELF-MOTIVATION

Infants gradually internalize their mothering sources' voice, touch, holding, and nurturing as a way of self-soothing. As older children accumulate positive experiences, they can also use these experiences—literally scenes of pleasure, achievement, and success—as a more sophisticated way of self-soothing.

Parents who validate their children's feelings help them to build this internal wealth of experiences that serve as a reservoir of self-soothing resources. They can also help children access these memories when they face a setback or other hurtful experiences. Knowing how to soothe yourself is an important element of emotional intelligence.

For example, on Easter Sunday, five-year-old Belinda runs into the living room where her parents are seated. Belinda is in great distress. She has smeared chocolate on her new Easter dress. Her mother gently holds her shoulders and asks Belinda what happened. Bit by bit, Belinda sobs out that she was at the neighborhood Easter egg hunt with Aunt Barbara and found a chocolate egg. When she started to eat it, it melted on her hands and got all over her dress.

Her mom validates Belinda's experience, beginning with sensory data. "I see you crying and having a tough time talking and breathing and you are looking down at the ground." Then she says, "I can imagine how sad you are, and you seem to feel some shame. Would you like a cuddle?"

Once Belinda's distress has subsided, Mom says, "Remember the red dress and shoes you wore over to Grandma and Grandpa's house last Christmas?" When Belinda nods, Mom can ask her to describe how pretty the dress was and to remember all the nice things her grandparents said about how beautiful she looked. Belinda might even be encouraged to go and look at the dress in the closet.

Many parents use future scenes like going to the ice cream store or toy store to change their distressed child's affect. Future scenes can be motivating and soothing, but I prefer to use scenes from the past. This teaches the child how to nourish herself with a positive experience she's already had.

Growing up in an environment where emotions are shamed precludes learning emotionally intelligent ways to self-soothe. I had many clients who told me they used self-sex from early in their childhood as a way to deal with their chaotic dysfunctional families. Many other addictions, including eating, drinking, drugging, and sexing, are dysfunctional ways to get self-soothing. Caregivers can offer their children a different way.

Emotional scenes can also be used for self-motivation. If I think of something I want to do, I can scan my past for times when I did something similar or tried something I had never done before.

Let's say a young girl wants to try out for a part in a school play. She's nervous, but then she remembers the time she jumped into the swimming pool or the first time she rode her bicycle alone. Both those memories help her to overcome her fear of trying out for the play.

Good emotional experiences provide a foundation for achievement orientation and goal seeking. If we support our children through their inevitable bad emotional experiences, those of failure and disappointment, they will develop resilience and adaptability. A lot of parents today expend huge amounts of energy trying to make sure their children never fail, thinking that will increase their self-esteem. But being able to pick yourself up again is the skill that really counts.

In addition to their caregiver's modeling and their actual experiences of success and failure, youngsters learn how to motivate themselves by reading, watching TV, and seeing movies about moral role models. These models aren't always human beings. *The Little Engine That Could* had a profound influence on me as a child! Remember how the engine kept repeating, "I think I can, I think I can," until he got over the mountain so the children could have toys for Christmas? The child passes through a period of symbolic play, often imitating his parents or his favorite TV characters. Out of these experiences and with the later development of competence and task completion in school, a child will develop a sense of purpose. Many a person winds up doing or being what he has envisioned in his childhood.

RESPECT FOR RULES AND AUTHORITY FIGURES: DEVELOPING GUILT AS THE GUARDIAN OF CONSCIENCE

An essential part of emotional intelligence is respect for law and order and respect for our fellow human beings. The respect for rules and authority begins as the child internalizes the dos and don'ts of polite behavior and is taught manners. Parents who treat their children with respect and who model good manners create the best environment for children to learn these lessons.

During the preschool period, children see rules as absolute and rigid. If development is arrested at this stage, the virtue of obedience can become a totalistic moral taskmaster. One psychologist calls this period "moral realism," because the rules seem to be independent of any context, outside the person, and unchangeable. Understanding moral realism should make caretakers careful to mollify the intensity of their enforcement of rules. Burning a child's finger with a lighted match to show what the fires of hell feel like, as many people told me had been done to them, is a way to raise torturers, not people who respect the rules. For a child, good-enough respect for the rules is the root of the virtue of obedience.

Validating Guidance as Discipline

We don't have to argue with seven- or eight-year olds about things they can't understand, but we can be respectful of them. Beginning at age seven, validating guidance is based on respect and sincere listening. We can listen to those in our care, and in areas where absolute boundaries are not necessary we can be willing to discuss things with them and even compromise. In his book *The Person,* psychiatrist Theodore Lidz writes, "Rigid and arbitrary parents and teachers foster fixation at the earlier levels of moral intelligence." Fixation at this level creates a form of moral retardation that distorts the development of a fully formed conscience. I'll discuss this further in chapter 12.

Guilt

Once children have internalized rules and prohibitions, they feel guilt when they violate them. Guilt is a healthy expression of the emotion of shame experienced in a moral context. We all need a sense of guilt as a guardian of conscience. Guilt moves us to make amends; it reminds us that breaking the rules does not bring joy. Guilt also helps habituate our appetite in the direction of right desire.

However, excessive rigidity and severe and austere rules create a neurotic sense of guilt. With this kind of guilt a person feels that she is always at fault, that whatever she does is not okay. Unhealthy guilt is the kind of guilt that cultures of obedience foster. Healthy guilt is "morality shame." Toxic guilt forms the feeling of "immorality shame."

In the following chapter, which is on the development of conscience, I will characterize this early period of emotional and moral development as the morality of constraint. It is the raw foundational stage in developing moral intelligence. But it is a stage that must be transcended if one is to become ethically mature. A moral life based on obedience to external rules is a base minimum. It requires no critical moral intelligence and cannot foster the internal strengths that make up virtues.

12

COMMITTING ADULTERY AT AGE EIGHT: HOW CONSCIENCE IS FORMED

[Children need]...a moral education which subtly, and by implication only, conveys to [them] the advantages of moral behavior, not through abstract ethical concepts, but through that which seems tangibly right and therefore meaningful to [them].
—Bruno Bettelheim

Children go through a period of moral realism which is the tendency to regard duty as independent of the mind, as imposing itself regardless of the circumstances in which the individual finds himself.
—Jean Piaget

There is no witness so dreadful, no accuser so terrible, as the conscience that dwells in the heart of every human being.
—Polybius

When I was seven years old, I was introduced to the sacrament of penance. In the Catholic Church, penance is based on the belief that a duly ordained priest, as the representative of Jesus Christ, has the power to forgive sins. A person goes to confession and confesses his sins; the priest then gives a penance, which usually involves saying some prescribed prayers. Children are not believed to be capable of serious sin before the age of seven, which is why the sacrament is introduced then.

Since the time of the Civil Code of Justinian, seven has been considered the age of reason. However, in light of our current understanding of brain development, the notion that reaching age seven makes a child capable of grievous sin and of serious moral responsibility has been radically challenged. No one believes anymore that a seven-year-old is fully responsible for behavior that would send him or her to eternal damnation.

My own experience with confession was proof that I didn't have the foggiest notion about much of the moral stuff that was being taught to me. In fact, I never knew what to confess, and I often made up things, since in Catholic school we were required to go to confession once a week.

One day I began the routine opening as prescribed: "Bless me, Father, for I have sinned." Then I said, "I committed adultery twenty-two times!" There was a long pause, after which the priest opened the screen of the confessional window (something they never did). He looked stunned and stared at me (which they also never did). After some questioning, he discovered that I thought adultery meant sassing or talking back to an adult. Since I had never confessed it, I thought I would give it a try.

My point here is not about Catholic religious practice; it's about mental development and our comprehension of the meaning of words and concepts at different stages. Clearly I had an active conscience—as well as a vivid imagination—at age eight. But how could it guide my behavior? How could I learn to apply the concepts I was being taught to the unique situations that would face me? How could I make genuine moral choices?

Knowing how to make good moral choices depends on having an informed and mature conscience. Chapter 11 focused on the early developmental stages that underlie emotional intelligence and moral intelligence. This chapter is about the thinking and reasoning that go into forming a good conscience.

INNATE CONSCIENCE

Robert Coles tells a story from the early days of school integration and civil rights. It's about a fourteen-year-old high school boy who was highly prejudiced, from a rough background, not very well read, a poor student—what we southerners call a "redneck." The boy wanted no part of school desegregation.

One day, as the boy walked down the hall, he saw that a group of white students had cornered one of the few African American males in the school. "You dirty nigger," they kept calling him. The fourteen-year-old was physically big. Suddenly he went over to the group and said, "Hey, cut it out," and the group stopped. When Coles asked him why he had done what he did, he answered, "Something in me just drew the line." Over the following year, the white boy befriended the African American boy. This experience changed his whole outlook on segregation.

What made this fourteen-year-old draw the line despite his conscious belief in segregation? I would describe his behavior as the result of the voice of his innate internal conscience. This innate predisposition may develop with knowledge and experience to become a more extensive boundary that will cry out or take action in the face of wrongdoing. Or it may be driven underground by the forces of social convention, repression, developmental defects, toxic shame, and the fear of not obeying a set of rigid, totalistic beliefs.

The ancients called the innate voice of conscience *synderesis,* which means roughly that human beings have an inborn sense that there is a good that is desirable and an evil that is undesirable. Wherever and whenever human beings have existed, historians and anthropologists have found evidence that they distinguished between good and bad behavior. Clinical data show that this sense emerges very early in life. It is not uncommon for a two- or three-year-old girl, suspected of being a victim of incest, who when questioned about it responds with projectile vomiting. She has no words or understanding to express what has been done to her. She simply knows it's wrong at the core of her being. She literally can't stomach it, and the affect of disgust takes over.

Developing the Innate Voice

Figure 12.1 gives you a rough outline of how the innate voice of conscience develops when it is nurtured by the other sources of moral intelligence I discussed in chapter 5.

Mutuality and trust are the foundation of empathic caring, which is the foundation for morality and the golden rule.

Early on, our affects of curiosity, interest, enjoyment, and pleasure are kept in balance by the affect of natural shame. Shame keeps us grounded in our finite limits, letting us know that we can and will make mistakes. As we develop autonomy and willpower, our choices need to be kept in check by shame.

Later, we develop a sense of guilt, which is the guardian of our conscience. Guilt first appears in relation to the internalized voices of our source figures. When our sense of guilt is fully developed, it becomes moral shame.

In the beginning, our moral shame is raw and somewhat unmerciful, a kind of external conscience. Our parents' relationship, their intimacy, their moral modeling, and their unified voices are the most important elements in the formation of external conscience. External conscience governs a morality of constraint. The psychologist Jean Piaget calls this stage "moral realism": "the tendency ... to regard duty ... [as] independent of the mind, as imposing itself regardless of the circumstances in which the individual finds himself." Children seem to regard rules and laws as autonomous and unwavering judges that exist completely outside of them.

As children's minds develop, they slowly learn to think more logically. At first the range of their logic is concrete rather than abstract. An important milestone is reached when school-age children begin to understand the intentions that initiate behavior. This ability softens their external conscience and expands their

Figure 12.1: STAGES IN THE FORMATION OF CONSCIENCE

POSITIVE MOTIVATION	STAGE	SAFEGUARDING AFFECTS AND VIRTUES
Kinship with all beings	Mature ethical sensibility guided by love and universal ethical principles	Love
Loyalty to your group: concern for common good	Respect for laws and the rights of others	Guilt as "morality shame"; care and justice
Acceptance by others; fairness	Morality of cooperation	Guilt as "morality shame"; care
Self-benefit; obey authority; rules of purity	Moral realism — following the rules rigidly	Guilt as "immorality shame"; care
Avoid punishment; win approval; harm no one	Manners and boundaries	Shame as embarrassment
Inborn drive to connect	Empathic mutuality founded on secure attachment, trust, and hope	Shame as shyness

sense of empathy, ushering in a morality of cooperation. Interacting with teachers and other children at school and in the neighborhood also lessens a child's egocentricity and helps him cooperate, share, and play fair with others.

Adolescence is heralded not only by an awakened sex drive but also by a new capacity for self-reflection, critical reasoning, and social interest. This period marks the beginning of a transition from a morality of cooperation to a more internalized morality that may ultimately grow into full ethical sensitivity. As the frontal lobes of the brain mature, the young person can view the future in a new way. He starts to develop foresight, a critical component of the virtue of prudence. The morality of constraint and the morality of cooperation are synthesized into an internalized conscience that becomes the foundation for the virtues of love and justice.

Types of Conscience

To develop a fully functioning virtue of prudence, innate conscience is not enough. One needs an *informed* conscience, by which I mean that a person has studied, questioned, and sought help from moral and spiritual mentors.

Even with such a sincere effort, however, a person's conscience can still have erroneous elements in it. (See Figure 12.2.) Our ancestors' honest belief in slavery is one example. Spanking children is another. Someone with a rigid conscience can be just but unmerciful or a person can have a scrupulous conscience that stems from fear of punishment and an obsessive-compulsive personality.

I was once assigned to assist a priest who had a scrupulous conscience. In the Catholic Mass, before the communion service the priest must consecrate the bread and wine in order to transform them into the body and blood of Christ. At the moment of consecration, the priest says certain brief Latin phrases which mean, "This is my body, this is my blood." The priests are instructed to pronounce every syllable slowly. Slowly is one thing. But the priest I assisted would sometimes take as long as thirty minutes to say these sentences. He had a scrupulous conscience.

A person may know the dictates of his conscience but be too

Figure 12.2: TYPES OF CONSCIENCE

CONSCIENCE CAN BE:	AS SHAPED BY:
Informed	Education, good moral examples, experience, moral imagination
Rigid	A concern with the letter of the law, justice without mercy
Scrupulous	An obsessive need to follow the law perfectly
Erroneous	Arrested cognitive development, cultlike indoctrination
Lax	Laziness, conformism, lack of curiosity, disinterest in truth
Dead	Failure to develop an internal sense of shame or guilt

lax or lazy to carry out what it demands. This is often the case with people who have studied about goodness and virtue but rarely have practiced being virtuous. These people have not learned to direct their will toward the good. Those who have been raised in cultures of obedience most often obey rules out of duty, obligation, and fear, but not out of an appetite for the good.

People Without a Conscience

Earlier I described what I called "affectional blindness." People who are termed "psychopathic" or "sociopathic" seem to have no shame, no guilt, and no conscience in relation to others. These people are mysterious. We know they have the innate affect of shame, but it doesn't seem to develop into moral shame or into the guilt that safeguards conscience. Nor do they develop empathy. I did several shows on *The Bradshaw Difference* in which I invited experts to discuss the origins of psychopathic or sociopathic behavior.

On one of these shows, which I titled "Raising Cain 'n' Abel," we interviewed parents who had waited years to adopt a child. Then they got a call that a three-year-old boy was available, but if they wanted him, they would be required to take his seven-year-old half brother as well. (The boys had the same father but different mothers.) The couple agreed, but during the first week the boys were in their home, the older boy tried to kill his younger brother. The parents grappled with this situation for several years before they admitted defeat and decided to send the older boy back to the adoption agency. It emerged that he had been raised by a crack-addicted prostitute mother who violated him sexually during his early childhood. While living with his adopting parents, he had several outbursts of violence at school, and one of his school counselors suggested that he had an antisocial personality disorder. At the adoption agency, this evaluation was supported by two different psychiatrists.

I discussed psychopathology or antisocial personality disorder at the beginning of chapter 3. There I mentioned the work of Jonathan Pincus, who concluded that more than 150 murderers he studied had evidence of both traumatic childhood abuse and neurological disturbance. There is still some question about how these two factors interact. There is no doubt that childhood abuse changes the brain and that some people seem to be born with neurological defects.

CONSCIENCE AND REASON

In the rest of this chapter, I will focus on the relationship between the normal developmental stages of human reasoning and the development of conscience and moral judgment. Without an understanding of how moral reasoning develops, we will fail to understand that many behaviors judged as morally bad are rooted in the normal limitations of children and adolescents' minds. Knowing how reasoning develops gives caretakers more realistic expectations, but it also gives us more effective ways to support the moral development of those in our care. Children are often expected to understand moral concepts that are simply beyond their mental capacities. We can, however, challenge them in ways that expand their moral understanding.

Uncertainty over the Effects of Moral Education

Much of the modern research on how conscience and moral judgment develop was motivated by the findings of two psychologists, Hugh Hartshorne and Mark May, who conducted a series of studies of moral education at the University of Chicago between 1928 and 1938. Their overarching question was whether existing approaches to moral education were achieving their goal, as measured by the prevalence of stealing, cheating, and lying. How effective were moral education programs in the home, schools, clubs (such as the Boy Scouts), and church groups of the time? In every study they arrived at the same conclusions:

- There is very little relationship between character training and actual moral behavior.
- Moral behavior is not consistent in individuals from one situation to another. A person who doesn't cheat in one situation may cheat in another.

- There is not necessarily a relationship between what people say about morality and the way they act. People who expressed great disapproval of stealing and cheating may actually steal and cheat as much as everyone else. Moreover, cheating is normally distributed around a moderate level—that is to say, nearly everyone cheats a little.

At the time of Hartshorne and May's study, the goal of most moral education was to teach respect for moral rules, so that they became the principles guiding behavior and decision making. The means of accomplishing this goal was to teach strict obedience: lecturing about these virtues, rewarding their practice, and punishing their omission. The most typical punishments were shaming and spanking. Hartshorne and May concluded that this type of moral education differed little from teaching the rules of table manners and social etiquette. It clearly did not have a consistent effect on moral behavior.

One of the most important consequences of Hartshorne and May's work was that it was a major stimulus for the research of Jean Piaget and Lawrence Kohlberg, who have attempted to give us detailed working models of the stages of moral development. In what follows, I'll briefly introduce you to their work, as well as to the critique of their work by one of Kohlberg's most prominent students, Carol Gilligan.

JEAN PIAGET

Jean Piaget was codirector of the Institute of Educational Science at Geneva, Switzerland, and a professor of experimental psychology at the University of Geneva when he attempted to grapple with Hartshorne and May's conclusions. Piaget was interested in how children formed moral judgments as their minds matured. He found that moral behavior could not be directly equated with intellectual development, because a person who feels at risk in a situation where punishment is possible might con his way out of it. Piaget wrote, "An intelligent scamp would perhaps give better answers than a slow-witted but really goodhearted little boy."

Piaget believed that the foundation of morality was mutuality. "Apart from our relations to other people," he once wrote, "there can be no moral necessity." Nevertheless, his major focus was on cognitive development and how it shapes moral judgment. He showed relatively little concern for the importance of affect (emotion) and appetite (will).

Neither Piaget, nor later Kohlberg, measured moral behavior itself. Instead, they were concerned with the reasons a person gives for what she is doing. For example, a mature adult and a young child might both resist stealing an apple, and they would both probably say that stealing an apple is wrong. How can we tell the difference in their moral maturity? For Piaget and Kohlberg, the only way to show the difference is to question them about *why* it is wrong to steal an apple. While this type of investigation is useful, it does not tell us what the person with greater moral maturity actually *does*. The adult may give more mature reasons for not stealing an apple, but without the virtue of honesty, she might go ahead and steal it anyway.

In considering the development of logical reasoning, Piaget concluded that while there is a pattern of sequential development, probably consistent with brain maturation, many other factors can also come into play. Each stage of brain maturity requires challenge, stimulation, healthy relationships, and a proper environment for development. A person's moral reasoning can be retarded or arrested at any stage of development. Fanatical terrorists exhibit a conscience that is arrested at the rigid stage of moral realism and a morality of constraint. We know that most of them have emerged from a closed environment subject to the will and authority of one leader. In such a context, there is no challenge, no stimulation, and no equal relationships.

Emerging from Mental Egocentrism

Child psychologist David Elkind, the former chairman of the Eliot-Pearson Department of Child Development at Tufts University, is considered by many to be the best at making Piaget's very clinical and difficult writings understandable to the nonclinician. Elkind has helped me to clarify Piaget's model by tracing the child's emergence from what he calls "mental egocentrism." Mental egocentrism is a form of subjective distortion of reasoning that continues until the brain is fully mature in late adolescence. It explains certain predictable errors and peculiarities in the moral judgment of children and adolescents. In what follows, I'll outline eight examples of this immature moral judgment that are normal during the preschool and school-age periods. I'll expand on these developmental limits when I discuss adolescence.

I. Separating Self from the External World

During the first two years of life, our major mental task is what Elkind calls the "conquest of the object." When a four- or five-month-old is playing with a toy that then disappears behind another toy, so that it is out of sight but still within reach, the infant stops looking for it. The child behaves as if the toy exists only as long as she is perceiving it. The common game of peek-a-boo is another example. For the infant, out of sight is out of mind, and each reappearance of Mom or Dad's face induces the same surprise and delight. Repeat the toy experiment toward the end of the child's first year, however, and the child will begin to look for the toy. She now understands that the object has an independent existence, and she can hold the object in memory when it is not present to her senses. As I noted in chapter 11, this milestone is also called "object constancy." With its achievement, the child takes the first step away from mental egocentrism.

Severely abused or neglected infants can develop a narcissistic disorder that distorts their ability to separate themselves from anyone or anything else. Everything is about them because there is nothing apart from them. Listening to the rantings of Charles Manson gives one the impression that nothing exists apart from him. Manson was violated sexually at this stage of development.

Object constancy is the beginning of an inner life. Since virtues are inner strengths, object constancy is a foundation for developing virtue.

2. The Power of Names and "Bad Words"

During the preschool years, the child begins to think in symbolic ways. According to Elkind, the child's symbolizing ability is evidenced by rapid growth in the acquisition and utilization of language; the appearance of symbolic play; and the first reports of dreams.

However, with these achievements the child is ensnared in a new egocentrism. Elkind says that children at this stage believe a name inheres in things, and an object can't have more than one name.

Names have power for small children. Preschoolers and children in the early grades like to call their playmates or siblings names. Names accompanied by "bad word" adjectival modifiers give a child a sense of magical power, especially because of their parents' reactions. Parents certainly need to give time-outs or use consequences for a foul-mouthed child, but it should be done without shaming. The less emotional power parents allow bad words or name-calling to have, the better.

3. Magical Thinking

Words and phrases have magical powers. Parents often support this by saying, "What's the magic word?" when they want a child to say "thank you" or "please." One of the most rewarded magical words is "try." Kids often learn that if they say "I tried," then they don't have to actually do it (like clean up a mess they made).

A second form of egocentric magical thinking is preschoolers' belief that Tigger and Winnie the Pooh (or the family dog) think, feel, and are motivated in the exact same way that they think, feel, and are motivated.

The magical thinking of preschoolers offers source figures an excellent opportunity to engage their imagination in stories and movies that teach a moral lesson. Early childhood is a time for nurturing moral imagination. But when it comes to religious matters, prudent education needs to avoid notions such as bodies burning for eternity in the fires of hell. There are lots of poems and stories we can use to nurture our children's moral imagination.

4. The Failure to Grasp Intention

Preschool children's mental egocentrism includes an inability to imagine the minds of others or to make moral judgments apart from what they can see. Piaget discovered this by telling children stories and asking them questions. One child accidentally breaks fifteen dishes, while another accidentally breaks two. Who should be punished the most? Most preschoolers will say, "The one who broke fifteen dishes."

Or, consider the following two examples: (1) There was a little boy named Julian. His father had gone out and Julian thought it would be fun to play with his father's inkwell. When he played with the pen, it leaked and made a tiny blotch on the tablecloth. (2) A boy named Augustus noticed that his father's inkwell was empty. One day, when his father was away, he decided to fill the inkwell in order to please his father. But while he was opening the ink bottle, he spilled a big blotch of ink on the tablecloth. In Piaget's studies, prior to the age of seven or eight, the children tended to judge guilt on the basis of material damage rather than intention. They asserted that the naughtier child was Augustus, because he made a larger blotch.

5. Harsh Rules and Punishments

Piaget also discovered that late-preschool- and early-school-age children believe that rules exist in their own right—that they have a life all their own independent of human judgment. Elkind believes that children first experience rules as absolute and unchangeable. Children accept what he calls moral realism because they believe their parents are omniscient. Until they reach the age of reason (age seven or eight) they are unable to put themselves in another person's shoes.

If you ask children at this age to give another misbehaving child a punishment, they can be rather severe. I once asked a five-year-old boy what the punishment should be for spilling a pitcher of milk. He told me that all the child's toys should be taken away from him. He said this without blinking an eye.

Moral realism, if arrested at this early stage, can lead to the moral retardation I referred to in chapter 11. Moral retardation is the root of moral totalism and of the kind of terrorism and brutality that characterizes moral or religious systems that emphasize obedience without question or content. A virtue is an excellence and is chosen from alternatives. It is based on choice, not constraint.

Much miscommunication and many disagreements among adults are rooted in the fact that people differ in their levels of cognitive maturity. If a person is arrested at the stage of moral realism, her moral understanding is rigid and inflexible, and she will have a difficult time dialoguing with a person who has achieved full mental maturity in late adolescence and/or early adulthood. They will be like people speaking two different languages.

6. Being Smarter Than Adults

When chilren reach the ability to reason they develop a new kind of mental egocentrism: they believe that they are smarter than their parents. Although they still believe the rules are absolute, they will begin to break them because they think they can get away with it. During this period of moral realism, a person's intentions make no difference, and while we know that intention alone does not make an act moral, for the pre-logical child, intentions don't seem to matter at all.

The school-age child can make an assumption, but she tends to hold on to her assumptions as if they were facts, even if new facts do not validate her assumptions. For example, a child catches his parent in a mistake, which is shocking to him. The literary critic Edmund Gosse describes the first time he realized his father was wrong about something. He says that the shock "was not caused by any suspicion that he was not telling the truth, but by the awful proof that he was not as I had supposed omniscient." The child makes the assumption that since she caught her parent in a mistake, she is smarter than the parent, and that if the parent was wrong in this one instance, the parent must be nearly wrong about everything, whereas if the child was right in this instance, she must be right about most things. Elkind calls this assumption "cognitive conceit."

7. Lying and Stealing

Cognitive conceit also shows up in children's moral behavior. School-age children will often steal and lie even though they know it is against the rules. Elkind writes, "For the child, breaking the rules is not primarily a moral matter but much more a matter of proving his cleverness by outwitting adults." The elementary school child's conscience is external in the sense that the child views the rules as outside rather than within himself. For example, in the story of Pinocchio, Jiminy Cricket is Pinocchio's external conscience, and Pinocchio's cavalier relationship to Jiminy illustrates the elementary school child's attitude toward adults' world of rules.

In my late childhood, I got in the habit of stealing. It is pretty clear to me now that my stealing came partly from cognitive conceit, but I also told myself that since we were poor, I had a right to steal. I continued stealing for several years. I never stole a whole lot. Finally one day I got caught. The man who caught me was merciful and let me pay back what I had stolen. That was the end of it for me.

Another consequence of cognitive conceit is children's use of humor in which adults are the butt of the joke. This is often interpreted as disrespect, but it really is not.

Children like to make fun of adult manners, including moral rules. A lot of nitpicking arguments between parents and children stem from cognitive conceit. Elkind describes one example:

An eight-year-old boy came to the dinner table with his hands dripping wet. When his mother asked why he had not wiped his hands he replied, "But you told me not to wipe my hands on the clean towels." His mother threw up her hands and said, "I said not to wipe your *dirty* hands on the towels."

Children get a big kick out of these exchanges, because they are exercising their new superior reasoning skills.

Stories for children abound in cognitive conceit. *Tom Sawyer, Alice in Wonderland,* and *Peter Pan* are stories in which adults are outwitted by children and made to look foolish. The appeal of *Peter Pan* even suggests that at some level children do not want to grow up to be dumb adults. Harry Potter is the new hero—a wizard who has all the magical powers school-age children wish they had.

Deep down, of course, children are still very emotionally dependent on their parents and fear time-outs or withholding of privileges. They know at an emotional level that they are not really superior.

8. Goodness of Adults

Elkind identified as another assumptive reality in early school age "the belief that adults are benevolent and well-intentioned." This is not a contradiction to the cognitive conceit I described earlier. The child believes that adults are benevolent and well-intentioned even though they are dumb.

This assumption—that the parent must be good—accounts for the difficulty therapists, social workers, and teachers have in getting disturbed children to say anything negative about their parents even when the child is clearly being abused. This also applies to the tenets of abuse, "might makes right," which the child internalizes. Later, it is hard to convince the child that might does not make right.

This belief in the benevolence of significant adults reinforces the importance of adults as moral models. Much of what a significant adult models, the child accepts as correct. In cultures of obedience, all adults are superior and should be obeyed. Imagine how this sets a person up to follow a cult leader or con man if his or her development is arrested at this stage of moral realism.

LAWRENCE KOHLBERG

The late Lawrence Kohlberg, a professor of education and social psychology at Harvard, was directly influenced by Piaget, although he went his own way, focusing solely on moral reasoning and following its development far beyond the ages that Piaget had considered.

His work, like that of Hartshorne and May before him, challenges the popular assumption that moral development can be fostered simply by teaching rules and norms that will then automatically be internalized. He disputed the way the growing child is trained merely to conform to accepted social rules and values. On the other hand, he also challenged the relativism that was becoming popular during the 1960s and 1970s—the notion that everyone should form their own values, which are nobody else's business. Instead, Kohlberg believed that his research had revealed a universal pattern, constant across cultures and through history, by which moral reasoning develops from the most basic level to the highest ability to resolve ethical dilemmas.

Kohlberg's Stages

Kohlberg's method went right to the heart of moral decision making in concrete situations. He asked people of all ages and of widely varying religions and cultures to comment on stories of moral dilemmas, asking them what the characters should do in each case. When he analyzed their responses, he identified six clearly distinguishable stages of moral reasoning that emerged universally.

In one of his most influential studies, Kohlberg followed the same group of eighty-four boys from early adolescence (ages ten to sixteen) through young manhood (they were twenty-two to twenty-eight years old at the end of his study), testing them at three-year intervals. He found that their moral thinking in response to the dilemmas changed in predictable ways, both as they expanded their life experience and, more importantly, as their moral assumptions were challenged.

Kohlberg believed that his data proved that people cannot understand moral reasoning that is more than one level higher than their current level, but also that they are cognitively attracted to the level just above them. They reach this higher level when some situation or idea creates a sense of conflict or disequilibrium that reveals the inadequacy of their thinking, or a respected person suggests a different way of looking at it. This means that if you are a parent, challenging your child's moral reasoning in a respectful and nonthreatening way can help inform the child's conscience.

I had a friend who was upset because his twelve-year-old was singing the praises of marijuana. She was not smoking it yet, but she allowed as how it was far better than drinking. Her dad gave her some stats on the health issues involved in smoking grass, showing her that it was more damaging to her lungs than cigarettes. He also got me to give him some letters written by kids in the drug abuse program I ran in L.A. These letters told a sad story of grades dropping dramatically and of many who dropped out of high school. This, fortunately, had an impact on her, and she actually changed her views on marijuana.

Kohlberg's stages trace an individual's moral growth in terms of his changing relationship to society. The first two stages describe what Kohlberg called a "preconventional morality." At these stages, people are motivated primarily to avoid personal harm and gain personal benefit. The third and fourth levels are more influenced by the accepted norms and expectations of society. They have a *conventional* orientation. The fifth and sixth stages are at a *postconventional* level. They support a morality that springs from a fully formed personal conscience, not bound by convention.

Here is a brief outline of Kohlberg's stages:

Stage 1: "avoid punishment" orientation. People at this stage respond to rules and are concerned with how authority will react, whether they will be punished or rewarded, and whether they will be labeled "good" or "bad." For example, a child is asked if he should obey his mother. He answers yes. When asked why, he says he doesn't want to get a spanking. In short, external consequences determine whether an action is good or bad. Decisions are based on blind obedience to an external power in an attempt to avoid punishment or seek reward.

Stage 2: "self-benefit" orientation. People at stage 2 realize that each individual has an idea of what is "right" or "best." They are concerned with the idea that one good turn (or bad turn) deserves another. For example, Paul is asked why he obeys God's rules. He answers, "So He will give me what I want." Another child answers, "So He'll protect me." Human relationships are built on the premise of exchanging favors or revenge. Fairness and sharing are practical issues. What is "fair" is doing something for others if they reciprocate. Self-interest is the compelling motive. Jimmy says, "If I let him play with my dump truck, he has to let me play with his tractor."

Stage 3: "acceptance by others" orientation. People see what is "right" from another's point of view as well as from their own. They are concerned with what others think. They strive for behavior that pleases others. At this stage, people are influenced by the feelings of others, what others expect and approve, and beliefs about what a virtuous person would do. This is the morality of maintaining good relationships and of conforming to the general will. Bobby says: "I should be nice to others because that's what's expected of a nice person."

Stage 4: "maintain the social order" orientation. People at stage 4 consider "right" from the perspective of what is best for society. They examine the consequences of their actions for the group and society. They value doing their duty, respect for authority, preserving the social order for its own sake, rules as determiners of "right" behavior, and fulfilling the requirements of authority and society. These individuals obey rules for their intrinsic value. Moral decisions are based on fixed rules that are seen as necessary to perpetuate the order of society. Stage 4 usually emerges in the teen years, when young people consider questions such as, "What does it mean to be a good member of my community, school, church, or society?" They understand that there is a lot more to morality than just living up to the expectations of their parents, teachers, and friends.

Kohlberg's first four stages comprise what we commonly call "morality." In these stages we do as we're told because of fear of authority (stage 1), for our own benefit (stage 2), in order to conform to the approved behavior of our social group (stage 3), or to conform to the laws of our community or religion (stage 4). We may be moral without ever having made independent moral decisions for ourselves. However, it is only at stages 5 and 6 that we reach full *ethical maturity*.

In order to be ethically mature, you must be your own person. For Kohlberg, such autonomy requires "a clear effort to define moral principles and values apart from the authority of groups or persons holding these principles and apart from the individual's identification with these groups."

> *Stage 5: "contract fulfillment" orientation.* Although individuals may hold different values, laws are established based on what people agree is the greatest common good of all concerned. The individual respects these impartial laws and agrees to abide by them. The society also agrees to respect the rights of the individual. The Declaration of Independence and the U.S. Constitution are based on these principles. The person at this stage looks like one at stage 4, but he has grown beyond a "law-and-order" mentality: he is aware of the larger principles behind the laws and may work to change laws he perceives as unjust.
>
> *Stage 6: "ethical principle" orientation.* The fully informed conscience is the directing agent of stage 6. Respect for each person's individuality is paramount, but the individual is to be guided by universal ethical principles, which are valid for all humanity. The person at this stage is committed to justice and feels an obligation to disobey unjust laws.

Kohlberg believed that this highest state is difficult to comprehend, and almost no one in his study consistently used this level of moral analysis. So Kohlberg turned to the writings of

Martin Luther King Jr. for an example of stage 6 reasoning, quoting key lines from King's famous "Letter from Birmingham Jail."

> One may well ask: "How can you advocate breaking some laws and obeying others?" The answer lies in the fact that there are two types of laws: just and unjust.... One has not only a legal but also a moral responsibility to obey just laws. Conversely, one has a moral responsibility to disobey unjust laws. To put it in the terms of St. Thomas Aquinas: an unjust law is a human law that is not rooted in eternal law and natural law. Any law that uplifts human personality is just. Any law that degrades human personality is unjust.... I submit that an individual who breaks a law that conscience tells him is unjust, and who willingly accepts the penalty of imprisonment in order to arouse the conscience of the community over its injustice, is in reality expressing the highest respect for law.

Kohlberg believed that the six stages he had discovered were invariant because the new structural whole, which supports each level of thinking, *is a complete reorganization of the mind*. The old way of thinking is gone and cannot return in a substantial way. It is as if one's entire mental landscape has been permanently changed. Once I clearly see the value of personal relationships and have experienced a sense of belonging, I can never go back to a purely egoistic motivation. Once I have experienced mutuality, belonging, and sharing, giving only for self-benefit will not be satisfactory.

The problem I, and many other people, have with Kohlberg's belief in invariance is that the facts contradict it. People at higher levels of moral thought still revert to lower-level moral behaviors at times. Kohlberg is almost equating knowledge and virtue.

A Conversation About Delinquency

I was fortunate enough to spend two days with Lawrence Kohlberg at a conference in Boston when I was the director of the

Palmer Drug Abuse Program in Los Angeles. I hoped to find some practical help in dealing with seven hundred teenagers who were endangering themselves and society.

I found Kohlberg to be a very complex man and hard to understand. At times he seemed to say that morality is based on the kind of moral intelligence I have been defining, which includes affect and intuition. He encouraged me to work with kids' emotions, and he really understood that addiction was about deep-seated shame. But he was also adamant about challenging teenagers' moral positions intellectually, in order to move them to higher levels of moral reasoning.

Kohlberg pointed me to some research that found a relationship between higher levels of moral reasoning, and moral behavior. For example, in experimental studies of cheating, the majority of subjects who were at lower stages cheated a great deal, while only a tenth of the subjects at higher stages did any cheating at all.

He also mentioned studies with prison populations that showed a high percentage of the inmates were fixated at stages 1 and 2. Later I read another study in which Kohlberg and a collaborator found that 83 percent of delinquent adolescents were stuck at one of Kohlberg's lowest two stages.

In our work with the Palmer group, we found positive changes over a three-year period when we challenged the way our teenagers reasoned. A lot of the youngsters were stuck at stage 2 (basically, "You scratch my back and I'll scratch yours"). I challenged them to pursue sobriety not only for themselves but also for the program as a whole. This became a powerful motivation. They prided themselves on building a strong community that would be there to help others.

IN A DIFFERENT VOICE

There have been several critiques of Kohlberg and Piaget, some of which I share and have mentioned above. Here I'll focus on the concerns of Carol Gilligan, who was on the Harvard faculty for more than thirty years and is now a professor at New York University.

Gilligan noted that on Kohlberg's scale, women consistently reached a lower level of moral development than men did. She also noted that most of his research had been done on men and boys. Were women inherently less morally mature than men, or did women's morality differ in some important way from the principles Kohlberg was measuring?

In her influential book *In a Different Voice*, Gilligan pointed out that many of the girls' answers were motivated by a morality of care and relationships, whereas Kohlberg's questions focused on a morality of rights and rules. Kohlberg's higher levels focused on an "ethics of justice," whereas women tended to hold themselves to a different standard, an "ethics of care." She pointed out, "Women not only define themselves in a context of human relationships but also judge themselves in terms of their ability to care." Many of the women's "wrong answers" in Kohlberg's study stemmed from their concern for relationships and their focus on caring.

Gilligan makes the case that when one *begins* with the study of women, a different description of moral development emerges: "In this conception, the moral problem arises from conflicting responsibilities rather than from competing rights and requires for its resolution a mode of thinking that is contextual and narrative rather than formal and abstract."

Gilligan's ideas are relevant to our discussion of prudence as a situational conscience that deals with the specific and ever-changing circumstances of moral choice. Fully developed moral intelligence, as I have defined it, is by nature "contextual and narrative"; it cannot be confined to a formal logical sequence.

Gilligan's starting point is that women have been shamed by being measured against concepts derived from the study of boys and men. She points out that Freud and others saw women as incomplete. Women's unique moral development is critically important for the moral life of all humans, and men have also suffered by the omission of women's moral voice. The two voices are not to be taken as polarized sexual stances so much as two different moral viewpoints that are applicable to all human beings. She points to an interplay of the two voices within each sex: a conception of morality concerned with care "centers moral development around the understanding of responsibility and relationships, just as the conception of morality as fairness ties moral development to the understanding of rights and rules." Both are necessary in achieving ethical maturity, and both depend on prudence. The two voices together give us the masculine/feminine wholeness we strive for in our shadow work.

As I was writing this brief presentation of Carol Gilligan's work, I realized that the two disparate modes of experience—justice (fairness) and care (harm no one)—were embodied in the experience of two young women, Stacey High and Marie Robards, whose story was widely reported and later became the focus of a feature in *Texas Monthly* magazine written by Skip Hollenbeck. I'll end this chapter by sharing it with you.

Poisoning Daddy

"Stacey," Marie asked, "do you think people can go through life without a conscience?"

Stacey answered, "Well, how about the kind of person who can look somebody in the eye and kill him in cold blood?"

This conversation took place one night in January 1994 between Stacey High and Marie Robards, who were inseparable best friends. It was their senior year in high school. They were studying Shakespeare's *Hamlet,* and they had come to the scene in which Hamlet's uncle Claudius, who had killed Hamlet's father to gain the throne, reveals his guilt.

This was Stacey's favorite soliloquy. Claudius, agonized, wonders whether he can ever repent of killing his brother. Stacey read the passage aloud, and when she finished she looked across at Marie and saw that her friend's hands were trembling and her face had turned pale. It was at this moment Marie asked Stacey her question about going through life without a conscience. At Stacey's reply, Marie collapsed to the floor and began to weep. Finally, after many questions from Stacey, the words came through her sobs: "My father, I poisoned him."

Stacey was a guest on my TV program *The Bradshaw Difference*. My aim was to follow the vagaries of her conscience as she grappled with the dilemma of her loyalty to her best friend and her obligation to achieve justice for Marie's father, Steven Robards.

Marie had not intended to kill her father. She had only wanted to make him sick. The trouble began the weekend before her sixteenth birthday, when she came home and found her stepfather with another woman. Marie had an unusually close relationship with her mother, Beth, and her relationship with her stepfather had been strained from the beginning. While Beth was devastated by her husband's affair, she chose to stay with him. Marie, however, could no longer tolerate him, and she went to live with her father, Steven.

Marie soon missed her mother and was constantly on the phone with her. By the following year, she wanted to go back to her mother, but she knew her stepfather would not let her. She was too proud to ask outright, so she began to formulate a plan that would force the issue. She had learned in her chemistry class that barium acetate was a poison. One day in February 1993, while her chemistry teacher was preoccupied, she stole some of the barium acetate. Marie had no idea how lethal this poison could be. She believed that if she put some of it in her father's food, it would make him very sick, and she could go and live with her mother. On February 18, she and her father bought some take-out Mexican food for dinner, and while he was out of the room, Marie put barium acetate in his refried beans. He died that night. She had unknowingly put twenty-eight times the lethal dose in his beans. The autopsy did not discover the poison, and the coroner attributed Steven Robard's death to a heart attack.

Marie told no one until the night in January 1994 when she and Stacey were studying *Hamlet*.

Stacey was deeply troubled and confused. For weeks she tried to keep Marie's story a secret. "When you're in high school it's, like, so important not to betray your best friends," she told me.

She did tell her mother, Libby, who also felt a tremendous struggle of conscience. Stacey and Libby pondered the issue. Marie was considered by everyone to be the near-perfect teenager. She was a straight-A student, played the clarinet in the band, and was extremely beautiful but dated very little and was committed to being a virgin until marriage. Stacey and Libby were both bothered by the idea that maybe Marie was very different from how she appeared. Stacey talked to the priest at her church without mentioning Marie's name. She also went to her school counselor several times, still keeping Marie's secret.

Libby had decided not to call the police. She felt that Stacey had to accept the responsibility to follow her own conscience. When I questioned Libby, she said, "I guess I knew that this was the moment in which Stacey was going to have to grow up." Stacey even talked to a policeman she knew, presenting the case in a disguised and hypothetical way. The priest, counselor, and policeman each urged Stacey to do a reality check and to realize that this was a matter beyond friendship and loyalty. Eight months after Marie's revelation, Stacy finally told her counselor Marie's name, which obligated the counselor to report the matter to the police. Marie was tried, convicted for the murder of her father, and sentenced to twenty-eight years in prison.

The process of finally telling her counselor Marie's name is a profile of how a person arrives at a prudential judgment. The virtue of prudence involves the two voices of loving care and justice, and for a long while Stacey struggled to reconcile her care for her friend with the demands of justice. In this book, I have presented both love and justice as the highest virtues and as the pinnacles of moral intelligence. But in some situations, even these supreme values may come into conflict, which makes the virtue of prudence an indispensable guide for our conscience. The job of prudence is to reason practically in accord with right appetite, which must include both fairness and loving care, and to decide on the action to take. If we have this ability and exercise it in matters both great and small, we have probably come as close to full ethical maturity as our imperfect humanity allows.

13

WERE YOU THERE WHEN JESUS SPANKED THE CHILDREN?: FAMILY, FATHERHOOD, AND CORPORAL PUNISHMENT

> Marriage and thus family are where we live out the most intimate and thus powerful of our human experiences. The family is the unit in which we belong...in which we create infinity through our children and in which we find a haven.
>
> —Judith Bardwick

> Psychological fathering is what the world is in need of more than ever in history. There is considerable psychological evidence that civilization will stand or fall with whether such fathering is available in sufficient quantity.
>
> —Edward V. Stein

> If a parent or teacher strikes a child, it's called discipline. If a child strikes a parent or teacher, it becomes assault.
>
> —Michael Marshall

In her book *The Way We Never Were: American Families and the Nostalgia Trap,* Stephanie Coontz challenges those who want to go back to the traditional family to "pick a ballpark date for the family they have in mind." One caveat: for whatever date you choose, the family of that period has to be accepted as a package deal.

For example, if you choose the colonial Puritan family with its strict discipline, lack of divorce, and subordination of the individual to the group, you must also accept the lower life expectancy and high mortality rates that made the average length of marriage about twelve years. One-third to one-half of all children experienced the death of at least one parent, and most families were blended as a result. "Disobedience by women or children was considered a small act of treason," Coontz writes, and punished harshly. Children were exposed to frank and detailed sexuality at an early age.

Or perhaps you choose the Victorian family of the 1830s and 1840s, "when women's roles were redefined in terms of domesticity rather than production, and men were labeled breadwinners (a masculine identity unheard of in colonial days), children were said to need time to play, and gentle maternal guidance supplanted the patriarchal authoritarianism of the past." But if you do, you'd better be sure you were part of the 20 percent who lived this way—the majority of families were poor and powerless to create the kind of domestic oasis that was the Victorian ideal.

The proliferation of textile mills meant that middle-class women no longer needed to spend untold hours producing fabric for clothing, but the cotton those mills used was produced by black slaves, including children, and women and children tended the spinning machines and looms. By the last third of the nineteenth century, many children were employed in crowded tenement sweatshops, making cigars or women's clothing. In 1900, 120,000 Pennsylvania children were working in mines or factories. In the South, children as young as six or seven were laboring in textile mills, working twelve-hour shifts.

Many more people would like to go back to the traditional family of the 1950s, the age of TV family shows such as *Leave It to Beaver* and *Ozzie and Harriet*. However, as Coontz points out, the reality of the 1950s families was far different from what the sitcom reruns portray. "A full 25 percent of Americans, forty to fifty million people, were poor in the mid-1950s," and food stamps and housing programs did not exist to provide a safety net. "Sixty percent of Americans over sixty-five had incomes below $1,000 in 1958 . . . a majority of elders also lacked medical insurance." And of course the Cleavers and the Nelsons were white, as was everyone in their world. There was a Hispanic gardener in *Father Knows Best,* but the character's name was Frank Smith.

In short, the idealized traditional family is a myth. As Stephanie Coontz says, "Families have always been in flux, and often in crisis." They have never lived up to nostalgic notions about "the way things used to be." If we are to find new solutions for the problems of our families, the first step is to stop trying to recapture a past that never existed.

A NEW UNDERSTANDING OF THE FAMILY

In 1975, a lecturer whose name I have forgotten changed my entire understanding of the family. His topic was the impact of an alcoholic parent, and I couldn't believe my ears as I heard my own alcoholic family described in minute detail. This man— whom I'd like to honor—described the family as a dynamic system governed by overt and covert rules that are more powerful than the individuals in the family. To help us understand how these systemic rules work, he asked us to imagine a mobile. The mobile is never perfectly at rest; its subtle motions represent the dynamic interactions of the family. But if we were to push on one part of the mobile, every other part would be thrown sharply out of balance and start to move. In families where the husband is alcoholic, the wife and children swing widely because of the impact of the father.

Systems thinking rests on the premise that the mobile always tries to find its gentle balance. When any family member is in trouble, all the rest are affected. This means that as the alcoholic father rejects his responsibilities, one or more other family members become super-responsible. For example, a male son, usually the eldest, may take his father's place, becoming a surrogate spouse to his mother. This picture fit my family to a T. My mother was super-responsible, as was my sister, and I became the breadwinner (I had my first job at ten years old) and surrogate spouse. I also took it upon myself to rescue the family's dignity. At a time when it seemed like every other family had a car, we had to ride the bus to church and school. So as the eldest son, I became the star and hero, making straight A's in school, excelling in sports, and becoming the class leader. The family was out of balance, and we were all struggling to make up for what was missing.

I had long been interested in family systems theory, but I had never applied it in a way that clarified my own alcoholic family. This lecture personalized my readings of the psychiatrists Murray Bowen and Ronald Laing, who both saw the family as a dynamic system. Shortly after that lecture, I read a book by my colleague at the Meadows, Claudia Black, called *It Will Never Happen to Me,* in which she discussed her alcoholic family in systems terms. I also read the works of Janet Woititz and Dr. Robert Ackerman on adult children of alcoholics.

A powerful experience with one of my best friends showed me the impact that a family systems approach could have. I had known this man for seventeen years. We had sobered up together. But I'd never really felt as close to him as I wanted to. Both of us were very guarded overachievers. One day after a tennis match, we were having lunch together. As he spoke he shared tender feelings about his son and his wife. After an hour conversation, I told him I was experiencing him differently. He was vulnerable and I felt closer to him. I asked him what had happened. He told me that his son had gone into treatment for alcoholism at the Meadows Treatment Center in Wickenburg, Arizona, and that the Meadows treatment demanded that the whole family come in for one week of the patient's five-week program. My friend had been so moved by family week that he went back for a five-week stay of his own. Then his wife went through the Meadows program. I knew his whole family well, and I experienced them as more close-knit and bonded after their treatment.

THE FUNCTIONAL FAMILY

What systems thinking makes clear is that the chief component of the family system is the marriage. The health of the marriage determines the health of the family. Long after the children grow up, the marriage will sustain the family.

Good Functional Family Rules

In systems thinking, the whole family is seen as a single organism, with its own personality, style, and needs. The needs include provisions for food, clothing, shelter, self-esteem, emotional warmth, an environment that supports self-actualization, and good boundaries. Above all, a functional family needs rules. Some suggestions for functional family rules are as follows:

1. Problems are acknowledged and resolved.
2. All members can freely and appropriately express their perceptions, feelings, thoughts, desires, and fantasies.
3. All relationships are dialogical. Each person is of equal value. Children's developmental limits are taken into account.
4. Communication is direct, congruent, and sensory-based, i.e., concrete, specific, and behavioral.
5. Family members can get most of their needs met.
6. Family members can be different.
7. Parents do what they say. They are self-disciplined disciplinarians.
8. Wherever appropriate, family roles are chosen and flexible.
9. All rules require accountability and consequences.
10. Violation of others' values leads to guilt.

11. Mistakes are forgiven and viewed as learning tools.
12. The family system exists for the individual's well-being.
13. Parents are in touch with their healthy shame. They know that they make mistakes and are humble.
14. While fun and spontaneity cannot be made into a rule, they are the fruit of all these rules.

The family is a single organism, but, as rule 12 states, it exists to promote individual autonomy. Isn't this a contradiction, and doesn't it fly in the face of our ideal of family union, support, and togetherness? One of the paradoxical aspects of functional and healthy families is that *as individualism increases, togetherness grows*. As people grow in solid selfhood they move toward wholeness, which makes real intimacy possible. We need separation in order to really know each other and have togetherness.

Why the Generation Gap Is Necessary

Every healthy family needs a generation gap. Family system theorists such as Bowen and Virginia Satir realized very early that in many marriages that are struggling and conflictual, one or both parents turn to one or more of their children to create a triangle that takes the heat off the marriage itself. For example, if one son is very talented, Mom and Dad may overfocus on him in order to avoid resolving their own problems. Another son may be a troublemaker. (Such a child is usually acting out the problems in the marriage.) The parents turn all their attention on their troublesome child, which protects them from having to confront themselves.

In another pattern, one parent may turn to one or more of the children to create an alliance or coalition against the other parent. If Dad is dissatisfied with the marriage, he may make his daughter his little princess or surrogate spouse, giving her far more time and attention than he gives his wife. Or he may turn to his son and make the child his best buddy, spending more time with him in sports or fishing trips than he spends with their mom. Likewise, Mom may make her daughter her sorority sister or make her son into her little man or surrogate spouse.

Whenever a child knows that he or she is more important to Dad than Mom is or more important to Mom than Dad is, a situation called "cross-generational bonding" is set up. This kind of bonding is destructive to the boundaries that every family needs. The major impact of cross-generational bonding (also called enmeshment) is that it damages a child's ego development. Enmeshed children have no boundaries between themselves and the parent they are overly bonded with. They feel their parent's feelings, not their own. They have no real sense of self-identity. Cross-generational bonding makes it much more difficult for the child to develop the solid sense of self and emotional intelligence that I described in chapter 11.

A Healthy Marriage

In a fully functional family, Mom and Dad get their needs met through their own inner resources and choices and through their work on establishing an intimate relationship with each other. The most significant person to Dad is Mom and vice versa. When parents are modeling intimacy and the virtue of love, the children experience what a good marriage is like. They have a model to use as a reference point.

Once a couple understands the dangers of cross-generational bonding, they have a moral responsibility to work on their marriage problems. Creating an intimate and healthy marriage has a direct impact on the formation of their children's conscience. Erik Erikson states: "It is not always understood that one of the main rationales for marital and familial loyalty is the imperative need for inner unity in the child's conscience." The parents need to create a complementary balance so that their children will internalize a unified voice as the foundation of their conscience. This does not mean that children of divorce will necessarily have a weak conscience. It means that a healthy relationship between a child's mother and father offers the best setting for forming their child's conscience. The voices of Mom and Dad also give their child an image of masculinity and femininity that is internalized as an inner voice. It is crucial for the development of a child's moral intelligence to incorporate the ethical example of parents who practice the virtue of love with all the kindness, respect, and care that goes with it.

DIVORCE, THEN AND NOW

When my parents divorced, my whole family felt ashamed. Adding to the shame was the fact that we were Catholic, and Catholics married for life. If they did divorce, they were never to marry again. My mother followed that law to her death.

Today, divorce is more accepted. (When my son was in school he actually felt somewhat different because his mother and I were still together, while almost all his friends had divorced parents.) In some ways, this is an improvement over the social ostracism my family felt. It is reasonable to end a marriage that injures and constrains one or both partners and for which remedies honestly tried have not worked. But make no mistake, divorce is a serious matter.

I have never met anyone who divorced who did not mourn and grieve for the death of a dream of what life could be like. Most people who divorce remarry and take on new obligations because the gain of belonging, of caring, and of being needed is greater than the "freedom" they are giving up. Many people also remarry the exact emotional replica of the person they divorced, especially if they haven't resolved the issues of the past and done the kind of deep feeling work I described in chapter 8. And divorce is often devastating to children. Beginning in the 1970s, some writers were describing divorce as "creative," freeing the individuals for expanded personal growth. There may have been something helpful in that thinking, but no one was dealing with the damaging, often brutal impact that divorce has on the children.

Children and Divorce

I remember riding my bike to baseball practice, crying so hard I could hardly see the street. My mother had unceremoniously announced that she had divorced my father. I'd known that their marriage was troubled, but the finality of their divorce caused me great anguish. It was never spoken about after that day.

Six years ago, I was flipping channels one evening and came upon a program describing a grief support group for children of divorce. As I watched, I started to tear up, and before I knew it, I was sobbing out loud. When I finally calmed down, it dawned on me that I had tapped into a reservoir of repressed grief over my parents' divorce. Then I remembered an evening many years earlier, when I was thirty-one, and had had too much to drink and began making a plan to get my parents together again. It seemed so logical in my drunken state, even though my father had been remarried for sixteen years.

Divorce not only tears the family apart; in many cases it means the complete loss of one parent, usually the father. In one study more than half of the children whose parents were divorced had never been in their father's new home. Forty-two percent had not seen their fathers in the previous year. When my parents divorced, I was enraged at my father. I refused to see him or speak to him. I gravitated to a group of fatherless guys and began my drinking and whoring with them. We constantly badmouthed our fathers to show that we didn't love them or need them. But I loved my father dearly, and as my life rolled on I missed him greatly. I remember one night in Galveston, Texas. I was in a restaurant with my group of guys, and I saw my father come in. He was with his new wife. I hadn't spoken to him in four years. It seemed crazy not to say hello, but I didn't. I just wanted to get out of the restaurant. I knew he hadn't seen me, so we got up and left. But I can still see him sitting there as I write this. I *really* wanted to say hello and talk to him.

It is a fact that many children of divorce who grow up without seeing a solid working marriage don't even know when a marriage is working and when it is not, and they end up with a far higher divorce rate in their own lives. I've not seen any statistics on this lately, but it happened to me and everyone I know, including my brother and my sister.

Why High Divorce Rates?

The divorce rate soared from the 1960s to the 1980s. Divorce figures are still high but have definitely stabilized somewhat since that time, when it seemed *everyone* was getting a divorce. But why do so many couples divorce? One reason may be that a couple has not worked through their childhood wounds and developmental dependency needs. Another may be that marriages potentially last longer than ever before. I mentioned earlier that in colonial times, the average marriage lasted about twelve years. Personal expectations were also lower then, sex roles were rigid, and great energy went into survival.

Another reason for the increase in divorce is increased employment and economic opportunity for women. According to anthropologist Helen Fisher, women have always initiated divorce more often when they have economic power. Today women have earning power as never before, and they now initiate more divorces than men.

At the same time, women generally will work harder at keeping the marriage together. Some argue that men are often treated with kid gloves by their wives and even by therapists when it comes to taking responsibility for marital relationships. Long centuries of male supremacy have created many unspoken rules relating to men's rights. Because of this, therapists often coddle their male clients and walk on eggshells to keep them coming to therapy. Many women are no longer willing to play by these unequal rules or to tolerate what psychotherapist Terrence Real calls "psychological patriarchy."

A factor that particularly concerns me is a kind of moral subjectivity that, as sociologist Judith Bardwick says, "has spawned the belief that commitment diminishes choice, narrows experience, and truncates growth." Hollywood celebrities are exalted for having glamorous marriages, affairs, divorces, and new marriages. This is advertised as the good life. To live life to the fullest without commitment is to be autonomous and free. We have been given a false image of the autonomous self, as if "autonomous" meant someone so intact and mature that he or she does not need anyone else. As Bardwick writes in her book *In Transition,* "I have never met any healthy person who is so autonomous as not to need anyone."

Marriage as a Permanent Commitment

Take a hard look at this notion that we can be freer and more self-actualized if we are free of commitment. Being intimate and committed involves revealing, needing, hearing, and giving. To act in these ways, we have to own our vulnerability; it takes the virtue of courage to be intimate and committed, allowing another person to truly know us. Intimacy and commitment involve risks but at the same time enhance confidence, reduce anxiety, and create a sense of belonging. "Divorce," says Bardwick, "means losing a sense of who you belong to and who belongs to you." Without the sense that you are terribly important to someone else, you can come to feel that nothing you do is important, because there is no one to do it for. Divorce destroys the anchorage of connection that we all need to flourish in the world.

Believing in marriage as permanent is exactly the opposite of seeing it as denying freedom and truncating growth. As Bardwick points out:

People may be far better able to grow when they are in a mutually committed relationship because feeling secure, they are better able to take risks. The more one trusts the relationship, the more one will protect it and, simultaneously, the more one will feel free to change within it.

FATHER LOSS

During the years I spent writing this book, I asked several hundred people what they thought the most important part of moral education was. Ninety percent answered, "Fathering." A few went on to tell me moving stories about what they had learned from their fathers, but far more spoke about the lack of connection with their fathers. They were talking about the impact of the absence of a father on their moral and emotional lives.

In his book *Finding Our Fathers,* Samuel Osherson writes, "The psychological or physical absence of fathers from their families is one of the great underestimated tragedies of our times." Millions of our children are living in fatherless homes as a result of death, desertion, divorce, illegitimacy, or emotional abandonment.

Growing up without a nurturing father has serious consequences for a child's moral development. In the movie *The Color Purple,* one of the women says, "I've never seen a child grow up right unless he had a pa." And the founder of modern psychotherapy, Sigmund Freud, wrote, "I could not point to any need in childhood as strong as that of a father's protection."

I certainly don't intend to denigrate the efforts that the majority of single mothers are making to give their children moral guidance. Nevertheless, the crisis in fathering has a direct impact on the moral confusion and distress we are experiencing today.

As a man who grew up without a father, I know the intimate truth of "father hunger," the longing for a strong father to provide safety, establish firm and fair limits, and offer approval and validation. I have longed for a father who could give me advice. I also know that there is something lacking in the foundation of my character that I've had to work very hard to try to rebuild.

Mother-Bonded Men

Father loss often pushes sons into the kind of enmeshed relationship with their mothers that I described in the discussion of cross-generational bonding. When a son is thrust into the closeness of surrogate spousehood, he is thrown into a deep conflict. First, he must enter a relationship far beyond his level of maturity and take on a set of adult marital issues, often becoming his mother's confidant and the recipient of her complaints about his father, as well as the nurturer and caretaker of her pain. Second, a boy must repress his emerging sexuality. His mother unconsciously (and in rare cases consciously) displaces her sexuality onto her son.

Throughout their lives, many boys who are mother-bonded remain perpetual Peter Pans who resist growing up and are unable to sustain a committed sexual relationship. They are highly seductive, often becoming sex and love addicts, but always ruled by the wound of their mother's engulfment. For them, to love a woman means to be engulfed in her pain. This requires taking care of her needs and giving up their own—with a price to be paid in resentment, withdrawal, or depression. When such men do marry, they often have moderate to severe intimacy dysfunction and become the replicas of their physically or emotionally absent fathers. Absentee, abusive, abandoning fathers beget sons who repeat the cycle.

As a counselor, I often found in digging deeper into destructive mother-son bonds that the mothers had unresolved sexual issues, either incest or experiences of sexual misconduct with their own fathers or with other male members of their extended family. Most of these mothers had not done the grief work necessary to heal their unresolved pain. Instead, they carried what some clinicians refer to as "sexualized rage"—the rage a woman feels when she is helpless and is being controlled and violated by her father, male relatives, or other male molesters. She carries this unresolved and often unconscious rage in her body. When a person is traumatized, she reacts by restricting her breathing, tightening her muscles, and dissociating imaginatively from the scene. Her body numbs out, but the violation remains imprinted in the neurological patterns of the brain and body. When a mother with sexualized rage inappropriately bonds with her son, he experiences his masculinity as the object of his mother's disgust and has difficulty developing a healthy sense of masculinity.

Mother-Bonded Girls

Girls who are abandoned by their fathers are also set up to take care of their mothers. They see firsthand the pain their mothers have suffered and may want no part of having intimacy with a male. Their mothers pass on their sexualized rage, deep sadness, and disappointment to their daughters. Some mothers model that the female sex is inferior; others model that it is superior. Both sexes, when mother-bonded, tend to use the other sex as a way of getting even with the mother who used them to take care of her pain, or with the father whose offender behavior deeply wounded the mother and the family.

A father's best gift is an underpinning of support that helps his daughter in two ways. First, he gives her confidence in her ability to achieve in the wider world. A mother can give her daughter the confidence to achieve in the world, but she can-not awaken her daughter's femininity the way a father can. Little girls like to be noticed by their fathers and are often coy and flirtatious with them. Older girls who have their father's approval are reassured that achievement will not diminish their femininity or attractiveness, despite many cultural messages to the contrary.

Figure 13.1: FATHER WOUNDS

MAN ⟶

I am not adequate—not a real man—unless I have a woman

I can't be happy as a man unless :
- I have a woman's wound to take care of
- I have a woman to take care of me
- I can control and dominate a woman

DEGRADED: My father was a no-good bum.
or
IDEALIZED: My father is a great man! I'll never be able to live up to his expectations and accomplish what he does.

I am not adequate—not a real woman—unless I have a man.

⟵ **WOMAN**

I can't be happy as a woman unless:
- I have a man to take care of me
- I have a man to take care of

DEGRADED: My father was rotten—he deserted my mother or dominated her.
or
IDEALIZED: No man can love me as much as my father—no man will be adequate compared to him.

Whether women idealize their absent fathers or condemn them, they maintain a picture of Daddy, and of men, that is somewhat drawn from fantasy. In my counseling practice I saw many women who needed some of their illusions about Daddy to survive. I think these fantasies helped in their childhood to dilute hopelessness and a sense of complete isolation. Yet my experience in exploring the feelings and fantasies of many women without fathers also revealed that their unrealistic expectations negatively affected their childhood, adolescence, and overall attitude toward self, relationships, career, and family.

Some of the effects of father abandonment and neglect on both boys and girls are:

- A fear of love—"If I love, the person may be taken away"
- Chronic detachment—the inability to establish goals or relationships because of internalized fear of abandonment
- Distancing from commitment
- Morbid extremes of dependency, codependency (enmeshment), or antidependency (isolation)
- Inability to imagine a relationship lasting
- Sadness and depression for which one has no appropriate explanation
- Chronic state of apathy—the denial of feeling altogether
- Inability to mourn, inability to love
- Romantic delusionism and serial romance—the inability to discern suitable partners, leading to poor choices, frequent replacement of partners, and a distorted view of love

Figure 13.1 sums up the relationship distortion that the father wound can create for both men and women.

Healing the Father Wound

During my work as a counselor, I found father loss to be a recurring theme in people's lives. The grief work I described in chapter 8 can be a model for grieving father loss. I also do a workshop specifically aimed at grieving father loss, particularly abandonment, abuse, and enmeshment such as cross-generational bonding. My workshop aims at making the hurts real, since we cannot heal something until we experience the hurt as real. A lot of childhood pedagogy of the past is now seen as abusive, even though it seemed normal to us as children. We cannot heal until we realize it actually *was* abuse.

After doing our own grief work, we need to turn to our father's woundedness. We need to demythologize our father. If a father was absent, violent, or present but not involved, the child (and the child in us) has unrealistic fantasies of the father's power. He, along with our mother, was our first higher power. We need to see that he does not have godlike power over us (although he may still be a dangerous abuser). Finally, we need to become the fathering source of our own lives. We also strongly recommend that workshop participants find support persons from whom they can learn to both get and give fathering. (See chapter 7 in my book *Creating Love* for a detailed presentation of this father work.)

We have to forgive our father (not condone his abuse) if we are to free ourselves from the energy it takes to keep resenting or idealizing him. Whether we consider him a monster or a saint, until we say goodbye, we can't grow up and be authentically present.

CORPORAL PUNISHMENT

I'd like to finish this chapter by examining corporal punishment, which I believe is the enemy of moral intelligence and also the cause of a great deal of cruelty and violence in the world.

Many people were spanked abusively by their fathers. Many mothers also spank, but the father has traditionally been seen as the administrator of discipline. I had many clients who suffered great anguish as they waited for their father to come home to spank them. I also had many clients who were battered as children by their fathers.

The beating, hitting, slapping, choking, pushing, pinching, shaking, threatening, ear pulling, mouth washing, and isolating of children are disciplinary traditions that go far back in human history.

Millions still believe that hitting and spanking are moral and ethical ways to raise their children. Nevertheless, studies are converging on the inherent danger of the chronic use of any type of corporal punishment. Children are fragile beings, and they can internalize, act out, and repeat these violent and abusive acts on others throughout their lives.

In the Catholic schools I attended, the nuns and priests had the unquestioned right to hit students with a paddle or with their bare hands. One day in the seventh grade, I was working in English class when I heard a loud jolting noise, and then another and another. I looked up to see the teacher slapping my friend Marshall's face repeatedly, twenty times or more. I felt myself sinking in my seat, trying to become invisible. My heart beat faster and I froze with fear. I wanted to cry out, but I was too afraid. I can still hear those blows to my friend's face as I write this. When she finally stopped, the nun went back to her desk at the front of the room and sat there trembling. Marshall's face was bleeding. She must have known that she had gone over the edge. Going over the edge is precisely the danger of corporal punishment. I had never witnessed such physical violence. The silence was terrible. All of the children in that class were victimized by her behavior. *A witness to violence is a victim of violence.* I will never forget that day.

Corporal punishment has been stopped in Catholic schools and for the most part in public schools, but it persists in the home. I spanked my son on two occasions. I felt awful afterward and realized that I had never seriously questioned the practice. It was commonplace in my childhood, and it is still commonplace among some groups of parents today.

On my talk show *The Bradshaw Difference,* one program was devoted to the subject of spanking children as a method of discipline. My featured guest was a school principal who had been spanking children at his school and had come under fire from many parents. On the program, we had people who agreed with the principal and people (including me) who were adamantly against spanking. When I asked the principal about his own childhood, he admitted that he had been spanked, on some occasions until he bled.

Why, after suffering the humiliation of such beatings, would this principal beat the children he was responsible for? He told me his parents had done their God-given duty and that he had turned out okay. My studies and experience suggest two other explanations. The first comes from the psychiatrist Alice Miller. In *Thou Shalt Not Be Aware,* she writes: "Parents who beat their children very often see the image of *their* parents in the infant they are beating." In other words, they are taking revenge on their own child for the hurt they suffered.

The second reason a child who has been beaten will beat his own and other children is that his powerful parent was godlike to him. A small child needs the love and protection of adults and cannot believe that his godlike parent could be wrong or bad. This sets up what is described clinically as a "compulsion to protect the parent." The child feels that he is bad and the parent is good. He therefore defends his parent's behavior. Physical abuse is often about unconscious revenge and about abuse that is accepted as normal. If you grow up with every kid in the family and neighborhood being spanked, you would probably believe that it is normal to spank children. Why would you question it?

On my TV show, I asked the principal and other spanking advocates how they decided how many times to hit their child, and also how they decided on the instrument of punishment. People did not agree on the instrument—belts, switches, canes, hairbrushes, and bare hands were mentioned. On the question of the number of blows administered, there was also no consistency. The school principal hedged, and I never got a straight answer out of him.

I ended the show by asking why we believe it is reasonable to hit small, vulnerable children when it is against the law to hit other adults, to use corporal punishment on convicted criminals, or even to hit animals.

Dissociation in Response to Violence

As I've noted, when a child is hurt and scared, he tends to hold his breath and tense his muscles. This creates a kind of body armor, a numbed-out feeling. If the abuse is chronic and reaches a certain threshold of tolerance, the child not only physically numbs out but also imaginatively leaves the scene. He automatically goes out of his body and fantasizes being in some other place.

A child who has numbed out and dissociated no longer feels or remembers what has happened. Here is a striking example from the book *Spare the Child,* written by Philip Greven, a professor of history at Rutgers University.

> I was physically punished as a child. One memory, representative of many, remains embedded ineradicably in my own mind. When I was about eight years old... [o]ne day I decided to see how deep a hole I could dig in the sand with a hose gushing full force.

To his delight, Philip dug a deep hole, but the hose became stuck in the ground. When he went to his mother, she told him he was in trouble and to wait until his father came home. Greven describes the waiting as an eternity for an eight-year-old expecting punishment. When his father came home, he freed the hose and then he came inside to spank Philip. Years later, his father reminded Philip of this incident,

> acknowledging how angry he had been at the time and recollecting that he had given him one of the hardest spankings of my life. When a man who weighs over two hundred pounds, stands six feet, and has huge hands spanks a small boy hard, it surely must hurt. Yet to this day, I have no conscious memory of the actual pain he inflicted and I felt. I only can remember the events that led up to the punishment itself. Amnesia has supressed the pain.

The subtitle of Greven's book is *The Religious Roots of Punishment and the Psychological Impact of Physical Abuse.* It is well researched and well argued, and I highly recommend it to any parents reading this book who are still spanking their children.

The Authority of the Bible

Christians often justify spanking by citing the authority of the Bible. By this they mean the Old Testament, because nothing in the New Testament supports spanking or other forms of corporal punishment. When parents brought their children to Jesus to be blessed, his disciples tried to keep them away, but Jesus was angry and asked that the children be brought to him. "Let the little children come to me, and do not forbid them; for of such is the Kingdom of God...I say to you whoever does not receive the Kingdom of God as a little child will by no means enter it" (Mark 10:14–15). Jesus loved children, and I can't in my wildest imagination visualize him spanking them. That is why I ironically entitled this chapter "Were You There When Jesus Spanked the Children?"

The major support for physical punishment is found in the

book of Proverbs. Ironically, the best-known saying—"spare the rod and spoil the child"—is not from the Bible at all, although it has a familiar proverbial ring. It is from Samuel Butler's long poem *Hudibras,* written in 1664. Proverbs 13:24 actually says, "He that spareth his rod hateth his son, but he that loveth him chasteneth him early." (As early as thirty months, according to the major Christian authority Dr. James Dobson.) Proverbs 19:18 instructs: "Chasten thy son while there is hope, and let not thy soul spare for his crying." (Dobson suggests that any crying over two minutes is a ploy, an attempt by the child to manipulate the parent.) Most of the physical punishment texts in Proverbs are attributed to Solomon; however, biblical scholars cite very close parallels to these proverbs in Egyptian and Assyrian texts. No one actually knows how much, if any, of Proverbs derives from Solomon himself.

But then comes the New Testament. As Philip Greven points out:

> One of the most profound and consequential transformations wrought by Christianity has been the radical change in the nature of God from Jehovah to Father. Christianity from the outset . . . cast[s] the central narrative of the life of Jesus in terms of the relationship of a father in heaven to his only son on earth. . . . Nowhere in the New Testament does Jesus approve of the infliction of pain upon children by the rod or any other such implement, nor is he ever reported to have recommended any kind of physical discipline of children to any parent.

It is primarily the fundamentalist sects who believe in the divine revelation of every word of the Bible and who therefore accept a literal reading of the book of Proverbs as divine truth. Consequently, much physical abuse does occur in fundamentalist congregations. The April 2, 2001, issue of *Time* magazine described a congregation in Atlanta, Georgia, run by the Rev.

Arthur Allen Jr. who beat their children so abusively that forty-one of its children were taken into custody by the state.

This is an extreme case, but the extreme can expose what is wrong with the very premise of spanking. Granted, many parents have spanked their children sparingly and have done so with control. But the practice is far too dangerous. I described a good Catholic nun who clearly lost control and traumatized a whole classroom of children with her slapping rampage. I remember thinking she might never stop hitting my friend, that she might kill him. Inherent in the permission to engage in corporal punishment is the possibility of being excessive. Even if a person found a scripture that endorsed only one swat, that one swat could be dangerous.

In his now-classic book *Dare to Discipline,* Dobson, founder of Focus on the Family and the Family Reseach Council, comments, "One of my greatest concerns in recommending corporal punishment (spanking) is that some parents might apply the thrashings too frequently or too severely." Dobson specifies that spankings should be reserved for the moment of the child's greatest antagonism. But who decides what the *greatest* moment of antagonism is? In another place, Dobson suggests that a spanking may not work because it is too gentle. He says, "A slap with the hand on the bottom of a multi-diapered thirty-month-old is not a deterrent to anything." Why? Because it doesn't *hurt* enough. In another place a mom asks Dobson what she should do with a child she spanks all the time but who continues to defy her. The answer seems obvious to me: the spanking doesn't work. Dobson tells her to "outlast" him, even if it "takes a repeated measure. The experience will be painful for both participants, but the benefits will come tomorrow and tomorrow and tomorrow." What Dobson is saying is that the mother needs to spank the child as long as it takes to bring him into submission. God knows what that could mean! It also seems clear that Dobson sees parenting as a battleground, and that spanking is the way to win the war.

Another book, *What the Bible Says About Child Training* by J. Richard Fugate, makes endless distinctions between chastisement and punishment. Christians are only to chastise, Fugate says. He exhorts his readers to avoid using belts, sticks, or open hands. According to Fugate, only the rod is prescribed by God. He never explains what exactly he means by the rod, but his broader point is clear: children must be absolutely under the authority of their parents, and any deviation is an act of defiance that must be corrected. The underlying belief seems as soul-killing as the hitting. I find the arguments in Fugate's book well-meaning but ultimately ridiculous. He makes endless distinctions based on Proverbs 13:24, 19:18, 22:15, 23:13–15, and 29:15. Those who take these passages literally bear a huge moral responsibility. I'll remind them that three-fourths of Christian biblical scholars see these passages specifically as reflections of a harsh and primitive code. If we no longer stone people to death for adultery, we should probably read these passages in a different way too.

Perfect Child, Wounded Adult

It is an amazing window into child rearing today to read the comments about Dobson's *Dare to Discipline* on Amazon.com. Amid the many impassioned messages pro and con, I was struck by an entry from a woman who told how she had been raised according to Dobson's instructions. In her Christian family, she said, her parents never hit her in anger or because they were frustrated. They always hit her in love. She grew up as a perfectly obedient child. Her parents were praised by other church members because their children were so obedient.

The not-so-visible results were that she grew up unable to recognize her own feelings, the ones she repressed while being spanked. Intense feelings felt so frightening that, she writes, "I resorted to hurting myself physically...in order to keep my feelings at bay." She hurt herself as her parents had hurt her. This is called "acting in." Other people who were spanked act *out* their feelings by hitting others, usually their own children.

This woman also wrote that she became an obsessive perfectionist, afraid to make a mistake, and that she struggled with relationships. She comments, "I grew up unable to say 'no' to people who loved me but also used me, dominated me and even hit me." Finally, she says that she has spent her adult life trying to re-parent herself and has learned many skills that she could have learned as a child.

Beyond Fundamentalism

According to *Time* magazine, a 1995 study by sociologist Murray Straus, of the Family Research Laboratory of the University of New Hampshire, showed that a majority of Americans still approve of corporal punishment, and 28 percent of parents strike their children with objects such as belts and paddles.

The American Academy of Pediatrics (AAP), the national professional organization for pediatricians, has taken a strong position against spanking. Among other things, it said: "Spanking is a less effective strategy than time-out or removal of privileges for reducing undesired behavior." They stated that many parents hit not because they think it is best for their kids; rather, the parents hit because they are angry, scared, or up to their eyeballs in frustration and don't know what else to do.

Nonetheless, in its most recent policy statement, the AAP acknowledges that up to 59 percent of pediatricians—their own membership—believe limited spanking is okay, and that more than 90 percent of parents have used it at one time or another.

In addition to opposing striking a child, the AAP includes this comment in its book for parents, *Caring for Your Baby and Young Child:*

If the spanking is spontaneous, parents should later explain calmly why they did it, the specific behavior that provoked it, and how angry they felt. They might apologize to their child for their loss of control, because that usually helps the youngster understand and accept the spanking.

For forty years, I have been advocating that parents apologize when they know they have hurt their children, whether physically or verbally. It is never too late for us to own our damaging behavior, and it is most helpful to our children's psyche. Up to age eight, most children, no matter how much they protest that their parents are being unfair, actually believe that they are bad and carry their abuser's shame. A parent's apology allows them to reduce their shame and realize that they are not bad.

I'd like to acknowledge here that, overall, permissiveness and neglect create more difficulties than an occasional spanking. I also know that many of you reading this who are living moral and ethical lives may have been spanked as children. The general conclusion of studies done on people who were spanked occasionally and seem to have grow up without deleterious effect is that success occurs primarily because of the parent's love, encouragement, and limit setting apart from the spankings. That is, *it was not the spanking that taught you anything.*

However, even if your family has spanked for generations, the extensive studies on spanking are unanimous: spanking is a form of child abuse and has serious consequences.

- Spanking works as a deterrent for conforming children who fear the rod. Their compliance is out of fear, not responsibility or cooperation.
- Spanking does not succeed with defiant children. Defiant children expect spankings. They learn to accept the spanking without reacting (often to show that they are tough). All parents can do is spank harder and longer, often resulting in severe abuse to the child.

- Children who are chronically spanked become sneaky and learn to lie. Their whole orientation is external. No internal virtue is developed.
- Homes can become a war zone when spanking is used as chronic discipline. The dinner table can set the stage for later eating disorders if children are hit for eating too fast or spilling food.
- Children follow their parents' example. Adults who hit children send a clear message: hitting others is acceptable under certain conditions. Children learn that the larger and more powerful you are, the more you can hit others, including smaller children.
- Spanking opens the floodgates to traumatic abuse, causing injury and breaking the law. Parents who approve of physical punishment abuse children at a rate four times greater than parents who do not approve of it.
- Children who are spanked often don't even know what they've done wrong, other than anger their parents somehow. They just "take it" and move on.

Chronic spanking also has cognitive effects. Murray Straus has shown that children under the age of four who were spanked more than three times a week showed a decrease in IQ. He concludes that the reason for this gap is that children who are spanked have less opportunity to build their reasoning, problem-solving ability, and language skills. "Children of non-spanking parents are far better behaved," says Straus. "They learn methods of controlling their anger that are not based on the fear of getting hit."

Moral intelligence cannot be learned through the use of external force. To stop spanking requires initiative, courage, and education. Physical punishment is destructive. True discipline is not. There are many different ways of disciplining, setting limits, and experiencing consequences for inappropriate behavior without spanking. (You will find some suggestions in chapters 11 and 14.)

Discipline has several dictionary definitions other than punishment. It means teaching, as well as a subject being taught. It means the experience that strengthens moral character. Since I believe with Aristotle and Aquinas that the virtuous life is the only true way to achieve happiness and human flourishing, the term *discipline* as I use it in this book means providing a rich and nourishing environment in which a person can develop her moral character and her own unique life of virtue. I believe that this is possible only by developing the virtue of prudence as the perfection of our innate moral intelligence.

In chapter 2 I suggested that our raw moral intelligence is a predisposition for the five major categories of universal morality: harming no one and caring and helping others when we can; fairness, which includes the real consequences when injustice is done; love and loyalty to one's family and to the larger community one chooses to be a part of (which certainly includes loving one's country); respect for just authority and just laws; and purity of mind, heart, and body. The great thing is that we are already predisposed toward these values.

In his book *The Road Less Traveled,* M. Scott Peck spoke of discipline as a set of techniques to reduce life's suffering and to enhance happiness. I don't see life as a quite the valley of suffering that he does, but in addition to developing our emotional intelligence, I like his four techniques for enhancing our happiness and reducing suffering: delay of gratification, acceptance of responsibility, dedication to truth, and balance. Peck believes that these can be learned by every healthy, normal child by the time he or she is ten years old. Peck's tenets really amount to teaching our children the boundaries of reality. They are the way to build our children's and our own self-worth and social interest, which were the goals of discipline set forth by psychiatrist Alfred Adler, whom I will discuss in chapter 14. I would stress that the world was made for us to be free in and as a place where we can find and nurture our true self, which means we must find our purpose and calling. The world of reality was also made for us to enjoy, and we need to laugh a lot and have fun while we are on the journey. There are many alternatives to corporal punishment to help our children develop their unique moral character, to love life, to love themselves, and to love their family and their neighbors.

Many good and well-intentioned people still believe that corporal punishment is a useful tool for morally educating their children. These folks believe it is biblically justified. Consider, however, that our founding fathers owned slaves and believed that such ownership was biblically justified. Today slavery is morally unthinkable. With everything we now know about the moral nature of the child, corporal punishment should become equally unthinkable.

14

THE HEART OF THE ORDER: CHARACTER AND FAMILY VALUES

We must give a certain character to our activities…
the habits we form in childhood make no small difference,
but rather they make all the difference.

—Aristotle

Character is a completely fashioned will.

—John Stuart Mill

Character refers to deep structures of personality that are particularly resistant to change.

—James Hillman

Liam Booth played for the Hollywood and Highland Stars in Toluca Baseball's Shetland Division. His coach, Paul Vercammen, described Liam as "a brown-haired boy, fair-skinned with little cherry cheeks every grandmother wants to pinch." He was born with a congenital heart defect, pulmonary atresia. He underwent four heart surgeries. At one point, Liam developed a potentially fatal staph infection, which no antibiotic seemed to be able to touch. Coach Vercammen writes, "Liam was on life support and in death's on-deck circle." Liam miraculously survived, and a year later, two months shy of his sixth birthday and with a donated pulmonary valve in his heart, he joined Vercammen's baseball team.

Liam was playing baseball on a team that cares about the children—not about winning at all costs. Coach Vercammen and all the parents join together to provide the youngsters with an experience of fun, camaraderie, and sportsmanship. When Liam was asked what he liked best about playing baseball, he answered, "Going to the dugout to be with my friends." Liam was able to occasionally hit the ball off the tee, but Vercammen and the team's other coach, Joe Campanella, tried endlessly to get Liam to hit a thrown pitch. He never succeeded, but nothing lessened his determination.

During the championship game, Liam came up to bat at a crucial moment—his team was behind, and there were two runners on and no outs. As Vercammen described it:

> Liam missed what I estimate was the 179th pitch to him this season. But on pitch 180, a thunderbolt seemed to strike the field. I heard it, a thwap, the unmistakable sound of wood smacking the ball. For the first time, Liam whacked a pitch fair, sending the ball halfway down the third-base line. [Our opponents] were stunned; both runners scored. Liam ended up safe and stood atop first base like an Olympic athlete on the gold medal platform.

Even the parents of the opposing team were crying in the stands as Vercammen gave Liam a high five—and then pulled the brim of his cap low so that no one could see the tears in his own eyes. The Stars went on to win the championship. As the subtitle of Vercammen's article reads, "Liam Booth might be smaller than the other members of his Toluca Lake Baseball team. And he might not connect with many pitches. But he's got hero written all over him."

I would add that he has character written all over him.

WHAT IS CHARACTER?

Character is who we are and what we believe in, as expressed in our actions and in how we live consistently from day to day. Character is the most enduring form in which our moral energy is channeled.

The Greek philosopher Heraclitus said that character is fate. The implication of his statement is that once our character is fully formed, it marks the boundaries of our destiny.

There is unquestionably something mysterious about each person's character. Even if we live quietly, without great public achievements, character is the unique manner in which we actualize our values. No one is exactly like anyone else. As James Hillman says in *The Soul's Code,* "Character is the mystery, and it is individual."

People of great character have three things in common:

1. Optimistic and undiluted moral energy that does not waver in the face of fear or adversity. They have the virtue of courage.
2. Self-discipline energized by willpower. They have the virtue of temperance.
3. Commitment to a core set of moral values that govern their style of living. These values are guarded by guilt and moved by the virtue of purpose.

While these virtues can be acquired throughout life, their foundation is built in childhood. After studying thousands of men and women, Bernice Neugarten, a social psychologist at the University of Chicago, concluded that the core pattern of character people form in their first seven years continues throughout their lives.

Moral Character Is Both Innate and Capable of Development

The great educators I discussed in chapter 4 saw that children have an innate moral intelligence, but they also saw how the external environment stimulates or retards its unfolding. This chapter picks up where chapter 11 left off, exploring how our children develop character as they move from the early world of the family into the wider world of neighborhood, school, and society. (See Figure 14.1.)

Our source figures have a major impact on moral character. Liam Booth embodies the energy, enthusiasm, and courage of his mother, Brenda, as well as the perseverance and dogged determination of his father, Bill. He definitely has his own unique character of hope, optimism, and joy.

Another component of every person's character is his or her temperament—certain innate behavioral biases due to different chemical patterns in the brain. In his book *Galen's Prophecy,* Jerome Kagan, a distinguished professor of psychology at Harvard, classifies these innate biases into four general categories: bold, timid, melancholy, and happy (upbeat).

Kagan's research established that up to 20 percent of children are what he called "behaviorally inhibited." They are finicky about new places or eating new foods, shy around strangers, prone to self-reproach, and anxious in social situations. Kagan theorizes that such children are born with a neurochemistry that makes the alarm system (the amygdala) in their emotional brain highly sensitive to arousal, while those on the bold end of the spectrum (about 40 percent of children) have an alarm system that is less easily excitable. There are also the cheerful types who seem to be chemically and emotionally constituted to see the doughnut, not the hole, while others—the dour and melancholy—see only the hole.

Temperament is relatively stable because of its genetic base, but every human quality can be changed through life experiences.

Figure 14.1:
THE BUILDING BLOCKS OF EMOTIONAL INTELLIGENCE:

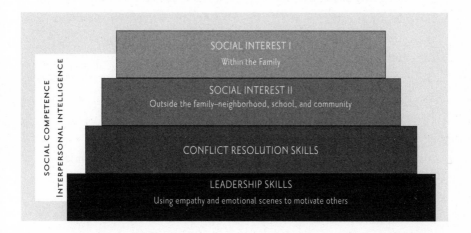

The brain is use-dependent and has great plasticity. Use dependency means that the more a new behavior is tried, such as speaking up despite shyness, the more the brain is capable of being assertive. This is a crucial point relative to moral intelligence. One could argue that a melancholy, depressive, or withdrawn temperament could be used as an excuse for asocial behavior. But Kagan is quite clear in his reply to such claims: "Put plainly, so that there is no confusion, every sane adult of average intelligence has the ability to moderate his or her asocial actions ... will is not undermined by temperament."

In addition to our innate temperament, three essential factors help shape our unique moral character. They are:

- The *ego strengths* that form the roots of the virtues of courage, temperance, and purpose, and of purpose's offspring, perseverance.
- *Parental leadership* that guides a child to develop three

qualities: healthy self-esteem (including the ego strengths mentioned above), social interest (which includes respect for parents, family members, and cultural and religious traditions), and respect for the rules and laws that come from legitimate authority. Parents also need to nurture their child's moral imagination. This includes supervising what their children read, the music they hear, what TV shows and movies they watch, their use of the Internet, and the video games they play.

- A *school environment* that fosters peer relationships, and expands the social skills of friendship, sharing, co-operating, and playing fair; increases respect for authority figures outside the family; teaches children the skills that prepare them to take on adult responsibilities; and an understanding of the wider culture of materialism and the cultural consensus of success (material success, physical beauty, and athleticism).

CHARACTER AND EGO STRENGTHS

Our ego functions in a way that is similar to the virtue of prudence in that it aims at establishing a measure of balance between our inner appetites/drives and the pressures coming from the outside world. The ego is the psychological organ of self-mastery and a guardian of human balance. A person with a weak ego lacks the ability to control his impulses. He also lacks the boundaries to say no and moderate those activities, substances, and things that in excess destroy meaningful experience and become vices.

Each of the essential components of character is rooted in an ego strength that is developed in a good-enough family environment during the first seven to ten years of our lives. A person who fails to develop these ego strengths as a young child can do remedial work and develop them later, though it is harder. An optimistic and undiluted energy that is unwavering even in the face of fear is the ego strength that forms the root of the virtue of courage. Self-discipline and learning to delay gratification are essential elements of character that are rooted in the ego strength of willpower, which forms the root of the virtue of temperance. The beginning of a commitment to a sound set of values is based on the ego strength of purpose, and purpose fuels the virtue of perseverance. I discussed courage, willpower, and purpose in chapter 11, but here I'd like to address the special challenges to the virtue of temperance that we face today. Certainly temperance ranks very high on the list of virtues that American society needs to reclaim.

Temperance and Our Consumer Culture

As a child I always dreamed of going on a shopping binge. Since my mom could barely make ends meet and often didn't, the only way I had to obtain things was by working. I began to work while I was still in elementary school, always giving part of my wages to my mother, and by high school I did manage to get the "right" clothes that my peer group demanded. I was never able to afford a car, though, and I consciously tried to do things to compensate. I was aware that I had a likeable personality, and being good in sports protected me greatly from being shamed.

Since then, having the "right" clothes, hairstyle, car, and so on has become even more rigid and demanding. I found this out when I took my children on the magical shopping trip I had always dreamed of. I gave them a generous limit and told them they could buy anything they wanted up to that amount. But what I'd hoped would be fun became an anxious ordeal. I discovered that my children considered only certain brands and stores acceptable. That was years ago; it's even worse today. The last time I took my granddaughter shopping, everything had to come from the Gap. This creation of approved objects of desire has a devastating effect on the virtue of temperance.

Desire is a basic part of our humanity, but it's important to recognize that our deepest appetites and longings can never be fully satisfied by the created order of the world. Someone once said, "Even after Shakespeare, Dante, and Mozart we say, 'Is that all?'" No finite, limited experience, object, or person can fill our transcendent longings. This is why human beings have always looked to some higher power—God as we understand God, or pure unconditional love—as the only possible source of our ultimate fulfillment.

Trying to develop temperance leads us to ultimately understand that things, material possessions, cannot satisfy that longing because it still remains after we possess an abundance of material goods.

The Organized Creation of Dissatisfaction

Today, however, we parents have to face powerful social forces that have organized to create dissatisfaction. Modern marketing leads us into what philosopher and literary critic René Girard calls "triangular desire." This means that we no longer genuinely choose the objects of our desire; rather we are socially pressured to want objects created by marketers. Cunning advertisers and public relations firms create the belief that certain items forge our identities as "cool!"

Adolescent and even preadolescent girls are lured by the way a certain Hollywood or music celebrity dresses. The boys are transfixed by the shoes some celeb tennis star or basketball player has endorsed. There is even a kind of temperance in all this; the outfit must be "just right," not "too far out" or "too straight." And children stake their quest for identity on these things. In high school, dressing like a punk, Goth, or prep gives teenagers the sense that they belong to a group. Every parent has experienced the intense emotional scenes their children enact when they don't have the "right" clothes or shoes to wear to school or the right music player or video game to show their friends. What should parents do?

Our job as parents is to acknowledge the role of these objects—without which our children and adolescents will be socially scorned or even ostracized—and our children's intense concerns while sending a clear message over and over again: "You are not what you own; your identity rests upon who you are." Even more important, we have to model this belief for them.

Examination of Conscience: Status Symbols

Before we can teach our children and adolescents that their identity is not determined by their possessions, we have to be sure we are not ourselves modeling triangular desire.

As Dr. Randall Smith, a theology professor at the University of St. Thomas in Houston, has written, "The same advertisers are at work on us, dividing the country into categories they label 'upward bound,' 'elite suburbs,' 'pools and patios,' or 'aging boomers.' A good advertising executive will be able to tell from your zip code where you shop and the kinds of things you are likely to buy." Our choices and tastes may feel intensely personal, when in fact we are being manipulated to want whatever will give us status or membership in a particular cultural group. I think it's important to note that these choices often feel authentic, as if they represented "our taste."

These fabricated objects of desire draw on the lusts and appetites we already own. Even though I understood intellectually exactly how this identity manipulation worked, the moment I had the money, I went for the status-symbol cars and clothes. It took me a good five years of being able to afford identity symbols such as the Versace suits or the Mercedes convertible before I truly realized how banal and empty they were as a way to fulfillment and happiness.

We parents fail when we model overconcern with social

status and put pressure on our children to "make it" by conforming to the success standards created by advertisers. We are relinquishing our role as parents and allowing the anonymous collective consumer culture to take our place. There is nothing wrong with fine things—just as long as we know and model that our identity is not based on what we own.

DISCIPLINE AS TEACHING SELF-ESTEEM AND SOCIAL INTEREST

Alfred Adler is considered one of the founding fathers of modern psychology. Adler's primary insight was that all healthy human development moves in the direction of self-esteem and social interest. A person grows morally when these two fundamental needs are met.

As Adler defined it, social interest includes:

- Respect for others
- Tolerance of others
- Interest in others
- Cooperation with others
- Courage
- Encouraging agreement
- A true sense of worth
- Willingness to share
- A feeling of belonging

According to Adler, one of the major reasons children misbehave or act antisocially is that they have become discouraged: They've lost their self-esteem because their needs have not been met or they have been toxically shamed, whether within the family or in the larger community. Lacking the courage of ego strength, discouraged children feel inferior, and in order to overcome their sense of inferiority and their feelings of being socially alienated, they spend their energy trying to get their needs met in abortive ways.

The late psychologist Rudolf Dreikurs developed Adler's insights into a pragmatic model of discipline that avoided power struggles and corporal punishment, while at the same time building the child's self-esteem, and social interest.

When children become discouraged, they turn to four basic types of manipulation, ranging from minor to major:

1. *Attention getting.* The discouraged child continually seeks proof of his approval or status, doing whatever is necessary to get attention. Most preschool children need a lot of attention, and it's normal for a child to seek reassurance of their significance to their parents. However, an extremely fearful and needy child will be felt as an annoyance and will engage in destructive attention-getting behavior, such as continually crying, interrupting, and temper tantrums. At this level, simply giving a child attention when he is misbehaving will generally stop the manipulative behavior. For a very needy child, however, even punishment can become a reward. Parents who threaten, yell, and spank need to take note of this.

2. *Power.* The discouraged child lacks confidence and feels powerless. As the need for power in a discouraged child intensifies, the caretakers will find themselves engaging in power struggles. The dinner table is one of the classic battlegrounds. The parent demands that the child eat all his food. The child refuses, and a stand-off takes place (sometimes for hours). A better strategy would be to withhold dessert or simply not make a child eat food she doesn't like. Whenever you start to think or say, "You can't get away with this," the child has achieved his goal of engaging you in a power struggle.

3. *Revenge.* At this level of discouragement children do things to hurt other children and make themselves as hateful as possible. Caretakers feel deeply hurt and outraged by the child and dislike them.

4. *Display of inadequacy.* The most discouraged children act stupid, inept, and indolent—even feeble-minded. The children assume real or imagined deficiency to safeguard prestige, and so that nothing will be expected of them. In essence, the child gives up and feels hopeless.

Unless parents learn to meet a child's legitimate needs for attention and some sense of personal power, these behaviors escalate. Attention getting, power, revenge, and inadequacy can become forms of violence later in life. One of the major issues in the marriages I counseled were power struggles; some involved severe emotional abuse, and a few physical abuse. Serial killers, who are highly motivated by attention and power, are covertly avenging real or imagined abuse. Some of the people who have gone on mass killing sprees have underlying feelings of being totally inadequate.

The Family as Organization

Dreikurs devoted his life to the development of democratic families and the diminishment of power struggles. He believed that the roots of violence were in families with discouraged and toxically shamed children as well as discouraged and immature parents. Parents use control and power because they've been taught control and power and feel inept without them. The same is true of cultures of obedience. Dreikurs believed that family life could be joyful and that virtue could be fostered by developing self-esteem and social interest.

The family is the place we first learn social interest. Like all organizational systems, families have a basic climate or environ-ment, shaped by six key factors:

1. *Flexibility.* When the family is flexible, it allows its members to be innovative in age-appropriate ways. Once when my wife and I were doing a workshop, my thirteen-year-old son rearranged the kitchen. It was quite a bit more functional the way he set it up, and we were glad he felt safe in taking the initiative.

2. *Responsibility.* Each member of the family is responsible in an age-appropriate way. Dreikurs recommends that the family have a weekly council meeting starting when the children are eight years old. The agenda is set by the par-ents, but it includes housework, lawn cutting, and other responsibilities within children's ability. No one is required to do the same job every week (except Dad and Mom). The family council sets goals to strive for as a family, and works to agree on its larger purpose in the community. The family also discusses vacations and ways to have fun to-gether.

3. *Standards and rules.* These are stated or written in con-crete, specific language. In the Dreikurs family council model, rules need to be agreed on. One essential rule is that all rules determined in the family council can be changed.

4. *Rewards and consequences.* There can be agreed-on re-wards for jobs well done. This is usually determined by parents, but everyone in the family has the right to com-ment or suggest awards. One child might agree to do the dishes for three months in order to get something he espe-cially wants. There are also agreed-upon consequences for failing to meet responsibilities or for breaking family rules.

5. *Clarity.* Each person in the family needs to know what is expected of him or her by the other members. Dad and/or Mom are the moneymakers, although as children are able, they can help out with part-time or summer jobs. If necessary, they may be asked to contribute to the household. If Dad and Mom have plenty, the children are guided in appropriate spending and taught money management.

6. *Commitment.* This involves an agreed-upon goal or common purpose for the family. This may simply mean treating each other with manners and respect. It may also involve loyalty. Commitment may not need to be formally expressed, although in some families it is constantly verbalized. I like a commitment to joy and looking for the positive side of things—certainly not to the neglect of real problems, but even then, sharing what lessons earlier problems taught a parent or the family as a whole can be useful.

Examination of Conscience: Family Goals

As the stewards of the family, parents need to be in unison on what they present as the agenda for their meetings. What would you like your family to be? What are you willing to let go of and what do you believe is necessary for you and your spouse to control? Consider how family meetings might enhance your love for one another. How can you make your family more lively and fun?

The Family Council and Discipline

Beginning at about seven or eight years of age, a child reaches the level of concrete logical thinking at which she is capable of grasping logical consequences such as withholding privileges. But even quite small children can grasp concrete, related consequences. The four-year-old who throws a block at his two-year-old brother is told in an authoritative way that his blocks will be taken away for a certain period every time he throws one. Or if six-year-old Alphonse leaves his toy radio-controlled car outside after being told a couple of times to put it in his room, the car is put in the attic for two weeks. There is a related consequence between the crime and the punishment. Once Alphonse can participate in the family council, he can have a say in deciding appropriate consequences.

The family council is democratic, but Mom and Dad are clearly the presidents. Still, all members of the family (at least seven or eight years old) have an equal vote. Younger children are welcome as long as they don't disrupt the meeting. When I first held the family council my son was two and he found the meeting boring.

The family gains experience in running the meetings, and as the children mature they are allowed more and more participation. When children realize that their vote really does count, they begin to take things more seriously, and when they are left with the undesirable chores because they were not present and therefore lost their vote, they will soon be coming to the council meetings. What Dreikurs found after much research and experimenting with actual families was that allowing children to participate in choosing their own consequences brought them a sense of self-worth.

In essence, the family council Dreikurs conceived of was a participatory democracy. The family was looked upon as belonging to all its members. The family as an entity had needs: money, food, a house (shelter), keeping the house in order, fun and recreation, and many other things. For Dreikurs these tasks should be shared age-appropriately by everyone in the family. The family council can decide on what kind of family it wants to be. One family gave each of their children a certain amount of money at Christmas (or any traditional time of giving) and had them donate a portion of that to a charity of their choice. Another family had all the members vote on a community charity they would all work on.

When a person agrees to a task that is important to the whole family (say, doing the dishes), then a consequence is discussed and voted on if the person fails to do that job. If consequences are to have an impact, the individual must be able to see the alternatives (choices) she is confronted with and accept the consequences imposed by the decision she makes. This teaches the child to be prudent and enhances her moral intelligence.

The council can also become a place where feelings can be safely expressed and outside problems are presented and help is received. Steven told his family council that he was being bullied on his way to school. The family came up with several suggestions, such as alternative routes and friendly conversation with the bullying child. None of these worked, and one day Steven was punched by the bully. At that point, Mom and Dad went to the school principal and the bullying was stopped. No solution works all the time, but if a child knows he has support and a place of refuge to help choose a course of action, it makes him feel safe.

PARENTAL LEADERSHIP

The family council is also a school for leadership, with the parents as role models. As you can see in Figure 14.1, leadership is one of the most important skills for social competence. My interest here is in moral leadership. Living a virtuous life that embodies and expresses your moral values is the best kind of parental leadership. A leader is able to motivate others by activating their emotions. Emotions move us, and great leaders know how to use words to trigger their followers' emotions and move them to action. Most of us will not be famous leaders, but we all have opportunities to be leaders in our families and our communities.

As part of his work on emotional and social intelligence, Daniel Goleman researched leadership styles. His work has been mostly in the business world, but it has important applications to parenting, teaching, coaching, and religious ministering.

Goleman identified six distinct styles of leadership:

1. Coercive: "Do what I tell you."
2. Authoritative: "Come with me."
3. Affiliative: "People come first."
4. Democratic: "What do you think?"
5. Pacesetting: "Do as I do now."
6. Coaching: "Try this."

Each style can work, and some are the best match for certain situations. For example:

1. Coercive: in a crisis or when people in our care are causing problems or have become troublemakers
2. Authoritative: when change requires a new vision or when a clear direction is needed
3. Affiliative: to heal rifts in a family team or organization to motivate people under stressful circumstances
4. Democratic: to get input from all the members of the family or team members
5. Pacesetting: to get quick results from a highly motivated and competent group of people
6. Coaching: to help a person improve behavior or performance, or develop long-term strengths

However, not all were equally effective when considered from the point of view of the *climate* of an organization, be it a fire department, office, church, or family. The affiliative, democratic, and coaching styles were all positive in building character (especially temperance and responsibility). But the authoritative was the most strongly positive, offering a strong model of a leader with purpose. The coercive and pacesetting styles were generally negative, although the coercive might be necessary in a crisis.

For example, if you have more than one child, learning to use an affiliative style of leadership may be very useful when your children get into their inevitable fighting and bickering. If your style is coercive, your older child will more often than not be coercive with his or her younger sibling(s). The affiliative style works very effectively with the conflict resolution model I will present shortly. You will have to take time to be the facilitator and teach the model to the warring siblings. Have your children each take a turn and present the facts about what's bugging them using "I" messages ("I saw you eat part of my candy. I feel like you're picking on me because you're bigger."). Help them express their feelings and say what they want ("I'm mad and I want you to give me some of yours."). Although the candy episode presented here is a pretty clear-cut case of boundary violation, the technique is worth teaching. It will take time and practice, but it builds honest communication.

Examination of Conscience: Leadership Styles

Try to recall the leadership styles your parents or grandparents used and what effect each style had on you. We often copy styles that were used on us that we didn't like. As I discussed in chapter 4, parents often do to their children what was done to them, as a form of revenge.

Looking at myself, I started out being the supernice dad coach, but in times of stress I resorted to coercive yelling and raging. I did not know how to contain anger. After a bout of rage I felt awful and went back to being a supernice dad. This is an ineffective and abusive style of leadership. I started to have some real success with the democratic family council when I learned how to contain my anger.

CONFLICT RESOLUTION

The backbone of social intelligence is conflict resolution. In chapter 10, I quoted John Gottman's statement that the essence of a good long-term relationship is the ability to argue well. Knowing how to argue well is the skill involved in resolving our inevitable differences. The fact that each of us is a unique person means that we will have differences of perception, opinions, beliefs, and values.

The best way for children to learn conflict resolution skills is for parents to model them. Unfortunately, many of us grew up in families that were under the shadow of a culture of obedience, and the remedies that were modeled for us were dysfunctional.

Dysfunctional Patterns

In the early years of my first marriage, I periodically raged at my wife and children. Once I realized how offensive and morally impotent this kind of behavior was, I was aware I had to do something about it, but I simply did not know how to contain my anger, and I had no models for remedying conflict. This is no excuse. We have a moral demand as caring human beings to learn better ways of resolving conflict. You can stop raging and yelling. I have. Rage and yelling are offender behavior (true forms of violence) and can have devastating effects on the people they are aimed at.

Other common dysfunctional approaches to conflict are what the psychologist Murray Bowen called "cutoffs," "triangulation," and "passive-aggressive behavior." The simplest form of cutoff is pouting silence—we simply refuse to speak to the person we are displeased with. Cutoffs can last a few hours, days, or in the worst cases years. I know of families where the cutoff by one person lasted for decades, even a lifetime.

Triangulation is an attempt to buffer the conflict. If I talk to my mother about my brothers' and sisters' faults, I do not have to face them directly. This can be dangerous because my mom may think I'm too harsh and tell my brother. He gets furious and blows up at me and cuts me off. Nothing gets resolved. All kinds of triangulations take place in families that do not have conflict resolution skills.

In chapter 10 I told you about Irma, who was enraged over her job and missed many weeks of work because of arthritis. Irma is an example of a person who saw no way to remedy her situation and turned her rage against herself in a passive-aggressive way.

We can also turn our passive-aggressive anger directly against another. The repressed anger is expressed obliquely, through seemingly unrelated behavior. If I am angry at my sister, I can accidentally break her favorite mirror or something else she really likes. Because it seems to be an accident (and I myself might even believe that it is), it's hard for my sister to be angry at me. All the while I've expressed my anger at her by breaking her cherished mirror.

For our individual health and for the health of our family, school, team, or organization, it is important for us to be straight about our feelings. Honest, self-responsible expression of feelings is the morally best way to connect with another person. Being honest about expressing our feelings to another builds trust. Even if you don't like what's being expressed, it's honest and the other person can be trusted. Yelling, raging, phony niceness, or silent withdrawal is the antithesis of emotional health.

Exercise: Dealing with Conflict

I have found the following model for dealing with conflict to be the single most helpful tool for my interpersonal life. It is a morally honest way to connect with another person. I've used it in my own life for the last twenty years. I've also used it when I worked with businesses, in marital counseling, and between parents and children.

Step One: Admit the Conflict

The first step is for the two people in conflict to admit that they have a conflict and decide on a time for working on a resolution to their quarrel. Generally an ongoing conflict in a family causes everyone anxiety. If you are using a democratic family council, the conflict can be put in the agenda for the next meeting, although most conflicts should be worked out privately (especially those between Mom and Dad). The council can be a place where conflicted partners express their willingness to reach a resolution or compromise. It's best when both parties are willing to come to a resolution. The person who is angry also needs to get clear about the scene or ongoing scenes that triggered the anger—as detailed a picture of the scene as possible.

Here's an example from my counseling practice. Henry is angry at his son Donald. The scene that triggered his anger was this one: Donald is on summer vacation. He is thirteen years old and has just finished seventh grade at a renowned and very expensive private school. Henry is a hardworking man, a bit rough at the edges and very successful financially in the meatpacking business. Donald has made it clear that he has no interest in his father's business, but Henry insists that Donald needs to get some experience in the work world. Donald says he wants to find his own job. Because of Donald's age, finding a job is a difficult task. Donald has spent the first month of summer vacation hidden away in his room listening to loud rap music. There have been several heated conversations between father and son over Don's failure to get a job and over the rap music that the father can't understand and hates. The most recent encounter ended in a prolonged shouting match with his father threatening to "beat the shit" out of Donald. Henry had to be restrained by his wife and a business friend who was spending the evening with them. The next day Henry called me for help, and I scheduled a counseling session for him and his son.

Step Two: Disclosure

Step two of the conflict resolution model involves the honest and clear disclosure of the scene that triggered the anger. Disclosure must be made in self-responsible statements, always in the first person.

Henry starts out well enough. "Wednesday night," he says to Donald, "we had a business customer over for cocktails and dinner. Shortly after supper we went to our living room to chat. The music from your room got louder and louder, so loud we could not have a civil conversation."

Now here's where Henry went off track. "I went upstairs and saw you and that friend of yours so out of it you couldn't hear me asking you to turn the music down. You and your deadbeat friend looked stoned to me. I told you that you were disgusting, a lazy bum that I've paid my hard-earned money to support and that I was going to kick your lazy ass. I still feel like doing it."

Donald sat glaring at his father, his eyes glazed in angry shame. At this point, my job was to stop the name-calling and contempt. So I asked Donald to leave the therapy session so I could work with Henry.

Now Henry was angry at me. "He needs the therapy, not me. What the hell are you doing?"

I validated Henry's upset and anger but told him it would be to his advantage to keep his son out of our counseling sessions for the next few weeks while I introduced a technique that I thought would help.

Step Three: The Awareness Wheel

The disclosure model I used with Henry was adapted from a book called *Alive and Aware* by Sherod Miller, Elam Nunally, and Daniel Wackman. Their book has great depth, and I want to acknowledge that I have simplified their model, which they called the "awareness wheel."

The awareness wheel begins with the *sensory data* that describe the scene or scenes that trigger our anger, distress, or fear. Then it asks us to focus on our *interpretation* of that data. The most important issue in conflict is the interpretation we make from the actual experience—the data we see or hear or touch. This interpretation is usually either an assumption (how a 13-year-old should act) or a *fantasy,* an act of the imagination, when it comes to knowing another person's intention. In this case, Henry stated that his son's friend was a deadbeat (this was the second time Henry had seen this friend). Henry also accused them of being stoned (he had no previous or actual data on that), he called his son disgusting and a lazy bum (Donald was a straight "A" student in a difficult school), and said he was wasting his father's money (Henry had insisted on Donald going to this school).

For practice, I had Henry go through the scene that had almost ended in physical violence. He said: "I had a business friend and customer over for dinner. During dinner I heard the music begin to play. After dinner my friend and I went to the living room for an after-dinner drink and I heard the music getting louder and louder—so loud we could hardly hear each other. I excused myself and went up to my son's room. The music was so loud that he couldn't hear me knocking on the door. Finally they opened the door and I saw one of them lying on a chair and the other on the bed, dressed in those baggy pants and shirts. Neither one of them spoke to me. I went over, lowered the music considerably and let them have it. I told them they were disgusting, lazy bums. My son told me not to talk to his friend that way. I yelled at him, he yelled back, and I threatened to kick the shit out of him. My wife and my friend came up and took me by the arm out of the room."

Imagining can be right or wrong, but it's always a fantasy since we have no way of getting under each other's skin or knowing for sure what is going on inside another person's mind.

After I got a pretty good picture of the scene, I asked Henry what he *imagined* was going on with his son. He said, "He's just spoiled and lazy." To which I countered with the *facts* about his academic excellence and his athletic achievement on the school's soccer team.

Then I asked Henry what he *felt* when he imagined his son using drugs and being a lazy bum. He said he felt *afraid* and angry. Now we were getting somewhere. "Afraid of what?" I asked. "I'm afraid I've let him down as a father; I'm afraid he's going to be a failure. I'm angry because he won't work for me; but mostly I'm angry cause I don't know how to motivate him," Henry replied.

Next I asked, "What do you *want* from him?" He said he wanted to know if he was involved with drugs and why he was resisting work.

Now the four-part disclosure of the awareness wheel was complete:

1. Sensory data—Henry had described what he saw and heard
2. Interpretation (fantasy)—he had enunciated his fantasies about his son
3. Emotion—he said he was afraid and angry
4. Volition—he said what he wanted

The awareness wheel asks us to speak with self-responsible "I" messages and say:

I saw, heard:
My interpretation (fantasy) of that data is:
My emotions, which come from my fantasy, are:
And my volition is: What I want from you.

At this point we were ready for Donald to join us in our next therapy session. When they were seated, I asked Henry to disclose himself according to the awareness wheel. His disclosure was not condemning, contemptuous, and shaming as it had been the first time around.

Owning his imaginative interpretation and telling his son that he was afraid that he had failed him, that he wanted the best for him but he did not know how to motivate him, allowed Donald to receive his father's disclosure unguardedly, without defenses, and to feel some compassion for his father's fear. Donald's whole body language was different when Henry finished his disclosure.

Step 4: Feedback

In this conflict resolution model, it's important for the one receiving the disclosure to report it back to the sender so that the sender is sure that the receiver heard him accurately. The psychologist Carl Rogers used this listening kind of validation as a key part of his therapy. Once the sender okays the feedback from the receiver, the receiver is free to respond.

Henry's son repeated what his father had said and went over and hugged him and assured him of his love for him. Donald said he enjoyed the rap music and that he hated the drug crowd. He had tried to get a job, but he was too young. He said he felt some fear about entering the work world.

Henry now mentioned two friends, one a grocery store manager, the other a psychiatrist. Each had told him they could hire Donald for the summer. Donald could be a grocery stock boy or he could clean three psychiatrist's offices in the evening. Donald wanted to think it over. It was agreed that Donald would listen to music with earphones. At Donald's suggestion, it was also agreed that he and his father would do something together (go fishing, go to a movie or sporting event) twice a month. We set up three more sessions, two weeks apart. I also had two extra sessions with Henry to review normal early teenage behavior. After the three follow-up sessions, things seemed to be reasonably stabilized.

This kind of mediating therapy for conflict resolution is not used enough in families or organizations. I've worked with law partners, clergymen, administrators and teachers, plant managers and front line supervisors using this model. It helps people be completely honest by staying under their own skin. To say I saw and heard, my fantasy is, I feel (whatever), and I want (whatever) allows the recipient of my disclosure to see what is going on inside of me. It demands listening as a way of contact and intimacy. And if they use it honestly, two people can greatly enhance their intimacy by clearly knowing how their partner is different from themselves.

This model can be used anywhere, with any group of people. Although I do not think a middle school child like Donald would use it with his buddies, it can help him understand that fantasy interpretation is at the root of many conflicts. We used this model quite effectively with the older teenagers in the L.A. drug program.

Parents need to be especially sensitive to using overly responsible "you" messages with their children. To a young child, parents are godlike. "You" messages can become godlike judgments that are nailed into a child's unconscious. "You are stupid" becomes a defining attribute for a child. The whole basket of parent tapes that many people carry around could be avoided if parents would be careful with their speech patterns and be rigorously honest by using "I" messages. I urge you to stop shaming and judging your children; I believe it's a moral duty. Many parental moralisms are seeds for their child's moral defects of character.

If children witness their parents' containment of emotion and nonshaming conflict resolution, they will have a model for resolving conflict. They will learn that they may not always get their way, but that they can work together toward a desired outcome. No parent will model conflict resolution perfectly all the time, and when caught off guard, people often regress to whatever they first learned in their family of origin. This model must be practiced and overlearned to become truly effective. Believe me: mastering nonshaming, rigorously honest conflict resolution is a moral gem.

MORAL IMAGINATION AND CHARACTER FORMATION

When I began this book with ten magnificent moral moments, I was trying to engage your moral imagination. Stories, poems, fables, and myths pertaining to virtue and virtuous people have always been one of the ways that parents and elders have attempted to educate those in their care. Guiding our children's moral imagination in our new age of electronic media is one of the most serious challenges to parental moral leadership. Please don't give up on this challenge.

Your family very likely has its own storehouse of family stories and sayings, and rather than try to suggest specific age-appropriate biblical stories and children's books, I'll simply recommend William J. Bennett's *The Book of Virtues* as a good place to start. This book is a true treasure for the moral imagination, divided into sections on self-discipline, responsibility, friendship, work, courage, perseverance, honesty, compassion, loyalty, and faith.

The Impact of the Information Revolution

Here, I'd like to focus on the impact of new technology on the moral imagination of our children. The information age, with its nonstop menu of movies, TV, and the Internet, has brought rich new resources as well as potent dangers to our children.

I can remember when everyone was talking about the enormous educational potential of television. In England, BBC-TV was launched with a public mission to transmit the best of British culture and history. PBS took up the same challenge in the United States, and *Sesame Street* and *Mr. Rogers' Neighborhood* became teachers to a whole generation of American children.

Then came the Internet, which was celebrated as the dawn of the "global village." We were going to give our children the best from all times and all cultures. But is that what we see on our TVs and computer screens today?

Unfortunately, network TV is not responsible to anyone but its sponsors, cable TV is not responsible to anyone but its paying customers, and both are accountable to only a minimal standard of social or moral responsibility.

This is a tragic thing because TV, the movies, the Internet, and all forms of media have changed our entire way of life. They have, to a large extent, replaced reading and storytelling as the primary nurturers of our moral intelligence. But parents can change that by reading to children early on and continuing to encourage children to read as they enter school.

Television as a Moral Teacher

Several years ago I was asked to present a one-day workshop for a group of criminal and civil judges in El Paso, Texas. The subject of the workshop was the relationship between media violence and actual violence. In other words, does violence on TV, in movies, and on the Internet cause actual acts of violence in society? (Video games are also a topic of debate; I will address those separately.)

In doing my research for the workshop, I found a book by Thomas Lickona entitled *Raising Good Children*. I was especially taken with one chapter, "Television as a Moral Teacher—and What to Do About It."

Lickona presented the research of Leonard Eron, then a psychologist at the University of Illinois, who pioneered the study of factors linked to aggression in children. Eron studied 875 eight-year-olds and did a follow-up on 475 of them ten years later. He looked at two primary factors: physical punishment and the amount of TV the eight-year-olds watched. The children who had been spanked were far more aggressive than those who had not been. But surprisingly, the single best predictor of aggression in the late teens was the amount of violent TV a child had watched at age eight. A later study of 750 children showed the same results—this time including increased aggression in girls, as well. Related research in Finland, Poland, and Australia came to the same conclusions. And these are only a few of many such studies.

Lickona also cites a comprehensive report from the National Institute of Mental Health that summarized more than 2,500 studies on television and behavior. The conclusion: "There is 'overwhelming evidence' of a causal link between children's watching TV and their performing violent acts."

I cohosted a late-night TV talk show for ten years. One of our guests was a paroled bank robber. He robbed his first bank after watching a TV show on bank robberies. He subsequently robbed fifty banks and shot two people before he was caught. His message was that his violence was a direct result of watching violence on TV.

What Children Learn from TV

Lickona lists the following as some of the potentially dangerous things children learn from TV:

1. *Violence isn't anything to get upset about.* Even if kids don't copy the violence on TV, they develop a ho-hum attitude toward it, primarily because it's disembodied and presented matter-of-factly.

2. *Put-downs are funny.* Put-downs are a huge and growing cause of interpersonal problems in children.

3. *It's a rotten world.* Television gives kids a jaundiced view of society. There is little respect for authority figures, and television focuses on bad news. It's a recipe for cynicism. I've personally been shocked by children's lack of respect for parents, teachers, and authority figures. (A friend recently called me to give him and his wife moral support because their seventeen-year-old daughter had been battered

by her nineteen-year-old husband. When the parents and I arrived at the couple's house, the daughter was belligerent because the police were taking the batterer to jail. They told her to sit down. She answered, "Why should I? I don't feel like it." The young husband was giving his father-in-law the finger from the backseat of the police car.) Studies have also found that heavy TV watchers are more fearful of the world and are apt to have violent dreams.

4. Adults are stupid. In sitcoms about families, the kids are always smarter than grown-ups. This of course plays into the cognitive conceit I discussed in chapter 12, but it also reinforces cynicism and disrespect.

5. Life is entertainment. I recently interviewed six experienced and devoted elementary school teachers. Each told me the same story: compared to when they entered the profession, children now expect and demand to be entertained, even in the classroom.

6. Sex is okay with just about anyone. In prime-time shows such as *Two and a Half Men* and *Sex & the City,* sex is casual and needs no commitment.

7. Things make you happy. If you have the right clothes, cars, and kind of house, you will be happy.

8. Violence is a way to get what you want. Rather than hard work, perseverance, and patience as a way to get what you want, use power, bullying, and violence to get them.

The reality shows point to the avid desire people have for getting on TV. Is this the highest aspiration we can offer our children? Is it so compelling that it's worth any amount of struggle and humiliation?

Lickona's book was too early to report data on Internet use. However, those of us who treat sexual addiction, as we do at the Meadows, see quite clearly that cybersex has grown exponentially. It is now estimated that pornography on the Internet makes more money than the three major TV networks put together.

The Video Game Plague

I recently gave a keynote address to a group of drug counselors and drug program administrators in Louisiana. This is where I met Lt. Col. Dave Grossman, a former Army Ranger and paratrooper who taught psychology at West Point and military science at Arkansas State University. He gave me a copy of his book *On Killing: The Psychological Cost of Learning to Kill in War and Society* and a book he wrote with Gloria DeGaetano, a recognized educator in the field of media violence, entitled *Stop Teaching Our Kids to Kill*. Lt. Col. Grossman has been an expert witness and consultant in several mass-murder cases, including that of Timothy McVeigh. *Stop Teaching Our Kids to Kill* is one of the most powerful, convincing, and frightening books I've read in a long time.

Grossman and DeGaetano offer detailed evidence for their claim that the primary blame for teen violence is to be laid on the makers of violent video games (called "murder trainers" by one expert), the TV networks, and Hollywood movie studios.

One incident reported by Grossman and DeGaetano shook me to the core:

Fourteen-year-old Michael Carneal steals a gun from a neighbor's house, brings it to school, and fires eight shots into a student prayer meeting that is breaking up. Prior to stealing the gun, he had never shot an actual handgun before. The FBI says that the average experienced law enforcement officer, in the average shoot-out, at an average range of seven yards, hits with approximately one bullet in five. So how many hits did Michael Carneal make? He fired eight shots; he got eight hits, on eight different kids. Five of them were head shots, and the other three were upper torso. The result was three dead and one paralyzed for life.

How does a child of fourteen who has never shot a handgun before acquire such expertise? According to Grossman, "Nowhere in the annals of law enforcement or military or criminal history can we find an equivalent achievement. The boy did this on his first try."

But in fact Michael Carneal had practiced killing literally thousands of people. His simulators were point-and-shoot video games that he played for hours and hours in video arcades and in the comfort of his own home. These games resemble the real thing—and in fact are being used by law enforcement agencies as part of their training.

Grossman and DeGaetano's book is a call to action for all concerned citizens—most especially parents, teachers, and school administrators. There are a growing number of media literacy and violence prevention organizations. Please get involved. If ever there were a moral question of deep social interest, it is this one, and our teenage kids are especially at risk.

Examination of Conscience: Media Use

The Greek philosopher Plato wrote eloquently about the importance of carefully educating the young. In *The Republic,* he said:

You know that the beginning is the most important part of any work especially in the case of a young and tender thing; for that is the time at which the character is being formed.... Shall we carelessly allow children to hear any casual tales [or watch any

TV shows], which may be devised by casual persons [?] . . . anything received into the mind at that age is likely to become in-
delible and unalterable; and therefore it is most important that
the tales which the young first hear should be models of virtuous
thought.

I remember my sixth grade baseball coach, Fred O'Conner,
taking the whole team to see the movie *The Pride of the Yankees,*
about the life of baseball great Lou Gehrig. Gehrig held the
record for the most consecutive games played until Cal Ripkin
broke it. He died of a mysterious disease (ALS) that is still called
"Lou Gehrig's disease." Gehrig was a model of loyalty, humility,
and perseverance throughout his life, and he demonstrated unusual courage in face of this terrible and painful disease. Most of
us boys were so moved we were crying (and trying not to let the
other guys see us). That one movie taught me more about loyalty,
humility, perseverance and courage than all the sermons I had
heard. Coach O'Conner understood the positive power of the
moral imagination.

Are you willing to use the V-chip and other ways to control
what your kid can watch? Reformers clamored for them, but
only a minuscule number of parents have used them. Are you
willing to set time limits on viewing or game playing, watch with
the kids, take the TVs out of the kids' bedrooms? Here's a chance
for you to exercise your virtue of prudence. Children will have a
tough time with peers if they aren't part of the TV culture, but
they don't have to be consumed by it.

Many of us are caught in the media trance ourselves. It is
powerful and compelling, and I urge parents to examine their
own conscience on these matters. Many of us are too hooked to
hit the off button or to be selective about what we watch. And
sometimes we're just as happy that our kids are occupied and out
of our hair. I struggled with these issues with my own children,
and I assure you I'm not trying to tell you what to do. But here's

a chance to make the right decision at the right time for the right reason.

Media Could Be an Influence for Good

It is important to add that vulnerable children and adolescents are most at risk, and that media violence can be an influence for good. Scientific evidence has established that screen portrayals of violence need not lead to reinforcement of aggressive attitudes and behaviors if the consequences of violence are demonstrated; if violence is shown to be regretted or punished; if the perpetrators are not glamorized and are shown to cause harm, pain, and human suffering; or if the act of violence is seen as justifiable.

Better yet, use the availability of DVDs to bring your children the best. A great movie for parents to share with their school-age children is *To Kill a Mockingbird,* the moving and powerful story of a man named Atticus Finch, played by actor Gregory Peck. Finch is a man of extraordinary moral character, and the drama is seen through the eyes of his two young children.

Try holding a family night several times a year to show your children the movies—or read them the books—that moved you as a child. It's a great way to let them know what you value.

SOCIAL INTEREST OUTSIDE THE FAMILY

My family had moved six times by the time I was nine years old. I stayed close to home and did not have a lot of social interaction until we had lived in the same house for more than four years. As I ventured into the neighborhood and went to the same school I became aware of the reality of social life outside the family. I slowly came to understand that other people had rules and norms that were different than my family's. I was popular at school, a straight-A student, and a good athlete. I quickly learned that these were marks of success in the world away from home. I also learned that I was poor and that my father's constant absences were due to his alcoholism.

The best thing I learned was what it was to have a friend.

When I was ten years old I used to sit on a curb on Huldy Street with my friend Bob Cagle and talk long into the night about the world of our future, what we wanted to do in life. My mom thought Bob was bad for me, since he had a home situation where he was pretty much unsupervised. But we saw the good in each other back then; children often do, much to their parents' chagrin. We shared many adventures together and learned how to share and be loyal to each other. Bob and I drifted apart in our late teens. But when I was in my first dark night of the soul, he was there for me. Then, some years later, I got a call from Bob saying he had read my book *Healing the Shame That Binds You,* and that it had helped him to understand his childhood. Although Bob had done well financially, he had some of the lingering shame issues that I had.

All in all, Bob has become a very successful man, married for life, raised several children, and now has a boatload of grandchildren. He is one of the finest men I've ever known. Bob and I will have lunch together this week, sixty-five years after we first met.

Earlier I referred to the deep mystery that surrounds the moral life. My mom thought Bob was headed down some dark road to failure. No one would have given a plugged nickle for my future during my drinking days. Yet in spite of many obstacles, and without any visible champions, two ten-year-old boys grew up to achieve what they had dreamed about on the curb of Huldy Street.

15

NAVIGATING ADOLESCENCE: WHY THE CONFLICT OF GENERATIONS IS NECESSARY

> The conflict between generations is inherent in social living and essential to social change.
>
> —Theodore Lidz

> I see no hope for the future of our people if they are dependent on the frivolous youth of today, for certainly all youth are reckless beyond words.... When I was a boy, we were taught to be discreet and respectful of elders—but the present youth are exceedingly wise and impatient of restraint.
>
> —Hesiod, ninth century B.C.

For two weeks during my junior year of high school, I lived in my best friend's car while he lived in a motel room with a girl in her late teens named Jackie, a much sought-after prostitute from Galveston's famed Post Office Street. It was a great coup to have gotten her to come home with us, but she liked my friend better than me. I spent two drunken weeks hoping I would receive some kind of sexual fruits from the arrangement, but I never did.

My junior year had disintegrated gradually. The previous summer I'd formed an alliance with four other guys—including my best friend—all fatherless and angry. After school started, I began missing baseball practice and spending more and more time at Parker's pool hall shooting pool and drinking beer. With my new peer group, I also began to frequent the Post Office Street brothels almost every other Saturday night.

This was the lowest point of my adolescence.

When I finally went home, my frantic mother grilled me about what I had been doing and badmouthed my best friend, calling him "trash" for the hundredth time. I made up some convoluted lie about what had happened. My mother finally gave up, too frazzled to care. I knew I could outlast her; she was at the point where it was easier for her to believe me.

I went to school the next day, a Friday. Instead of my usual straight A's, my third-semester report card showed the first C and D I'd ever gotten in my life. And, as I'd known would happen, I was kicked off the varsity baseball team. I had real potential as a catcher. I had been scouted by the St. Louis Cardinals in my sophomore year. But I was already on probation because I'd missed too many practices. Cutting school was the last straw. This would be the end of my baseball career.

All that weekend, I stayed in my room. I felt terrible shame and more alone than I had ever been in my life. I was lost and confused about who I was and where I was headed. I felt like I was no damn good. I was violating all the values I had been taught. I hated what I was doing. There were many times I didn't want to go drinking, and I really disliked going to Post Office Street. The sex was never fulfilling. But I was too scared to tell my buddies for fear they would turn on me and exclude me.

I felt I had nowhere to turn. My father was gone, and while I idolized my grandfather, he was a rigid Catholic, and I could not talk to him about anything other than golf or Notre Dame football. The priest who was my homeroom teacher was supposed to be my spiritual director, but he had molested me three times and continued to stalk me, regularly asking me to go to dinner or the movies with him. I thought his sexual exploitation was my fault, and I knew my mother and grandfather would not believe me if I told them what had happened. Or if they did believe me, it would scandalize them, and I would feel horrible if I disrupted their neat and tidy faith.

In the midst of this chaos, I helped my mother financially and even gave my little brother his allowance. My mother had never gotten over her divorce, and she sometimes cried for hours in her room with the door locked. I felt I was responsible for her pain, and I hated that burden.

I was still going to church every Sunday and on holy days. I also went to confession and prayed a lot—mostly apologizing for the mess I was in. My harsh conscience told me I was morally corrupt, but deep down I wanted to be good.

I was in the full vortex of what I would later understand to be my adolescent identity crisis. Mine was quite extreme, but it contained many of the elements of the normal adolescent transition. It also contained many elements of moral intelligence.

In this chapter, I'd like to examine the adolescent transition in the context of the sources of moral intelligence that I've discussed throughout this book, including ego strength (character), environment, moral models, conscience, experience (experimentation), emotional intelligence, and religion.

My observations come not only from my own adolescence but also from a dozen years of teaching adolescents in both high school and college, and also from running a teenage drug abuse program in Los Angeles. My own troubled youth gave me a lot of empathy for the kids I taught. They were at times joyous and wonderful, and at other times they seemed like outpatients from the local asylum. Knowing that the brain in not fully developed until the early twenties makes a lot of adolescent behavior easier to understand.

THE ADOLESCENT BRAIN

Provided earlier development has been normal, the ability to think abstractly starts at about age twelve, and it will continue to develop for several more years, reaching its maturation at anywhere from eighteen to the early twenties. In chapter 12, I pointed out that our thinking can expand only if it is challenged.

Lack of education, whether because of poverty, dropping out of school, or living in a cultlike family or religious group, can inhibit mental expansion.

Normal adolescence opens the door to what Piaget called "formal operational thinking." Adolescents can think about thinking; they become conscious that they are conscious. They can also come up with a purely ideal or hypothetical construct, such as "What if no one had to die?" and speculate about it.

This means that *the future becomes a problem for the first time*. The adolescent's new mental ability can be painful because the future presents fearful unknowns and because the ability to reflect on one's own thought process brings an often excruciating sense of self-consciousness. This newfound mental ability ushers in what Erik Erikson called an "ego identity crisis."

For Erikson the ego identity crisis describes and characterizes the tasks that should be achieved during the adolescent transition to adulthood, and like every developmental crisis, it is a time of heightened potential and severe vulnerability and risk.

While no one completely knows his or her true self by the end of adolescence, young people who have developed the social interest I discussed in chapter 14 have a good sense of how they are perceived by others; if they have also achieved good ego strengths (good self-esteem) prior to adolescence, they have the foundation upon which they can develop a strong and enduring sense of ego identity. Strong ego identity is the inner structure of strong moral character.

The low point in my own adolescence was a dramatic version of Erikson's identity crisis. Going into high school, I was severely shame-based. On the outside, I was at the top of my class academically and a better-than-average athlete, but on the inside I felt flawed and defective and was horribly ashamed of my family. Shame-based people have boundary problems. If you feel like an imposter, flawed and defective, then you have trouble really standing for anything—you have no real values. Your only values are outside of you. This was partially true for me. I needed to belong, but deep down I also had a gut-level knowledge that I was on the wrong track.

Even with decent self-esteem, adolescent thinking can be confused. Because the teenager's mind is able to hypothesize and create imaginative alternatives, there is a tendency to get lost in these processes. Teachers and parents need to help teenagers focus their minds and realistic imaginations on future goals that are achievable.

In their late teens, the ability to futurize that has been made possible by the maturing frontal lobes brings up the question of the meaning of one's life—the call of one's destiny. "Who am I? Why am I here? Where am I going? What is my legacy?" These are the implicit—or explicit—questions that torment adolescents.

The true self emerges slowly throughout one's lifetime. In early childhood it must often be hidden or repressed. As the adolescent starts leaving home, interacting with and getting feedback from friends, and beginning to date potential mates, the true self clamors to emerge—sometimes in troubling or confusing ways. Young people must cope with a myriad of new choices as they experiment with their newly developed physical, emotional, and mental abilities.

As a teacher, I never wanted to discourage experimentation and curiosity, because we never know for sure where the urges of the true self will lead. At the same time, I was aware that many adolescents ignore the difference between mental constructs and the "real thing." Many kids told me they were going to be major league baseball players or movie stars or TV news anchors, without the slightest notion of what it really takes to achieve such positions. They were also attracted to ideologies even though they didn't know the practical results of those ideologies. They just hadn't lived enough to see that the "master plan" may not play out so well in the real world.

When I was a child, parents and teachers often put down kids' aspirations quite harshly: "What makes you think you know so much?" "You'll never make a living doing that." By the time my son was in school, we'd started to tell children, "You can be anything," which, in a way, can be just as cruel. Our job is to (temperately) help young people keep their feet in the real world while they build concretely step by step toward some of their dreams. We do not want to crush their dreams. Their ability to see what does not yet exist moves us all forward.

When I taught high school, I often counseled students to seek out experiences related to their goal. Joe, a senior, thought he wanted to be a lawyer, so I helped him get a job in a law office the summer after he graduated. He enjoyed his summer and went to law school after college. But even a negative experience can be valuable. I started college intending to major in pre-med and had a summer job in a medical lab after my freshman year. I found out that I did not want to be a doctor.

Many adolescents are remarkably lacking in curiosity about things outside their comfort zone. They're happy to just get by. This also applies to their moral intelligence. The apathetic teen conforms to his or her dogmatic religious or moral beliefs without questioning them.

It is critical to our sense of integrity and competence to know what we can and can't do, what we know and don't know. This knowledge is a boundary that keeps a person on track. As I said in chapter 9, having a solid self-identity requires an accurate view of our strengths as well as our weaknesses. Many of us are so busy beating ourselves up for what we lack that we fail to value the things that are already part of our character. This goes for how we view our children as well. In the midst of my own adolescent identity crisis, I took for granted that I knew the value of hard work and perseverance and had already formed a strong identity as a reliable worker. But this has stood me in good stead in all the years since.

SEPARATING FROM PARENTS

I'll never forget the day that my sweet, loving, obedient son walked out of his room and "pubertied" on me. He announced that he was moving to the garage apartment behind the house and that he expected absolute privacy. He had a certain disdain in his eyes as he looked at me. I seemed to have become a vampire, and from that day forward he almost held up a crucifix when I was in his presence. It's quite an adjustment to have your darling child suddenly see you as Dracula and speak to you in monosyllabic grunts. This went on for eight years. Then, starting at age twenty-five, he slowly emerged as a loving adult, even though he likes to do things his own way.

The inner urge of puberty is toward separation and true selfhood. This usually takes the form of separation from the family, especially the parents, which is hard on the latter, especially when youngsters have been very close earlier on. As parents, we often feel guilty—where did we go wrong? Yet as the great Yale psychiatrist Theodore Lidz writes:

> Needing to free himself from the attraction to a parent, the adolescent usually begins to deny the attractiveness of the parent by devaluing the parent's attributes, but he has other unconscious reasons for derogating his parents. Movement toward adulthood requires the youth to overcome his desires to remain dependent, as well as his feelings that his parents are more capable of directing his life than he is himself.

The parents and their standards must be seriously questioned as the adolescent begins to reconnect with his true self. This inner urge to separate is why the peer group now replaces the parents in terms of a place of belonging and in terms of the rules and norms one must be loyal to.

THE "PEER GROUP PARENT" AS ENVIRONMENT

As the peer group becomes our children's primary environment, we have to pray that they will choose their friends based on the values they have learned from us. Don't think your children will follow what you say—they are more likely to follow what you actually do.

The "peer group parent" helps the teenager begin to leave home, and leaving home is probably the hardest thing that any of us have to do. Leaving home is not just about moving to an apartment or a new city; it is also about separation from the bonds of emotional attachment that created our foundational mutuality. The peer group becomes our new secure attachment figure. That is why it has so much power over the teenager.

Much of the intensity of this separation has to do with how the teenager has negotiated his or her earlier developmental dependency needs. In fact, faulty bonding in earlier stages of development will make adolescence much more difficult. I hate to say it, but in many cases there's not a lot parents can teach in terms of moral virtue that they haven't already taught. As a new secure attachment bond, the peer group offers a sense of belonging. This is why youngsters who have been abused, neglected, or abandoned find the allure of gangs or deviant groups so compelling. The peer group, whether it is a gang or a church group, gives the young person a sense of security and belonging, as well as a new family of affiliation. The peer group can also be a hard taskmaster. I did things that I really didn't want to do because I was afraid the group would reject me. On a positive note, my peer group absolutely rejected the use of hard drugs or narcotics of any kind.

The peer group is powerful, but it isn't almighty. Parents are certainly not helpless. If you think your adolescent has moved into a truly dangerous peer group, you need to intervene. I was involved in many cases where parents were able to save their child from the harmful influence of a toxic peer group. Today there are some excellent peer group programs and teen treatment centers that offer a drug-free peer group.

In Houston, for example, we now have Archway Academy, which offers a supportive, sober environment for students recovering from alcohol and drug addiction. Archway was established by a group of committed Houstonians involved in twelve-step adolescent peer group treatment programs who recognized a compelling need for a school that would address the unique needs of this special group. Church groups are also an excellent place for teenagers to find support and grow morally.

I remember three occasions during my years as a therapist when big powerful men cried like babies in my office because their daughters seemed incorrigible. These men had spent several years and lots of money trying to get their daughters off drugs, and the girls were still rebelling and using drugs. When my friend John found out that his sixteen-year-old daughter was smoking pot daily and hanging out with a sexually promiscuous girl, he gave her a choice: she could either go to the Palmer Drug Abuse Program in Houston or leave home. This was a drastic gamble, but it worked. The best love you can dispense when you are aware that your child is in with a bad group is "tough love." Sometimes after parents have done all they know how to do, they just have to pray.

When a teen entered the drug program I ran in Los Angeles, we told the parents to back off. Backing off meant that the parents had to stop lecturing or trying to control their teenager's drug use. We took on the kids and used powerful peer group pressure to keep them in line. We later offered therapy groups for parents and found that most of them were in a bad place in their marriage. Children and adolescents often act out the anger or pain that is not being dealt with in their parents' marriage. As I've said, the marriage is the chief component of the family. Some kids act out in dramatic ways to get help for their parents.

If you're worried about your child's peer group, first take a rigorously honest look at yourself and your marriage. Don't minimize or deny your problems. Look at your own alcohol and prescription drug use. Get help for yourself and/or your marriage. A family-oriented therapeutic approach is the best. I involved the whole family when I ran my hospital in California. The Meadows treatment center, where I am a senior fellow, has a family week as an integral part of their treatment. Nothing changes until something changes—and that may mean the parents as well as the child.

MODELS AND CHOICES

By late adolescence, young people are beginning to realize that they have a lot to learn. They often seek out a mentor or experienced person they want to emulate. This person may be one of their parents. Frequently it is a person who excels in a vocation that they admire or are curious about. Some know exactly what they want to do and seek out people who can help them move toward their goals.

I found over and over again that the more integrity and ethical sensibility a mentor or adult model had, the more powerful his or her influence was. The kids in the drug program often told me they wanted to be drug counselors. I discouraged this, feeling they were in the glow of their recovery and might be taken in by their attachment to me or one of the other counselors. However, I did encourage several youngsters to become teachers. They had lots of emotional intelligence and were bright and very interested in helping others.

The choice of vocation can seem overwhelming to young people today. It's not like the days when Dad was a farmer or tradesman and the son knew he'd follow in his dad's footsteps, or a girl knew she would run the household like her mother. Many teenagers attach themselves to rock singers, movie stars, or celebrity athletes and make idols out of them. Attaching to an idol has a religious intensity and may cover up a youngster's religious confusion.

Teenagers today are also under enormous pressure to go to college straight out of high school, but when I was a university professor I often found that young people who worked for a couple of years before entering higher education were better prepared and did much better work. They were also less likely to get into the middle of a major and be just as confused about their future as when they started.

We have made college degrees a form of magic in our culture. This needs to be kept in perspective. Vast numbers of happy and successful people (successful by their own definition) never went to college, and many of our most creative and innovative people do not have advanced degrees. There is no question that higher education usually confers substantial economic benefits over a lifetime. But in recognition of this, we are shoehorning thousands of kids into studies in which they have no interest and little chance of succeeding. A different approach, and one of the most critical things we can do for our adolescents, is helping them identify what they like and make a commitment to it.

One factor that makes good choices difficult is the ambivalence adolescents feel. They are no longer children and they are not yet adults. During this period, moral regressions often take place as a refuge from the new choices and emotional turmoil involved in growing up, finding an identity, and leaving home.

At any other time in life, the personality fluctuations of normal adolescence would be highly abnormal and might indicate the need for psychological help of some kind. In adolescence, an adult structure of personality and personal identity is emerging, and it takes its own time to do so. The individual adolescent is highly motivated to experiment and is in no hurry to shut down the process of discovery.

Anna Freud writes:

It is normal for an adolescent to behave for a considerable length of time in an inconsistent and unpredictable manner... to love his parents and to hate them... to be deeply ashamed to acknowledge his mother before others and, unexpectedly, to desire heart-to-heart talks with her; to thrive on imitation of and identification with others while searching unceasingly for his own identity; to be more idealistic, artistic, generous, and unselfish than he ever will be again, but also the opposite: self-centered, egoistic, calculating.

Their confusion and ambivalence is why I often felt I was with a group of outpatients from the local asylum. I'm a strong believer in adolescents going to work at the legal age. Work gives a young teenager a sense of self-esteem. It teaches them about the real world. It gives them a sense of control.

RUMBLINGS OF REBELLION: INTERNALIZING CONSCIENCE

About a year to a year and a half after pubescence, peer group conformity solidifies, and this is often the period when the revolt against and questioning of parental, religious, moral, and cultural dictates begins.

This adolescent crisis has a meaning in terms of your teenager's conscience. It is the young person's move to become morally and religiously self-reliant. Previously it was not so much they who believed as their family or the people around them. Now is the time for them to grow up morally and religiously— to internalize their beliefs and assume responsibility for them. Until this point their morality and faith have been borrowed ones; now they must have the strength to stand alone. This takes courage, and many adolescents (especially those from cultures of obedience) will cop out and simply conform to their parents' moral and religious beliefs without any critical reflection.

If teenagers are willing to take that stand—owning their beliefs and dealing with the responsibilities that these beliefs demand—a crisis often takes place and their old morality and faith are shaken. This is the time when teenagers are particularly vulnerable to a secret society or a cult, an authoritarian religion, or any other group that offers certainty. The choice that leads to one's own informed conscience is often a lonely one.

As much as parents, teachers, and others may dislike adolescent rebellion, when it is honest it is an act of moral courage and an essential step toward a mature conscience. Teenagers are developing their own virtue of prudence. Their critique of their parents' culture and religious beliefs often marks a transition to a deeper ethical maturity.

This is one reason that I subtitled this chapter "Why the Conflict of Generations Is Necessary." For example, homophobia was and is institutionalized in religion and was routine even among people of goodwill in past generations, while today it is losing some of its hold. Though it is not gone by any means— there are still too many ugly incidents—more people are realizing that being gay or lesbian is rooted in a genetic predisposition. In the latest revision of my book *Healing the Shame That Binds You*, I presented the latest clinical proof for this in a section called "The Gay Brain." Biologists have shown that nature is filled with species that engage in same-sex relations; the proportion of gays and lesbians has remained constant throughout human history. The current generation of teens and young adults has formed a group conscience that is far more tolerant and sane than that of previous generations.

In chapter 12, I gave you only a glimmer of the struggle that Stacey High went through in deliberating and finally acting on the dictates of her own conscience. I would call her ultimate choice—to report her best friend for the murder of her father—a fully prudent decision. She was in no way coerced by any outside authority, whether a parent, priest, school counselor, or law enforcement official, although each represented one of the major sources from which conscience is fully formed. Each of these sources of instruction—parental, religious, educational, and legal—is external to us, but each represents a voice or voices that are internalized and form a unified voice of deliberation when we consult our conscience. This is how conscience becomes informed.

In the final analysis, however, an ethically mature choice is one that we make for ourselves. Stacey made a free choice on the basis of her fairly informed internalized conscience. Stacey had been through the kind of rebellion that I described earlier in this chapter. The situation she found herself in with her friend Marie would have been a tough one for any person. Stacey's appetite, her will, was oriented to do the right thing. Murder was wrong. She followed her conscience.

The moral goal of adolescence is the virtue of fidelity. Erik Erikson describes fidelity as the ability "to perceive and to abide by values established by a living system" that one has internalized. The virtue of fidelity takes one beyond morality as a strict adherence to external rules and is the marker of each person's degree of internalized conscience and ethical maturity. The virtue of fidelity simply means that one has internalized a set of values that one is faithful and loyal to—that informs one's conscience.

EXPERIMENTATION (EXPERIENCE)

The affect interest (or curiosity) is the energy of life itself. Adolescence brings with it lots of new choices, and adolescents need to experiment and try things out—including the wild outfits, hair, and body adornments that cause so much adult consternation. The peer group will often set the boundaries of experimentation. I never forgot a kid who was about six foot two, skinny as a rail, not so hot-looking, wearing a T-shirt that said "I grok" on the front and "Go naked" on the back. I could barely control my laughter at the thought of him naked, and the other kids also found him a bit much, but he was dead serious. Sometimes the experimentation can be dangerous. I remember chug-a-lugging a half pint of gin one night to win a bet. I thought I was going to die.

Since adolescents can futurize in ways they've never been able to do before, uncertainty about their personal future becomes a huge problem. Often it's so huge that it brings intense anxiety. Kids find that drinking, drugging, or any other kind of mood alteration eases this pain. Some youngsters are strong enough to let things ride for a while; some are just apathetic.

All of this experimentation and experience involves choices. It is only by exercising choice that we can garner the experience that will be the fodder of our wisdom. My drinking and sexing taught me the utter barrenness of addiction. Addiction is rightly called spiritual and moral bankruptcy. Unfortunately, there are many who will have to experience this for themselves before they can make better choices. Achieving moral intelligence is not a neat and tidy enterprise. It is riddled with pain and joy. And as I pointed out earlier, there is a sense of mystery in the moral life. Later in my drinking life I drove my car while I was completely blacked out, probably a hundred times. Why am I alive? Thank God I didn't kill some innocent victim. Why didn't I quit after these experiences of amnesia? That's the mystery.

Some youth have a pretty good handle on what they want to do and where they want to go. They are disciplined and conscientious. If your child is like this, you are fortunate indeed. The kids I taught in high school felt free to come and talk to me rather than the school counselor. Some had a pretty concrete plan about the university they wanted to attend and what their career choice was. Most talked about the pressure their parents were putting on them to choose a career. I emphasized the value of being curious, often encouraging them to hold off going to college. Many young people are okay with uncertainty for a while. They want to experiment. They need to experiment. Then there are kids who get lost. Some had gotten into drugs and couldn't see the forest for the trees. Kids like this are extremely hard to reach. Sometimes parents just have to let go and pray with all their might. One thing I saw over and over again was that the kids who seemed the worst, turned out to be the most extraordinary when they got it together.

LONELINESS

I remember a phrase from a book I read years ago: "In its innermost depth, youth is lonelier than old age." I believe this is one of the major issues facing adolescents today. Perhaps it has always been a part of growing up. I've told you about my utter loneliness after my two-week episode during junior year of high school. I had no one to talk to. The sense of loneliness is often very intense in families where there is divorce, especially where the father is out of the picture. (Both boys and girls need their father to talk to, but girls often have a caring closeness with their mother and can talk to her.) One kid told me he felt like a three-year-old whose parents had left him in the grocery cart and never came back. Then there's the boy or girl who is not physically attractive or athletically inclined. This is the one for teachers and counselors to look for, to befriend, and to be there to talk to.

Earlier I spoke about Dr. Robert Coles' work on the religious and moral life of children. I found the following passage in *The Moral Intelligence of Children* extremely poignant.

> To cheat and lie is to be alone; to knock oneself out with drugs is to be alone; to sleep with men because they want to knock you up, you and a million others on a sexual assembly line that passes for life, is to be alone, even as to behave like that to women is to be alone; and finally, to shoot to kill in order to survive and prevail (just barely, and so often only for a short time) is to be murderously alone.

And here's the voice of Delia, a troubled teen: "Alone, with nothing to hold on to, no one you'd ever want to hold on to." Delia had a beloved grandmother who modeled a good life for her. "She'd tell us about the Bible and all the adventures in it," she told Coles, "and she'd say we can have our own adventures. She said God was waiting on us, to help us have them." But her grandmother died when Delia was seven years old, and she was left without any nurturing source figure. Her remaining grandfather was a drunk, and her parents were drug addicts who were serving long sentences in prison. Delia slowly fell into moral troubles: lying, cheating, abusing drugs, and being cynical and mean toward other children. Delia described her state of mind to Coles as a persistent loneliness with no moral rules to hold on to and no one she trusted or respected enough to guide her.

Unfortunately, there are many Delias in our schools, adolescents trapped in loneliness. I saw this when I was teaching. The aggressive troublemakers made more noise, but they weren't the ones you really worried about the most. It was the sad, silent, almost pitiful passivity of some of the students that got to me. Passivity is a sign of hopelessness.

I especially remember Eddie. Teachers hear about troublesome students in the faculty lounge long before they have them in class, and no one could motivate Eddie. There were some political reasons Eddie was allowed to remain in this fine prep school, but he seemed impervious to learning. He always just barely passed each subject. He didn't bother anyone. He just did nothing.

For the first few weeks that Eddie was in my senior religion class, he sat and stared into space. One day I realized he was staring at the clock on the wall and writing something down. I was friendly to Eddie and treated him with respect, asking for his thoughts on whatever subject we were discussing, but he usually had no opinion. Then one day about six weeks into the year, he handed me some papers after class and asked me to look at them. When I got around to them I was really astonished. He had written several poems. One was about the mystery of time. He made references to the hands of our classroom clock, and the poem was rich and deep. I asked him to stay after school to talk with me, and we went on to discuss his poems on several different occasions. By the second quarter, Eddie was actively participating in class.

SHAME AND THE IMAGINARY AUDIENCE

Some studies suggest that what was a clear decline in emotional intelligence (kids being lonely and depressed, more angry and unruly, more prone to worry, and more impulsive and aggressive) has greatly improved in the last decade. This is good news. But there are still some very real problems. I have about twenty teacher acquaintances at all levels of school who are greatly concerned about the violence, impulsiveness, and aggressiveness of the students. Teaching is at times chaotic. Several say that adolescents (including girls) seem more shameless and disrespectful of authority than ever before. Half of these teachers have taken early retirement, commenting that they "just can't take it anymore." Some say the classroom is a war zone.

In part this is a result of the interaction of shame (and youngsters' efforts to avoid it) with the late twentieth century's suspicion of authority and rejection of any absolute or totalistic system of religion or morality.

Shame is one of the dominant affects during adolescence. Young teenagers look, sound, and feel awkward in their transforming bodies, and their extreme self-consciousness makes them incredibly vulnerable. I had terrible acne as an adolescent, and had I not been quite smart, a good athlete, and a strong leader, I would have been subject to ridicule and put-downs. Even with my popularity, I cannot remember a moment that I was not acutely aware of my acne. The only time I felt okay was when I was drinking.

Any departure from the peer group culture can result in

painful exposure and loss of status. Because all adolescents fear being exposed (shamed), they will gang up on anyone who is flawed (fat, dumb, thin, awkward, nerdy) and scapegoat him or her. Gays and lesbians are especially vulnerable during this period. School administrators have a tough time monitoring bullies because they are sneaky. Unfortunately, coaches and teachers will sometimes even participate in the bullying.

The terror that children feel when they are being scapegoated is excruciating, and it is estimated that 135,000 students stay home from school each day because of their fear of being ridiculed and, in many cases, physically hurt. It is clear that part of the motive for the killings by the students at Columbine High School in 1999 was revenge for the ridicule and teasing they had received from bullying athletes at their school.

The mental egocentrism of early and middle adolescence ups the ante on this kind of social judgment. Puberty makes adolescents so narcissistically preoccupied with their own physical appearance and personality that they have trouble being present to others.

Psychologist David Elkind writes: "Since he [the adolescent] fails to differentiate between what others are thinking about and his own mental preoccupations, he assumes that the other people are as obsessed with his behavior and appearance as he is himself." Young adolescents anticipate every social situation in terms of how others will react to them. In this sense, they are continually constructing or reacting to an imaginary audience. The wish to be left alone and have privacy at home may be related to adolescents' belief that their imaginary audience knows them as well as they know themselves and is aware of every blemish and flaw. No wonder our children pass us by with monosyllabic words or grunts on their way to their room. This idea of an imaginary audience also explains the dominance of toxic shame, which is the feeling of being exposed without the ability to cover up.

Adolescents are not only self-critical, however. They can also be self-admiring and think (or want to think) that others admire them equally. This may be a way, from a purely cognitive point of view, to account for the loudness, weird dress, and grandiose attention-getting behavior some adolescents engage in. To return to the Columbine killings, the murderers made videotapes of themselves in advance as if to let the world know how clever and extraordinary they were.

Corresponding to the imaginary audience is another mental construct that complements it. Some adolescents feel that since they are important to so many people (the imaginary audience), their own feelings must be special and unique. Only they can suffer with such agony and intensity and only they can experience such rapture. Elkind calls this the "personal fable." The personal fable can easily become a part of an adolescent's ego identity. I had people in midlife come to counseling still clinging to some aspect of their personal fable.

This uniqueness often leads to the belief in personal immortality or invulnerability. "Death will happen to others but not to me," I heard a youngster say when I ran my teenage drug program in Los Angeles. Sexually active teenagers may refuse to take precautions because they are convinced that they would never get pregnant or cause a pregnancy.

Knowing about and understanding the fact that teenagers construct a personal fable does not excuse immoral behavior, but it can help us to understand the dynamics behind it.

RELIGIOUS READINESS

Adolescents experiment with roles, new activities, sexuality, fantasy, and ideas. With their maturing brain, they can question things they've never questioned before. Since the future is an urgent issue for the first time, adolescents also wonder about death, the afterlife, heaven, hell, and salvation. They raise questions such as why we are here, where we are going, and how God can allow poor people and children to suffer. This makes adolescence the time of greatest religious readiness.

At the same time, adolescents' relationship with their imaginary audience fuels the search for a place of sacred refuge, a place to be alone and not judged. Teenagers often have a very intimate relationship with God, which becomes a new bond of absolute security outside the family and the peer group. The need to be guarded from exposure leads to an I-thou relationship with God as a personal confidant whom the teenager looks to for direction, guidance, and support. God was my constant confidant and judge during adolescence.

Adolescence is a time of genuine religious seeking. The personal fable may be the form it takes for some youngsters, but that does not diminish the seriousness of the quest. The personal fable can also fuel the bravado of denial, in which adolescents boast of disbelief in God to their parents and refuse to go to church or follow the rules of their childhood religion. This achieves separation big time, but it's not really about religion.

Adolescents who have been brought up in a rigid culture of obedience are less likely to seriously question their faith than those who have been less severely morally indoctrinated. Teens who live in a culture of obedience have rarely experienced other religious groups or worshiped in another religious community. Their thinking has not been challenged, and they may very well be arrested at a concrete, literal level of cognitive function.

As I discussed in chapter 12, both Piaget and Kohlberg asserted that people do not automatically advance in their moral thinking. They must be challenged, and they must experience the blocks or contradictions in the position they are holding. Otherwise religion can become a form of avoidance—when the absurdity of a position is revealed, faith is called on to bail the person out. When I ran my addiction recovery unit, the John Bradshaw Center at Ingleside Hospital in Los Angeles, our toughest challenge was treating what I call "religious addicts." When God becomes a drug, the therapist has to develop a stronger-than-usual rapport with the patient. Then the question becomes one of what the patient is going to trust—religious slogans or the therapist. When a person is indoctrinated early on, the religious slogans function like posthypnotic suggestions. Most religious addicts come from families that embody cultures of obedience. Their moral doctrine is totalistic and the language of their religion is loaded. Such language takes the most complex human problems and reduces them to simplistic slogans. These have to be challenged in therapy. People cannot escape the bondage of totalism until their beliefs are challenged and shown to be inadequate, contradictory, or contrary to reality.

For adolescents living in ambivalence, the totalistic choice can solve all their problems. Promises of afterlife and heavenly rewards take all the uncertainty out of the future. This is why such systems are attractive to the indoctrinated and unindoctrinated alike. Adolescents who succumb to absolute, totalistic moral and religious beliefs behave much better than those who are honestly questioning and criticizing their childhood faith. But the conscience of the conformist is not really an informed conscience. It does not lead to the development of the virtue of fidelity as Erikson defined it.

When I chose to be a Catholic priest, the decision brought me a sense of certainty. When I took my first religious vows of poverty, chastity, and obedience, I was told that my soul was now free of original sin and all my failures were forgiven. If I died, I would go straight to heaven. After the vows ceremony, I drove with my mother, aunt, and uncle from Rochester, New York, to Toronto, Canada. In my book *Creating Love,* I described my elation during that drive. I was twenty-two years old, and I prayed that we would have a car wreck and die. I figured my mother, aunt, and uncle had not made it to my heights of sanctity but that God would be sure to take them in anyway. In *Creating Love* I called this the "mystified love of God," in contrast to what I called "genuine soulful love." I have to tell you that I now see that kind of mystified love and faith as out-and-out erroneous, but vast numbers of Christians and Muslims still believe in similar doctrines.

Adolescents who are not brainwashed by a totalistic religious childhood are free to question those aspects of their faith that they find troublesome. Some put religion aside for a while, exploring philosophy and other things that are intellectually challenging. Most ultimately come back to the religion of their family as a spiritual home, even though they may not believe certain doctrines or follow all the prescribed rituals.

Some youngsters grow up with no religious guidance. In a way this can be a blessing, because they are free to investigate on their own and to find the spiritual models that are most congruent with their own conscience. They may investigate Asian religions, explore the ethical precepts of yoga, or adopt a practice of Buddhist mindfulness. I know many who have found their religious truth this way.

There is no doubt that everyone needs something greater than themselves to believe in. This is the fruit of the natural affect of good shame. As we grow older shame lets us feel our limitations, our need for help, and the fact that we do not know it all. As we mature and encounter suffering, fate, and death, we experience the awe and wonder of life and develop modesty and humility. We experience our finitude. The philosopher Nietzsche called shame the source and safeguard of spirituality.

THE DEVELOPMENT OF HEALTHY SEXUALITY

We are sexual beings from the moment of our birth. Without the innate drive of lust, the human race would die out in a hundred years. Lust is largely dormant during our preteen years, but most have some experiences of sex play before the sex drive fully emerges.

From our earliest awareness of sex, curiosity, excitement, and desire are bound up with vulnerability and shame. I remember a girl named Marilyn and me in a chinaberry tree when we were six years old. I had just showed her mine and she was about to show me hers. My heart was pounding, and then I heard my mother's booming voice of condemnation. I was shamed to the core.

I remember the titillating excitement that gripped me two years later when several of us neighborhood kids were playing in a girl named Greta's garage. Someone suggested that we *pretend* we were naked and smoking. It was an incredible turn-on, and I eagerly looked forward to doing it whenever possible, although I felt guilty for even having such thoughts.

The emergence of full sexual arousal moves the young teenager to experiment. For boys, the first experience of climax and ejaculation is awesome—somewhat frightening and at the same time desirable. The person experiencing sexual release knows that the world has changed; the ante has been raised, and adulthood makes its presence known like a slap in the face.

Self-Sex

During my adolescence I experienced periods of almost obsessive masturbation. It's hard to think of any other normal human activity that has been mystified and demonized as much as masturbation.

There has been a pervasive folk belief—often supported by medical and religious teachings—that masturbation causes insanity. During the Victorian era, this belief was shared by the educated and promulgated as fact by psychiatrists and physicians.

Contemporary teenagers are likely to be better informed, but masturbation continues to be a source of much anguish to many adolescents. I well remember my own cyclical struggles with shame and guilt: the vows to stop followed by periods of continence, and then beginning the cycle all over again. At one point I didn't care if I went bald or lost my eyesight—folklore that remained even after the insanity threat had faded. I figured I could still do it blind and bald!

There is no question that masturbation can become compulsive and that it is a "drug of choice" for many sex addicts. During adolescence, however, it has the positive effect of allowing young people to relieve sexual tension and impulses safely. It can allow them the quiet needed for study and help them avoid teenage pregnancy or delay marriage until they are more mature. A lot of shame, guilt, and confusion vanish when teenagers are given good information about the normalcy of masturbation.

Premarital Sex

Adolescents are also caught between strong religious prohibitions about premarital sex and a casual public acceptance of sexual intercourse on some sitcoms and in the movies.

I've talked to many teenage boys and girls who are active sexually and who are taking no precautions to prevent pregnancy. I've urged them to be continent, or at least to practice safe sex. I've told them horror stories about how pregnancy has ruined people's lives, especially those of young women, setting off a chain of serious consequences that lasted literally for generations. Still, the teenagers were convinced that they would never get pregnant and that they need not take precautions to prevent conception. I saw this as an example of their personal fable. Girls often romanticize babies as "someone to love who will love me" and fantasize how the baby will bind the father to them.

I have seen so much tragedy associated with teenage sex that I believe it is imperative to aid youngsters in deciding to be abstinent. Realistically, there are ways to prevent or at least postpone teenage sexual activity. Many people may object to my strong belief in abstinence. I would like them to meet some of the thirteen-year-old girls who are living alone with new babies because they were abandoned by the boy or man who got them pregnant. I did several TV programs on *The Bradshaw Difference* where we interviewed a number of these young girls. They were unanimous in their opposition to premarital sex in high school. I also interviewed a large sampling of college-age women who had babies and were left to raise them by themselves. I have listened to many family histories of early pregnancies, which were repeated for three and four generations with disastrous consequences. My family was one of them.

Before offering any advice, let me be clear that my sexuality was very damaged and affected the first half of my life. In school the nuns taught us that sex was beautiful, but their actions belied that. In the third grade, one nun used to read an examination of conscience before going to confession. She would stutter and tremble on sentences such as "Did I touch myself impurely?" It seemed mysterious and bad to me, so bad she couldn't even say the words.

My mother, father, sister, and I lived in my grandparents' home for the first six years of my life. My grandmother, my mother, and one of my aunts had been sexually violated by my maternal great-grandfather. Each of these women had "sexualized rage," a disgust for men and sex. I remember my grandmother saying, "Men think with their penis." At five years old, I found this very confusing. I remember walking around and having a chat with my penis. I wanted to know what it thought about certain things. When I got no answer, I concluded that I had a dumb, mute penis.

My father was absent all the time and I soon assumed the role of my mother's confidant and surrogate spouse. Having no father as a role model, I picked up my mother, grandmother, and aunt's disdain for men. Their sexualized rage and disgust caused my mirror neurons to flash with the feeling that *I* was disgusting, especially when I was sexual in any way.

My sexual experimentation with women began in the eighth

grade. I ran around with six other boys from fatherless homes and angry mothers, and I went with them to Galveston's Post Office Street, a string of brothels a few blocks long. Having sex with hardened prostitutes is hardly an exercise in healthy sexuality. And I've already mentioned being molested by two Catholic priests, one in high school and one in the seminary.

This early sexual history, coupled with my six-year sexual addiction, is not a pretty picture. I am sure it does not inspire you to eagerly await my advice. However, I have practiced healthy, monogamous sex for the past twenty-seven years. What I learned during my recovery from sexual addiction was how much I objectified women. Similarly, female sex addicts objectify men. In recovery meetings, we talked about objectification. Is John a nice person, or is he buttocks and a penis? Is Mary a lovely woman, or is she just a set of breasts, a vagina, and buttocks? It seems somewhat pathetic to have relationships with pieces of paper or electronic images, as do those who have compulsive self-sex with pornography, but is a real-life partner any more real to a sex addict? Many sex addicts see their partners as objects of conquest or status symbols to fan their own ego. The media and movies continually sexually objectify women and men. Some have argued that because of this our whole culture is sexually addicted. What I believe unequivocally is that sex addicts know nothing about sex, because loving intimacy is the core of healthy sexuality. Loving sexual intimacy is *both* ecstatically carnal and deeply spiritual. It has the quality of holding, nurturing, wholeness, and playfulness. Later in this chapter I describe the beautiful way the philosopher Max Scheler described healthy sex as developing from healthy shame, understood as modesty, awe, reverence, and the experience of wholeness.

So what can we do to help our teenage children choose abstinence?

- We can let them know that the majority of their peers are not engaging in intercourse. Adolescents are motivated by peer group norms. They want to be seen as cool, and they often push themselves way past their readiness or comfort zone to fit in.

- We can give explicit information about safe sex and birth control without condoning premarital sexual activity.
- We can model sexual propriety and privacy. Parents need to have good boundaries in their own sex life. If either parent is having an affair, the family knows about it, even though the knowledge may be unconscious. I wrote about this in my book *Family Secrets*. Kids also know—without being told—when their parents have a good sexual relationship.
- We can do everything possible to monitor what they view on TV and the Internet. Parents need to be aware of their own issues with cybersex or pornography.
- We can be honest about our own adolescent sexual experiences or failures. It's imperative to talk about teen pregnancy, especially if parents have been involved in it themselves. Adolescents value personal disclosure and honesty.
- The family or school can get teenagers involved in projects that make them feel valuable and worthwhile. My goddaughters went to Ireland after their junior year in high school and worked with handicapped elders. It was such a powerful experience that they volunteered to return after their senior year, before going to college. These girls have great self-esteem. It has been shown that the most promiscuous boys and girls have low self-worth, often using sex to feel wanted.

I'll end with an interesting idea proposed by William Damon, the director of the Center on Adolescence at Stanford University. Damon offers a model for a neighborhood contract, where town-hall-style meetings and committees devise guidelines for neighborhood children. He believes that all parents share certain common values no matter what their background. Nobody, he says, wants their kids to have premarital sex, steal, lie, or cheat. This idea has not yet caught on nationwide, but I hope some of my readers will seek out Damon's 1997 book, *The Youth Charter: How Communities Can Work Together to Raise Standards for All Our Children.*

RESPECTFUL ENGAGEMENT

William Damon believes as I do, that until late adolescence, moms and dads are the authorities in the family. As children reach adolescence, Damon suggests what he calls "respectful engagement." Engagement means that parents discuss moral issues directly, but it is not finger-wagging. The child is encouraged to express his or her point of view and the parent's job is to listen honestly and respectfully and try to understand why the child sees things differently. In the final analysis, however, the issue is not up for grabs. The authoritative figure that bears the responsibility has the final say. Respectful engagement can work in family council meetings, especially as children reach higher levels of maturity.

My experience with this was in the context of the family council. My daughter wanted to stay out on weekends without a curfew. We discussed this respectfully. I expressed my fears about nightlife in Houston, Texas. She asked us why we didn't trust her judgment. I told her that was not the issue. I said, "There are three of us in on this, your mother, me, and you, and all of us have emotions." We agreed that every hour she was out after midnight she would call us and let us know exactly where she was. Her mother and I set the ultimate boundary at 2:30 A.M. That really worked for us.

Premarital teenage sex is a serious problem, but the belief that premarital sexual relations among teenagers are becoming rampant or universal is not true. No one knows for sure what the frequency of sexual intercourse is among high school students, but a recent survey I saw showed that the majority of boys and girls had not engaged in intercourse by the end of high school. As promiscuous as I was in high school, I never had sex with a nice girl—that is, a girl I dated. When I taught high school during the late 1950s, the majority of students were not having intercourse. On the other hand, one citation for a very large recent study showed that just over 70 percent of both high school men and women have engaged in oral sex. Our new generation seems to believe that oral sex is not really sex. Someone will have to explain this to me.

The Development of Healthy Sexuality

I believe that our culture is sexually obsessive and I know a thousand stories of people whose lives have been ruined because of their sexual acting out. The media, pornography, sex movies, massage parlors, phone sex, and especially cybersex are shameless models for our youth. Too many of our politicians, religious figures, and celebrities model immoral behavior to our adolescents.

My own thinking about healthy sexuality was strongly influenced by my recovery work and by the work of the early-twentieth-century German philosopher Max Scheler.

In Scheler's model, healthy sexuality develops out of healthy shame, defined as modesty, awe, and reverence. In this sense, shame is a marker of the spiritual. It safeguards the spirit because it lets us know that we are tiny specks in a miraculous universe. To have sex with a sense of healthy shame means that we are cognizant of the sacredness of our partner and of the act that we are involved in. The phallic and vaginal mysteries of conception and generation comprise the deepest mysteries of life itself.

Healthy shame *forms, directs, and fulfills* the sex drive. It forms it because it inhibits the pleasure and excitement that a young teenager's autoerotic experimentation brings. Without a sense of shame, there would be no limit to autoeroticism.

During puberty, with the full awakening of the sex drive, a teenager experiences lust as well as the awe and the numinousness of sex. Puberty brings a sense of self-identity as a sexual person, someone who embodies the generative mysteries of life. As adolescents experience their true self-emergence, they feel the desire for mutuality with a sexual partner. But in healthy courtship, the movement is from lust to attraction and from attraction to attachment, commitment, and intimacy. Healthy sexuality is best achieved when people feel they can give themselves in sexual love in a committed relationship without fearing they will lose themselves.

Shame fulfills the sexual drive in sexual intercourse as a caring experience of the whole person. Such an experience may result in the choice of marriage or not. In being married, a couple may choose to experience the mystery of pregnancy and childbirth.

As a couple deepens their love, they deepen the sexual expression of that love. They come to the realization that sexual satisfaction is best when both partners are fully and passionately engaged. Shame, writes Max Scheler, is the "conscience of love." The word that Scheler uses, *shame,* has the same meaning as the Greek word *aidos,* which Aristotle uses to describe lovers gazing into each other's eyes. *Aidos* means awe and reverence. Shame as awe and reverence is the conscience of love.

I think that Scheler may betray a hint of German Victorianism here. Couples in committed relationships and marriages often work out their sex lives less sacramentally than Scheler implies. His discussion of sexuality gives too little attention to the physical pleasure, playfulness, experimentation, and joy that sex can bring to a relationship. Nor does commitment guarantee fulfilling sex. I have counseled many couples where one partner was clearly using the other. There can be sex addiction and co-sex addiction (COSA) in a marriage, just as there can be emotionally and spiritually fulfilling sex in an honest relationship when two people are not married. Many teenage girls are unknowingly entering the path of co-sex addiction.

FAILED ELDERSHIP AND MORAL ALONENESS

Think of yourself as an idealistic adolescent struggling with the advent of puberty. You are being urged to be virtuous, to exercise self-control. You are looking for heroes or heroines, someone who will awaken your true self-identity. Suddenly you're caught up in months of news frenzy about your president, a man you could admire and want to be like. He goes on TV and lies to the American people. He's committing adultery inside the White House with an intern only six and a half years older than his own daughter. The leader of the free world, the most powerful man in the world, is betraying his wife in front of the whole country. You see an *A&E Biography* on John F. Kennedy and the prostitutes provided him by the "Rat Pack" in Las Vegas. Another *A&E Biography* shows Nixon getting suitcases of money from Vegas mobsters. Clinton and Kennedy are likable, highly articulate, and charismatic, but are they ethical role models?

Let me conclude this chapter by focusing again on the moral aloneness Robert Coles described. I've discussed the media as an immoral teacher of sexual acting out and violence, as well as the moral ineptitude of the American educational system to teach emotional intelligence, nurture moral intelligence, and form character.

Teenagers read about politicians' sexual improprieties and witness how other self-righteous politicians use these to go after their rivals. They hear about and see police brutality—offenses by those who are supposed to be pillars of conscience and law. Then the door flies open about the clergy and shocking scandals involving pedophilia and other types of sexual abuse. Our military has paid huge amounts of money to settle sexual harassment suits, as well as suits for rape and uncontrolled sexual abuse as well as murder. We are overwhelmed with the exposure of many corporations as citadels of greed.

Amidst all this, there are some examples that our young people—and all the rest of us—can look up to. As heinous as September 11 was, it showed the tremendous goodness and virtue of the common man and woman. Our firefighters, our police officers, and the thousands of ordinary citizens who volunteered under desperate conditions were not after publicity, vacation homes, or hoards of money. They showed us the kind of moral virtue and ethical maturity that our children hunger for and need in order to grow into their full human nature.

Thousands of years before those tragic events, Aristotle and Aquinas made it abundantly clear that the single most important teacher of virtue is a virtuous person.

Albert Schweitzer, who devoted his whole life to caring for others and for the sanctity of life itself, wrote: "Example is not the main thing in influencing others. It is the only thing."

I shudder to think what the course of my own life would have been had I not had a grandfather and mother who stood for unflinching values. Some of those values I've taken issue with, but others saved my life. I truly believe I never would have stopped my alcoholism without the power of their voices in the depths of my conscience.

Many of our youth are discouraged and demoralized. To develop virtues such as courage, self-control, willpower, and purpose, we need the moral energy of those we are bonded with in mutuality. This is what Delia had lost—her grandmother's "moral energy." I have many similar stories I could tell you about demoralized youth. I listened to them over and over when I taught high school and ran the drug rehabilitation program in Los Angeles. I agree with Robert Coles that "there is no question that absent parents, detached parents, haunt these narratives and the lives they portray—and the result is not only psychological pain but moral loss."

With such parents, Coles points out, a young person's conscience is "not likely to grow up strong and certain." When all parents model for their children is a "feeble, contradictory, compromised moral life, no wonder their children find their own often truculent way to follow suit. I say 'truculent' because a child can be quite angry at being denied the protection of a strong guiding conscience, at being left morally rudderless." *Are teenagers acting out their rage at their elders' betrayal?* Is their shamelessness a mirror of their elders' shamelessness? For my own part, I have no trouble owning my own moral failures and how they let my children down.

I also must say that I have witnessed many adolescents who behaved in a virtuous and admirable way. I saw many of the youngsters in our drug program change radically, especially when their parents changed. I have no doubt that we can foster a new age of virtue and ethical sensibility. Whoever you are, I implore you to make the choice to live the life of virtue. Our youth, perhaps your own children, are crying out for your moral modeling.

Our youngsters are the future of the world. Carl Sandburg says it well in a speech he gave in 1937:

> One thing I know deep out of my time—youth when lighted and
> alive and given a sporting chance is strong for struggle and not
> afraid of any toils or punishments or dangers or deaths.

What shall be the course of society and civilization across the next hundred years?

For the answers read if you can the strange and baffling eyes of youth.

A LAST WORD

Recorded history is a war-torn killing field spawned by totalistic religions and moralities who believe they are the righteous (the good) and have the duty to destroy those who do not believe as they do (the evil). The loyalty to our own kin is so deeply rooted in our evolutionary inheritance that it makes "loving the stranger" humankind's greatest moral challenge.

Meeting that challenge is impossible without the enhancement of virtue, which gives us an ethically sensitive "second nature," enabling us to overcome the self-righteous propensity of our raw moral intelligence.

The Christian apostle Paul urged us to grow up and give up our childish ways of thinking (1 Cor. 13:11). This is clearly the appointed time to take *adult* responsibility for finding the common bond of humanity with our sisters and brothers on planet Earth. Without love and compassion for each other, it is a pipe dream to believe that power, greed, hatred, prejudice, and the desire for ethnic cleansing will not inevitably lead to a nuclear solution. Jesus told his followers that they could do greater things than he did (John 14:12). A universal reclaiming of the golden mean of virtue, one small individual act at a time, may well be the second sacred incarnation—this time of all the gods.

SELECTED READINGS

Albom, Mitch. *Tuesdays with Morrie.* New York: Doubleday, 1998. This is a book filled with Morrie Schwartz's wisdom, which he garnered from experience rather than book learning.

Anthony, E. James, and Bertram T. Cohler. *The Invulnerable Child.* New York: Guilford Press, 1987. While the authors admit that there is no completely invulnerable child, they have pioneered the research on children who have been able to survive dysfunctional families and neighborhoods thanks to strong coping abilities, resiliency, creativity, and competence.

Aquinas, Thomas. *Basic Writings of Saint Thomas Aquinas.* Ed. Anton C. Pegis. New York: Random House, 1945. The material I have used is from Vol. 2, Section XII, which is a discussion of virtues and vices. The material is from the *Summa Theologica,* I–II, Questions 49–89. I spent years studying Thomas Aquinas, and it was well worth it. He is one of the great philosophical and theological minds of all time.

Aristotle. *The Nicomachean Ethics.* Translated by David Ross and revised by J. L. Ackrill and J. O. Urmson. New York: Oxford University Press, 1998. This represents Aristotle's most mature thought. Aristotle also wrote an earlier ethical treatise, called the *Eudmenian Ethics,* in which his thought was much closer to Plato's.

Beauregard, Mario, and Denyse O'Leary. *The Spiritual Brain: A Neuroscientist's Case for the Existence of the Soul.* New York: HarperCollins, 2008.

Bennett, William J. *The Book of Virtues.* New York: Simon & Schuster, 1993. This book, as its title indicates, is a treasury of great moral stories, annotated with very helpful comments. I'm personally grateful to William Bennett for having the courage to do the laborious work it took to produce *The Book of Virtues,* as well as a second book entitled *The Moral Compass.*

Bettelheim, Bruno. *The Use of Enchantment: The Meaning and Importance of Fairy Tales.* New York: Vintage Books, 1977. A book that can help you stimulate your child's moral imagination.

Black, Claudia. *Changing Course: Healing from Loss, Abandonment and Fear.* 2nd ed. Center City, MN: Hazelden, 2002.

———. *Deceived: Facing Sexual Betrayal, Lies and Secrets.* Center City, MN: Hazelden, 2009. Addresses the current epidemic of co-sex addiction (COSA).

Bowlby, John. *A Secure Base.* New York: Basic Books, 1988. Bowlby has been the central figure in the understanding of secure attachment as the foundation of healthy human development.

Bradshaw, John E. *Bradshaw On: Healing the Shame That Binds You.* Deerfield Beach, FL: Health Communications, 1988. This is my extensive treatment of healing toxic shame.

———. *Bradshaw On: The Family.* Deerfield Beach, FL: Health Communications, 1988. This book outlines the theory of family systems in depth and describes types of dysfunctional families.

———. *Creating Love: A New Way of Understanding Our Most Important Relationships.* New York: Bantam, 1992. This is my work on secret or covert beliefs about love that each of us carries from our family of origin, and offers ways to make our needs conscious through critical evaluation.

———. *Family Secrets: The Path from Shame to Healing.* New York: Bantam, 1995. The book shows in detail how what is unexpressed in the family system will be carried by the family members, especially the children.

———. *Homecoming: Reclaiming and Healing Your Inner Child.* New York: Bantam, 1990. This book outlines the developmental stages of human dependency needs and offers several ways to work on grieving your unmet needs.

Buber, Martin. *Good and Evil.* Trans. Ronald Gregor Smith. Saddle River, NJ: Prentice Hall, 1981. Buber is one of the great philosophical and theological minds of our time. He has shown how shameless people hide in moral righteousness and religiosity.

Canning, Maureen. *Lust, Anger, Love: Understanding Sexual Addiction and the Road to Healthy Intimacy.* Naperville, IL: Source Books, 2008.

Carnes, Patrick. *Out of the Shadows: Understanding Sexual Addiction.* 3rd ed. Center City, MN: Hazelden, 2001.

Coles, Robert. *The Moral Intelligence of Children.* New York: Random House, 1997.

_____. *The Moral Life of Children.* New York: Atlantic Monthly Press, 1986. Robert Coles is a prolific writer and researcher. He has studied children of many ethnic groups and won a Pulitzer Prize for his five-volume Children of Crisis series. Coles has continued the work of Steiner and Montessori to give us great insights into the moral intelligence of children. He is one of my true heroes.

Comte-Sponville, André. *A Small Treatise on the Great Virtues.* New York: Metropolitan Books, 2001. André Comte-Sponville is one of the most important of a new wave of French philosophers and is the author of five highly acclaimed books on classical philosophy. At many points while I was writing this book, André's depth and clarity helped me move out of a stuck place. His influence on my understanding of the nature of virtues is everywhere apparent.

Coontz, Stephanie. *The Way We Never Were: American Families and the Nostalgia Trap.* New York: Basic Books, 2000.

Csikszentmihalyi, Mihaly. *Creativity.* New York: HarperPerennial, 2007. This is an important contribution to the psychology of discovery and invention. Mihaly calls the height of creativity the state of "flow."

Damasio, Antonio. *Descartes' Error.* New York: Putnam, 1994.

_____. *The Feeling of What Happens.* New York: Harcourt, 1999. Damasio's books are two of the best brain stories of the decade. They embody a lifetime of research by one of the leading neuroscientists of our time. Damasio has proved convincingly that when there is damage to certain parts of our brain, choice is impaired. Without freedom of choice, no moral act is possible.

Damon, William. *The Youth Charter: How Communities Can Work Together to Raise Standards for All Our Children.* New York: The Free Press, 1997.

Darwin, Charles. *The Expression of the Emotions in Man and Animals.* New York: D. Appleton and Company, 1913. Darwin's works are a turning point in human awareness, helping us to see shame as one of the things that distinguishes us from other animals. This is a critical issue in the understanding of moral intelligence.

De Becker, Gavin. *The Gift of Fear: And Other Survival Signals That Protect Us from Violence.* New York: Dell, 1999. Gavin De Becker is an expert on danger and violence. His book shows quite well how fear serves as a type of discernment.

deMause, Lloyd. *Foundations of Psychohistory.* New York: Creative Roots, 1982. deMause has been relentless in uncovering data to show that civilizations are created directly in relation to the way we treat our children.

Dobson, James. *The New Dare to Discipline.* Carol Stream, IL: Tyndale House, 1996.

Doidge, Norman. *The Brain That Changes Itself: Stories of Personal Triumph from the Frontiers of Brain Science.* New York: Penguin, 2007.

Dreikurs, Rudolf. *The Challenges of Parenthood.* New York: Meredith Press, 1948.

Dreikurs, Rudolf, Bernice Brunia Grunwald, and Floy C. Pepper. *Maintaining Sanity in the Classroom: Classroom Management Techniques.* 2nd ed. Philadelphia: Taylor and Francis, 1998. This book offers numerous techniques for avoiding power struggles at school and enhancing students' sense of caring for themselves and caring for and cooperating with others.

Dreikurs, Rudolf, and Vicki Soltz. *Children: The Challenge.* New York: Hawthorn Books, 1964. Dr. Dreikurs is a psychiatrist who became the leading exponent of Adlerian psychology. His concepts of logical or natural consequences versus punishment and the democratic family show us excellent ways to avoid power struggles with children as well as authoritarian coercion. His methods are proven and will work to foster your child's moral intelligence if you are willing to put the effort into using them.

Edmunds, Francis. *An Introduction to Steiner Education: The Waldorf School.* Rev. ed. London: Sophia Books, 2004.

Erikson, Erik H. *Insight and Responsibility.* New York: Norton, 1964. The essay "Human Strength and the Cycle of Generations" contains Erikson's connection of his theory of the developmental stages of ego strength with the roots of virtues. I used this essay extensively in part 3 of this book. I have been a student of Erikson's for forty years, and I believe his depth and wisdom have stood the test of time. The more I study his work, the more I understand his brilliance.

——. *Childhood and Society.* New York: Norton, 1950.

——. *Adulthood.* New York: Norton, 1978. This is a group of essays on adulthood in various parts of the world.

——. *Identity: Youth and Crisis.* New York: Norton, 1994.

Erikson, Erik H., Joan M. Erikson, and Helen Q. Kivnick. *Vital Involvement in Old Age.* New York: Norton, 1986.

Eyre, Richard, and Linda Eyre. *Teaching Your Children Values.* New York: Fireside, 1993. This book is a rich resource of practical teachable moments for parents to teach values. I like the Eyres' strong emphasis on parental modeling.

Fairlie, Henry. *The Seven Deadly Sins Today.* Notre Dame, IN: University of Notre Dame Press, 1978. A rather righteous presentation of the history and nature of the seven deadly sins.

Farber, Leslie H. *The Ways of the Will: Selected Essays.* Ed. Robert Boyers and Anne Farber. New York: Basic Books, 2000.

Fisher, Helen. *Anatomy of Love: A Natural History of Mating, Marriage, and Why We Stray.* New York: Ballantine, 1994. Fisher is an excellent science popularizer. Here she discusses the brain chemistry involved in being in love and the mature love-based attachment.

Fosha, Diana. *The Transforming Power of Affect: A Model for Accelerated Change.* New York: Basic Books, 2000. Presents a theory of accelerated-dynamic experiential psychotherapy. I welcome this theory, which is very similar to what Pia Mellody and I have been doing for the past thirty-five years.

Freud, Anna. "Adolescence" in *Adolescence and Psychoanalysis: The Story and the History.* Ed. Maja Perret-Catipovic and François Ladame. London: Karnac Books, 1998.

Fromm, Erich. *The Heart of Man: Its Genius for Good and Evil.* Ed. Ruth Nanda Anshen. New York: Harper & Row, 1964. Fromm believes in the natural goodness of human beings. He gives a very powerful account of the psychological roots of evil.

Gardner, Howard. *Intelligence Reframed: Multiple Intelligences for the 21st Century.* New York: Basic Books, 1999. This book is an expanded discussion of Gardner's theory of multiple intelligences, which he presented in *Frames of Mind* (1983). In this latter book, Gardner discusses moral intelligence in some detail.

Gauld, Joseph E. *Character First*. New York: Prima Lifestyles, 1995. A description of the Hyde School, a powerful model for developing moral intelligence in our children.

Gilligan, Carol. *In a Different Voice: Psychological Theory and Women's Development*. Cambridge: Harvard University Press, 1982. Carol Gilligan gives a rich and persuasive account of female moral development, but her work is not aimed specifically at gender. Rather, it addresses polarity and wholeness, making it clear that moral intelligence must be grounded in the male/female polarity, synthesizing an ethics of rights with an ethics of caring.

Goleman, Daniel. *Emotional Intelligence*. New York: Bantam, 1995. This bestseller makes it clear that emotional intelligence is more important than IQ for living life joyfully. It also discusses the essential core from which moral intelligence develops.

Gordon, David, and Maribeth Meyers-Anderson. *Phoenix: Therapeutic Patterns of Milton H. Erickson*. Cupertino, CA: Meta Publications, Inc., 1981. The books Milton Erickson wrote and the books about him are too numerous to detail. His therapeutic skills were the epitome of practical reasoning at its best. Filled with examples of Erickson's approach to therapy, this is my favorite book explaining his work.

Gottman, John M., and Nan Silver. *The Seven Principles for Making Marriage Work*. New York: Three Rivers Press, 2000. This book is a practical guide for building the virtue of love and its role in sustaining a marriage. Gottman has probably done more actual research on marriage than any other psychologist in the country. He gives you the real deal.

Greven, Philip. *Spare the Child: The Religious Roots of Punishment and the Psychological Impact of Physical Abuse*. New York: Vintage, 1992. Greven presents the religious roots of corporal punishment, offering a biblical exegesis of the justification for corporal punishment. He shows clearly that there is no justification for the physical punishment of children in the New Testament. He also outlines the consequences of physical punishment that include anxiety and fear, anger and hate, melancholy and depression, dissociation, paranoia, sadomasochism, domestic violence and more. Every parent needs to read this well-documented scholarly book.

Grossman, Dave. *On Killing: The Psychological Cost of Learning to Kill in War and Society*. New York: Back Bay Books, 1996. If you ever have a chance to hear Lt. Col. Grossman lecture, do not pass it up. He is a powerful communicator and will move you to take action against violence in movies, TV, and video games.

Grossman, Dave, and Gloria DeGaetano. *Stop Teaching Our Kids to Kill: A Call to Action Against TV, Movie, and Video Game Violence*. New York: Crown, 1999. Their book offers incontrovertible evidence, based on recent data and major scientific studies, that violence in TV, video games, and movies is conditioning children to be violent and to lack the awareness of the consequences of violence; indeed, they are teaching the very mechanics of killing.

Haley, Jay. *Problem-Solving Therapy*. 2nd ed. San Francisco: Jossey-Bass, 1987. Another excellent book on Milton Erickson.

Hartshorne, Hugh, and Mark Arthur May. *Studies in Deceit: Book One, General Methods and Results*. Manchester, NH: Ayer, 1975.

Hillman, James. *The Soul's Code: In Search of Character and Calling*. New York: Warner Books, 1996. This is a bestseller that everyone deserves to read. The autobiographical material Hillman has assembled is proof positive of Slavin and Kriegman's concept of the true self. People simply cannot be encapsulated by psychological and philosophical theories that predict how they should be. We are all more than anyone's mind can fathom.

Holt, John. *How Children Fail*. Rev. ed. New York: Perseus Books, 1982. This book has been around for a long time. As a high school teacher, I welcomed it with open arms. Holt shows what any good teacher knows from experience: that the authoritarian coercive type of teaching that we are still using will truncate the human spirit.

———. *How Children Learn*. Rev. ed. New York: Perseus Books, 1982. This book should be required reading for school board members and for any politician who dares to mention the word *education*.

Hunter, James Davison. *The Death of Character*. New York: Basic Books, 2000. I admire Hunter's courage in confronting the spineless, egotistical subjective moral relativism that dominates areas of our life.

Kagan, Jerome. *Galen's Prophecy: Temperament in Human Nature.* Boulder: Westview Press, 1998. This is an easy-to-read presentation of temperament and underscores the importance of innate predispositions in our personality.

Kaufman, Gershen. *The Psychology of Shame: Theory and Treatment of Shame-Based Syndromes.* 2nd ed. New York: Springer Publishing Company, 2004. Along with Donald Nathanson, Kaufman is the best authority on Silvan Tomkins' affect theory.

Kohlberg, Lawrence. "Stages in Moral Development as a Basis for Moral Education." In *Moral Education: Interdisciplinary Approaches.* ed. C. M. Beck, B. S. Crittenden, and E.V. Sullivan. Toronto: University of Toronto Press, 1971. To my knowledge, this is the clearest presentation that Kohlberg gave of his theory of moral stages.

LeDoux, Joseph. *The Emotional Brain: The Mysterious Underpinnings of Emotional Life.* New York: Touchstone, 1996. LeDoux's book is the foremost modern guide to understanding how our emotional life operates, in spite of the unknowns that still abound in our understanding of the brain. Certainly this book is a critical resource for understanding the nature and development of moral intelligence as I've described it.

Lerner, Harriet. *The Dance of Intimacy: A Woman's Guide to Courageous Acts of Change in Key Relationships.* New York: HarperPerennial, 1989. An excellent book for understanding the dynamics of family systems and how our families impact our lives.

Levine, Peter, and Ann Frederick. *Waking the Tiger: Healing Trauma: The Innate Capacity to Transform Overwhelming Experiences.* Berkeley: North Atlantic Books, 1997. Levine explores the dynamics of animals in the wild and their resiliency in trauma, effectively arguing that the human animal is endowed with similar instinctual faculties. Levine's work altered the way we perceive trauma, normalized its symptoms, and introduced new and valuable methods for overcoming traumatic incidents.

Lickona, Thomas. *Raising Good Children: From Birth Through the Teenage Years.* New York: Bantam, 1994.

Lidz, Theodore. *The Person: His and Her Development Throughout the Life Cycle.* New York: Basic Books, 1976. The book is a tremendous resource for looking in-depth at the entire life cycle.

Lifton, Robert Jay. *Thought Reform and the Psychology of Totalism: A Study of Brainwashing in China.* Chapel Hill: University of North Carolina Press, 1989. This book shows how totalistic authoritarian systems can cause the numbing of emotions and total mind control. If you want insight into how a culture of obedience can operate, read this book.

Lillard, Paula Polk. *Montessori: A Modern Approach.* New York: Schocken Books, 1972.

Maritain, Jacques. *The Range of Reason.* New York: Scribner, 1952. Maritain was for a long time the leading interpreter of Thomas Aquinas' thought.

May, Gerald G. *Will and Spirit.* San Francisco: HarperCollins, 1982. An extremely enlightening discussion of the difference between willingness or right appetite and willfulness.

Mayeroff, Milton. *On Caring.* Ed. Ruth Nanda Anshen. New York: Harper and Row, 1971. This is a wonderful book. My fundamental understanding that all virtues flow from caring for ourselves and others as an inner state of being comes from reading Mayeroff's book.

Mellody, Pia, and Lawrence S. Freundlich. *The Intimacy Factor: The Ground Rules for Overcoming the Obstacles to Truth, Respect, and Lasting Love.* New York: HarperOne, 2004.

Mellody, Pia, Andrea Wells Miller, and J. Keith Miller. *Facing Codependence: What It Is, Where It Comes From, How It Sabotages Our Lives.* New York: HarperOne, 2003.

———. *Facing Love Addiction: Giving Yourself the Power to Change the Way You Love.* New York: HarperOne, 2003. Pia Mellody's work forms the core of treatment at the Meadows in Wickenberg, Arizona.

Miller, Alice. *For Your Own Good: Hidden Cruelty in Child-Rearing and the Roots of Violence.* Trans. Hildegarde Hannum and Hunter Hannum. New York: Farrar, Straus and Giroux, 1983. Alice Miller is the most important writer I have read in the last forty years. Her earlier book *The Drama of the Gifted Child* opened my eyes to why I could be so successful yet feel so disconnected. Miller saw clearly the damage a narcissistically deprived mother could do to her child in their initial attachment. Miller also exposed the hidden dangers in patriarchal parenting based on blind obedience, or what she described as "obedience without content."

————. *Thou Shalt Not Be Aware: Society's Betrayal of the Child.* New York: Farrar, Straus and Giroux, 1998.

Montessori, Maria. *The Absorbent Mind.* Trans. Claude A. Claremont. New York: Owl Books, 1995.

————. *From Childhood to Adolescence.* New York: Schocken Books, 1973. Discusses the moral characteristics of the child from seven to twelve years.

————. *The Montessori Method.* New York: Schocken Books, 2008.

————. *The Secret of Childhood.* New York: Ballantine, 1972.

Moore, Thomas. *The Soul of Sex: Cultivating Life as an Act of Love.* New York: HarperPerennial, 1999.

Muller, Wayne. *Legacy of the Heart: The Spiritual Advantages of a Painful Childhood.* New York: Fireside, 1993.

Nathanson, Donald L. *Shame and Pride: Affect, Sex, and the Birth of Self.* New York: Norton, 1992. Nathanson is an expert psychotherapist who came into contact with Silvan Tomkins' affect theory and has taken on the mission of presenting Tomkins to the world. He is the founding director of the Silvan Tomkins Institute. Although I feel like a novice, I have a deep sense of the revolutionary importance of Tomkins' work. Nathanson has made Tomkins' theory understandable for me.

Osherson, Samuel. *Finding Our Fathers.* New York: Contemporary Books, 2001. Osherson has shown how damaging the loss of the father can be for a child.

Owens, Joseph. *A History of Ancient Western Philosophy.* New York: Appleton Century Crofts, 1959. A comprehensive survey of ancient philosophy, to late-antiquity.

Piaget, Jean. While Piaget is controversial and difficult to read, he has made a large contribution to our understanding of how the mind develops. There are a number of excellent interpreters of Piaget's thought that have been helpful, including:

Duska, Ronald F., and Mariellen Whelan. *Moral Development: A Guide to Piaget and Kohlberg.* New York: Paulist Press, 1975.

Elkind, David. *Children and Adolescents: Interpretive Essays on Jean Piaget.* New York: Oxford University Press, 1981. The most helpful resource on interpreting Piaget is the child psychologist

David Elkind. He is my resource for examples I used of the various stages of cognitive egocentrism in children and adolescents.

Pulaski, Mary Ann Spencer. *Understanding Piaget: An Introduction to Children's Cognitive Development.* New York: Harper & Row, 1971.

Pieper, Josef. *Prudence.* New York: Pantheon Books, 1959. Pieper has written books on each of the four cardinal virtues. He is an avid follower of Thomas Aquinas and an excellent interpreter of Aquinas' thought.

Pletcher, Claudine, and Sally Bartolameolli. *Relationships from Addiction to Authenticity: Understanding Co-Sex Addiction—A Spiritual Journey to Wholeness and Serenity.* Deerfield Beach, FL: Health Communications, 2008. COSA is a painful addiction that is only now becoming fully understood. For a full discussion of this subject, read this groundbreaking book.

Restak, Richard. *The New Brain: How the Modern Age Is Rewiring Your Mind.* New York: Rodale, 2004. This book contains the new studies I used on the exceptionally performing brain.

Richards, Mary Caroline. *Toward Wholeness: Rudolf Steiner Education in America.* Middletown, CT: Wesleyan University Press, 1980. This book is the best overall presentation of Rudolf Steiner's thought and the Waldorf approach. It also gives a brief chronology of Steiner's life and work and an extensive bibliography. Though I have no firsthand knowledge of how Steiner's principles are reflected in Waldorf Schools today, I'd like to see his ideas begin to be incorporated in public school education.

Ridley, Matt. *The Origins of Virtue: Human Instincts and the Evolution of Cooperation.* New York: Viking, 1997. Ridley is an excellent writer and makes the very complex topic of evolutionary biology quite understandable. He argues convincingly for an evolved instinct for cooperation.

Sanford, John A. *Evil: The Shadow Side of Reality.* New York: Crossroad, 1982. John Sanford is an Episcopal priest and a certified Jungian analyst. He is also a gifted theologian. More than anyone, Sanford has helped me grasp the danger of being overidentified with the image of being good.

———. *The Invisible Partners: How the Male and Female in Each of Us Affects Our Relationships*. Mahwah, NJ: Paulist Press, 1980.

Scheler, Max. "Shame and Feelings of Modesty" in *Person and Self-Value: Three Essays*. Ed. and partially trans. M. S. Frings. New York: Springer, 1987.

Schore, Allan N. *Affect Dysregulation and Disorders of the Self*. New York: Norton, 2003.

———. *Affect Regulation and the Repair of the Self*. New York: Norton, 2003. Schore is a leading figure in the neuroscience of affect and attachment dysfunction. My information on the right brain in chapter 3 is heavily indebted to his work.

Schwartz, Jeffrey, and Sharon Begley. *The Mind and the Brain: Neuroplasticity and the Power of Mental Force*. New York: Harper Perennial, 2003. This book contains Schwartz's revolutionary clinical work on how the will can change the brain.

Seligman, Martin E. P., et al. *The Optimistic Child*. New York: Houghton Mifflin, 1995. This book offers a psychological basis for the virtue of hope.

Siegel, Daniel J. *The Developing Mind: How Relationships and the Brain Interact to Shape Who We Are*. New York: Guilford Press, 1999. Siegel's work is a critical addition to the neuroscientific understanding of the relationship between the mind and the brain.

Simon, Sidney B., Leland W. Howe, and Howard Kirschenbaum. *Values Clarification*. Rev. ed. New York: Warner Books, 1995. This book is based on the process theory of the philosopher John Dewey. It shows how a person can choose values prudently.

Slavin, Malcolm Owen, and Daniel Kriegman. *The Adaptive Design of the Human Psyche: Psychoanalysis, Evolutionary Biology, and the Therapeutic Process*. New York: Guilford Press, 1992. Slavin and Kriegman's groundbreaking work provides an evolutionary foundation for the universal belief in a "deep self" or soul.

Sölle, Dorothee. *Beyond Mere Obedience: Reflections on a Christian Ethic for the Future*. Minneapolis: Augsburg, 1970. Theologian Dorothee Sölle makes a compelling case in this book for the dangers of any kind of absolute obedience.

Standing, E. M. *The Montessori Revolution in Education*. New York: Schocken Books, 1967.

Stein, Edward, ed. *Fathering, Fact or Fable?* Nashville: Abingdon Press, 1977. This book is a compilation of essays on the issues around absentee fathers and the importance of a male figure in a child's life.

Stern, Karl. *The Flight from Woman.* New York: Paragon House Publishers, 1986. Dr. Stern's book was an inspiration to me on my personal journey. He shows how the rejection of the feminine, understood as one's emotions and vulnerability, can lead to serious problems. He analyzes the philosopher Descartes, whose famous statement, "I think, therefore I am," was the foundation of his metaphysics and the beginning of what has been called "rationalism," placing emotion in an inferior position in human actualization.

Tomkins, Silvan S. *Affect Imagery Consciousness.* 2 vols. New York: Springer, 1962. Though his ideas are extremely valuable, I find Tomkins' writing so difficult that I have come to my understanding of him through Donald Nathanson and Gershen Kaufman.

Unell, Barbara C., and Jerry L. Wyckoff. *20 Teachable Virtues.* New York: Perigee, 1995. This is a very practical and helpful book for parents and teachers. The authors give copious examples of teachable moments where modeling and discussion can be quite effective.

van der Kolk, Bessel A., Alexander C. McFarlane, and Lars Weisaeth, eds. *Traumatic Stress: The Effects of Overwhelming Experience on Mind, Body, and Society.* New York: Guilford Press, 2006. Van der Kolk's essay, "The Black Hole of Trauma," gives a good overview of how trauma damages a person's ability to be "authentically present" and how foresight is damaged. The whole book is quite comprehensive.

Wakerman, Elyce. *Father Loss: Daughters Discuss the Man That Got Away.* New York: Doubleday, 1984. Wakerman presents several interviews with women showing how the loss of their father has affected their lives.

West, Kenneth. *21 Deadly Myths of Parenting and 21 Creative Alternatives.* Tulsa, OK Council Oak Books, 1990. This book offers a detailed description of how time-outs work in disciplining children. It also offers a variety of alternatives to spanking and shaming. It includes the Dreikurian materials I presented in the text.

Woodman, Marion. *Addiction to Perfection: The Still Unravished Bride.* Toronto: Inner City Books, 1982. Marion Woodman is a deeply insightful Jungian analyst. She shows how the inhuman demands of perfectionism, as embodied in a totalistic culture, can cause severe damage to human personality.

Wright, Robert. *The Moral Animal*. New York: Pantheon Books, 1994. Wright names the genre of this book as the "new science of evolutionary psychology." He argues powerfully that although many of our moral sentiments have a deep biological basis, we still have a strong tendency to deceive ourselves about our goodness.

Zweig, Connie, and Jeremiah Abrams, eds. *Meeting the Shadow: The Hidden Power of the Dark Side of Human Nature*. New York: Jeremy P. Tarcher/Putnam, 1991. This book is replete with essays explaining Carl Jung's concept of the shadow as the dark side of the personality and offering a rich understanding of why owning the shadow is the ultimate ethical problem.

ACKNOWLEDGMENTS

I'm a teacher by profession and my job is to synthesize the work of others, the truly germinal thinkers that have created our collective consciousness. It is a nice feeling to stand on the shoulders of those that have come before me, especially those unbelievably gifted Greek philosophers, Heraclitus, Democritus, and Aristotle, who understood the moral intelligence that was necessary for the life of virtue. The great medieval thinker and synthesizer of his day, St. Thomas Aquinas, followed in their footsteps and added a theological glow to their vision.

Only now have the neuroscientists of the last four decades given their insights a sure footing in the brain. I am grateful to Charles Darwin, Silvan Tomkins, Paul Ekman, Donald Nathanson, Gershen Kaufman, Joseph LeDoux, Antonio Damasio, Allan N. Schore, Daniel J. Siegel, Jeffrey Schwartz, and Daniel Goleman for their work in understanding the importance of affect as the primary source of human behavior, especially as it relates to consciousness, free will, and choice. In Selected Readings you will find many more authors and books that I am thankful for. I take full responsibility for my interpretations of these thinker's great works.

Thanks go to Maria Montessori, whose seminal truths about children are far from being fully understood. Thanks to my colleagues at the Meadows, Claudia Black, Pia Mellody, Maureen Canning, Bessel van der Kolk, Peter A. Levine, and Bob Fulton.

Thanks to the great cognitive researchers, Jean Piaget, Lawrence Kohlberg, Carol Gilligan, and David Elkind. Thanks also to my two most important mentors, Erik Erikson and Ashley Montagu.

I thank my loving wife, Karen, for all the time, help, and support she has given me. Writing a book is especially trying on a relationship.

Also to Reverend Michael Falls, my friend of forty years, George and Claudine Pletcher, Bob Cagle, Barney Cearly, and the "Kindergarten Boys" for sixty-five years of love and sharing. Thanks for your patience in having to hear about this book for five years.

So many people have taught me so much by the power of their being: my son John, whose honesty and work ethic are sterling; my stepdaughter Brenda, whose courage and perseverance amaze me; and stepson Brad, whose humor and creativity are superb. My thanks to my granddaughter Kori for her love; and to my grandsons: Liam for his unbelievable courage; and Jackson for his incredible spirit and all the books he's written.

My thanks to the great Bantam team for their support over many years and four books, especially president and publisher Irwyn Applebaum and master publicity director Barb Burg. Finally, I really have no words to describe my editor, Toni Burbank, who has a unique skill for getting to the heart of the matter. I cannot thank her enough.

INDEX

ABOUT THE AUTHOR

For more than forty years, John Bradshaw has combined the roles of counselor, author, theologian, management consultant, and public speaker, becoming one of the leading figures in the fields of addiction/recovery and family systems.

Born in Houston, Texas, into a troubled family and abandoned by his alcoholic father, John became an academic overachiever and an out-of-control teenager. He studied for the Roman Catholic priesthood at a seminary run by the religious order of St. Basil, where he remained for nine years, leaving just prior to being ordained. During this time he earned degrees in psychology and theology from the University of Toronto. It was also during this time that a high school drinking problem became a full-fledged addiction.

On December 11, 1965, John took a drastic step—he committed himself to Austin State Hospital. After six days he signed himself out of the hospital and entered an alcohol recovery program. Soon afterward he began to lecture at a local church and before long was in demand as a teacher, counselor, speaker, and corporate consultant.

In 1986, with the airing of *Bradshaw On: The Family*, John became a public television phenomenon, with a total of six public television series and two specials that reached millions of viewers. In 1996, he also appeared on national network TV in his syndicated talk show *The Bradshaw Difference*. Throughout this period, he also gave talks and multiday workshops attended by thousands of people at a time.

His previous books include *Bradshaw On: The Family* (a #1 *New York Times* bestseller), *Healing the Shame That Binds You* (a *New York Times* bestseller), *Homecoming* (a #1 *New York Times* bestseller), *Creating Love* (a #1 *New York Times* bestseller), and *Family Secrets*.

He is currently Senior Fellow at the Meadows, a leading addiction treatment center in Wickenburg, Arizona, and makes presentations nationwide on the inner child and feeling work he pioneered. The father of four children and stepchildren, and grandfather of three, he resides in Houston, Texas, with his wife, Karen Ann. He has become a true elder who has personally guided some half-million participants in his unique healing work, and whose bestselling books and TV series have reached many millions more throughout the world. In 2001, the editors and readers of *Common Boundary* magazine named John one of the 100 most influential writers on psychology and spirituality in the twentieth century.

John Bradshaw conducts lectures and workshops throughout the world. Information about upcoming lectures, workshops, and keynote addresses, or to purchase CDs or DVDs of John's workshops or lecture series, including his PBS series, is available at:

johnbradshaw.com
Within the United States: 800-6-BRADSHAW
Outside the United States: 713-771-1300
Facsimile: 713-771-1362

To contact John Bradshaw:

John Bradshaw
PO Box 667147
Houston, Texas 77266-7147
or
youcanheal@aol.com